Adobe Illustrator

2022 release

Adobe

Classroom in a Book®

The official training workbook from Adobe

Brian Wood

Adobe Illustrator Classroom in a Book® (2022 release)

Adobe Press is an imprint of Pearson Education, Inc. For the latest on Adobe Press books, go to www.adobepress.com. To report errors, please send a note to errata@peachpit.com. For information regarding permissions, request forms and the appropriate contacts within the Pearson Education Global Rights & Permissions department, please visit www.pearson.com/permissions.

Adobe Inc., 345 Park Avenue, San Jose, California 95110-2704, USA

Cover Illustration: Petra Eriksson, Barcelona, Spain

ISBN-13: 978-0-13-762215-3
ISBN-10: 0-13-762215-5

1 2021

WHERE ARE THE LESSON FILES?

Purchase of this Classroom in a Book in any format gives you access to the lesson files you'll need to complete the exercises in the book.

1   Go to adobepress.com/IllustratorCIB2022.

2   Sign in or create a new account.

3   Click Submit.

Note: If you encounter problems registering your product or accessing the lesson files or web edition, go to adobepress.com/support for assistance.

4   Answer the questions as proof of purchase.

5   The lesson files can be accessed through the Registered Products tab on your Account page.

6   Click the Access Bonus Content link below the title of your product to proceed to the download page. Click the lesson file links to download them to your computer.

Note: If you purchased a digital product directly from adobepress.com or peachpit.com, your product will already be registered. However, you still need to follow the registration steps and answer the proof of purchase question before the Access Bonus Content link will appear under the product on your Registered Products tab.

CONTENTS

1   GETTING TO KNOW THE WORK AREA   28

2   TECHNIQUES FOR SELECTING ARTWORK   58

3   USING SHAPES TO CREATE ARTWORK FOR A POSTCARD   82

8 USING COLOR TO ENHANCE ARTWORK 210

12 USING BRUSHES TO CREATE AN AD   **328**

13 EXPLORING CREATIVE USES OF EFFECTS AND GRAPHIC STYLES   **356**

GETTING STARTED

Adobe® Illustrator® is the industry-standard illustration application for print, multimedia, and online graphics. Whether you are a designer or a technical illustrator producing artwork for print publishing, an artist producing multimedia graphics, or a creator of web pages or online content, Adobe Illustrator offers you the tools you need to get professional-quality results.

About Classroom in a Book®

Adobe Illustrator Classroom in a Book® (2022 release) is part of the official training series for Adobe graphics and publishing software developed with the support of Adobe product experts. The features and exercises in this book are based on Illustrator (2022 release).

The lessons are designed so that you can learn at your own pace. If you're new to Adobe Illustrator, you'll learn the fundamentals you need to master to put the application to work. If you are an experienced user, you'll find that Classroom in a Book® also teaches some more advanced features, including tips and techniques for using the latest version of Adobe Illustrator.

Although each lesson provides step-by-step instructions for creating a specific project, there's room for exploration and experimentation. You can follow the book from start to finish or do only the lessons that correspond to your interests and needs. Each lesson concludes with a review section to quiz you on the main concepts covered.

Prerequisites

Before beginning to use *Adobe Illustrator Classroom in a Book® (2022 release)*, you should have working knowledge of your computer and its operating system. Make sure that you know how to use the mouse and standard menus and commands and also how to open, save, and close files. If you need to review these techniques, see the printed or online documentation for macOS or Windows.

Installing the program

● **Note:** When instructions differ by platform, macOS commands appear first and then the Windows commands, with the platform noted in parentheses. For example, "press Option (macOS) or Alt (Windows), and click away from the artwork."

Before you begin using *Adobe Illustrator Classroom in a Book® (2022 release)*, make sure that your system is set up correctly and that you've installed the required software and hardware.

You must purchase the Adobe Illustrator software separately. For complete instructions on installing the software, visit helpx.adobe.com/support/illustrator.html. You must install Illustrator from Adobe Creative Cloud onto your hard disk. Follow the onscreen instructions.

Fonts used in this book

The Classroom in a Book lesson files use fonts that are included with your Creative Cloud subscription, and trial Creative Cloud members have access to a selection of fonts from Adobe for web and desktop use.

For more information about Adobe fonts and installation, see the Adobe HelpX article at helpx.adobe.com/creative-cloud/help/add-fonts.html.

Online Content

Your purchase of this Classroom in a Book includes online materials provided by way of your Account page on adobepress.com. These include:

Lesson files

To work through the projects in this book, you will need to download the lesson files using the following instructions.

Web Edition

The Web Edition is an online interactive version of the book providing an enhanced learning experience. Your Web Edition can be accessed from any device with a connection to the Internet, and it contains:

- The complete text of the book.

- Hours of instructional video keyed to the text. Throughout the lessons, content that is available only as video content is marked with a video icon (■◀).

- Interactive quizzes.

Accessing the lesson files and Web Edition

You must register your purchase on adobepress.com to access the online content:

1   Go to adobepress.com/IllustratorCIB2022.

2   Sign in or create a new account.

3   Click Register.

4   Answer the question as proof of purchase.

5   The lesson files can be accessed from the Registered Products tab on your Account page. Click the Access Bonus Content link below the title of your product to proceed to the download page. Click the lesson file link(s) to download them to your computer.

The Web Edition can be accessed from the Digital Purchases tab on your Account page. Click the Launch link to access the product.

● **Note:** If you purchased a digital product directly from adobepress.com or peachpit.com, your product will already be registered. However, you still need to follow the registration steps and answer the proof of purchase question before the Access Bonus Content link will appear under the product on your Registered Products tab.

Restoring default preferences

Note: If finding the preferences file proves difficult, please contact brian@ brianwoodtraining.com for assistance.

The preferences file controls how command settings appear on your screen when you open the Adobe Illustrator program. Each time you quit Adobe Illustrator, the position of the panels and certain command settings are recorded in different preference files. If you want to restore the tools and settings to their original default settings, you can delete the current Adobe Illustrator Prefs file. Adobe Illustrator creates a new preferences file, if one doesn't already exist, the next time you start the program and save a file.

You must restore the default preferences for Illustrator before you begin each lesson. This ensures that the tools function and the defaults are set exactly as described in this book. When you have finished the book, you can restore your saved settings, if you like.

To delete or save the current Illustrator preferences file

Tip: To quickly locate and delete the Adobe Illustrator preferences file each time you begin a new lesson, create a shortcut (Windows) or an alias (macOS) to the Adobe Illustrator 26 Settings folder.

The preferences file is created after you quit the program the first time and is updated thereafter. *After launching Illustrator*, you can follow these steps:

1 Exit Adobe Illustrator.

2 Locate the preferences file:

   • On macOS, locate the file named Adobe Illustrator Prefs as follows: <OSDisk>/Users/<username>/Library*/Preferences/ Adobe Illustrator 26 Settings/en_US**/Adobe Illustrator Prefs

   Tip: To locate the correct Library folder on macOS, go to the Finder, press the Option key, and choose Go > Library from the menu at the top. Without pressing the Option key, the Library menu item does not appear in the Go menu.

   • On Windows, locate the file named Adobe Illustrator Prefs as follows: <OSDisk>\Users\<username>\AppData\Roaming\Adobe\ Adobe Illustrator 26 Settings\en_US**\x64\Adobe Illustrator Prefs

   Note: On Windows, the AppData folder is hidden by default. You will most likely need to enable Windows to show hidden files and folders. For instructions, refer to your Windows documentation.

   For more information, refer to the Illustrator help: helpx.adobe.com/illustrator/using/setting-preferences.html.

   If you can't find the file, that's because either you haven't started Adobe Illustrator yet or you have moved the preferences file. The preferences file is created after you quit the program the first time and is updated thereafter.

3 Copy the file and save it to another folder on your hard disk (if you want to restore those preferences) or delete it.

4 Start Adobe Illustrator.

*On macOS, the Library folder is hidden by default. To access this folder, in the Finder press the Option key, and choose Library from the Go menu in the Finder.

**The folder name may be different depending on the language version you have installed.

To restore saved preferences after completing the lessons

1   Exit Adobe Illustrator.

2   Delete the current preferences file. Find the original preferences file that you saved and move it to the Adobe Illustrator 26 (or other version number) Settings folder.

Note: You can move the original preferences file rather than renaming it.

Additional resources

Adobe Illustrator Classroom in a Book® (2022 release) is not meant to replace documentation that comes with the program or to be a comprehensive reference for every feature. Only the commands and options used in the lessons are explained in this book. For comprehensive information about program features and tutorials, please refer to these resources:

Adobe Illustrator Tutorials: helpx.adobe.com/illustrator/tutorials.html (accessible in Illustrator by choosing Help > Illustrator Tutorials) is where you can find and browse tutorials on Adobe.com.

Adobe Illustrator Learn & Support: helpx.adobe.com/support/illustrator.html (accessible in Illustrator by choosing Help > Illustrator Help) is where you can find and browse tutorials, help, and support on Adobe.com.

Adobe Community: community.adobe.com lets you tap into peer-to-peer discussions, questions, and answers on Adobe products.

Resources for educators: adobe.com/education and edex.adobe.com offer valuable information for instructors who teach classes on Adobe software. Find solutions for education at all levels, including free curricula that can be used to prepare for the Adobe Certified Associate exams.

Adobe Illustrator product home page: See adobe.com/products/illustrator.html.

Adobe add-ons: exchange.adobe.com/creativecloud.html is a central resource for finding tools, services, extensions, code samples, and more to supplement and extend Adobe Creative Cloud.

Adobe Authorized Training Partners

Browse a wealth of courses offered worldwide by our Adobe Authorized Training Partners at learning.adobe.com/partner-finder.html.

WHAT'S NEW IN ADOBE ILLUSTRATOR (2022 RELEASE)

Adobe Illustrator (2022 release) has new and innovative features to help you produce artwork more efficiently for print, web, and digital video publication. The features and exercises you'll learn about in this book are based on the Illustrator 2022 release. In this section, you'll preview many of these new features.

Apply 3D effects and materials

3D effects in Illustrator are all new in this release. You can apply 3D effects like Rotate, Revolve, Extrude and Inflate from the Effect menu. You can also adjust lighting and shadows in the new 3D and Materials panel.

You can add texture to artwork using default materials in the 3D and Materials panel or materials you create in the *.Sbsar format. You can also choose from free (and paid) community and Adobe materials on the substance3D.adobe.com/assets website.

Share for collaborative commenting

Share a link to your Illustrator document with others to review your documents. Reviewers with the link can view shared documents and add comments for feedback. The initiator can then view all comments in the Comments panel with the shared document open in Illustrator on the desktop.

Activate missing fonts seamlessly

If you turn this option on, Adobe fonts used in a document are automatically activated in the background when documents are opened.

Find what you need with the Discover panel

Search through tools, Help content, and more as you explore in-app self-guided content, including hands-on tutorials.

Other enhancements

The following are other enhancements in Illustrator (2022 release):

- **Select same text**—Selecting similar text based on font family, font size, text color, and more have been added to the Select > Same menu.

- **Simplified variable-width strokes**—When you edit strokes with variable-width strokes, fewer anchor points are now applied.

- **Place linked cloud documents**—You can now link, embed, relink, and update Photoshop Creative Cloud files in Illustrator.

- **Support for HEIF or WebP formats**—You can now open or place High Efficiency Image Format (HEIF) or WebP format files in Illustrator.

Adobe is committed to providing the best tools possible for your publishing needs. We hope you enjoy working with Illustrator (2022 release) as much as we do.

—The Adobe Illustrator Classroom in a Book® (2022 release) team

A QUICK TOUR OF ADOBE ILLUSTRATOR (2022 RELEASE)

Lesson overview

In this interactive demonstration of Adobe Illustrator (2022 release) you'll get an overview of the main features of the application.

This lesson will take about 45 minutes to complete. To get the lesson files used in this chapter, download them from the web page for this book at adobepress.com/IllustratorCIB2022. For more information, see "Accessing the lesson files and Web Edition" in the Getting Started section at the beginning of this book.

Begin to get comfortable with some of the essential features of Adobe Illustrator as you create an advertisement.

Starting the lesson

For the first lesson of this book, you'll get a quick tour of the most widely used tools and features in Adobe Illustrator, offering a sense of the many possibilities. Along the way, you'll create artwork for an art supply advertisement. First, you'll open the final artwork to see what you will create in this lesson.

Note: If you have not already downloaded the project files for this lesson to your computer from your Account page, make sure to do so now. See the "Getting Started" section at the beginning of the book.

Note: If finding the preferences file proves difficult, contact brian@brianwoodtraining.com for assistance.

1   To ensure that the tools and panels function exactly as described in this lesson, delete or deactivate (by renaming) the Adobe Illustrator preferences file. See "Restoring default preferences" in the "Getting Started" section at the beginning of the book.

2   Start Adobe Illustrator.

3   Choose File > Open, or click Open in the Home screen that is showing. Open the L00_end.ai file in the Lessons > Lesson00 folder.

4   Choose View > Fit Artboard In Window to see an example of the art supply ad you'll create in this lesson. Leave the file open for reference, if you'd like.

Creating a new document

In Illustrator, you can start a new document using a series of preset options, depending on your needs. In this case, you will save the ad you create for social media, so you will choose a preset from the Web presets to start.

1   Choose File > New.

2   In the New Document dialog box, select the Web preset category at the top of the dialog box.

You could choose from a blank document preset size to start, but in this case, you'll make the ad a specific size. In the Preset Details area on the right, change the following:

- Enter a name for the document in the blank space under "Preset Details": **SocialMedia_ad**
- Width: Select the Width value, and type **1080** (pixels).
- Height: Select the Height value, and type **1080** (pixels).

3   Click Create, and a new, blank document opens.

4 Choose File > Save As.

5 If the Cloud Document dialog box opens, click Save On Your Computer to save the file on your computer (locally).

● **Note:** Learn more about what a cloud document is in Lesson 1, "Getting to Know the Work Area."

6 In the Save As dialog box set the following options:

- Leave the name as SocialMedia_ad.ai.
- Navigate to the Lessons > Lesson00 folder.
- Leave Adobe Illustrator (ai) chosen from the Format menu (macOS) or Adobe Illustrator (*.AI) chosen from the Save As Type menu (Windows).
- Click Save.

● **Note:** The figures in this lesson were taken using macOS and may look slightly different from what you see if you are using Windows.

7 In the Illustrator Options dialog box that appears, leave the Illustrator options at their default settings, and then click OK.

8 Choose Window > Workspace > Essentials, and then choose Window > Workspace > Reset Essentials to reset the workspace.

9 Choose View > Fit Artboard In Window.

The white area you see is called the *artboard*, and it's where your artwork will go. Artboards are like pages in Adobe InDesign or physical papers on a desk. Your document can have multiple artboards, and each can be a different size.

Drawing shapes

● **Note:** Explore how to make and edit all kinds of different shapes in Lesson 3, "Using Shapes to Create Artwork for a Postcard."

Shapes are the cornerstone of Illustrator, and you'll create many of them in the coming lessons. To start your project, you'll make several shapes that will become a marker in the ad.

1   Select the Rectangle tool (▢) in the toolbar on the left.

2   Move the pointer into the top center of the artboard, and drag to make a small rectangle that will become the marker tip. As you drag, you'll probably see a gray measurement label showing the size of the shape. That is a part of Smart Guides, which are turned on by default. When the gray measurement label next to the pointer shows a width of around 80 pixels and height of approximately 110 pixels, release the mouse button.

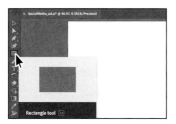 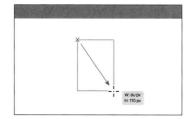

Now you'll make a copy of the rectangle below it, to make the top part of the body of the marker.

3   Choose Edit > Copy, and then choose Edit > Paste In Place to paste a copy on top of it.

4   To move it down, drag the rectangle by the solid blue dot in the center. You'll see a vertical magenta alignment guide as you drag, telling you the copy is aligned with the original. See the figure for how far to drag.

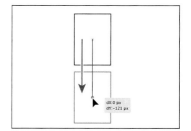

5   Below the new rectangle, drag to make a much larger rectangle.

For a reference, the rectangle I made is 280 pixels wide and about 600 pixels tall. See the figure for approximately how big.

6   Press and hold on the Rectangle tool to see a menu of tools. Select the Ellipse tool from that menu.

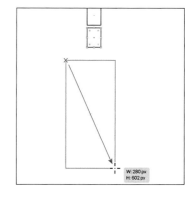

7 Press the Shift key and drag to make a perfect circle that fits within the largest rectangle. Release the mouse button and then the key.

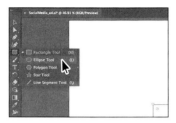
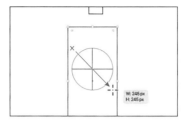

Editing shapes

Most shapes are *live*, which means you can edit them without switching away from the tool you're drawing with. Next you'll edit the circle, and then the larger rectangle. The edits you will make will be more exacting.

● **Note:** Learn more about editing shapes in Lesson 3, and Lesson 4, "Editing and Combining Shapes and Paths."

1 With the circle still selected, drag it from the blue dot in the center so the left edge aligns (snaps) to the left edge of the larger rectangle.

A vertical magenta guide will show when the circle is aligned with the rectangle.

2 To make the circle as wide as the rectangle, pressing the Shift key, drag the point on the right side of the box around the circle, to the right. When the pointer snaps to the right edge of the rectangle, release the mouse button and then the key.

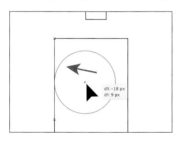
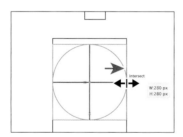

3 With the circle still selected, drag it up from the blue dot in the center so the center of the circle aligns (snaps) with the top of the larger rectangle.

Magenta guides will show when the circle is aligned with the rectangle.

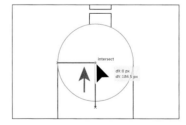

4 Select the Selection tool (▶) in the toolbar on the left to edit the other shapes.

5 Click in the largest rectangle to select it. Drag the bottom middle point on the box down to make the rectangle taller until you see a height of about 670 pixels in the gray measurement label next to the pointer.

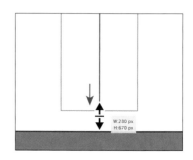

6 To move the two smaller rectangles in place, click one of the rectangles, and then Shift-click the other.

7 Drag them onto the circle, making sure they are centered on the circle. A vertical magenta guide will show when it is. Use the figure as a reference.

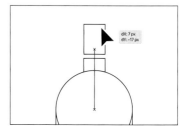

8 Choose File > Save to save the document.

Combine shapes using the Shape Builder tool

● **Note:** Learn more about working with the Shape Builder tool in Lesson 4.

The Shape Builder tool (⊕) is used to create more complex shapes by merging and removing simpler shapes. Next you'll merge the circle, larger rectangle, and one of the smaller rectangles to make the body of the marker.

1 Starting in an empty area of the artboard, drag across the three shapes to select them.

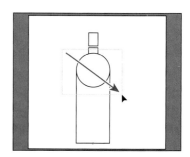

2 Select the Shape Builder tool (⊕) in the toolbar on the left.

3 Move the pointer to roughly where you see the pointer in the first part of the following figure. Drag through all of the shapes to combine them, following the second part of the figure for where to drag. Release the mouse button, and the shapes are combined.

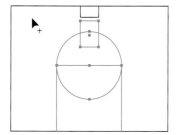
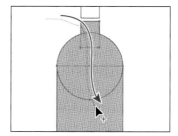
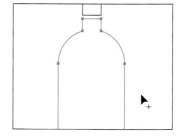

Now you'll round a few of the corners on the bottle. To round only a few, you need to select certain anchor points using the Direct Selection tool.

The blue squares on the selected shape are called *anchor points*. They are used to control the path's shape.

Note: Learn more about paths and anchor points in Lesson 7, "Drawing with the Pen tool."

4   Select the Direct Selection tool (⊳) in the toolbar.

You will also see a bunch of double circles called *corner radius widgets*. They control the roundness of the corners. To round two corners at once, you will select the anchor points on just those corners.

5   Drag across the two anchor points you see in the following figure.

6   Drag either double-circle away from the shape to round the corners as much as you want.

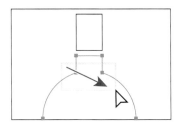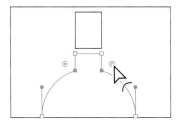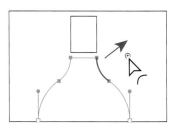

If you drag far enough, the paths will turn red, telling you that's as much as you can round the corners.

7   Save the file by choosing File > Save.

Applying and editing color

Applying color to artwork is a great way to express yourself creatively. Shapes you create can have a stroke (border) that goes around the edge and can be filled with a color. You can apply and edit swatches, which are saved colors that you make or that come with each document by default.

Note: Learn more about fill and stroke in Lesson 8, "Using Color to Enhance Artwork."

1   Select the Selection tool (▶) in the toolbar.

2   Click the small marker tip rectangle to select it.

3   Click the white color box (□) to the left of the word "Fill" in the Properties panel. In the Swatches panel that opens, ensure that the Swatches option (▦) is selected at the top. Move the pointer over the color swatches, and a tool tip appears, telling you the name of the swatch. Click an orange color with the tool tip ("R=247, G=147, B=30") to change the fill color.

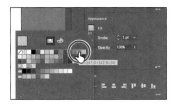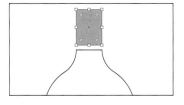

While you can use the default swatches, you can also create your own colors and save them as swatches to reuse later.

Note: Going forward, you'll find you need to hide panels such as the Swatches panel before you continue. You can press the Escape key to do this.

4 To remove the stroke (border) on the shape, in the Properties panel, click the down arrow for the stroke weight until it is gone.

5 Select the marker body shape to change its fill color as well.

6 Click the Fill color box (□) to the left of the word "Fill" in the Properties panel. In the Swatches panel, click to apply a lighter orange color to the marker tip. Leave the Swatches panel showing. Now you'll edit that color.

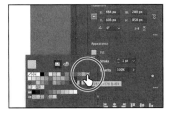 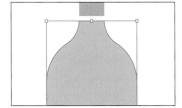

7 Double-click the swatch you applied in the Swatches panel (it has a white border around it).

8 In the Swatch Options dialog box, select Preview to see the change to the marker body. Drag the G (Green) slider to the right to give the color some more yellow and make it a bit lighter. The swatch is made of red, green, and blue colors.

9 Click OK to save the change you made to the swatch.

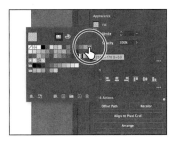 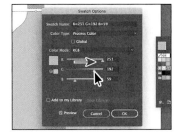

10 To remove the stroke (border) on the shape, in the Properties panel, click the down arrow for the stroke weight until it is gone.

Transforming artwork

From rotating and scaling to moving, shearing, and reflecting, transforming artwork in Illustrator will allow you to create unique and creative projects.

Now you'll reshape the marker tip, and then make some copies of the whole marker, change the color, and rotate them.

1 Click the small marker tip rectangle to select it.

2 Select the Direct Selection tool (▷) in the toolbar and click the upper-left corner point on the shape to select it. Release the mouse button, and then drag that selected corner point down to give the marker tip a chiseled look.

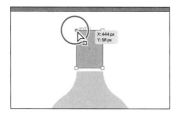 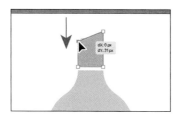

3 Select the Selection tool (▶) in the toolbar.

4 To deselect everything, choose Select > Deselect.

5 To select both shapes on the artboard, choose Select > All On Active Artboard.

6 Click the Group button toward the bottom of the Properties panel on the right.

   Grouping treats the selected objects as one. The next time you want to select both the marker tip and the body you can simply click one to select them as a group.

Note: If your marker is not in the middle of the artboard, go ahead and drag it into the middle.

7 Choose Edit > Copy and then Edit > Paste to make a copy.

8 Drag the copy to the left, as in the figure.

9 To rotate the copy of the marker, move the pointer just off a corner of the box around it. When you see curved arrows, drag counter clockwise to rotate it a little.

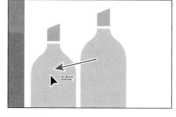

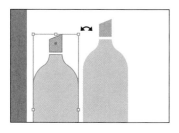 

With one marker copy in place, you'll make another copy and flip it so it's on the other side of the original marker.

10 With the marker still selected, make a copy by choosing Edit > Copy. This time, choose Edit > Paste In Place to make a copy right on top of the original.

11 To flip the copy, in the Properties panel, click the Flip Horizontally button (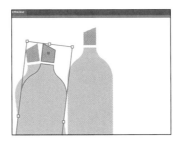).

12 Press the Shift key, and drag the marker to the right of the marker in the middle. Release the mouse button and then the key. Leave the marker selected.

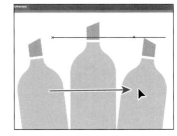

Recoloring artwork

In Illustrator, you can easily recolor artwork using the Recolor Artwork option. Next, you'll recolor the two marker copies.

1 Shift-click the marker on the far left to select both.

● **Note:** If you click anywhere in the document, the Recolor Artwork dialog box will close. To open it again, make sure the markers are selected, and then click the Recolor button in the Properties panel.

2 Click the Recolor button toward the bottom of the Properties panel to open the Recolor Artwork dialog box.

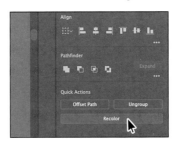
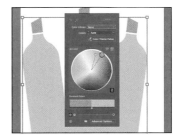

You can see the two colors from the bottle—the orange and lighter orange, as circles on the color wheel in the middle of the dialog box. Recolor artwork lets you change color in selected artwork. Now, you'll show the swatches that are in the document and then change the two orange colors.

3 Choose Document Swatches from the Color Library menu at the top of the panel.

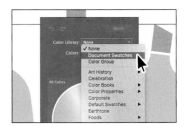

The color wheel now shows the swatches you saw when editing the fill color of artwork in the Properties panel. You can drag the little color circles in the color wheel to change the corresponding color in the selected art. But, by default, dragging one color circle drags all together.

4   To edit the two colors independently, click the link icon (⬚) beneath the color wheel to turn it off. It will look like this after you click it: ⬚. It's circled in the first part of the following figure.

5   Now, drag each of the orange circles, one at a time, into a different red color to change the artwork.

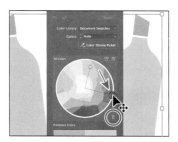 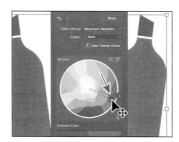

6   Click in an empty are of the document window to hide the Recolor Artwork dialog box.

7   To select all of the markers, choose Select > All On Active Artboard.

8   Choose Object > Group to group them all together.

    If you need to edit one of the markers, you can always click the Ungroup button in the Properties panel to break the markers apart again.

9   Choose Select > Deselect.

10 Choose File > Save.

Creating and editing a gradient

Gradients are two or more colors that gradually blend one into another over a distance that you can apply to the fill or stroke of artwork. Next, you'll up your color game and apply a gradient to a banner. Then you will add some text to it.

● **Note:** Learn more about working with gradients in Lesson 11, "Gradients, Blends, and Patterns."

1   Choose View > Zoom Out so it's easier to see the edges of the artboard.

2   Press and hold the mouse button on the Ellipse tool (◯) in the toolbar, and select the Rectangle tool (▭) from the menu of tools.

3   Starting on the left edge of the artboard, drag across to the right edge, making a rectangle the width of the artboard and with a height of approximately 375 pixels.

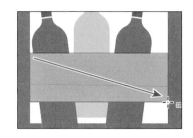

4   In the Properties panel, click the Fill color box, and select the white-to-black swatch with the tool tip "White, Black."
Leave the Swatches panel showing.

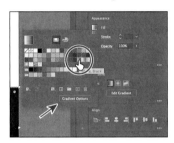

5   At the bottom of the Swatches panel, click the Gradient Options button to open the Gradient panel. An arrow is pointing to the button in the previous figure.

You can drag the Gradient panel by the title bar at the top to move it around.

6   In the Gradient panel, do the following:

• Click the Fill box to make sure you are editing the fill (circled in the figure).

• Double-click the little black color stop (⬤) on the right side of the gradient slider in the Gradient panel (an arrow is pointing to it in the figure).

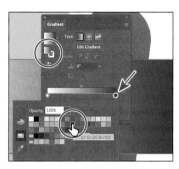

• Click the Swatches button (▦) in the panel that appears. Select a dark blue swatch.

• Double-click the little white color stop (◻) on the left side of the gradient slider in the Gradient panel (an arrow is pointing to it in the figure).

• Select a lighter blue swatch.

There are a lot of creative possibilities with gradients, from applying gradients to the stroke (border) of objects to making color transparent (see-through).

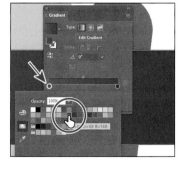

7   Click the X at the top of the Gradient panel to close it.

Editing strokes

A *stroke* is the outline (border) of artwork such as shapes and paths. There are a lot of appearance properties you can change for a stroke, including width, color, dashes, and more. In this section, you'll adjust the stroke of the banner rectangle.

Note: Learn more about working with strokes in Lesson 3.

1 With the rectangle still selected, click the word "Stroke" in the Properties panel.

In the Properties panel, when you click an underlined word, more options appear in a panel.

2 In the Stroke panel, change the following options:

- Stroke Weight: **11 pt**
- Click Align Stroke To Inside (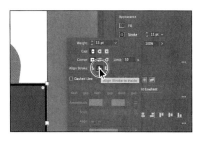) to align the stroke to the inside of the rectangle edge.

3 In the Properties panel, click the Stroke color box (■), and select the white swatch.

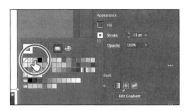

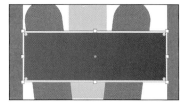

4 Choose Select > Deselect.

Creating with the Curvature tool

With the Curvature tool (✐), you can draw and edit smooth, refined paths and also straight lines. In this section, you'll explore the Curvature tool while creating a marker scribble.

Note: Learn more about working with the Curvature tool in Lesson 6, "Using the Basic Drawing tools."

1 Select the Curvature tool (✐) in the toolbar. Before you start drawing, you'll remove the fill and change the stroke color.

2 Click the Fill color box (■) to the left of the word "Fill" in the Properties panel. In the Swatches panel, click to apply the None (⬚) swatch to remove the fill.

3 Click the Stroke color box (▢) to the left of the word "Stroke" in the Properties panel. In the Swatches panel, click to apply an orange swatch.

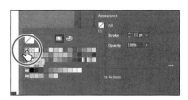

4   Move the pointer into the middle of the marker tip (see the first part of the following figure). Click and release to start drawing a shape.

5   To make a serpentine shape (like an "s"), move the pointer to the left, and click and release (see the second part of the figure). Move the pointer away after clicking to see a curving path.

Every time you click, you are creating what is called an *anchor point*. As described earlier, anchor points you add (the circles you see on the path) control the shape of the path.

6   Make a scribble by clicking to the right, to the left, and then to the right. See the figure for where I clicked.

7   Press the Esc key to stop drawing.

With the path selected, next you'll change the order of the artwork and put the path behind everything else on the artboard.

8   Click the Arrange button in the Quick Actions section of the Properties panel. Choose Send To Back to stack it behind everything. Leave it selected.

Applying a brush

With brushes, you can decorate paths with patterns, figures, brush strokes, textures, or angled strokes. You can also modify the brushes provided with Illustrator and create your brushes. Next, you'll apply a brush to the path you just drew to make it look more like a marker scribble.

1   Select the Selection tool (▶) in the toolbar.

2   With the path you drew still selected, choose Window > Brush Libraries > Artistic > Artistic_Ink. It's toward the bottom of the long menu that displays.

3 Scroll in the Artistic_Ink panel, and click the brush named "Marker" to apply it.

In the panel that opens, you see some brushes that come with Illustrator.

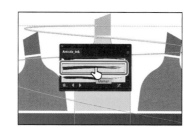

4 Change the Stroke Weight in the Properties panel to 6 pt by clicking the up arrow to the right of the word "Stroke."

5 Close the Brushes panel by clicking the X in the top corner of the panel.

6 Choose File > Save.

Working with type

Next you'll add text to the project and make some formatting changes to it.

● **Note:** Learn more about working with type in Lesson 9, "Adding Type to a Project."

1 Select the Type tool (**T**) in the toolbar on the left, and click in the large rectangle with the gradient fill. Placeholder text will appear with the selected placeholder text, "Lorem ipsum."

2 Type **ART SUPPLIES** in capital letters.

The text will be small and hard to read against the gradient. You'll remedy that next.

3 Select the Selection tool (▶) so the text object is selected.

4 Click the Fill color box (■) in the Properties panel. In the Swatches panel, click to apply an orange color.

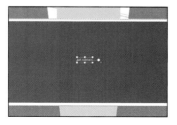

5 In the Character section of the Properties panel, select the font size, and type **73**. Press Return or Enter to accept the size change.

6 In the same section of the Properties panel, change the Tracking (▧) value by selecting the value in the field and typing **30** (highlighted in the following figure). Press Return or Enter to accept the change. Tracking is how you can adjust spacing between characters. Leave the text selected.

Warping text

● **Note:** Learn more about warping text in Lesson 9.

You can create some great design effects by warping text into different shapes using envelopes. You can make an envelope out of an object on your artboard, or you can use a preset warp shape or a mesh grid as an envelope.

1 With the Selection tool selected and the text still selected, copy and paste the text by choosing Edit > Copy and then Edit > Paste.

2 Drag the two text boxes so they are still within the bounds of the rectangle and stacked one on top of the other.

3 Select the Type tool, move the pointer over the top text, and triple-click to select it. Type **CRAFTY**.

4 Select the Selection tool (▶) so the CRAFTY text object is selected.

5 Change the font size to **190** in the Properties panel on the right.

6   Choose Object > Envelope Distort > Make With Warp to open the Warp Options dialog box. In that dialog box, change the following:

  • Style: Arch (*not Arc*)

  • Bend: **20%**

7   Click OK. The text is now in a shape, but is still editable.

8   With the Selection tool selected, drag the curved text and the "ART SUPPLIES" text into position.

9   Choose Select > Deselect.

▶ **Tip:** To edit the warp options again in the Warp Options dialog box, click the Warp Options button in the Quick Actions section of the Properties panel.

Working with effects

Effects alter the appearance of an object without changing the base object. Next you'll apply an effect to a sale sticker you make.

● **Note:** Learn more about effects in Lesson 13, "Exploring Creative Uses of Effects and Graphic Styles."

1   Press and hold on the Rectangle tool (▢) in the toolbar, and select the Ellipse tool (◯). Over the top of the banner rectangle, Shift-drag to make a circle like the one in the figure. Release the mouse button and then the key.

2   Click the Fill color in the Properties panel. In the panel that opens, select a color. I chose a light blue.

3   In the Properties panel, click the Choose An Effect button (![fx]), and choose Distort & Transform > Zig Zag.

4   In the Zig Zag dialog box, select Preview to see your changes, if it isn't already selected, and then set the following options:

- Size: **9 px**
- Absolute: Selected
- Ridges Per Segment: **9**
- Points: Corner

 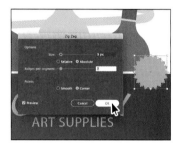

5   Click OK.

Adding more text for practice

Now for a little practice! Try adding some text on top of the circle. You'll apply formatting you've already learned and a few more options. Here are the steps:

1   Select the Type tool (**T**), and click to add some text. To replace the text, type **30%**, press Enter or Return, and then type **OFF**.

2   Select the Selection tool (▶) so the text object is selected.

3   Set the following options in the Properties panel:

- Change the fill color to white.
- Change the font size to **60 pt**.
- Change the Leading (circled in the figure) to **50**. This changes the distance between the lines of text.
- In the Paragraph section of the Properties panel (below the formatting options you just set), click Align Center (![icon]) so the text is center aligned.

4 Drag the text so it is approximately centered on the circle.

5 Shift-click the blue circle to select the text and the blue circle.

6 Click the Group button in the Quick Actions section of the Properties panel to keep them together as a group.

● **Note:** If your circle is too small, press the Shift key and drag a corner to make it larger. Release the mouse button and then the key.

Aligning artwork

Illustrator makes it easy to align or distribute multiple objects relative to each other, the artboard, or a key object. In this section, you'll move artwork into position and align some of it to the center of the artboard.

● **Note:** Learn more about aligning artwork in Lesson 2, "Techniques for Selecting Artwork."

1 With the Selection tool (▶) selected, click to select the group of markers.

2 To select more content, press the Shift key, and click the banner rectangle, the "CRAFTY" text, and the "ART SUPPLIES" text.

3 Click the Align To Selection menu (▦▾) in the Properties panel to the right of the document, and choose Align To Artboard from the menu. Any content you apply an alignment to will now align to the edges of the artboard.

4 Click the Horizontal Align Center button (▤) to align the selected artwork to the horizontal center of the artboard.

5 If necessary, drag the marker scribble and the sale bug into position.

6 Choose File > Save, and then choose File > Close.

1 GETTING TO KNOW THE WORK AREA

Lesson overview

In this lesson, you'll explore the Illustrator workspace and learn how to do the following:

- Open an Adobe Illustrator file.

- Understand cloud documents.

- Work with the toolbar.

- Work with panels.

- Reset and save your workspace.

- Use view options to change the display magnification.

- Navigate multiple artboards and documents.

- Rotate the canvas view.

- Explore document groups.

 This lesson will take about 45 minutes to complete. To get the lesson files used in this chapter, download them from the web page for this book at adobepress.com/IllustratorCIB2022. For more information, see "Accessing the lesson files and Web Edition" in the Getting Started section at the beginning of this book.

By learning how to navigate the workspace easily and efficiently, you'll be able to make the most of the extensive drawing, painting, and editing capabilities of Adobe Illustrator. The workspace consists of the Application bar, menus, toolbar, Properties panel, Document window, and other default panels.

Introducing Adobe Illustrator

In Illustrator, you primarily create and work with vector graphics (sometimes called *vector shapes* or *vector objects*). *Vector graphics* are made up of lines and curves defined by mathematical objects called vectors. You can resize vector graphics to cover the side of a building or to use as a social media icon, without losing detail or clarity.

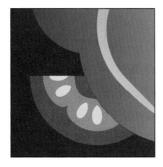

An example of vector artwork.

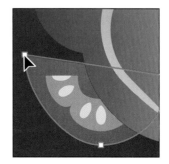

Editing vector artwork.

Vector graphics maintain crisp edges when printed to a PostScript printer, saved in a PDF file, or imported into a vector-based graphics application. As a result, vector graphics are the best choice for artwork like logos that will be used at various sizes and in various output media.

 **Tip:** To learn more about bitmap graphics, search for "Importing bitmap images" in Illustrator Help (Help > Illustrator Help).

Illustrator also allows you to incorporate *bitmap images*—technically called *raster images*—that are made up of a rectangular grid of picture elements (pixels). Each pixel is assigned a specific location and color value. Pictures you take on your phone camera are considered raster images. Raster images can be created and edited in a program like Adobe Photoshop.

Example of a raster image and a zoomed-in portion to show the pixels.

Opening an Illustrator file

In this lesson, you'll begin exploring Illustrator by opening a document. First, you'll restore the default preferences for Adobe Illustrator. This is something you will do at the start of each lesson in this book to ensure that the tools function and the defaults are set exactly as described in this lesson.

1 To delete or deactivate (by renaming) the Adobe Illustrator preferences file, see "Restoring default preferences" in the "Getting Started" section at the beginning of the book.

2 Double-click the Adobe Illustrator icon to launch Adobe Illustrator.

   With Illustrator open, you will see the Home screen showing resources for Illustrator, and more.

3 Choose File > Open or click the Open button in the Home screen.
   In the Lessons > Lesson01 folder on your hard disk, select the L1_start1.ai file, and click Open to open the design.

   You will use the L1_start1.ai file to practice navigating, zooming, and investigating an Illustrator document and the workspace.

4 Choose Window > Workspace > Essentials, make sure it's selected (a checkmark appears next to the name if selected), and then choose Window > Workspace > Reset Essentials to reset the workspace.

   The Reset Essentials command ensures that the workspace, which includes all of the tools and panels, is set to the default settings. You'll learn more about resetting the workspace in the section "Switching workspaces."

5 Choose View > Fit Artboard In Window.

   An *artboard* is the area that contains artwork that will be output and is similar to a page in Adobe InDesign or Microsoft Word. This command fits the whole artboard (the purple area in the figure) into the Document window so you can see the whole design.

Note: If finding the preferences file proves difficult, please email me (brian@ brianwoodtraining.com) for assistance.

Note: If you have not already downloaded the project files for this lesson to your computer from your Account page, make sure to do so now. See the "Getting Started" section at the beginning of the book.

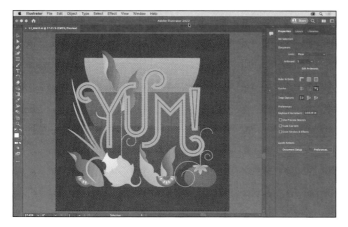

Understanding cloud documents

You can save your Illustrator documents as cloud documents. A cloud document is an Illustrator document that is stored in Adobe Creative Cloud and can be accessed anywhere you sign in to Illustrator.

After you create a new document or open a document from your hard drive, you save the file to the cloud by choosing File > Save As. The first time you do this, you will see a Cloud Document dialog box with options to save as a cloud document or save to your computer. Click the Save To Creative Cloud button.

Note: If instead of the Cloud Document dialog box you see the Save As dialog box and want to save as a cloud document, you can click the Save Cloud Document button.

In the dialog box that appears, you can change the name and click the Save button to save the document to the cloud. If you change your mind and want to save the file locally, you can click On Your Computer in that dialog box.

When working on cloud documents, changes are automatically saved, so the document is always up to date. In the Version History panel (File > Version History), you can access previously saved versions of a document. You can bookmark and name specific versions so they show in the Marked area of the panel, and open a version in a new window to see changes. Unmarked versions are available for 30 days and marked versions are available indefinitely.

If you want to open a cloud document, choose File > Open. In the Open dialog box, click Open Cloud Document. You can then open a cloud document from the dialog box that appears.

When you launch Illustrator, you can click Your Files from the Home screen to view documents saved to the Creative Cloud. From there, you can open and organize them.

Exploring the workspace

When Illustrator is launched and a file is open, the menus, Application bar, toolbar, and panels appear on the screen. The arrangement of these elements is called a *workspace*. When you first start Illustrator, you see the default workspace, which you can customize how you like. You can create and save multiple workspaces—one for editing and another for viewing, for example—and switch between them as you work.

A. Application bar

B. Panels

C. Toolbar

D. Document window

E. Status bar

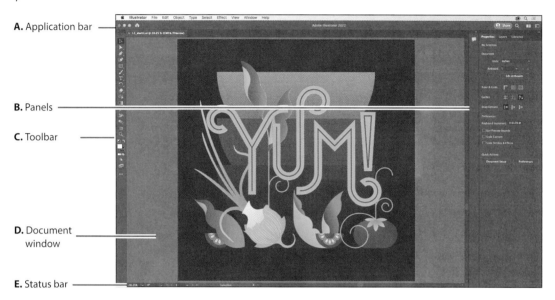

A. The **Application bar**, across the top by default, contains application controls, the workspace switcher, and search. On Windows, the main menu bar items appear *inline* with the Application bar—see the following figure.

Note: The screen captures in this lesson were taken using macOS and may look slightly different from what you see, especially if you are using Windows.

B. **Panels** help you monitor and modify your work. Certain panels are displayed by default in the panel dock on the right side of the workspace, and you can display any panel by choosing it from the Window menu.

C. The **toolbar** contains tools for creating and editing images, artwork, artboard elements, and more. Related tools are grouped together.

D. The **Document window** displays the file(s) you're working on.

E. The **Status bar** appears at the lower-left edge of the Document window. It displays information, zooming, and navigation controls.

Getting to know the toolbar

The toolbar on the left side of the workspace contains tools for selecting, drawing, painting, editing, and viewing, as well as the Fill and Stroke boxes, drawing modes, and screen modes. As you work through the lessons, you'll learn about the specific function of many of these tools.

▶ **Tip:** You can turn the tool tips on or off by choosing Illustrator > Preferences > General (macOS) or Edit > Preferences > General (Windows) and selecting or deselecting Show Rich Tool Tips.

1 Move the pointer over the Selection tool (▶) in the toolbar. Notice that the name (Selection tool) and keyboard shortcut (V) display in a tool tip, as well as in most cases, more information about the tool.

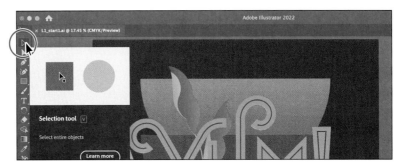

2 Move the pointer over the Direct Selection tool (▷). Press and hold until a tool menu appears, and then release the mouse button. Click the Group Selection tool (▷⁺) in the menu to select it.

Any tool in the toolbar that displays a small triangle contains additional tools that can be selected this way.

▶ **Tip:** You can also select hidden tools by pressing the Option key (macOS) or the Alt key (Windows) and clicking the tool in the toolbar. Each click selects the next hidden tool in the tool sequence.

3 Press and hold the Rectangle tool (▭) to reveal more tools. Click the arrow at the right edge of the hidden tools panel to separate the tools from the toolbar as a separate floating panel of tools that you can access easily.

4 Click the Close button (X) in the upper-left corner (macOS) or upper-right corner (Windows) of the floating tool panel to close it. The tools return to the toolbar.

Next, you'll learn how to resize and float the toolbar. In the figures in this lesson, the toolbar is a single column by default. You may initially see a double-column toolbar, depending on your screen resolution and workspace, and that's okay.

5 Click the double arrow in the upper-left corner of the toolbar to either expand the single column into two columns or collapse the two columns into one (depending on your screen resolution).

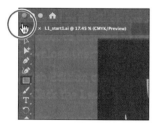

▶ **Tip:** You can also double-click the title bar at the top of the toolbar to switch between two columns and one column.

● **Note:** When the toolbar is floating, be careful not to click the X or it will close! If you close it, choose Window > Toolbars > Basic to reopen it.

6 Click the same double arrow again to collapse (or expand) the toolbar.

7 Drag the toolbar into the workspace by the dark gray title bar at the top of the toolbar or by the dashed line beneath the title bar. The toolbar is now floating in the workspace.

8 Drag the toolbar to the left side of the Application window using either the solid bar at the top of the toolbar or the dashed line just below the solid bar.

When the pointer reaches the left edge, a translucent blue border, called the *drop zone*, appears. Release the mouse button to dock the toolbar neatly into the side of the workspace.

Finding more tools

In Illustrator, the default set of tools that appears in the toolbar does not include every available tool. As you make your way through this book, you'll explore other tools that you'll need to know how to access. In this section, you'll see how to access these other tools.

1 Click Edit Toolbar (**⋯**) at the bottom of the toolbar.

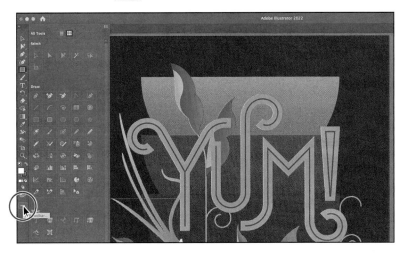

A panel appears that shows all of the available tools. The tools that appear dimmed (you can't select them) are already in the default toolbar. You can drag any of the remaining tools into the toolbar, where you can then select and use them.

2 Move the pointer over a tool that is dimmed, like the Selection tool, at the top of the tools list (you may need to scroll up).

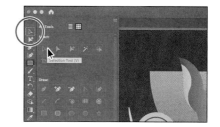

The tool is outlined in blue in the toolbar. If you hover over a tool like the Ellipse tool, which is nested within the Rectangle tool, the Rectangle tool will be outlined, showing you where it is.

3 Scroll in the list of tools until you see the Shaper tool ( ). To add it to the toolbar, drag the Shaper tool onto the Rectangle tool. When a highlight appears around the Rectangle tool, release the mouse button to add the Shaper tool.

4 Press the Escape key to hide the extra tools.

The Shaper tool will now be in the toolbar until you remove it or reset the toolbar. Next, you'll remove the Shaper tool. Later in the book, you will add tools to learn more about them.

5 Click Edit Toolbar ( ) at the bottom of the toolbar again to show the panel of extra tools. Drag the Shaper tool anywhere onto the panel and release the mouse button to remove the Shaper tool from the toolbar.

▶ **Tip:** After clicking Edit Toolbar, you can reset the toolbar by clicking the panel menu icon ( ) and choosing Reset.

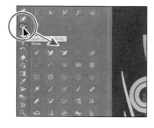 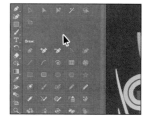

6 Press the Escape key to hide the extra tools.

Working with the Properties panel

When you start Illustrator for the first time and open a document, you'll see the Properties panel on the right side of the workspace. The Properties panel displays properties for the active document when nothing is selected. It also displays appearance properties for content you select. It's a panel you'll use quite a bit; it puts all of the most commonly used options in one place.

Using the Properties panel, you'll change the color of artwork in the poster.

1 Select the Selection tool (▶) in the toolbar, and look in the Properties panel on the right.

At the top of the Properties panel, you will see "No Selection." This is called the Selection Indicator. It's a great place to see what type of content is selected (if any). With nothing selected in the document, the Properties panel shows the current document properties and program preferences.

2 Move the pointer into the top bowl shape in the document, and click to select it.

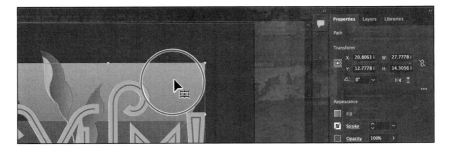

In the Properties panel, you should now see appearance options for the selected artwork, which is a path, as indicated by "Path" at the top of the panel. You can change the size, position, color, and much more for the selected artwork.

Tip: Words that are underlined in the Properties panel show more options when you click them.

3 Click the color box to the left of the word "Fill" in the Properties panel to show a panel of colors.

4 In the panel that shows, make sure the Swatches option is selected at the top (circled in the figure), and then click another color to apply it.

5 Press Escape to hide the panel.

6 Choose Select > Deselect to deselect the bowl shape.

The Properties panel once again shows document properties and program preferences when nothing is selected.

Working with panels

Panels like the Properties panel give you quick access to many of the tools and options that make modifying artwork easier. All of the panels available in Illustrator are listed alphabetically in the Window menu. Next, you'll experiment with hiding, opening, and closing panels.

1 Click the Layers panel tab to the right of the Properties panel tab.

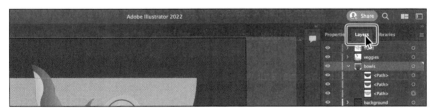

The Layers panel is grouped with two other panels—the Properties panel and the Libraries panel. They are all part of the same panel group.

2 Click the double arrow at the top of the dock to collapse the panels.

You can use this method of collapsing the panels to create a larger area for working on your document. You'll learn more about docking in the next section.

Tip: To show a panel that is not currently visible, choose the panel name from the Window menu. A checkmark to the left of the panel name indicates that the panel is already open and in front of other panels in its panel group. If you choose a panel name that is already selected in the Window menu, the panel and its group either close or collapse.

Tip: To expand or collapse the panel dock, you can also double-click the panel dock title bar at the top.

3 Drag the left edge of the docked panels to the right until the panel text disappears.

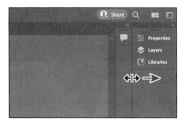 

This hides the panel names and collapses the panel dock to icons only. To open a panel that is collapsed as an icon, you can click a panel icon.

4 Click the double arrow again to expand the panels.

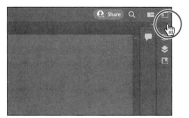 

5 Choose Window > Workspace > Reset Essentials to reset the workspace.

You'll learn more about resetting and switching workspaces in the section "Switching workspaces."

Moving and docking panels

Panels in Illustrator can be moved around in the workspace and organized to match your working needs. Next, you'll open a new panel and dock it with the default panels on the right side of the workspace.

1 Click the Window menu at the top of the screen to see all of the panels available in Illustrator. Choose Align from the Window menu to open the Align panel and the other panels grouped with it by default.

Panels you open that do not appear in the default workspace are free-floating. That means they are not docked and can be moved around. You can dock free-floating panels on the right or left side of the workspace.

2 Drag the Align panel group by the title bar above the panel names to move the group closer to the docked panels on the right.

Next, you'll dock the Align panel with the Properties panel group.

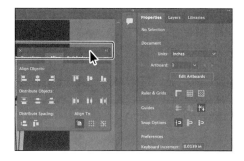

3 Drag the Align panel by the panel tab onto the Properties, Layers, and Libraries panel tabs on the right. When a blue highlight appears *around* the entire panel dock, release the mouse button to dock the panel in the group.

When dragging a panel to the dock on the right, if you see a blue line *above* the docked panel tabs before releasing, you'll create a new panel group rather than docking the panel with the existing panel group.

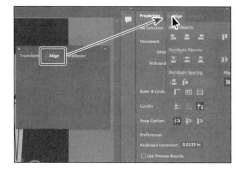

4 Click the X at the top of the Transform and Pathfinder panel group, which is free-floating, to close it.

Aside from adding panels to the dock on the right, you can also remove them.

5 Drag the Align panel by the panel tab, to the left, away from the dock of panels, and release the mouse button.

6 Click the X at the top of the Align panel to close it.

7 Click the Libraries panel tab on the right to show that panel, if the panel isn't already showing.

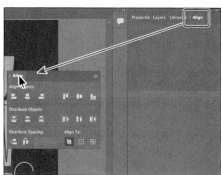

Scaling the Illustrator interface

When you launch Illustrator, it identifies your screen resolution and adjusts the application scale factor accordingly. You can scale the user interface of Illustrator based on your screen resolution to make the tools, text, and other UI elements easier to see.

Choose Illustrator > Preferences > User Interface (macOS) or Edit > Preferences > User Interface (Windows) to change the UI Scaling settings. The change will take place after restarting Illustrator.

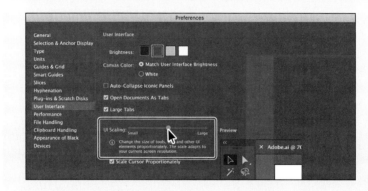

Switching workspaces

Illustrator comes with a host of workspaces that are tailored to a variety of tasks. As you've seen, you can also customize the parts of the default Essentials workspace, like the toolbar and panels. As you make changes, like opening and closing panels and changing their position (among other things), you can save that particular arrangement as a workspace—and switch between them while you work.

Next, you'll switch workspaces and learn about some new panels.

Tip: You can also choose Window > Workspace and choose a workspace.

1 Click the workspace switcher (▣) on the right end of the Application bar above the docked panels to change the workspace. See the first part of the following figure.

You'll see a number of workspaces listed, each with a specific purpose, that will open panels and arrange the workspace accordingly.

Tip: Press Tab to toggle between hiding and showing all panels. You can hide or show all panels at once, except for the toolbar, by pressing Shift+Tab to toggle between hiding and showing them.

2 Choose Layout from the workspace switcher menu to change workspaces.

You'll notice a few major changes in the workspace. One of the biggest is the Control panel, which is now docked at the top of the workspace, just above the Document window (it's highlighted in the following figure). Similar to the Properties panel, it offers quick access to options, commands, and other panels relevant to the currently selected content.

Also, notice all of the collapsed panel icons on the right side of the workspace. In workspaces, you can create groups of panels that are stacked on top of others. That way, a lot more panels are visible.

3   Choose Essentials from the workspace switcher (▢) above the docked panels to switch back to the Essentials workspace.

4   Choose Reset Essentials from the workspace switcher in the Application bar.

    When you switch back to a previous workspace, it remembers any changes you made, like selecting the Libraries panel. To completely reset a workspace to its default settings, the Essentials workspace in this case, you'll need to reset it.

▶ **Tip:** To delete workspaces you create, choose Window > Workspace > Manage Workspaces. Select the workspace name, and click the Delete Workspace button.

▶ **Tip:** To change a saved workspace, reset the panels as you'd like them to appear and then choose Window > Workspace > New Workspace. In the New Workspace dialog box, name the workspace with a new, unused name. If you name a new workspace with a name that's already in use, a message appears in the dialog box warning that you will overwrite an existing workspace with the same name if you click OK.

Saving a workspace

So far, you've reset the workspace and chosen a different workspace. You can also arrange the panels the way you like and save your own custom workspace. Next, you'll dock a new panel and create your own workspace.

1   Choose Window > Artboards to open the Artboards panel group.

2   Drag the Artboards panel by the panel tab onto the Properties panel *tab* at the top of the docked panels on the right. When a blue highlight appears around the entire panel dock, release the mouse button to dock the Artboards panel and add it to the existing panel group.

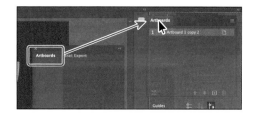

3 Click the X at the top of the free-floating Asset Export panel to close it.

4 Choose Window > Workspace > New Workspace. Change its name to **My Workspace** in the New Workspace dialog box, and click OK.

The name of the workspace could be anything, as long as it makes sense to you.
The workspace named "My Workspace" is now saved with Illustrator until you remove it.

5 Choose Window > Workspace > Essentials, and then choose Window > Workspace > Reset Essentials.

Notice that the panels return to their default number and positions after choosing Reset Essentials.

6 Choose Window > Workspace > My Workspace.

7 Toggle between the two workspaces using the Window > Workspace command, and return to the Essentials workspace before starting the next exercise.

Using panel and context menus

Most panels in Illustrator have more options available in a panel menu, found by clicking the panel menu icon (▤ or ▤) in the upper-right corner of a panel. These additional options can be used to change the panel display, add or change panel content, and more. Next, you'll change the display of the Swatches panel using its panel menu.

1 With the Selection tool (▶) selected in the toolbar on the left, click the bowl shape again.

2 Click the Fill color box, to the left of the word "Fill," in the Properties panel.

3 In the panel that appears, called the Swatches panel, make sure that the Swatches option (▦) is selected toward the top of the panel. Click the panel menu icon (▤) in the upper-right corner, and choose Small List View from the panel menu.

  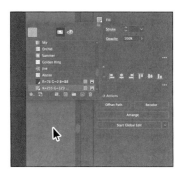

This displays the swatch names, together with thumbnails. Because the options in the panel menu apply only to the active panel, only the Swatches panel view is affected.

4 Click the same panel menu icon (▤) in the panel showing, and choose Small Thumbnail View to return the swatches to their original view.

In addition to the panel menus, context-sensitive menus display commands relevant to the active tool, selection, or panel. Usually the commands in a context menu are available in another part of the workspace, but using a context menu can save you time.

5 Press Escape to hide the Swatches panel.

6 Choose Select > Deselect so the bowl shape is no longer selected.

7 Move the pointer over the dark gray area surrounding the artwork. Then, right-click to show a context menu with specific options.

The context-sensitive menu you see may contain different commands, depending on what the pointer is positioned over.

▶ **Tip:** If you move the pointer over the tab or title bar for a panel and right-click, you can close a panel or a panel group from the context menu that appears.

Adjusting the brightness of the user interface

As with Adobe InDesign and Adobe Photoshop, Illustrator supports a brightness adjustment for the application user interface. This is a program-wide preference setting that allows you to choose a brightness setting from four preset levels.

To edit the user-interface brightness, you can choose Illustrator > Preferences > User Interface (macOS) or Edit > Preferences > User Interface (Windows).

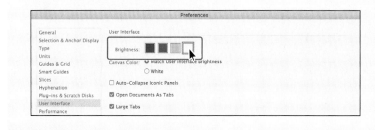

Changing the view of artwork

While working in files, it's likely that you'll need to change the magnification level and navigate between artboards. The magnification level, which can range from 3.13% to 64000%, is displayed in the title bar (or document tab) next to the filename and in the lower-left corner of the Document window.

There are a lot of ways to change the zoom level in Illustrator, and in this section you'll explore several of the most widely used methods.

Using view commands

▶ **Tip:** The keyboard shortcut for the View > Zoom In command is Command and + (macOS) or Ctrl and + (Windows). You can zoom out using the keyboard shortcut Command and − (macOS) or Ctrl and − (Windows).

View commands are found in the View menu and are an easy way to enlarge or reduce the view of artwork.

1   Choose View > Zoom In twice to enlarge the display of the artwork.

Using the viewing tools and commands affects only the display of the artwork, not the actual size of the artwork. Each time you choose a Zoom option, the view of the artwork is resized to the closest preset zoom level. The preset zoom levels appear in a menu in the lower-left corner of the Document window, identified by a down arrow next to a percentage.

▶ **Tip:** Choose View > Actual Size to display the artwork at actual size.

2   Choose View > Fit Artboard In Window to see the entire poster again.

By choosing View > Fit Artboard In Window or by using the keyboard shortcut Command+0 (macOS) or Ctrl+0 (Windows), the entire artboard (page) is centered in the Document window.

3   Click the sliced tomato beneath the "M" in "YUM" to select it. Choose View > Zoom In.

If you have artwork selected, using the View > Zoom In view command will zoom in to what is selected.

4   Choose View > Fit Artboard In Window.

5   Choose Select > Deselect so the tomato is no longer selected.

Using the Zoom tool

In addition to the View menu options, you can use the Zoom tool (Q) to magnify and reduce the view of artwork to predefined magnification levels.

1 Select the Zoom tool (Q) in the toolbar, and then move the pointer into the Document window.

Notice that a plus sign (+) appears at the center of the Zoom tool pointer.

2 Move the Zoom tool pointer over the whole tomato, and click once.

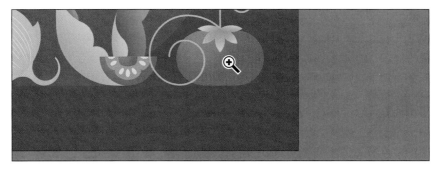

The artwork is displayed at a higher magnification, depending on your screen resolution. Notice that where you clicked is now in the center of the Document window.

3 Click two more times on the tomato.

The view is increased again, and you'll notice that the area where you clicked is centered in the document window.

4 With the Zoom tool still selected, press the Option (macOS) or Alt (Windows) key. A minus sign (–) appears at the center of the Zoom tool pointer. With the Option or Alt key pressed, click the artwork twice to reduce the view of the artwork.

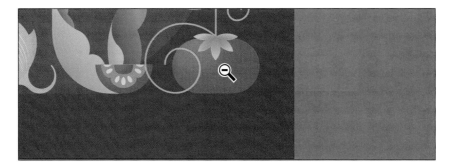

Using the Zoom tool, you can also drag in the document to zoom in and out. By default, if your computer meets the system requirements for GPU performance and it's enabled, zooming is animated. To find out if your computer meets the system requirements, see the sidebar "GPU performance" following this section.

5 Choose View > Fit Artboard In Window.

6 With the Zoom tool still selected, drag from the left side of the document to the right to zoom in. The zooming is animated. Drag from right to left to zoom out.

If your computer does not meet the system requirements for GPU performance, you will instead draw a dotted rectangle, called a *marquee*, when dragging with the Zoom tool.

7 Choose View > Fit Artboard In Window to fit the artboard in the Document window.

The Zoom tool is used frequently during the editing process to enlarge and reduce the view of artwork. Because of this, Illustrator allows you to select the Zoom tool using the keyboard at any time without first deselecting any other tool you may be using.

- To access the Zoom tool using your keyboard, press spacebar+Command (macOS) or Ctrl+spacebar (Windows).

- To access the Zoom Out tool using your keyboard, press spacebar+Command+Option (macOS) or Ctrl+Alt+spacebar (Windows).

Tip: With the Zoom tool selected, if you move the pointer into the Document window and press the mouse button for a few seconds, you can zoom in using the animated zoom.

Note: In certain versions of macOS, the keyboard shortcuts for the Zoom tool (Q) open Spotlight or the Finder. If you decide to use these shortcuts in Illustrator, you may want to turn off or change those keyboard shortcuts in macOS System Preferences.

GPU performance

The Graphics Processing Unit (GPU), found on video cards and as part of display systems, is a specialized processor that can rapidly execute commands for manipulating and displaying images. GPU-accelerated computing offers faster performance across a broad range of design, animation, and video applications.

This means you get a big performance boost: Illustrator runs faster and more smoothly than ever before.

This feature is available on compatible macOS and Windows computers. It is turned on by default, and options can be accessed in Preferences by choosing Illustrator > Preferences > Performance (macOS) or Edit > Preferences > Performance (Windows).

To learn more about GPU performance, visit helpx.adobe.com/illustrator/kb/gpu-performance-preview-improvements.html.

Panning in a document

In Illustrator, you can use the Hand tool (✋) to pan to different areas of a document. Using the Hand tool allows you to push the document around much like you would a piece of paper on your desk. This can be a useful way to move around in a document with a lot of artboards or when you are zoomed in. In this section, you'll access the Hand tool a few different ways.

1   Press and hold on the Zoom tool in the toolbar, and select the Hand tool (✋).

2   Drag down in the Document window. As you drag, the artboard and artwork on it moves with the hand.

    As with the Zoom tool (🔍), you can select the Hand tool with a keyboard shortcut without first deselecting the active tool.

● **Note:** The spacebar shortcut for the Hand tool (✋) does not work when the Type tool (T) is active and the cursor is in text. To access the Hand tool when the cursor is in text, press the Option (macOS) or Alt (Windows) key.

3   Click any other tool except the Type tool (T) in the toolbar, and move the pointer into the Document window. Hold down the spacebar on the keyboard to temporarily select the Hand tool, and then drag to bring the artwork back into the center of your view. Release the spacebar.

4   Choose View > Fit Artboard In Window.

Panning with the Navigator panel 🎬

To learn about a different way to pan around in a document, check out the video *Panning with the Navigator panel*, which is part of the Web Edition. For more information, see the "Web Edition" section of "Getting Started" at the beginning of the book.

Viewing artwork

When you open a file, the artwork is displayed in Preview mode, which is in vector form. Illustrator offers other ways of viewing your artwork, such as outlined and rasterized. Next, you'll take a look at the different methods for viewing artwork and understand why you might view artwork each of these ways.

When working with large or complex illustrations, you may want to view only the outlines or paths of objects in your artwork. That way, the artwork doesn't have to be redrawn each time you make a change. This is called Outline mode. Outline mode can also be helpful for selecting objects, as you will see in Lesson 2, "Techniques for Selecting Artwork."

▶ **Tip:** You can press Command+Y (macOS) or Ctrl+Y (Windows) to toggle between Preview and Outline modes.

1   Choose View > Outline.

    Only the outlines of objects are displayed. You can use this view to find and select things that might be hiding behind other objects.

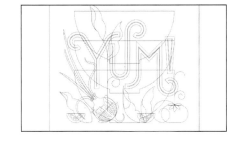

With Outline mode still active, choose View > Preview (or GPU Preview) to see all the attributes of the artwork again.

2 Choose View > Pixel Preview.

3 Select the Selection tool, and click the tomato you selected earlier.

4 Choose 400% from the zoom level menu in the lower-left corner of the application window to more easily see the edges of the tomato.

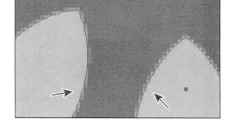

Pixel preview shows you how the artwork would look if it were rasterized and viewed onscreen in a web browser. Note the "jagged" edge on some of the artwork. Arrows are pointing to it in the figure.

5 Choose View > Pixel Preview to turn off Pixel preview.

6 Choose View > Fit Artboard In Window to make sure that the artboard is fit in the Document window, and leave document open.

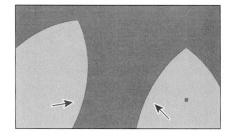

Navigating multiple artboards

As you may recall, artboards contain artwork that will be output, similar to pages in Adobe InDesign. You can use artboards to crop areas to be output or for placement purposes. Multiple artboards help create various things, such as multi page PDFs, printed pages with different sizes or different elements, independent elements for websites, video storyboards, or individual items for animation in Adobe Animate or Adobe After Effects.

Illustrator allows for up to 1000 artboards within a single file (depending on their dimensions). Multiple artboards can be added when you initially create an Illustrator document, or you can add, remove, and edit artboards after the document is made. Next, you will learn how to navigate a document that has a few artboards.

1 Choose File > Open. In the Open dialog box, navigate to the Lessons > Lesson01 folder, and select the L1_start2.ai file on your hard disk. Click Open to view another version of the poster.

Tip: You'll learn about another method for navigating artboards, the Artboards panel, in Lesson 5, "Transforming Artwork."

2 Choose View > Fit All In Window to fit all artboards in the Document window. Notice that there are two artboards in the document; they contain two versions of the L1_start1.ai artwork.

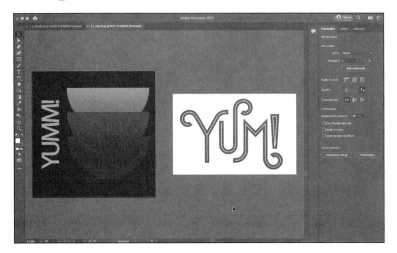

You can arrange the artboards in a document in any order, orientation, or size—they can even overlap. Suppose that you want to create a four-page brochure. You can create different artboards for every page of the brochure, all with the same size and orientation. They can be arranged horizontally or vertically or in whatever way you like.

3 Select the Selection tool (▶) in the toolbar, and click to select the red "YUM" text on the right.

4 Choose View > Fit Artboard In Window.

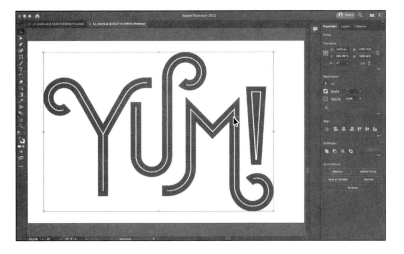

When you select artwork, it makes the artboard that the artwork is on the *active*, or selected, artboard. By choosing the Fit Artboard In Window command, the currently active artboard is fit into the Document window. The

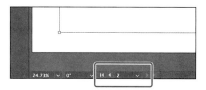

active artboard is identified in the Artboard Navigation menu in the Status bar in the lower-left corner of the Document window. Currently it's artboard 2.

5 Choose Select > Deselect to deselect the artwork.

6 Choose 1 from the Artboard menu in the Properties panel.

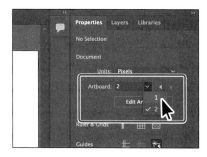

Notice the arrows to the right of the Artboard menu in the Properties panel. You can use these to navigate to the previous (◀) and next (▶) artboards. Those arrows plus a few others also appear in the Status bar below the document.

7 Click the Next navigation button (▶) in the Status bar below the document to view the next artboard (artboard 2) in the Document window.

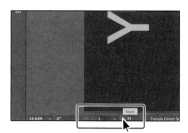

The Artboard menu and navigation arrows always appear in the Status bar below the document, but they appear in the Properties panel only when not in Artboard Editing mode, the Selection tool is active, and nothing is selected.

Rotating the view

Projects like packaging designs, logos, or any that contain rotated text can be easier to work on when you rotate them temporarily. Think of a large drawing on paper. If you wanted to edit part of the drawing, you might turn the paper on your desk. In this section, you'll see how to rotate the canvas with the Rotate View tool and edit some text.

1 Choose 1 from the Artboard menu in the Properties panel to fit the artboard with the purple background in the document window.

2 Press and hold on the Hand tool in the toolbar, and select the Rotate View tool (🖐️).

▶ **Tip:** To automatically align the canvas view to a rotated object, you can choose View > Rotate View to Selection to rotate the canvas.

3 Drag clockwise in the Document window to rotate the entire canvas. As you drag, press the Shift key to rotate the view in 15-degree increments. When you see −90 degrees in the measurement label, release the mouse button and then the key.

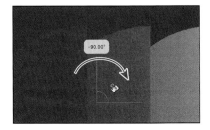

The artboards, which are on the canvas, rotate as well.

4 Select the Type tool (**T**) in the toolbar. Now you'll edit the "YUMM" text by adding another "M." Click in between the Ms in the blue "YUMM!" text to insert the cursor. Type a capital **M**. The text now reads "YUMMM!"

When finished, you can reset the canvas.

5 Select the Selection tool, and click in an empty area to deselect.

6 Click the −90° you see in the Status bar below the document to show a menu of canvas rotation values. Choose 0 from that menu to set the canvas back to the default rotation.

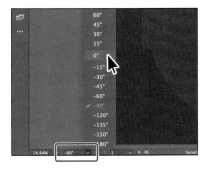

▶ **Tip:** To reset the rotated canvas view, you can also press the Esc key, choose View > Reset Rotate View, or press Shift+Cmd+1 (macOS) or Shift+Ctrl+1 (Windows).

Arranging multiple documents

In Illustrator, all workspace elements, such as the panels, Document window, and tools, are grouped in a single integrated window called the Application frame, which lets you treat the application as a single unit. When you move or resize the Application frame or any of its elements, all elements within it respond to each other so none overlap.

When you open more than one document in Illustrator, they appear as tabs at the top of the Document window. You can arrange the open documents in other ways, such as side by side, so that you can easily compare or drag items from one document to another. You can also use the Window > Arrange menu to display your open documents in various configurations quickly.

You should currently have two Illustrator files open: L1_start1.ai and L1_start2.ai. Each file has its own tab at the top of the Document window. These documents are considered a group of Document windows. You can create document groups to associate files while they are open.

1   Click the L1_start1.ai tab at the top of the Document window to show the L1_start1.ai document.

2   Drag the L1_start1.ai document tab *directly to the right* of the L1_start2.ai document tab. Release the mouse button to see the new tab order.

Dragging the document tabs allows you to change the order of the documents. Ordering tabs may be helpful if you use the document shortcuts to navigate to the next or previous document. See the tip to the right.

To see both of the documents simultaneously, maybe to drag artwork from one to the other, you can arrange the Document windows by cascading or tiling them. Cascading allows you to stack different document groups. Tiling shows multiple Document windows at one time, in various arrangements. Next you'll tile the open documents so that you can see both documents at one time.

3   Choose Window > Arrange > Tile.

The available space in the Application frame is divided between the documents.

Note: If you don't drag directly to the right, you may undock the Document window and create a new group. If that happens, choose Window > Arrange > Consolidate All Windows.

Tip: You can cycle between open documents by pressing Command+~ (next document) and Command+Shift+~ (previous document) (macOS) or by pressing Ctrl+F6 (next document) and Ctrl+Shift+F6 (previous document) (Windows).

4 Click in the Document window on the left to activate the document, and choose View > Fit Artboard In Window. Do the same for the Document window on the right.

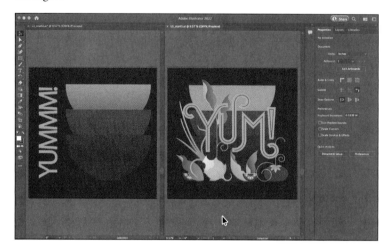

With documents tiled, you can drag artwork between documents, which copies that artwork from one document to another.

To change the arrangement of the tiled windows, you can drag document tabs to other positions. However, it's easier to use the Arrange Documents menu to quickly arrange open documents in a variety of configurations.

5 Click Arrange Documents (⊞) on the ride side of the Application bar to display the Arrange Documents menu. Click the Consolidate All button (▢) to bring the documents back together.

In the Arrange Documents (⊞) menu, you can tile the documents like you did when choosing Window > Arrange > Tile. You get more options on how to tile them (vertically or horizontally).

6 Click the Close button (X) on the L1_start1.ai document tab to close the document. If a dialog box appears asking you to save the document, click Don't Save (macOS) or No (Windows).

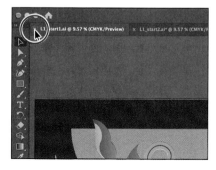

7 Choose File > Close to close the L1_start2.ai document without saving.

Review questions

1   Describe two ways to change the view of a document.

2   How do you save panel locations and visibility preferences?

3   Describe a few ways to navigate between artboards in Illustrator.

4   How can you rotate the canvas view?

5   How is arranging Document windows helpful?

Review answers

1   You can choose commands from the View menu to zoom in or out of a document or to fit it to your screen; you can also use the Zoom tool (Q) in the toolbar and click and drag over a document to enlarge or reduce the view. In addition, you can use keyboard shortcuts to magnify or reduce the display of artwork.

2   You can save panel locations and visibility preferences by choosing Window > Workspace > New Workspace to create custom work areas and to make it easier to find the controls you need.

3   To navigate between artboards in Illustrator, you can choose the artboard number from the Artboard Navigation menu at the lower left of the Document window. With nothing selected and while not in Artboard Editing mode, you can choose the artboard number from the Artboard menu or use the Active Artboard arrows in the Properties panel. You can use the Artboard Navigation arrows in the Status bar in the lower left of the Document window to go to the first, previous, next, and last artboards. You can also use the Artboards panel to navigate to artboards, or you can use the Navigator panel to drag the proxy view area to navigate between artboards.

4   To rotate the canvas view, drag in the Document window with the Rotate View tool (✋), choose a rotate value from the Rotate View menu in the Status bar, or (bonus!) choose a rotate value from the View > Rotate View menu.

5   Arranging Document windows allows you to tile windows or to cascade document groups (the process for cascading wasn't discussed in the lesson). This can be useful if you are working on multiple Illustrator files and you need to compare or share content between them.

2 TECHNIQUES FOR SELECTING ARTWORK

Lesson overview

In this lesson, you'll learn how to do the following:

- Differentiate between the various selection tools and use selection techniques.

- Recognize Smart Guides.

- Save selections for future use.

- Hide, lock, and unlock items.

- Use tools and commands to align shapes and points to each other and the artboard.

- Group items.

- Work in Isolation mode.

- Arrange objects.

This lesson will take about 45 minutes to complete. To get the lesson files used in this chapter, download them from the web page for this book at adobepress.com/IllustratorCIB2022. For more information, see "Accessing the lesson files and Web Edition" in the Getting Started section at the beginning of this book.

Selecting content in Adobe Illustrator is one of the more essential things you'll do. In this lesson, you'll learn how to select objects using selection tools; protect objects by grouping, hiding, and locking them; align objects to each other and the artboard; and much more.

Starting the lesson

Creating, selecting, and editing are the cornerstones of working with artwork in Adobe Illustrator. In this lesson, you'll learn the fundamentals of selecting, aligning, and grouping artwork using different methods. You'll begin by resetting the preferences in Illustrator and opening the lesson file.

● **Note:** If you have not already downloaded the project files for this lesson to your computer from your Account page, make sure to do so now. See the "Getting Started" section at the beginning of the book.

1 To ensure that the tools function and the defaults are set exactly as described in this lesson, delete or deactivate (by renaming) the Adobe Illustrator preferences file. See "Restoring default preferences" in the "Getting Started" section at the beginning of the book.

2 Start Adobe Illustrator.

3 Choose File > Open. Locate the file named L2_end.ai, which is in the Lessons > Lesson02 folder that you copied onto your hard disk, and click Open.

This file contains the finished illustration that you'll create in this lesson.

4 Choose File > Open to open the L2_start.ai file in the Lessons > Lesson02 folder on your hard disk.

You'll save this starter file so you can work on it.

5 Choose File > Save As.

When saving in Illustrator, you may see the dialog box at right. If you do, you can choose to save either to the Creative Cloud as a cloud document or to your computer. To learn more about saving as a cloud document, visit the sidebar "Understanding cloud documents" in Lesson 1, "Getting to Know the Work Area."

For this lesson, you'll save the lesson file to your computer.

6 If the Cloud Document dialog box opens, click Save On Your Computer to show the Save As dialog box.

7 In the Save As dialog box, name the file **SaveWildlife.ai**, and save it in the Lessons > Lesson02 folder. Leave Adobe Illustrator (ai) chosen from the Format menu (macOS) or Adobe Illustrator (*.AI) chosen from the Save As Type menu (Windows), and click Save.

8 In the Illustrator Options dialog box, leave the Illustrator options at their default settings, and click OK.

9 Choose Window > Workspace > Essentials, make sure it's selected, and then choose Window > Workspace > Reset Essentials to reset the workspace.

Selecting objects

Whether creating artwork from scratch or editing existing artwork in Illustrator, you'll need to become familiar with selecting objects. It will help you to understand better what vector artwork is all about. There are many methods and tools for selecting and editing, and in this section, you'll explore the most widely used, which are the Selection (▶) and Direct Selection (▷) tools.

Using the Selection tool

The Selection tool (▶) lets you select, move, rotate, and resize objects. In this section, you'll become familiar with it.

1 Choose 2 Pieces from the Artboard Navigation menu below the Document window.

This should fit the artboard on the right into the Document window. If the artboard *doesn't* fit in the window, you can choose View > Fit Artboard In Window.

2 Select the Selection tool (▶) in the toolbar on the left. Move the pointer over the different artwork on the artboards, but don't click.

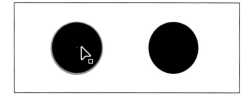

The icon that appears next to the pointer as it passes over objects (▶) indicates that there is artwork under the pointer that can be selected. When you hover over an object, that object is also outlined in a color, like blue in this instance.

3 Move the pointer over the edge of one of the black circles.

A word such as "path" or "anchor" might show next to the pointer because Smart Guides are on by default (View > Smart Guides). Smart Guides are temporary snap-to guides that help you align, edit, and transform objects or artboards. You'll learn more about Smart Guides in Lesson 3, "Using Shapes to Create Artwork for a Postcard."

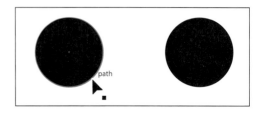

● **Note:** The bounding and anchor points in this lesson are larger to make them easier to see. To learn how you can do that, see the sidebar "Changing the size of anchor points, handles, and the bounding box display."

4 Click anywhere inside the black circle on the left to select it.

A bounding box with eight handles appears around the selected circle. The *bounding box* can be used to make changes to content, such as resizing or rotating. The bounding box also indicates that an item is selected and ready to be modified. The color of the bounding box indicates which layer the object is on. Layers are discussed more in Lesson 10, "Organizing Your Artwork with Layers."

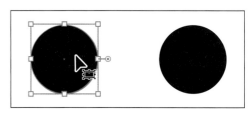

5 Click in the black circle on the right.

Notice that the circle on the left is now deselected and only the circle on the right is selected.

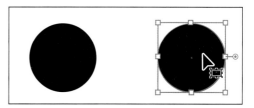

6 Pressing the Shift key, click in the circle on the left to *add* it to the selection, and then release the key.

Both circles are now selected, and a larger bounding box surrounds them.

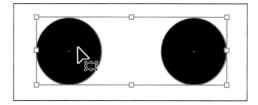

7 Move the circles a short distance by dragging from inside either selected circle. Because both circles are selected, they move together.

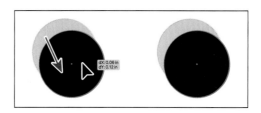

As you drag, you may notice that magenta lines appear. These are called *alignment guides*. They are visible because Smart Guides are turned on (View > Smart Guides). As you drag, the objects align to other objects in the document. Also notice the measurement label (gray box) next to the pointer that shows the object's distance from its original position. Measurement labels also appear because Smart Guides are turned on.

Selecting and editing with the Direct Selection tool

Shapes and paths are composed of anchor points (sometimes just called *points*) and path segments. Anchor points control the shape of a path segment and work like pins holding a wire in place. A shape, like a square, is made of at least four anchor points on the corners with path segments connecting the anchor points.

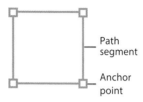
Path segment

Anchor point

One way to change the shape of a path or shape is by dragging its anchor points. The Direct Selection tool (▷) lets you select anchor points or paths within an object so you can reshape them. Next, you'll become familiar with selecting anchor points using the Direct Selection tool to reshape a few leaves.

1 Select the Direct Selection tool (▷) in the toolbar on the left. Click inside one of the bamboo leaves to see its anchor points.

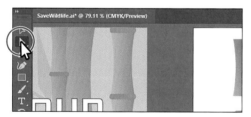 

Notice that the anchor points are all filled with a blue color, which means they are all selected. For this section, you may want to zoom in to the selected shape.

2 Choose View > Zoom In a few times so it's easier to see the leaf up close.

3 Move the pointer directly over the anchor point on the end of the leaf.

With the Direct Selection tool selected, when the pointer is right over an anchor point, the word "anchor" appears. Also notice the little white box next to the pointer (▷). That small dot that appears in the center of the white box indicates that the cursor is positioned over an anchor point.

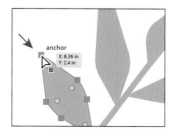

4 Click to select that anchor point, and then move the pointer away from it.

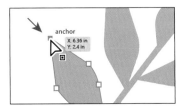 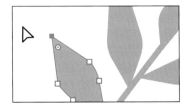

Notice that only the anchor point you clicked is now filled with blue, indicating that it's selected. The other anchor points in the shape are now hollow (filled with white), indicating that they are not selected.

Note: The gray measurement label that appears as you drag the anchor point has the values dX and dY. *dX* indicates the distance that the pointer has moved along the x-axis (horizontally), and *dY* indicates the distance that the pointer has moved along the y-axis (vertically).

5 With the Direct Selection tool still selected, move the pointer over the selected anchor point, and then drag it to make the leaf longer.

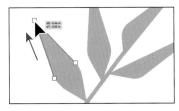 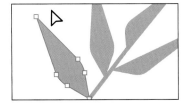

6 Try clicking another point on the shape. Notice that when you select the new point, the previous point is deselected.

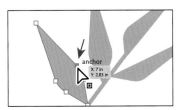

7 Choose Select > Deselect so the leaf anchor point is no longer selected.

Changing the size of anchor points, handles, and the bounding box display

The anchor points, handles, and bounding box points may be difficult to see at times. In the Illustrator preferences, you can adjust the size of those features.

By choosing Illustrator > Preferences > Selection & Anchor Display (macOS) or Edit > Preferences > Selection & Anchor Display (Windows), you can drag the Size slider to change the size.

Selecting with a marquee

Another way to select content is by dragging across what you want to select (called a *marquee selection*), which you'll do next.

1   Select the Selection tool (▶) in the toolbar. Move the pointer above and to the left of the leaf shapes. Drag across them to create a marquee that overlaps at least part or all of them. Release the mouse button.

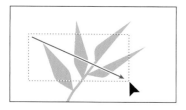 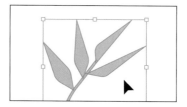

When dragging with the Selection tool (▶), you need to encompass only a small part of an object to select it.

2   Choose Select > Deselect, or click where there are no objects.

Now you'll use the Direct Selection tool to select multiple anchor points in the circles by dragging a marquee around anchor points.

3   Select the Direct Selection tool (▷) in the toolbar. Drag across the tops of the two green leaves you see in the first part of the following figure, and release the mouse button.

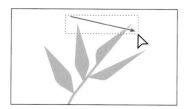 

4   Move the pointer over one of the selected anchor points at the top of the leaves. When you see the word "anchor," drag it to see how they move together.

You can use this method when selecting points so that you don't have to click exactly on the anchor point that you want to select.

5   Choose Select > Deselect and then choose File > Save.

Hiding and locking objects

Selecting artwork may be more difficult when there are objects stacked one on another or when there are multiple objects in a small area. In this section, you'll learn a common way to make selecting objects easier by locking and hiding content. Next, you'll attempt to drag across artwork to select it.

1   Choose 1 Final Artwork from the artboard navigation menu in the lower left.

2   With the Selection tool (▶) selected, move the pointer into the green area to the left of the panda artwork and then drag across the panda to select it. Release the mouse button.

Notice that you dragged the large green shape, rather than selecting the head of the panda.

3   Choose Edit > Undo Move.

4   With the large green background shape still selected, choose Object > Lock > Selection, or press Command+2 (macOS) or Ctrl+2 (Windows).

Locking objects prevents you from selecting and editing them.

5   Click the "PROTECT OUR WILDLIFE" text, and lock it as well by choosing Object > Lock > Selection.

6   Drag across the head of the panda again, this time selecting the whole thing *and* the bamboo in the background.

 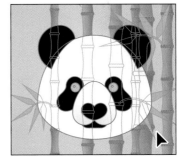

The panda is selected, but so is the bamboo in the background. Since we don't need to do anything with the bamboo, we can hide it temporarily so we can focus on other artwork.

7 Choose Select > Deselect.

8 Click the bamboo in the background to select all of it.

The bamboo is made of many shapes and is grouped, so it's treated as a single object. You'll learn about groups soon.

9 Choose Object > Hide > Selection, or press Command+3 (macOS) or Ctrl+3 (Windows).

The bamboo is now hidden so that you can more easily focus on other objects.

Unlocking objects

If you find you want to edit something that is locked, you can unlock it later. In this case, the text needs to move down a little. To do that, you need first to unlock it.

1 Choose Object > Unlock All to unlock everything in the document.

The green shape in the background and the "PROTECT OUR WILDLIFE" text are unlocked and are selected.

2 Choose Select > Deselect.

3 Drag the text down a little to reposition it.

► **Tip:** In Lesson 10, you'll learn how to unlock individual objects like the green shape in the background using the Layers panel.

Unlocking individual objects

You can unlock all locked objects in the document at once, use the Layers panel to unlock individual objects, or turn on a program preference and unlock individual objects in the document.

- Choose Illustrator > Preferences > Selection & Anchor Display (macOS) or Edit > Preferences > Selection & Anchor Display (Windows). Select the Select And Unlock Objects On Canvas option, if it isn't already selected. Click OK.

- A small lock icon appears on selected content that is locked. You can click that lock icon to unlock it.

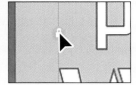

Selecting similar objects

Using the Select > Same command, you can select artwork based on similar fill color, stroke color, stroke weight, and more. The stroke of an object is the outline (border), and the stroke weight is the width of the stroke. Next, you'll select several objects with the same fill and stroke applied.

1   Choose View > Fit All In Window to see all the artwork at once.

2   With the Selection tool (▶), click to select one of the larger green "bamboo" shapes on the right.

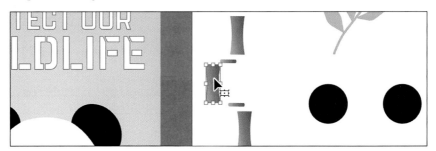

3   Choose Select > Same > Fill Color.

    All the shapes with the same fill color are now selected.

    You can save a selection if you know that you need to reselect a series of objects again. Saved selections are a quick way to make the same selection later. Selections you save are saved only with this document.

    You'll save the current selection next.

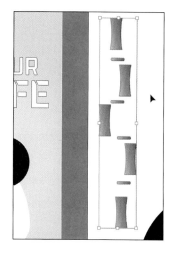

Tip: In Lesson 14, you'll learn about another method for selecting similar artwork using Global Edit.

4   With the shapes still selected, choose Select > Save Selection. Name the selection **Bamboo** in the Save Selection dialog box, and click OK.

    Now that you've saved it, you'll be able to choose this selection quickly and easily from the bottom of the Select menu when you need it.

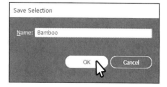

5   Choose Select > Deselect, and then choose File > Save.

Selecting in Outline mode

By default, Adobe Illustrator displays all artwork with its paint attributes, like fill and stroke (border), showing. However, you can view artwork in Outline mode to display artwork so that the appearance is removed and only outlines (or paths) are visible. Outline mode can be useful if you want to more easily select objects within a series of stacked objects.

1   Choose Object > Show All to see the bamboo on the artboard on the left you previously hid.

2   To lock the bamboo, choose Object > Lock > Selection.

3   Choose View > Outline to view artwork as outlines.

4   With the Selection tool (▶), back on artboard 1, click within one of the curved shapes that surround the eyes on the panda to try to select it.

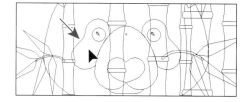

You can't select it! To select in Outline mode, you can click the object's edge or drag a marquee across the shape to select it. Also, in Outline mode, you may see a small X in the center of some of the shapes. If you click that X, you can select the shape. With lots of shapes in one place, clicking the X can be challenging.

▶ **Tip:** You could have also clicked the edge of one of the shapes, pressed the Shift key, and clicked the edge of the other to select both.

5 With the Selection tool selected, drag across the very top of the curved shapes surrounding the eyes to select them.

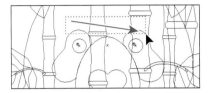 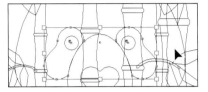

Notice that the bamboo is not selected. That's because it was locked.

6 Press the Up Arrow key several times to move both shapes up a little bit.

7 Choose View > Preview (or GPU Preview) to see the painted artwork.

Aligning objects

Illustrator makes it easy to align or distribute multiple objects relative to each other, the artboard, or a key object. In this section, you'll explore the different options for aligning objects.

Aligning objects to each other

One type of alignment is aligning objects to each other. This can be useful if, for instance, you want to align the top edges of a series of selected shapes to each other. Next you'll align the green bamboo shapes to each other.

1 Choose Select > Bamboo to reselect the green shapes on the right artboard.

2 Click the Next Artboard button (▶) in the lower-left corner of the Document window to fit the artboard with the selected green shapes in the window.

3 Click the Horizontal Align Center button (▣) in the Properties panel on the right.

Notice that all of the selected objects moved to align to the horizontal center of the shapes.

4 Choose Edit > Undo Align to return the objects to their original positions. Leave the objects selected for the next section.

Aligning to a key object

A *key object* is an object that you want other objects to align to. This can be useful when you want to align a series of objects and one of them is already in the perfect position. You specify a key object by selecting all the objects you want to align, including the key object, and then clicking the key object again. Next, you'll align the green shapes using a key object.

1   With the shapes still selected, click the leftmost shape with the Selection tool (▶). See the first part of the following figure.

    That object is now the key object. When selected, the key object has a thick outline indicating that other objects will align to it.

2   Click the Horizontal Align Center button (▣) in the Properties panel again.

● **Note:** The key object outline color is determined by the layer color that the object is on. You'll learn about layers in Lesson 10.

Notice that all of the selected shapes moved to align to the horizontal center of the key object.

3   Click the key object to remove the blue outline, and leave *all* of the green shapes selected. An arrow is pointing to it in the following figure.

● **Note:** If you accidentally deselect some or all of the shapes, to reselect them choose Select > Deselect and then choose Select > Bamboo.

The next time you align the selected content it won't align to the key object.

Distributing objects

Distributing objects means you equally distribute the spacing between the centers or edges of those objects. Next, you will make the spacing between the green bamboo shapes even.

● **Note:** You'll need to hide the panel to continue. To do that, press the Escape key. I won't always tell you to hide these panels, so it's a good habit to get into.

1 With the green shapes still selected, click More Options (●●●) in the Align section of the Properties panel (circled in the figure). Click the Vertical Distribute Center button (⊟) in the panel that appears.

Distributing moves all of the selected shapes so that their centers are spaced an equal distance apart.

2 Choose Edit > Undo Align.

3 With the shapes still selected, click the topmost shape of the selected shapes to make it the key object.

4 Click More Options (●●●) in the Align section of the Properties panel (circled in the following figure). Ensure that the Distribute Spacing value is 0 (zero), and then click the Vertical Distribute Space button (⊟).

Distribute Spacing distributes the spacing between selected objects, whereas the Distribute Objects alignments distribute the spacing between the center points of selected objects. The value you can set is a great way to set a specific distance between objects.

5 Choose Select > Deselect, and then choose File > Save.

Aligning anchor points

Next, you'll align two anchor points to each other using the Align options. Like setting a key object in the previous section, you can also align anchor points to a key anchor point you select.

1   Select the Direct Selection tool (◢), and select the black shape at the bottom of the artboard on the right to see its anchor points.

2   Click the lower-left corner point of the shape (see the first part of the following figure). Press the Shift key, and click to select the lower-right point of the same shape to select both anchor points (second part of the following figure).

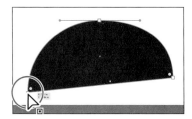 

The last selected anchor point is the *key anchor point*. Other points will align to this point.

3   Click the Vertical Align Top button (▢) in the Properties panel to the right of the document.

 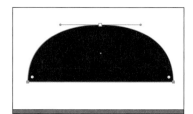

The first anchor point selected aligns to the second anchor point selected.

4   Choose Select > Deselect.

Aligning to the artboard

You can also align content to the active artboard (page) rather than a selection or a key object. Aligning to the artboard aligns each selected object separately to the edges of the artboard. Next, you'll align the black shape to the artboard that contains the final artwork.

1 Select the Selection tool (▶), and click the larger black shape at the bottom of the artboard to select it.

2 Choose Edit > Cut to copy the shape and remove it from the artboard.

3 Click the Previous artboard button (◀) in the lower-left corner of the Document window to navigate to the first (left) artboard in the document, which contains the final artwork.

4 Choose Edit > Paste to paste the shape in the center of the Document window.

5 Click the Align To button (▣▾) in the Align section of the Properties panel, and make sure that Align To Artboard is chosen in the menu that appears.

Any content you align will now align to the artboard.

6 Click the Horizontal Align Center button (▤), and then click the Vertical Align Bottom button (▥) in the Align section of the Properties panel to align the black shape to the horizontal center and vertical bottom of the artboard.

The black shape will be on top of the other artwork. Later, you will put it behind the head of the panda.

7 Choose Select > Deselect, and then choose File > Save.

Working with groups

You can combine objects into a group so that the objects act as a single unit. That way, you can move or transform several objects without affecting their individual attributes or positions relative to each other. It can also make selecting artwork easier.

Grouping items

Next you'll select multiple objects and create a group from them.

1 Choose View > Fit All In Window to see both artboards.

2 Choose Select > Bamboo to select the green shapes on the right artboard.

3 Click the Group button in the Quick Actions section of the Properties panel on the right to group the selected artwork together.

▶ **Tip:** After this step is performed, the Group button in the Properties panel now shows as Ungroup. Clicking the Ungroup button will remove the objects from a group.

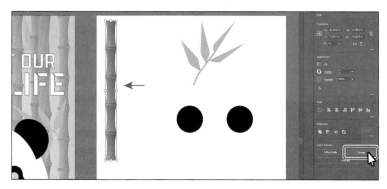

4 Choose Select > Deselect.

5 With the Selection tool (▶) selected, click one of the green shapes in the new group. Because they are grouped together, all are now selected.

6 Drag the group of bamboo shapes close to the top of the artboard on the left.

Next you'll align the bamboo group to the top of the artboard.

7 With the group still selected and Align To Artboard (▣▾) chosen from the Align To menu in the Properties panel on the right, click the Vertical Align Top button (▥).

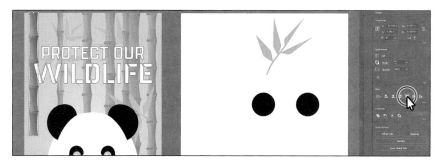

8 With the Selection tool selected, press the Shift key, and then drag the lower-right corner of the bounding box down to the bottom of the artboard to make the bamboo shapes larger. When the pointer reaches the bottom of the artboard, release the mouse button and then the key.

Editing a group in Isolation mode

Isolation mode lets you isolate groups to easily select and edit specific objects or parts of objects without having to ungroup the objects. When in isolation mode, all objects outside the isolated group are locked and dimmed so that they aren't affected by your edits. Next, you will edit a group using Isolation mode.

1   With the Selection tool (▶), drag across the green bamboo leaves on the right artboard to select them.

2   Click the Group button at the bottom of the Properties panel to group them together.

3   Double-click one of the leaves to enter Isolation mode.

● **Note:** You'll learn more about layers in Lesson 10.

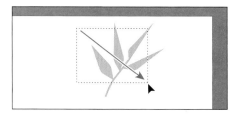

Notice that the rest of the content in the document appears dimmed (you can't select it). At the top of the Document window, a gray bar appears with the words "Layer 1" and "<Group>." That bar indicates that you have isolated a group of objects on Layer 1, and they are now temporarily ungrouped.

4   Click to select any of the leaves. Click the Fill color box in the Properties panel on the right, and making sure the Swatches option (▦) is selected in the panel that appears, click to select a different green color.

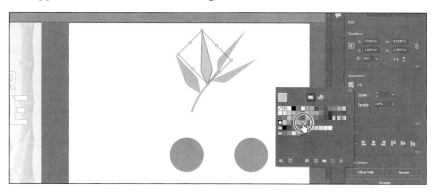

5   Double-click outside the shapes within the group to exit Isolation mode.

You can also click the gray arrow in the upper-left corner of the Document window or press the Escape key when in Isolation mode. The leaves are once again grouped, and you can also now select other objects.

6 Click to select the leaf group, and leave it selected for the next section.

Creating a nested group

Groups can also be *nested*—grouped within other objects or grouped to form larger groups. Nesting is a common technique and a great way to keep associated content together. In this section, you'll explore how to create a nested group.

1 Drag the group of leaves onto the bamboo on the left artboard.

2 Shift-click the bamboo group to select it as well.

3 Choose Object > Group.

You have created a *nested group*—a group that is combined with other objects or groups to form a larger group.

4 Choose Select > Deselect.

Tip: Instead of either ungrouping a group or entering Isolation mode to select the content within, you can select with the Group Selection tool (⯈⁺). Nested within the Direct Selection tool (⯈) in the toolbar, the Group Selection tool lets you select an object within a group, a single group within multiple groups, or a set of groups within the artwork.

5 With the Selection tool, click the leaves to select the nested group.

6 Double-click the leaves to enter Isolation mode. Click to select the leaves again, and notice that the leaf shapes are still grouped. This is a nested group.

7 Choose Edit > Copy and then Edit > Paste to paste a new group of leaves.

8 Drag them lower onto the bamboo.

9 Press the Escape key to exit Isolation mode; then click a blank area of an artboard to deselect the objects.

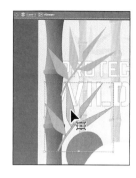

Exploring object arrangement

Illustrator puts objects one on top of another in order as you create them, beginning with the first object created. This ordering of objects, called *stacking order*, determines how they display when they overlap. You can change the stacking order of objects in your artwork at any time, using either the Layers panel or the Arrange commands.

Arranging objects

Next you'll work with the Arrange commands to finish the panda artwork.

1 With the Selection tool (▶) selected, click the black shape at the bottom of the artboard on the left.

2 Click the Arrange button in the Properties panel. Choose Send To Back to send the shape behind all of the other shapes.

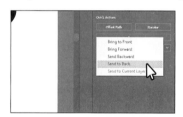

3 Click the Arrange button again, and choose Bring Forward as many times as necessary to bring the black shape on top of the large blue-green background shape and the bamboo shapes. I chose it three times.

Now you'll move the eyes into place and practice arranging.

4 Drag across both black circles on the artboard on the right to select them.

5 Pressing the Shift key, drag a corner to make them smaller. When the measurement label shows a width of approximately 1.2 inches (pretty small). Release the mouse button and then the key.

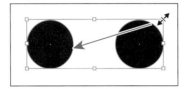 

6 Drag both circles onto the panda head.

7 Choose View > Zoom In a few times to zoom into the circles.

8 Choose Select > Deselect, and then drag each circle into the yellow of the eyes. With one of the circles selected, choose Send Backward from the Arrange menu in the Properties panel on the right, as many times as you need. I chose it three times.

9 Repeat the previous step for the other black circle—dragging it onto the other yellow eye.

10 Choose View > Fit Artboard In Window to center the poster in the Document window.

11 Choose File > Save and then File > Close.

Review questions

1 How can you select an object that has no fill?

2 Explain how you can select an item in a group without ungrouping.

3 Of the two selection tools (Selection [▶] and Direct Selection [▷]), which allows you to edit the individual anchor points of an object?

4 What should you do after creating a selection that you are going to use repeatedly?

5 To align objects to the artboard, what do you first need to change in the Properties panel or Align panel before you choose an alignment option?

6 Sometimes you are unable to select an object because it is underneath another object. Explain a way to get around this issue.

Review answers

1 You can select an object that has no fill by clicking the stroke or by dragging a marquee across any part of the object.

2 You can double-click the group with the Selection tool selected to enter Isolation mode, edit the shapes as needed, and then exit Isolation mode by pressing the Escape key or by double-clicking outside of the group. Read Lesson 10 to see how you can use layers to make complex selections. Also, using the Group Selection tool (▷⁺), you can click once to select an individual item within a group (not discussed in the lesson). Click again to add the next grouped items to the selection.

3 Using the Direct Selection tool (▷), you can select one or more individual anchor points to change the shape of an object.

4 For any selection that you anticipate using again, choose Select > Save Selection. Name the selection so that you can reselect it at any time from the Select menu.

5 To align objects to an artboard, first choose the Align To Artboard option.

6 If your access to an object is blocked, you can choose Object > Hide > Selection to hide the blocking object. The object is not deleted. It is just hidden in the same position until you choose Object > Show All. BONUS! You can also use the Selection tool (▶) to select an object that's behind other objects by pressing the Command (macOS) or Ctrl (Windows) key and then clicking the overlapping objects until the object you want to select is selected.

3 USING SHAPES TO CREATE ARTWORK FOR A POSTCARD

Lesson overview

In this lesson, you'll learn how to do the following:

- Create a new document.
- Use tools and commands to create a variety of shapes.
- Understand Live Shapes.
- Create rounded corners.
- Work with drawing modes.
- Use Image Trace to create shapes.
- Simplify paths.

This lesson will take about 60 minutes to complete. To get the lesson files used in this chapter, download them from the web page for this book at adobepress.com/IllustratorCIB2022. For more information, see "Accessing the lesson files and Web Edition" in the Getting Started section at the beginning of this book.

Basic shapes are essential to creating Illustrator
artwork. In this lesson, you'll create a new document
and then use the shape tools to create and edit a
series of shapes for a postcard.

Starting the lesson

In this lesson, you'll explore the different methods for creating artwork using the shape tools and other methods to add artwork to a postcard for a farmers market.

Note: If you have not already downloaded the project files for this lesson to your computer from your Account page, make sure to do so now. See the "Getting Started" section at the beginning of the book.

1 To ensure that the tools function and the defaults are set exactly as described in this lesson, delete or deactivate (by renaming) the Adobe Illustrator preferences file. See "Restoring default preferences" in the "Getting Started" section at the beginning of the book.

2 Start Adobe Illustrator.

3 Choose File > Open. Locate the file named L3_end.ai, which is in the Lessons > Lesson03 folder that you copied onto your hard disk, and click Open.

This file contains the finished illustrations that you'll create in this lesson.

4 Choose View > Fit All In Window; leave the file open for reference, or choose File > Close.

Creating a new document

To start, you'll create a new document for the postcard that you'll add artwork to.

1 Choose File > New to create a new document.
In the New Document dialog box, change the following options:

- Select the **Print** category at the top of the dialog box.

- Select the Letter blank document preset, if it isn't already selected.

You can set up a document for different kinds of output, such as print, web, video, and more, by choosing a category. For example, if you are designing a web page mockup, you can select the Web category and select a document preset (size). The document will be set with the units in points (most likely), the color mode as CMYK, and the raster effects to High (300 ppi)—all optimal settings for a print document.

2 On the right side of the dialog box, in the Preset Details area, change the following:

- Enter a name for the document in the blank space under Preset Details: **Postcard**.

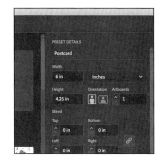

The name will become the name of the Illustrator file when you save it later.

- Units: Choose **Inches** from the units menu to the right of the Width field.

- Width: Select the Width value, and type **6**.

- Height: Select the Height value, and type **4.25**.

- Orientation: **Landscape** (⬛).

- Artboards: **1** (the default setting).

You'll learn about the Bleed option shortly. At the bottom of the Preset Details section on the right side of the New Document dialog box, you will also see Advanced Options and More Settings (you may need to scroll to see it). They contain more settings for document creation that you can explore on your own.

3 Click Create to create a new document.

With the document open in Illustrator, now you'll save it.

4 Choose File > Save As. If the Cloud Document dialog box opens, click Save On Your Computer to save the document locally.

5 In the Save As dialog box that opens, make sure that the name of the file is Postcard.ai, and save it in the Lessons > Lesson03 folder. Leave Adobe Illustrator (ai) chosen from the Format menu (macOS) or Adobe Illustrator (*.AI) chosen from the Save As Type menu (Windows), and click Save.

Adobe Illustrator (.ai) is called a native format and is your working file. That means it preserves all Illustrator data so you can edit everything later.

Tip: If you want to learn more about these options, search for "Save artwork" in Illustrator Help (Help > Illustrator Help).

6 In the Illustrator Options dialog box that appears, leave the options at their default settings, and click OK.

The Illustrator Options dialog box is full of options for saving the Illustrator document, from specifying a version for saving to embedding any files that are linked to the document.

7 Choose Window > Workspace > Essentials (if it's not already selected).

8 Choose Window > Workspace > Reset Essentials to reset the panels and settings for the Essentials workspace.

9 Click the Document Setup button in the Properties panel (Window > Properties).

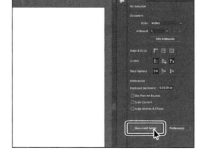

The Document Setup dialog box is where you can change document options like units, bleeds, and more after a document is created. You will typically add bleed to artboards for printed artwork that needs to be printed all the way to the edge of the paper. *Bleed* is the term used for the area that extends beyond the edge of the printed page, and it ensures that no white edges show up on the final trimmed page.

10 In the Bleed section of the Document Setup dialog box, change the value in the Top field to **0.125 in**, either by clicking the up arrow button to the left of the field once or by typing the value, which should make all four fields change. Click OK.

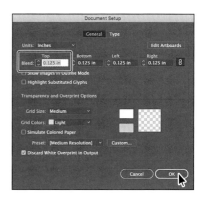

11 Choose View > Fit Artboard In Window to fit the artboard (page) in the Document window.

The area between the red line around the artboard and the edge of the white artboard is the bleed area.

Working with basic shapes

In the first part of this lesson, you'll create a series of basic shapes, including rectangles, ellipses, and polygons. Shapes you create are composed of *anchor points* with paths connecting the anchor points. A basic square, for instance, is composed of four anchor points on the corners with paths connecting those anchor points (see the upper figure at right). A shape is referred to as a *closed path* because the ends of the path are connected.

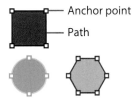

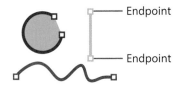

Examples of closed paths.

A path, like a line, can also be *open*. An open path has distinct anchor points on each end, called *endpoints* (see the figure at right). You can fill open and closed paths with color, gradients, or patterns.

Examples of open paths.

Creating rectangles

You'll start this lesson by creating a bowl to contain fruit. You'll build the bowl from a few rectangles, and you'll explore creating them using two distinct methods.

1   Select the Rectangle tool (▭) in the toolbar on the left.

First we'll create the larger rectangle that will be the main body of the bowl.

2   Move the pointer into the artboard. Press the mouse button, and drag down and to the right to create a rectangle that is taller than it is wider. Release the mouse button. Don't worry about the size right now. You'll adjust it shortly.

As you drag to create shapes, the tool tip that appears next to the pointer is called the *measurement label* and is part of Smart Guides (View > Smart Guides). It shows the width and height of the shape as you draw.

3   Move the pointer over the small blue dot in the center of the rectangle (called the *center point widget*). When the pointer changes (▸⊞), drag the shape into the bottom half of the artboard, roughly centered horizontally.

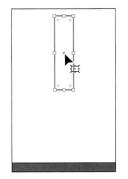

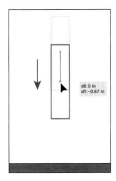

Next, you'll create a smaller rectangle to serve as the base of the bowl.

4 With the Rectangle tool still selected, click anywhere in the document to open the Rectangle dialog box. Change the Width to **1** inch and the Height to **0.1** inches. Click OK to create a new rectangle.

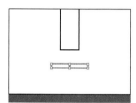

Creating a rectangle with the Rectangle dialog box is useful when you know the size of the shape you need. For most drawing tools, you can either draw with the tool or click to create a shape of a specific size.

● **Note:** Since the rectangle is small, it may be challenging to drag from the center point. As you go through the lessons, you'll zoom in and out to make it easier to select things.

5 Move the pointer over the center point widget, and drag the rectangle below the first rectangle.

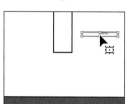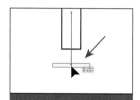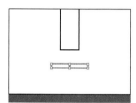

You'll move both shapes into their final positions shortly.

Editing rectangles

All of the shape tools, except for the Star tool and Flare tool, create Live Shapes. Live Shapes have attributes such as width, height, rotation, and corner radius that are editable without switching from the drawing tool you are using.

With two rectangles created, you'll make some changes to the first.

1 Select the Selection tool (▶) in the toolbar.

2 Click in the larger rectangle you created to select it. Drag up from the middle point on the top of the rectangle to make it taller. *As you drag*, press the Option (macOS) or Alt (Windows) key to resize the top and bottom together. When you see a height of approximately 3 inches in the measurement label (the gray tool tip next to the pointer), release the mouse button and then the key.

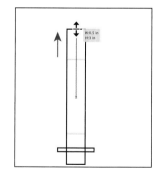

3 To rotate the shape, move the pointer just off of a corner on the shape. When you see rotate arrows (↰), drag clockwise to rotate the shape. As you drag, press the Shift key to constrain the rotation to increments of 45 degrees. When an angle of 270 shows in the measurement label, release the mouse button and then the key. Leave the shape selected.

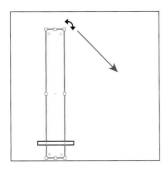
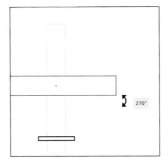

4   In the Transform section of the Properties panel on the right, make sure
    Maintain Width And Height Proportions to the right of Width (W:) and Height
    (H:) is *deselected* (it looks like this: 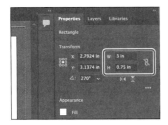). Select the Height (H:) value, and type
    0.75. Press Return or Enter to accept the change.

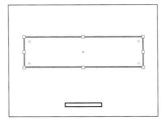

The Maintain Width And Height Proportions setting is useful when you change
the height or the width and want the other value to change proportionally.
The options in the Transform section of the Properties panel help transform
selected shapes and other artwork precisely. You'll learn more about those
options in Lesson 5, "Transforming Artwork."

By default, shapes are filled with white and have a black stroke (border). Next,
you'll change the color of the larger rectangle to brown to suggest a bowl made
of dark wood, like walnut.

5   Click the Fill color box in the Properties panel on the right. In the panel that
    opens, make sure that the Swatches option (⊞) is selected at the top. Select
    a brown color to fill the rectangle. I chose a brown with a tool tip that shows
    "C=50 M=50 Y=60 K=25" when you hover the pointer over the color.

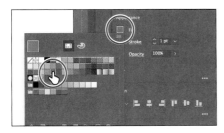
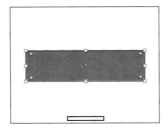

6   Press the Escape key to hide the Swatches panel before moving on.

7   Click the Stroke color box in the Properties panel, make sure that the Swatches option (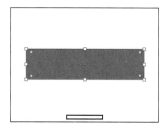) is selected, and select None to remove the stroke from the rectangle. Press the Escape key to hide the Swatches panel before moving on.

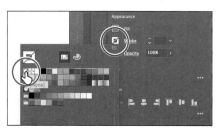

8   Choose Select > Deselect, and then choose File > Save to save the file.

Rounding corners

The rectangles you created don't look very much like a bowl. Luckily it's easy to round off the corners of rectangles to make more interesting—and practical— shapes. In this section, you'll round all the corners of the smaller rectangle.

1   Click the smaller rectangle to select it.

2   Choose View > Zoom In as many times as necessary until you see the Live Corners widgets (⊙) in each corner of the rectangle.

   If you are zoomed out far enough, the Live Corners widgets are hidden on the shape.

● **Note:** If you drag until you see a red arc, in the next step the value won't change when you click the up arrow since the maximum is already achieved.

3   Drag any of the Live Corners widgets (⊙) in the rectangle toward the center to round the corners a little.

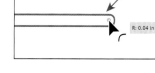

   The more you drag toward the center, the more rounded the corners become. If you drag a Live Corners widget far enough, a red arc appears on the shape, indicating you've reached the maximum corner radius.

4   In the Properties panel to the right, click More Options (●●●) in the Transform section to show more options. Ensure that Link Corner Radius Values is on (🔗) (an arrow is pointing to it in the figure), and click the up arrow for any of the Radius values as many times as you can until the value no longer increases (the maximum radius value is achieved). If necessary, click in another field or press the Tab key to see the change to all corners.

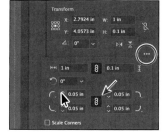

Aside from changing the corner radius, you can also change the corner type. You can choose between Round (default), Inverted Round, and Chamfer.

5   With the options still showing in the Properties panel, click the corner type for each of the bottom corners, and choose Chamfer.

6   Press the Escape key to close the options panel.

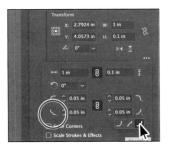

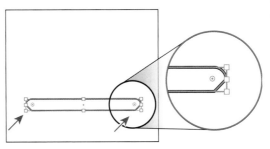

▶ **Tip:** You can also double-click a Live Corners widget in a shape to open the Transform panel as a free-floating panel.

7   Click the Fill color box in the Properties panel on the right. In the panel that opens, make sure that the Swatches option (▦) is selected at the top. Select a brown color to fill the rectangle. We chose a brown that is darker than the brown of the larger rectangle.

8   Click the Stroke color box in the Properties panel, make sure that the Swatches option (▦) is selected, and select None to remove the stroke from the rectangle.

9   Choose Select > Deselect.

Rounding individual corners

Next, you'll explore rounding the individual corners of a rectangle.

1   Choose View > Fit Artboard In Window.

2   Click the larger rectangle to select it.

The Live Corners widgets (◉) should be showing in the corners of the shape.

● **Note:** You should be getting used to hiding panels, like stroke color, first—then you can access the menu items.

3   Select the Direct Selection tool (▷) in the toolbar. With the shape still selected, double-click the lower-left Live Corners widget (◉). In the Corners dialog box, click the up arrow for the Radius value until the value stops changing (the maximum value is reached). Click OK.

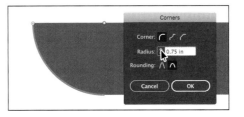

▶ **Tip:** You can Option-click (macOS) or Alt-click (Windows) a Live Corners widget in a shape to cycle through the different corner types.

Notice that only one corner changed. The Corners dialog box allows you to also select an extra option called *Rounding* to set absolute versus relative rounding (see the previous figure). Absolute (⌒) means the rounded corner is exactly the radius value. Relative (⌒) bases the radius value on the angle of the corner point.

4 Click the lower-right Live Corners widget (⊙) to select just that one Live Corners widget. See the first part of the following figure.

5 Drag that widget (⊙) to round the corner until you see the red color on the path, indicating that the corner is as round as it can get.

  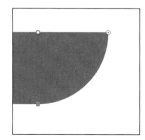

6 Select the Selection tool (▶) in the toolbar, and drag the larger rectangle so that it touches the smaller rectangle and is aligned horizontally with the smaller rectangle.

A magenta line will appear in the center of both shapes when they are aligned.

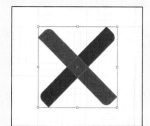

7 Choose Select > Deselect, and then choose File > Save.

Drawing on a grid for alignment

A grid is a series of horizontal and vertical lines for you to create artwork on. The grid appears behind your artwork in the illustration window. It does not print.

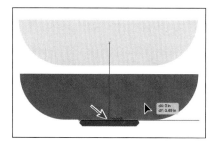

- To show or hide the grid, choose View > Show Grid or View > Hide Grid.

- To snap objects to gridlines, choose View > Snap To Grid, select the object you want to move, and drag it to the desired location.

- When the object's boundary comes within 2 pixels of a gridline, it snaps to the line.

- To specify the spacing between gridlines, grid style (lines or dots), grid color, or whether grids appear in the front or back of artwork, choose Illustrator > Preferences > Guides & Grid (macOS) or Edit > Preferences > Guides & Grid (Windows).

—From Illustrator Help

Creating and editing ellipses

Next, you'll create a few ellipses with the Ellipse tool (⬭) to make a pear. The Ellipse tool can be used to create ellipses and perfect circles.

1   Press and hold the mouse button on the Rectangle tool (▭) in the toolbar, and select the Ellipse tool (⬭).

2   Above the bowl, on the left side of the artboard, drag to make an ellipse with an approximate width of 0.6 inches and a height of 0.75 inches.

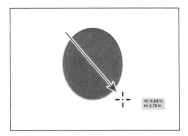

   Now you'll draw a perfect circle and start drawing so it's perfectly aligned with the center of the ellipse you just made. Drawing it where you want it, instead of drawing it and moving it, saves you steps.

3   With the Ellipse tool still selected, move the pointer just below the edge of the ellipse, aligned with the center of it. A magenta guide will appear when the pointer is aligned with the horizontal center (see the first part of the following figure).

4   Now, to draw the shape from the center, press Option+Shift (macOS) or Alt+Shift (Windows), and drag to create a circle that has an approximate width and height of 1 inch. As you drag the pointer, you can tell it's a perfect circle when magenta crosshairs appears within. Release the mouse button and then the keys.

> **Tip:** The Shift key constrains the ellipse to a perfect circle, and the Option/Alt key lets you draw from the center of the shape.

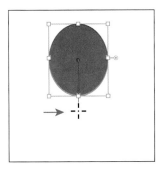
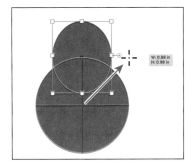

5   To keep the shapes together, select the Selection tool (▶), and drag across both shapes to select them. Click the Group button in the Quick Actions section of the Properties panel to the right.

   Grouping treats content like a single object, which makes it easier to move the currently selected artwork. You'll group other content you create going forward for the same reason.

6 Click the Fill color box in the Properties panel on the right. In the panel that opens, make sure that the Swatches option (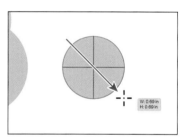) is selected at the top. Select a green color to fill the shapes in the group.

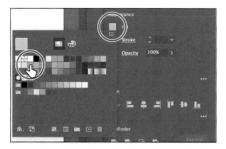
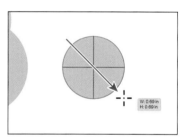

7 Choose Select > Deselect, and then choose File > Save.

Creating and editing circles

Next, you'll create three perfect circles with the Ellipse tool (⬭) to create an apple. For one of those circles, you'll explore the Live Shapes feature that allows you to create a pie shape.

1 Select the Ellipse tool (⬭), and, to the right of the pear, press and drag to begin drawing an ellipse. As you drag, press the Shift key to create a perfect circle. When the width and height are both roughly 0.7 inches, release the mouse button and then the Shift key.

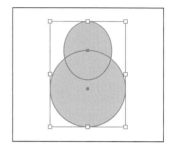

Without switching to the Selection tool, you can reposition and modify an ellipse with the Ellipse tool, which is what you'll do next.

2 With the Ellipse tool selected, move the pointer over the center point of the circle. To make a copy of the circle, press Option (macOS) or Alt (Windows) and drag to the right a little. Release the mouse button and then the key when the circles overlap a bit.

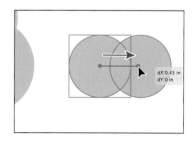

You'll create one more circle by drawing it. This new circle needs to be as wide as the two circles you already have, so you'll align the circle with them as you draw it.

3 Move the pointer over the left edge of the left-most circle. When you see "anchor" next to the pointer, press and drag down and to the right to draw a circle. As you drag, press the Shift key. When it's as wide as the two circles, a magenta Smart Guide appears on the right edge. Release the mouse button and then the key.

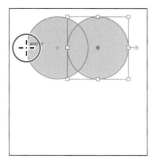 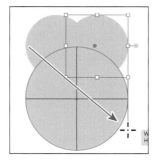

4 With the ellipse selected, note the pie widget (─◉) projecting from the anchor point on the right side of the ellipse. Drag that pie widget counterclockwise around the top of the ellipse—don't worry about how far.

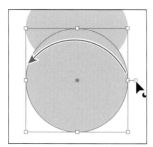 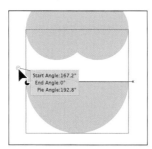 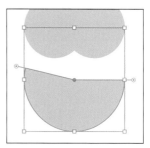

Dragging the pie widget allows you to create a pie shape. After dragging the widget initially and releasing the mouse button, you will then see a second widget. The widget you dragged controls the start angle. The widget that now appears on the right side of the ellipse controls the end angle.

5 In the Properties panel to the right, click More Options (•••) in the Transform section to show more options. Choose 180° from the Pie Start Angle (◖) menu. Press the Escape key to hide the panel.

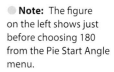 **Note:** The figure on the left shows just before choosing 180 from the Pie Start Angle menu.

 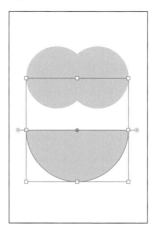

6   Move the pointer over what *was* the center of the half ellipse. Drag the shape up over the two smaller circles. When it's aligned horizontally and vertically centered with the two circles, magenta alignment guides and the word "intersect" will most likely appear next to the pointer.

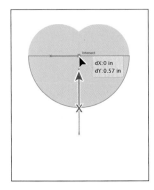

7   Select the Selection tool in the toolbar, and drag across all three circles to select them.

8   Click the Fill color in the Properties panel, and make sure that the Swatches option (▤) is selected in the panel that appears. Select a red color with a tool tip of "C=15 M=100 Y=90 K=10."

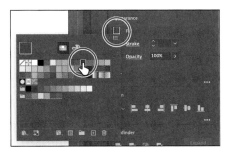
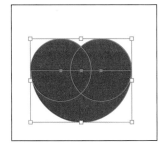

Later in this lesson, you'll create an orange (the fruit) using a copy of the half circle from the apple as a starting point.

9   Click in an empty area of the artboard to deselect.

10 To make a copy of the half circle, press Option (macOS) or Alt (Windows), and drag it into an empty area of the artboard. Release the mouse button and then the key.

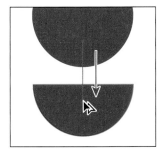

Changing stroke width and alignment

Strokes are visible outlines or borders of an object or path. You've edited shape fills in this lesson but haven't done much with strokes aside from removing them. You can easily change the color of a stroke or the weight of a stroke to make it thinner or thicker. You'll do that next.

1   With the Selection tool (►) selected, click the smaller rectangle that is the bottom of the bowl.

2   Choose View > Zoom In a few times.

3 Click the word "Stroke" in the Properties panel to open the Stroke panel. In the Stroke panel, change the stroke weight of the selected rectangle to **2**. Click the Align Stroke To Inside button (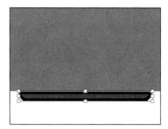) to align the stroke to the inside edge of the rectangle.

● **Note:** You may notice in the selected artwork that you see only the corner points of the bounding box. It depends on the zoom level of your document.

Aligning a stroke to the inside of a shape can be a great way to ensure that the stroke doesn't overlap the shape above.

4 Click the Stroke color box in the Properties panel, make sure that the Swatches option () is selected, and select a lighter brown color.

5 Choose Select > Deselect.

Creating a polygon

Using the Polygon tool (⬡), you can create shapes with multiple straight sides. By default, the Polygon tool draws hexagons (a six-sided shape) drawn from the center. Polygons are also Live Shapes, which means attributes such as size, rotation, number of sides, and more remain editable after you create them. Now you'll create a polygon to make a series of leaves.

1 Choose View > Fit Artboard In Window to fit the artboard in the Document window.

2 Press and hold on the Ellipse tool (◯) in the toolbar, and select the Polygon tool (⬡).

3 Choose View > Smart Guides to turn them off.

4 Move the pointer in a blank area of the artboard. Drag to the right to begin drawing a polygon, but *don't release the mouse button yet.* Press the Down Arrow key once to reduce the number of sides on the polygon to five, and don't release the mouse button yet. Hold down the Shift key to straighten the shape. Release the mouse button and then the key. Leave the shape selected.

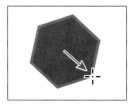
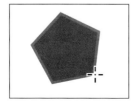

Notice that you didn't see the gray measurement label (the tool tip), since it's part of the Smart Guides that you turned off. The magenta alignment guides are also not showing, since the shape is not snapping to other content on the artboard. Smart Guides can be useful in certain situations, such as when more precision is necessary—maybe you want to know how large the shape is—and can be toggled on and off when needed.

5   To change the fill color, click the Fill color box in the Properties panel, and make sure that the Swatches option (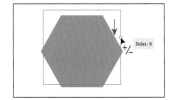) is selected in the panel that appears. Select a green color with a tool tip of "C=85 M=10 Y=100 K=10."

6   Click the Stroke color box in the Properties panel, make sure that the Swatches option (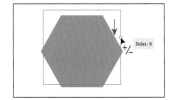) is selected, and select None to remove the stroke from the shape.

7   Choose View > Smart Guides to turn them back on.

8   With the Polygon tool still selected, drag the side widget (◇) on the right side of the bounding box down to change the number of sides to 6.

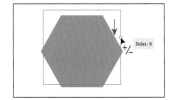

Editing the polygon

Now you'll edit the polygon and create a rounded leaf from it.

1   To rotate the polygon, move the pointer just off a corner of the bounding box around the shape. When the pointer changes to a rotate arrow (↰), drag counterclockwise. As you drag, press the Shift key to constrain the rotation to multiples of 45 degrees. When you see an angle of 90° in the measurement label next to the pointer, release the mouse button and then the key.

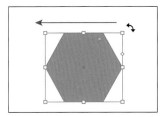
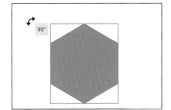

2   To change the size of the polygon, move the pointer over a corner and drag. As you drag, press the Shift key to change the width and height proportionally (together).

When the measurement label shows a height of approximately 0.65 inches, release the mouse button and then the key. Depending on how big your polygon was to start, you will make it either larger or smaller in this step to match the height we suggest.

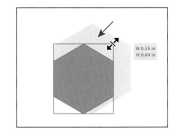

3 In the Transform section of the Properties panel on the right, make sure Maintain Width And Height Proportions to the right of Width (W:) and Height (H:) is deselected (it looks like this: 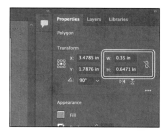) so you can change the values independently. Select the Width (W:) value and type **0.35**. Press Return or Enter to accept the change.

With the leaf shape (polygon) now created, you'll round some of the corners to make it look a little more natural.

4 With the polygon selected, choose View > Zoom In a few times to zoom in to it.

If you look at the polygon right now, with the Selection tool (▶) selected, you'll see a single Live Corners widget (◉) in the shape. If you were to drag that widget, all of the corners would be rounded.

5 Select the Direct Selection tool (▷) in the toolbar. You should now see Live Corners widgets in each corner. You'll only round four of the corners.

6 Drag across the four anchor points in the middle of the shape (see the following figure). With those anchors selected, you should see the Live Corners widgets for them.

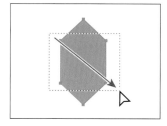 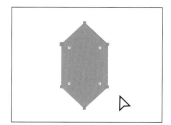

7 Drag one of the selected Live Corners widgets toward the center of the shape. Keep dragging past the center until you see the red lines, indicating that you can't round them anymore.

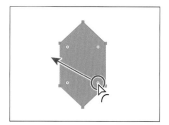 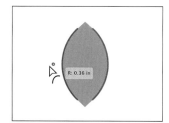 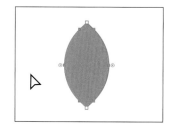

Creating a star

Next, you'll use the Star tool (☆) to create a few stars that will become flowers. Currently, the Star tool doesn't create Live Shapes, so editing the star after the fact can be more difficult. When drawing with the Star tool, you'll use keyboard modifiers to get the number of points you want and change the radius of the star's arms (the length of the arms). Here are the keyboard modifiers you'll use in this section when drawing the star:

- **Arrow keys:** Pressing the Up Arrow or Down Arrow key adds or removes arms from the star, respectively, as you draw it.
- **Shift:** This straightens the star (constrains it).
- **Command (macOS) or Ctrl (Windows):** Pressing this key and dragging while creating a star allows you to change the radius of the arms of the star (make the arms longer or shorter).

Next you'll create a star. This will take a few keyboard commands, so *don't release the mouse button* until you are told.

1   Press and hold on the Polygon tool (⬡) in the toolbar, and select the Star tool (☆). Move the pointer to the right of the leaf.

► **Tip:** You can also click in the Document window with the Star tool (☆) and edit the options in the Star dialog box instead of drawing it.

2   Press and drag to the right to create a star shape. Notice that as pointer moves, the star changes size and rotates freely. Drag until the measurement label shows a width of about 1 inch and then stop dragging. *Don't release the mouse button!*

3   Press the Down Arrow key once to decrease the number of points on the star to four. *Don't release the mouse button!*

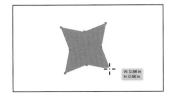

4   Press Command (macOS) or Ctrl (Windows), and start dragging again, this time toward the center of the star a short distance. This keeps the inner radius constant, making the arms shorter. Drag until the star looks something like the figure and then stop dragging, *without releasing the mouse button*. Release Command or Ctrl but *not the mouse button*.

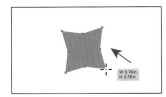

5   Press the Shift key. When the star straightens out, release the mouse button and then the key.

Editing the star

With the star created, next you'll transform and copy the star.

1 Select the Selection tool (▶), press the Shift key, and drag a corner of the star bounding box toward the center. When the star has a width of approximately 0.4 inches, release the mouse button and then the key.

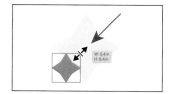

2 Select the Star tool (☆). Press the Shift key, and draw a new star that's a little smaller than the first. Release the mouse button and then the key.

   Notice that the new star has the same basic settings as the first star you drew.

3 To rotate the star, in the Transform section of the Properties panel, change the Rotate value by selecting the value and typing in **45**. Press Return or Enter. To scale the star, make sure Maintain Width And Height Proportions to the right of Width (W:) and Height (H:) is *selected* (it looks like this: 🔒). Select the Height (H:) value, and type **0.14**. Press Return or Enter to accept the change.

4 Change the fill color of the smaller star in the Properties panel to a yellow.

5 Select the Selection tool (▶), and drag the smaller star into the center of the larger star.

6 Click in an empty area of the artboard to deselect, and then click the larger star, and change the fill color to white.

7 Drag across the star shapes to select them, and then click the Group button in the Properties panel to group them together.

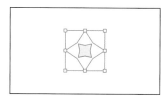

8 Choose File > Save.

Drawing lines

Next, you'll create a line, known as an *open path*, with the Line Segment tool. This line will become the surface that the bowl rests on. Lines created with the Line Segment tool are Live Lines, and similar to Live Shapes, they have many editable attributes after they are drawn.

1 Choose View > Fit Artboard In Window.

2 Press and hold on the Star tool (✩) in the toolbar, and select the Line Segment tool (╱).

3 To the right of the bowl, press and drag up to draw a line. As you drag, press the Shift key to constrain the line to a multiple of 45 degrees. Notice the length and angle in the measurement label next to the pointer as you drag. Drag until the line is around 2 inches in length.

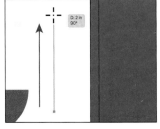

4 With the new line selected, move the pointer just off the top end. When the pointer changes to a rotate arrow (↶), press and drag down until you see an angle of 0 (zero) in the measurement label next to the pointer. That will make the line horizontal.

Lines rotate around their center point by default.

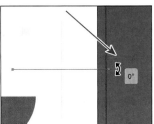

5 Select the Selection tool (▶) in the toolbar, and drag the line by the center point to just below the bowl. When it is touching the bottom of the bowl and it is aligned horizontally with the bowl—you'll see a vertical alignment guide when the line is aligned with the bowl—release the mouse button.

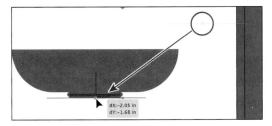

This line represents a table that the bowl is sitting on, so make sure the line touches the bottom of the bowl.

6 With the line selected, change the stroke weight to **2 pt** in the Properties panel to the right of the document.

7 Click the Stroke color box in the Properties panel, and make sure that the Swatches option (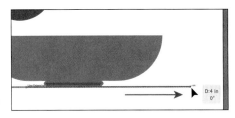) is selected in the panel that appears. Select a brown color with a tool tip of "C=35 M=60 Y=80 K=25."

Next, you'll change the width of the line you just dragged into position. Since it's already centered on the bowl and you want to make it wider, you'll resize it from the center so you don't have to reposition it after resizing.

8 To change the length of the line from the center, move the pointer over one of the ends, press Option (macOS) or Alt (Windows), and drag away from the center. Drag until the line is 4 inches, and release the mouse button and then the key.

> ● **Note:** If, as you drag the end of the line, the line is rotating, you can press the Shift key as you drag to constrain it to horizontal.

If you drag a line in the same trajectory as the original path, you will see the words "Line Extension" and "on" appear at opposite ends of the line. These appear because the Smart Guides are turned on.

9 Drag across the two shapes that make up the bowl and the line beneath. Click the Group button in the Properties panel to keep the artwork together.

Using Image Trace to convert raster images into editable vector art

In this part of the lesson, you'll learn how to work with the Image Trace command, which converts a raster image, like a JPEG, into editable vector artwork. Tracing can help turn something you drew on paper—for instance, a raster logo, a pattern or texture, or hand-drawn type—into editable vector art. In this section, you'll trace a picture of a lemon to get shapes.

1 Choose File > Place. In the Place dialog box, select the lemon.jpg file in the Lessons > Lesson03 folder on your hard disk, leave all options at their defaults, and click Place.

2 Click in an empty part of the artboard to place the image. It won't fit on the artboard, but that's okay.

3 To center the selected image in the Document window (since it's rather large), choose View > Zoom Out.

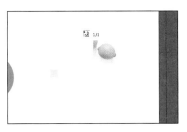

Note: You can also choose Object > Image Trace > Make, with raster content selected, or begin tracing from the Image Trace panel (Window > Image Trace).

4 With the image selected, click the Image Trace button in the Properties panel to the right of the document, and choose Low Fidelity Photo from the menu.

This converts the image into an image tracing object. That means you can't edit the vector content yet, but you can change the tracing settings or even edit the image you just placed in Photoshop and then see the updates if the image is linked to the Illustrator file.

5 Choose Silhouettes from the Preset menu that's showing in the Properties panel.

The Silhouettes preset will trace the image, forcing the resulting vector content to turn black. This is useful when you want to get the main shape from the tracing. An image tracing object is made up of the original source image and the tracing result, which is the vector artwork. By default, only the tracing result is visible. However, you can change the display of both the original image and the tracing result to best suit your needs in the View menu you will see in the Image Trace panel you open next.

Tip: The Image Trace panel can also be opened by choosing Window > Image Trace.

6 Click the Open The Image Trace Panel button (▣) in the Properties panel.

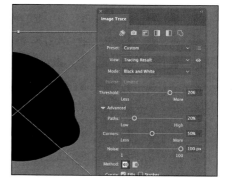

The buttons along the top of the Image Trace panel are saved settings for converting the image to grayscale, black and white, and more. Below the buttons at the top of the Image Trace panel, you will see the Preset menu. This is the same menu as in the Properties panel. The Mode menu allows you to change the color mode of resulting artwork (color, grayscale, or black and white). The Palette menu is also useful for limiting the color palette or for assigning colors from a color group.

Tip: You can deselect Preview at the bottom of the Image Trace panel when modifying values so Illustrator won't apply the trace settings to what you are tracing every time you make a change.

7 In the Image Trace panel, click the triangle to the left of the Advanced options to reveal them. Change the following options in the Image Trace panel, using these values as a starting point:

- Threshold: **206** (Any pixels that are darker than the threshold value are converted to black.)

- Paths: **20%** (For path fitting. A higher value means a tighter fit.)
- Corners: **50%** (The default setting—a higher value means more corners.)
- Noise: **100 px** (Reduce noise by ignoring areas of a set pixel size. A higher value means less noise.)

8 Close the Image Trace panel.

9 With the lemon tracing object still selected, click the Expand button in the Properties panel.

The lemon is no longer an image tracing object but is composed of shapes and paths that are grouped together.

Cleaning up traced artwork

Since the lemon image has been converted to shapes using the Image Trace command, you can now refine the shapes to make the lemon look better.

1 With the lemon artwork selected, click the Ungroup button in the Properties panel to break apart the different shapes and edit them separately.

2 Deselect the artwork by choosing Select > Deselect.

3 Click the extra shape that was traced. Use the figure as a guide. Press Delete or Backspace to remove it.

4 Click the lemon shape to select it. To change the color, click the Fill color box in the Properties panel. In the panel that opens, make sure that the Swatches option (🔲) is selected at the top. Select a yellow color to fill the lemon.

To make the edges a little bit smoother, you'll apply the Simplify command. The Simplify command reduces the number of anchor points that the path is made of without affecting the overall shape too much.

5 With the lemon selected, choose Object > Path > Simplify.

6 In the Simplify options that appear, by default the Reduce Anchor Point slider is set to an auto-simplified value. Drag the slider to the left to remove a few more points.

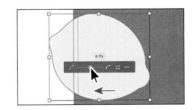

You can drag the slider to the left to reduce the anchor points and further simplify the path. The position and value of the slider specify how closely the simplified path matches the curves of the original path. The closer the slider is to the minimum value on the left, the fewer the anchor points there are, but the path will most likely start to look different. The closer the slider is to the maximum value on the right, the closer the precision of the original curve.

7 Click More Options (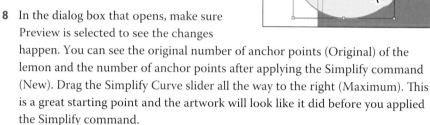) in the Simplify options to open a dialog box with more options.

8 In the dialog box that opens, make sure Preview is selected to see the changes happen. You can see the original number of anchor points (Original) of the lemon and the number of anchor points after applying the Simplify command (New). Drag the Simplify Curve slider all the way to the right (Maximum). This is a great starting point and the artwork will look like it did before you applied the Simplify command.

9 Drag the slider to the left until you see New: 5 pts (circled in the figure). You'll need to drag a little and then release to see the New value change. Click OK.

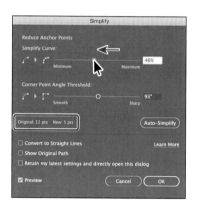

For the Angle Threshold, if the angle of a corner point is less than the angle threshold, the corner point is not changed. This option helps keep corners sharp, even if the value for Curve Precision is low.

Note: If the Angle Threshold you see is different from the figure, that's okay. You can change it to match the figure if you like.

10 To scale the lemon, press the Shift key, and drag a corner to make it smaller. When you see a width of the approximately 1.2 inches in the tool tip, release the mouse button and then the key.

11 Drag the lemon into an empty area of the artboard.

12 Choose File > Save.

Working with drawing modes

Tip: You can cycle through the drawing modes by pressing Shift+D.

Illustrator has three different drawing modes available that are found at the bottom of the toolbar: Draw Normal, Draw Behind, and Draw Inside. Drawing modes allow you to draw shapes in different ways.

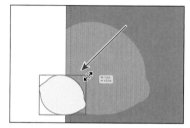

- **Draw Normal mode:** You start every document by drawing shapes in Normal mode, which stacks shapes on top of each other.

- **Draw Behind mode:** This mode allows you to draw behind all artwork on a selected layer if no artwork is selected. If artwork is selected, the new object is drawn directly beneath the selected object.

- **Draw Inside mode:** This mode lets you draw objects or place images inside other objects, including live text, automatically creating a clipping mask of the selected object. You'll learn more about masks in Lesson 15.

Placing artwork

Next you'll place artwork from another Illustrator document that contains text shapes and artwork you will use to create another piece of fruit.

1 Choose File > Open. In the Open dialog box, select the artwork.ai file in the Lessons > Lesson03 folder on your hard disk, and click Open.

2 Select the Selection tool (▶) in the toolbar. To select all of the content, choose Select > All On Active Artboard. Choose Edit > Copy.

3 Click the Postcard.ai tab to return to the postcard document.

4 Choose View > Fit Artboard In Window.

5 Choose Edit > Paste to paste the "FARM FRESH" text and part of the artwork for an orange.

6 Choose Select > Deselect.

Tip: The orange group is made of a circle drawn with the Ellipse tool, a star drawn with the Star tool, and a series of lines drawn with the Line Segment tool.

Using Draw Inside mode

Now you'll add the artwork of the orange you copied from the artwork.ai file to the inside of the red half-circle using the Draw Inside drawing mode. This can be useful if you want to hide (*mask*) part of the artwork.

1 Click the red half-circle copy you made earlier when creating the apple.

2 Click the Fill color box in the Properties panel on the right. In the panel that opens, make sure that the Swatches option (▦) is selected at the top. Select an orange color to fill the shape. I chose the color with the tool tip "C=0 M=50 Y=100 K=0."

3 With the orange half-circle selected, choose Draw Inside from the Drawing Modes menu (◉), near the bottom of the toolbar.

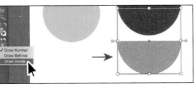

This button is active when a single object is selected (path, compound path, or text), and it allows you to draw within the selected object only. Notice that the orange shape has a dotted open

Note: If the toolbar you see is displayed as a double column, you will see all three of the drawing modes as buttons toward the bottom of the toolbar.

rectangle around it, indicating that Draw Inside mode is still active. You can draw, place, or paste content into a shape with Draw Inside mode active. The shape you are about to add content inside of does not need to be selected.

4   Select the Selection tool (▶), and click the artwork of the orange (the fruit) you pasted to select it. Choose Edit > Cut to cut the selected artwork from the artboard.

5   Choose Edit > Paste.

    The artwork is pasted within the orange half circle since it was selected when entering Draw Inside mode.

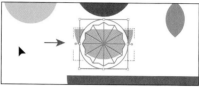

▶ **Tip:** You can separate the artwork again by choosing Object > Clipping Mask > Release. This will make two objects, stacked one on another.

6   Click the Drawing Modes button (⊙) toward the bottom of the toolbar. Choose Draw Normal.

    When you are finished adding content inside a shape, you can choose Draw Normal so that any new content you create will be drawn normally (stacked rather than drawn inside).

7   Choose Select > Deselect and then choose File > Save..

Editing content drawn inside

Next you'll edit the orange artwork inside of the shape to see how you can later edit content inside.

1   With the Selection tool (▶) selected, click to select the orange artwork you pasted. Notice that it selects the half-circle shape instead.

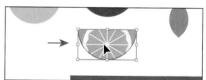

    The half-circle shape is now a mask, also called a *clipping path*. The half-circle shape and the orange pasted artwork make a *clip group* and are treated as a single object. If you look at the top of the Properties panel, you will see Clip Group. As with other groups, if you would like to edit the clipping path (the object containing the content drawn inside it) or the content inside, you can double-click the Clip Group object.

2   With the clip group selected, click the Isolate Mask button in the Properties panel to enter Isolation mode and be able to select the clipping path (half-circle shape) or the orange pasted artwork within.

3 Click the orange pasted artwork within the map boundaries, and drag it to be more centered in the half-circle.

4 Press the Escape key to exit Isolation mode.

5 Choose Select > Deselect.

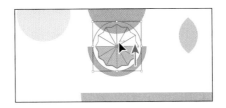

Working with Draw Behind mode

Throughout this lesson, you've been working in the default Draw Normal mode (without knowing it!). Next, you'll draw a rectangle that will cover the artboard and go behind the rest of the content using Draw Behind mode.

1 Click the Drawing Modes button () at the bottom of the toolbar, and choose Draw Behind.

As long as this drawing mode is selected, every shape you create using the different methods you've learned will be created behind the other shapes on the page. The Draw Behind mode also affects placed content (File > Place).

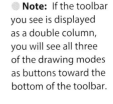

Note: If the toolbar you see is displayed as a double column, you will see all three of the drawing modes as buttons toward the bottom of the toolbar.

2 Press and hold on the Line Segment tool (╱) in the toolbar, and select the Rectangle tool (▢).

3 Move the pointer off the upper-left corner of the artboard where the red bleed guides meet. Press and drag to the lower-right corner of the red bleed guides.

4 With the new rectangle selected, click the Fill color box in the Properties panel. Make sure that the Swatches option (▦) is selected, and then change the fill color to a gray color with the tool tip "C=0 M=0 Y=0 K=20."

5 Press the Escape key to hide the panel.

6 Choose Object > Lock > Selection to lock the rectangle.

7 Click the Drawing Modes button () toward the bottom of the toolbar. Choose Draw Normal.

Finishing up

To finish the postcard, you'll move the artwork into position on the artboard, rotate some, and make copies.

1   Choose View > Fit Artboard In Window to see the entire artboard, if necessary.

2   Select the Selection tool (▶) and click one of the red shapes in the apple. Press the Shift key, click the remaining two shapes, and then release the key.

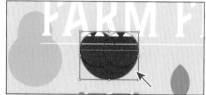

3   Click the Group button in the Properties panel to group the apple shapes together.

4   Drag each piece of fruit and the text into position.

5   Make copies of the fruit and leaf artwork. To do so, click each piece of artwork, and choose Edit > Copy and then Edit > Paste.

6   To rotate a group, you can move the pointer just off a corner of the selected artwork and drag when you see the rotate arrows (↶↷).

Note: If you don't see the Arrange button in the Properties panel, you can also choose Object > Arrange and choose an arrangement option.

7   To bring artwork in front of other artwork, click the artwork to select it. Click the Arrange button in the Properties panel, and choose Bring To Front.

    Artwork that is behind other artwork was created first.

8   Choose File > Save.

9   To close all open files, choose File > Close a few times.

Review questions

1   When creating a new document, what is a document category?

2   What are the basic tools for creating shapes?

3   What is a Live Shape?

4   Describe what Draw Inside mode does.

5   How can you convert a raster image into editable vector shapes?

Review answers

1   You can set up a document for different kinds of output, such as print, web, video, and more, by choosing a category. For example, if you are designing a web page mockup, you can select the Web category and select a document preset (size). The document will be set with the units in pixels, the color mode as RGB, and the raster effects to Screen (72 ppi)—all optimal settings for a web design document.

2   There are five shape tools in the Essentials workspace: Rectangle, Ellipse, Polygon, Star, and Line Segment (the Rounded Rectangle and Flare tools are not in the toolbar in the Essentials workspace).

3   After you draw a rectangle, ellipse, or polygon (or rounded rectangle, which wasn't covered) using a shape tool, you can continue to modify its properties, such as width, height, rounded corners, corner types, and radii (individually or collectively). This is what is known as a Live Shape. The shape properties, such as corner radius, are editable later in the Transform panel, in the Properties panel, or directly on the art.

4   Draw Inside mode lets you draw objects or place images inside other objects, including live text, automatically creating a clipping mask of the selected object.

5   You can convert a raster image into editable vector shapes by selecting it and then clicking the Image Trace button in the Properties panel. To convert the tracing to paths, click Expand in the Properties panel, or choose Object > Image Trace > Expand. Use this method if you want to work with the components of the traced artwork as individual objects. The resulting paths are grouped.

4 EDITING AND COMBINING SHAPES AND PATHS

Lesson overview

In this lesson, you'll learn how to do the following:

- Cut with the Scissors tool.
- Join paths.
- Work with the Knife tool.
- Outline strokes.
- Work with the Eraser tool.
- Create a compound path.
- Work with the Shape Builder tool.
- Work with Pathfinder effects to create shapes.
- Work with the Reshape tool.
- Edit strokes with the Width tool.

 This lesson will take about 45 minutes to complete. To get the lesson files used in this chapter, download them from the web page for this book at adobepress.com/IllustratorCIB2022. For more information, see "Accessing the lesson files and Web Edition" in the Getting Started section at the beginning of this book.

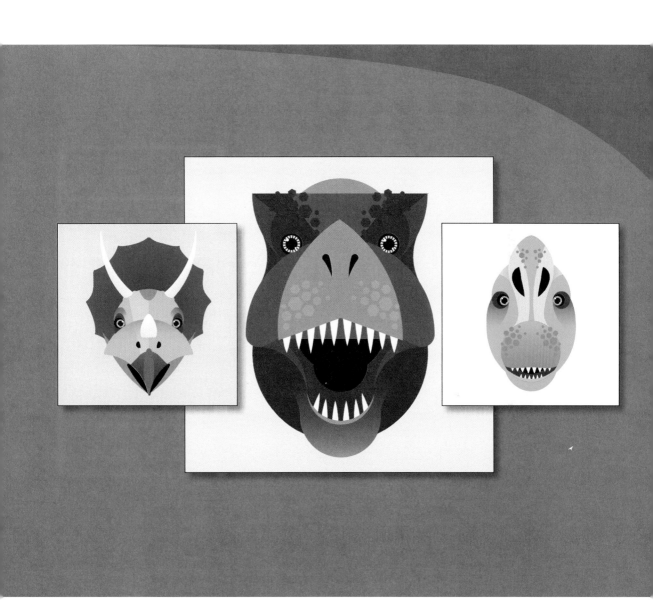

Soon after you begin creating simple paths and
shapes, you will most likely want to use them to
create more complex artwork. In this lesson, you'll
explore how to edit and combine shapes and paths.

Starting the lesson

In Lesson 3, you learned about creating and making edits to basic shapes. In this lesson, you'll take basic shapes and paths and learn how to edit and combine them to create artwork for a few dinosaur illustrations.

Note: If you have not already downloaded the project files for this lesson to your computer from your Account page, make sure to do so now. See the "Getting Started" section at the beginning of the book.

1   To ensure that the tools function and the defaults are set exactly as described in this lesson, delete or deactivate (by renaming) the Adobe Illustrator preferences file. See "Restoring default preferences" in the "Getting Started" section at the beginning of the book.

2   Start Adobe Illustrator.

3   Choose File > Open. Locate the file named L4_end.ai, which is in the Lessons > Lesson04 folder that you copied onto your hard disk, and click Open. This file contains the finished artwork.

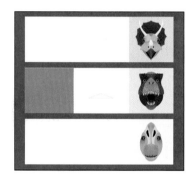

4   Choose View > Fit All In Window; leave the file open for reference, or choose File > Close (I closed it).

5   Choose File > Open. In the Open dialog box, navigate to the Lessons > Lesson04 folder, and select the L4_start.ai file on your hard disk. Click Open.

6   Choose File > Save As. If the Cloud Document dialog box opens, click Save On Your Computer to save it locally.

Tip: By default, the .ai extension shows on macOS, but you can add the extension on either platform in the Save As dialog box.

7   In the Save As dialog box, change the name to **Dinosaurs.ai** (macOS) or **Dinosaurs** (Windows), and choose the Lesson04 folder. Leave Adobe Illustrator (ai) chosen from the Format menu (macOS) or Adobe Illustrator (*.AI) chosen from the Save As Type menu (Windows), and then click Save.

8   In the Illustrator Options dialog box, leave the Illustrator options at their default settings, and click OK.

9   Choose Window > Workspace > Reset Essentials.

Note: If you don't see Reset Essentials in the Workspace menu, choose Window > Workspace > Essentials before choosing Window > Workspace > Reset Essentials.

Editing paths and shapes

In Illustrator, you can edit and combine paths and shapes in various ways to create your artwork. Sometimes that may mean starting with simpler paths and shapes and using different methods to produce more complex paths. The methods and tools you will use include working with the Scissors tool (✂), the Knife tool (✐), and the Eraser tool (◆), outlining strokes, joining paths, and more.

Cutting with the Scissors tool

Several tools allow you to cut and divide shapes. You'll start with the Scissors tool (✂), which splits a path at an anchor point or on a line segment to create an open path. Next, you'll cut a shape with the Scissors tool and reshape it.

1   Click the View menu, and make sure that the Smart Guides option is selected. A checkmark appears when it's selected.

2   Choose 1 Dino 1 from the Artboard Navigation menu in the lower-left corner of the Document window. Choose View > Fit Artboard In Window to make sure the artboard fits in the document window.

3   Select the Selection tool (▶) in the toolbar, and click the purple shape with the yellow stroke on the left side of the artboard.

4   Press Command and + (macOS) or Ctrl and + (Windows) three times to zoom in to the selected artwork.

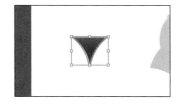

After you modify this shape, you'll add it to the dinosaur head on the right side of the same artboard to complete the beak.

5   With the shape selected, in the toolbar press and hold on the Eraser tool (◆), and select the Scissors tool (✂).

6 Move the pointer over the top edge of the shape, in the middle (see the first part of the following figure). When you see the word "intersect" and a vertical magenta line, click to cut the path at that point, and then move the pointer away.

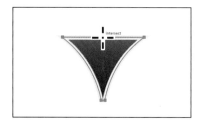 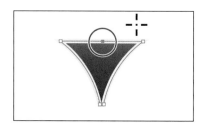

● **Note:** To learn more about open paths and closed paths, see the section "Working with basic shapes" in Chapter 3.

Cuts made with the Scissors tool must be somewhere on a line or a curve rather than on an end point of an open path. When you use the Scissors tool to click the stroke of a closed shape, like the shape in this example, the path is cut where you click so that it becomes an open path.

7 Select the Direct Selection tool (▷) in the toolbar. Move the pointer over the selected (blue) anchor point, and drag it up.

 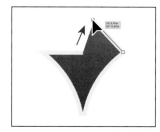 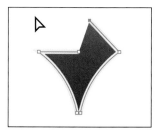

8 From where you originally cut the shape, drag the other anchor point up and to the left until a magenta alignment guide shows, indicating it's aligned with the other anchor point you just dragged.

 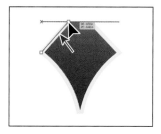 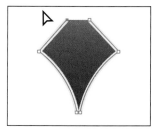

Notice that the stroke (the yellow border) doesn't go all the way around the shape. That's because cutting a shape with the Scissors tool makes an open path. If you only want to fill the shape with a color, it doesn't have to be a closed path. It is, however, necessary for a path to be closed if you want a stroke to appear around the entire fill area.

Joining paths

Suppose you draw a "U" shape and later decide to close the shape, essentially joining the ends of the "U" with a straight path. If you select the path, you can use the Join command to create a line segment between the end points, closing the path.

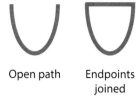

Open path   Endpoints joined

When more than one open path is selected, you can join them to create a closed path. You can also join selected end points of two separate paths. Next, you'll join the ends of the path you just edited to create a closed shape again.

1   Select the Selection tool (▶) in the toolbar. Click away from the path to deselect it, and then click in the purple fill to reselect it.

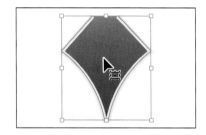

This step is important because only one anchor point was left selected from the previous section. If you were to choose the Join command with only one anchor point selected, an error message would appear. By selecting the whole path, when you apply the Join command, Illustrator simply finds the two ends of the path and connects them with a straight line.

▶ **Tip:** If you wanted to join specific anchor points from separate paths, select the anchor points, and choose Object > Path > Join or press Command+J (macOS) or Ctrl+J (Windows).

2   Click the Join button in the Quick Actions section of the Properties panel.

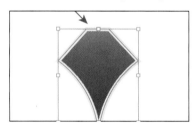

When you apply the Join command to two or more open paths, by default Illustrator first looks for and joins the paths that have end points located closest to each other. This process is repeated every time you apply the Join command until all paths are joined.

▶ **Tip:** In Lesson 6, you'll learn about the Join tool (✄), which allows you to join two paths at a corner, keeping the original curve intact.

3   In the Properties panel, change the stroke to 0 by clicking the down arrow icon until the stroke is removed.

Next, you'll round the corners on the top of the shape.

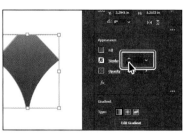

4 Select the Direct Selection tool (▷) in the toolbar, and drag across the top of the shape to select the top two anchors.

5 Drag one of the corner radius widgets toward the center of the shape to round the corners.

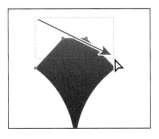  

6 Choose Select > Deselect, and then choose File > Save.

Cutting with the Knife tool

You can also use the Knife tool (🔪) to cut vector artwork. Using the Knife tool, you drag across a shape, and instead of creating open paths, you end up with closed paths.

1 Press the spacebar to access the Hand tool, and drag in the document window to see the green shape to the right.

2 With the Selection tool (▶) selected, click the green shape.

Any objects selected will be cut by the Knife tool. If nothing is selected, it will cut any vector objects it touches.

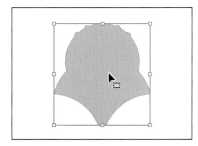

3 Click Edit Toolbar (•••) at the bottom of the toolbar. Scroll in the menu that appears and toward the bottom of the menu you should see the Knife tool (🔪). Drag the Knife tool directly onto the Scissors tool (✂) in the toolbar. When the Scissors tool shows a highlight, release to add the Knife tool to the list of tools.

4 Press the Escape key to hide the menu.

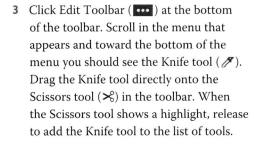  

5 With the Knife tool now selected in the toolbar, move the Knife pointer () above the selected shape. Drag in a "U" shape to cut into the shape.

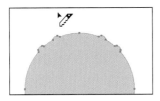 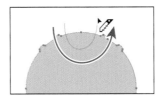 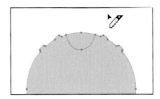

6 Choose Select > Deselect.

7 Select the Selection tool (▶), and click the new shape on the top (see the following figure).

8 Click the Fill color box in the Properties panel, make sure the Swatches option (⬚) is selected in the panel that appears, and click to select a darker green. I chose the color named "Dark green."

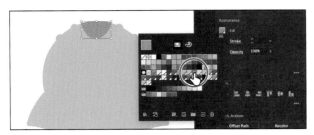

9 Choose Select > Deselect.

Cutting in a straight line with the Knife tool

By default, as you just saw, dragging across a shape with the Knife tool makes a free-form cut that is not straight. Next, you'll see how to cut artwork in a straight line with the Knife tool to give the dinosaur head (the green shape) a highlight.

1 With the Selection tool (▶) selected, click the large light green shape.

2 Select the Knife tool (✐). Move the pointer just above the top of the shape. Press the Caps Lock key to turn the Knife tool pointer into crosshairs (-¦-).

The crosshairs pointer is more precise and can make it easier to see exactly where you begin cutting.

Note: Pressing the Option/Alt key keeps the cut straight. Adding the Shift key (Option/Alt-Shift) constrains the cutting to a multiple of 45°.

3 Press and hold Option+Shift (macOS) or Alt+Shift (Windows), and drag down all the way across the shape to cut it into two. Release the mouse button and then the keys.

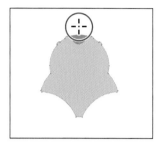 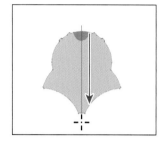

4 Press and hold Option (macOS) or Alt (Windows), and drag down from the top of the shape, at a slight angle, all the way across the shape to cut it into two. Release the mouse button and then the key. This way, you can cut in a straight line in any direction.

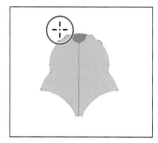 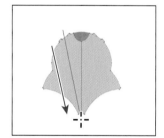

5 Choose Select > Deselect.

6 Select the Selection tool (▶), and click the middle shape you just created (see the first part of the following figure).

7 Click the Fill color box in the Properties panel, make sure the Swatches option (▦) is selected in the panel that appears, and click to select a lighter green.

 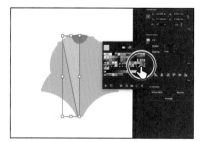

8 Drag across all of the green shapes to select them.

9 Click the Group button in the Quick Actions section of the Properties panel.

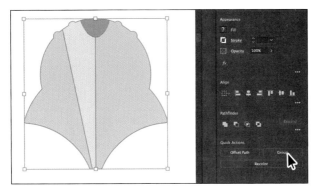

10 Press the Caps Lock key to turn off the pointer crosshairs.

Outlining strokes

A path, like a line, can show a stroke color but not a fill color by default. If you create a line in Illustrator and want to apply both a stroke and a fill, you can outline the stroke of a path, which converts it into a closed shape (or compound path). Next, you'll outline the stroke of a line so you can erase parts of it in the next section to make the final part used to complete the first dinosaur.

1 Press the spacebar to access the Hand tool, and drag in the document window to see the purple circle to the right.

2 With the Selection tool (▶) selected, click the path of the purple circle.

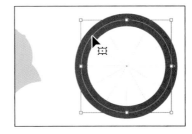

To erase part of the circle and make it look like a dinosaur frill, the circle will need to be a filled shape, not a path. For an example of what a frill looks like, see the figure at the start of the next section, "Using the Eraser tool." You should also see a set of gray lines that look like the spokes of a wheel. Those are just guides used for erasing. They were created by duplicating a straight line several times, and individually rotating each line 30° from the last.

3 Choose Object > Path > Outline Stroke.

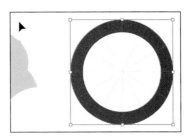

This creates a filled shape that is a closed path. Next, you'll erase parts of the shape.

Using the Eraser tool

Note: You cannot erase raster images, text, symbols, graphs, or gradient mesh objects.

The Eraser tool (◆) lets you erase areas of your vector artwork. You can use the Eraser tool on paths, compound paths, paths inside Live Paint groups, and clipping content. Without any objects selected, you can erase any object that the tool touches across all layers. If any artwork is selected, only that artwork can be erased.

Next, you'll use the Eraser tool to erase part of the selected shape so it looks like a triceratops frill (see the figure at right).

1 Press and hold down the mouse button on the Knife tool (✎), and select the Eraser tool (◆) in the toolbar.

Tip: With the Eraser tool selected and nothing selected in the document, you could also click the Tool Options button at the top of the Properties panel to see the options dialog box.

2 Double-click the Eraser tool (◆) in the toolbar to edit the tool properties. In the Eraser Tool Options dialog box, change Size to **30 pt** to make the eraser larger. Click OK.

You can change the Eraser tool options, depending on your needs.

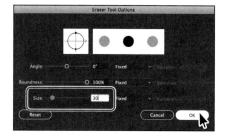

3 Move the pointer above the selected purple circle. Between two guide lines, drag in a "U" shape to create a scallop.

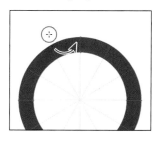
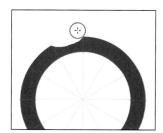
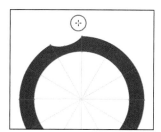

When you release the mouse button, part of the shape is erased, and the shape is still a closed path. To finish, you'll erase the bottom of the circle shape.

4 Repeat this around the circle as you see in the figure, leaving the bottom intact.

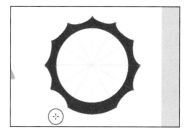

5 Move the pointer as in the first part of the following figure. Drag back and forth across the bottom of the purple circle to erase it.

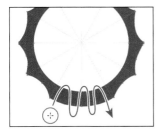 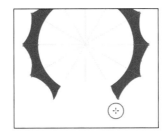 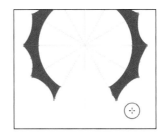

Erasing in a straight line

You can also erase in a straight line, which is what you'll do next.

1 Press the spacebar to access the Hand tool, and drag in the document window to see the partially complete dinosaur to the right.

2 With the Selection tool (▶) selected, click the cream-colored nose horn.

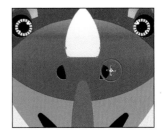

3 Choose View > Zoom In a few times to see more detail.

4 Double-click the Eraser tool (◆) to edit the tool properties. In the Eraser Tool Options dialog box, change Size to **20 pt** to make the eraser smaller. Click OK.

5 With the Eraser tool (◆) selected, move the pointer to where you see the red "X" in the first part of the following figure. Press the Shift key, and drag straight across to the right. Release the mouse button and then the Shift key.

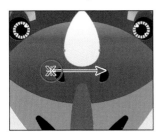 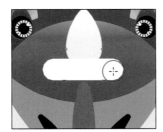 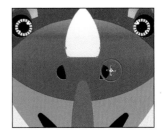

If nothing is erased, try again. Also, it may look like you erased other parts of the shape, but if nothing else was selected, you didn't.

6 Choose File > Save.

Assemble the first dinosaur

To complete the dinosaur you see, you'll drag and position the artwork you have worked on to this point.

1 Choose View > Fit Artboard In Window.

2 With the Selection tool (▶) selected, drag the purple shape onto the beak of the dinosaur.

3 Drag the green group of shapes onto the head (see the following figure).

4 Drag the purple frill onto the purple circle behind the head.

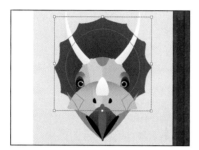

5 If the purple frill covers any of the artwork, click Arrange toward the bottom of the Properties panel, and choose Send Backward a few times until it looks like the figure.

Creating a compound path

Compound paths let you use a vector object to cut a hole in another vector object. If you were to select two vector objects, the "cutting" object is the top object. Whenever I think of a compound path, I think of a doughnut shape created from two circles. Holes appear where paths overlap. A compound path is like a group, and the individual objects in the compound path can still be edited or released (if you don't want them to be a compound path anymore).

Next, you'll create a compound path to provide some art for a dinosaur's eyes.

1 Choose 2 Dino 2 from the Artboard Navigation menu in the lower-left corner of the Document window.

2 With the Selection tool (▶) selected, select the gray circle on the far left of the artboard, and drag it into the center of the larger yellow circle to its right.

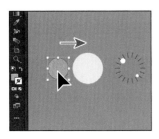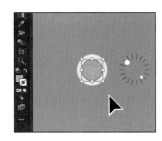

Smart Guides help you align the circles. You can also select the two circles and align them to each other using the Align options in the Properties panel.

3 Drag across the gray circle and yellow circle to select both.

4 Choose Object > Compound Path > Make, and leave the artwork selected.

▶ **Tip:** You can still edit the original shapes in a compound path like this one. To edit them, select each shape individually with the Direct Selection tool (▷), or double-click the compound path with the Selection tool, to enter Isolation mode and select individual shapes.

You can now see that the gray circle has seemingly disappeared, and you can see through the yellow shape to the aqua background shape. The gray circle "punched" a hole in the yellow shape. With the shape still selected, you should see "Compound Path" at the top of the Properties panel to the right.

5 Drag the group of lines just to the right of the yellow shape into the center of the yellow shape.

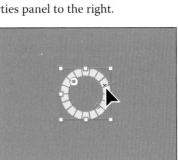

The group of lines should be on top of the yellow circle. If it isn't, choose Object > Arrange > Bring To Front.

6 Drag across the eye shapes to select them.

7 Choose Object > Group.

8 Choose Select > Deselect and then choose File > Save.

Combining shapes

Creating more complex shapes from simpler shapes can be easier than creating them with drawing tools like the Pen tool. In Illustrator, you can combine vector objects in different ways. The resulting paths or shapes differ depending on the method you use to combine the paths. In this section, you'll explore a few of the more widely used methods for combining shapes.

Start by creating a shape

Before you can jump into combining shapes, you'll create a triangle. Then you'll combine it with a few other shapes that are already there. Those shapes will then become the last part of the dinosaur. Before you create the triangle, you'll swap the selected fill and stroke colors so that the fill becomes the stroke for the new shape you make.

1 To swap the fill and the stroke of the shape so that the fill becomes the stroke, click the Swap Fill And Stroke button toward the bottom of the toolbar.

   Having a stroke on the shape you are about to draw, rather than a fill, will make it easier to see a gray guide path.

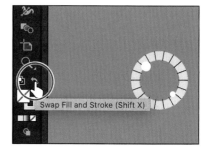

2 Press and hold on the Rectangle tool and select the Polygon tool in the toolbar.

3 To the right of the eye shapes, in the middle of the artboard, you'll see a few yellow shapes. Starting in the center of the yellow circle, drag to create a polygon. While dragging, press the down arrow a few times until the shape has three sides (triangle). Drag until the shape is as wide as the gray triangle guide, press the Shift key to straighten it, and release the mouse button and then the key.

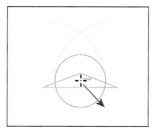
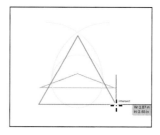

4 Drag the top edge of the triangle down to snap to the guide triangle, and drag the bottom bounding point up to snap to the same guide triangle.

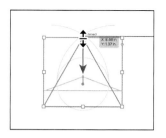 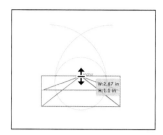 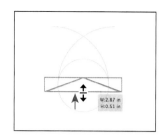

Working with the Shape Builder tool

The first method you'll learn for combining shapes involves working with the Shape Builder tool (⬡). This tool allows you to visually and intuitively merge, delete, fill, and edit overlapping shapes and paths directly in the artwork. Using the Shape Builder tool, you'll create a more complex shape for another dinosaur head from a series of simpler shapes you create.

1   Select the Selection tool (▶), and drag across the yellow paths and the shape you made. The gray guide path for the triangle is locked, so it won't be selected.

2   Change the stroke weight to **5 pt** in the Properties panel. Change the stroke color to the color named Orange to make it easier to see.

    To edit shapes with the Shape Builder tool (⬡), they need to be selected. Using the Shape Builder tool, you will now combine, delete, and paint these simple shapes to create a single shape.

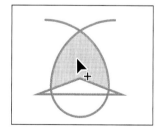

▶ **Tip:** You can also press the Shift key, and drag a marquee across a series of shapes to combine them. Pressing Shift+Option (macOS) or Shift+Alt (Windows) and dragging a marquee across selected shapes with the Shape Builder tool (⬡) allows you to delete a series of shapes within the marquee.

3   Select the Shape Builder tool (⬡) in the toolbar. Move the pointer off the left side of the shapes, and drag to the right. Release the mouse button to combine the shapes.

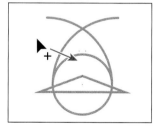 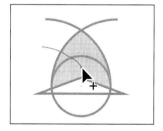 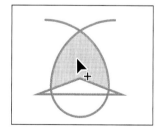

When you select the Shape Builder tool, the overlapping shapes are temporarily divided into separate objects. As you drag from one part to another, a red outline appears, showing you the resulting shape when the shapes are merged together. The red outline, in this case, is challenging to see since it's red on an orange stroke.

Next, you'll delete a few shapes. You may want to zoom in to the shapes.

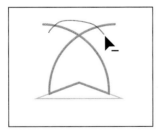 **Note:** When you position the pointer over the shapes, make sure you see the mesh within those shapes before clicking to delete.

4 With the shapes still selected, hold down the Option (macOS) or Alt (Windows) key. Notice that, with the modifier key held down, the pointer shows a minus sign (▶_). Click in the *middle* of the shape on the far left, not the stroke, to delete it. *Zoom in if you need.* Refer to the figure to see which shape to remove.

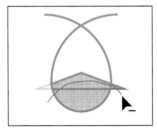 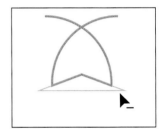

5 Move the pointer below the shapes. Hold down the Option (macOS) or Alt (Windows) key, and drag through the rest of the bottom shapes. Release the mouse button and then the key to remove those shapes.

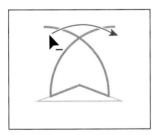 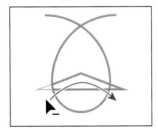 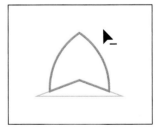

6 Option-drag (macOS) or Alt-drag (Windows) across the two curved paths to delete them. Refer to the figure to see what to remove.

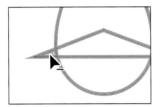 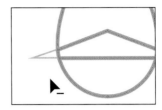

7 Select the Selection tool. To swap the fill and the stroke of the shape so that the stroke becomes the fill, click the Swap Fill And Stroke button toward the bottom of the toolbar.

Assemble the second dinosaur

To complete the second dinosaur, you'll drag and position the artwork you have worked on to this point.

1 Choose View > Fit Artboard In Window.

2 With the Selection tool (▶) selected, drag the yellow eye into place on the dinosaur and the orange shape onto the nose. Don't worry about exact positioning. Leave the last orange shape selected.

3 Choose View > Zoom In a few times to zoom in to the dinosaur.

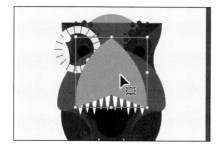

4 To arrange the orange shape behind the other artwork on the nose, click Arrange in the Properties panel, and choose Send Backward as many times as necessary. I had to choose it three times.

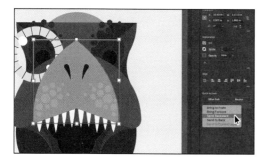

5 Click the yellow circle around the eye, and to resize it, press the Shift key, and drag a corner. Release the mouse button and then the key. Drag it into place.

6 To make a copy, Option-drag (macOS) or Alt-drag (Windows) the eye to the other side. Release the mouse button and then the key.

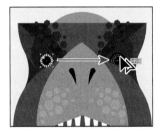 

7 Choose Select > Deselect, and then choose File > Save.

Combining objects using Pathfinder effects

Pathfinder effects, found in the Properties panel or the Pathfinder panel (Window > Pathfinder), are another way to combine shapes in a variety of ways. By default, when a Pathfinder effect such as Unite is applied, the original objects selected are *permanently* transformed.

1 Choose 3 Dino 3 from the Artboard Navigation menu in the lower-left corner of the Document window.

2 With the Selection tool (▶) selected, drag across the three ellipses with the black strokes to select them all.

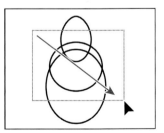

You need to create a combined shape for the dinosaur head to the right. You will use the Properties panel and those shapes to create the final artwork.

3 With the shapes selected, in the Pathfinder section of the Properties panel on the right, click the Unite button () to *permanently* combine the three shapes into a path.

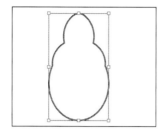

Note: The Unite button in the Properties panel produces a similar result as the Shape Builder tool by combining multiple shapes into one.

4 Choose Edit > Undo Add to undo the Unite command and bring all of the shapes back. Leave them selected.

▷ **Tip:** Clicking More Options (•••) in the Pathfinder section of the Properties panel will reveal the Pathfinder panel, which has more options.

Understanding shape modes

In the previous section, the pathfinders made a permanent change to the shapes. With shapes selected, Option-clicking (macOS) or Alt-clicking (Windows) any of the default set of pathfinders showing in the Properties panel creates a compound shape rather than a standard shape (path). The original underlying objects of compound shapes are preserved. As a result, you can still select each original object within a compound shape. Using a shape mode to create a compound shape can be useful if you think that you may want to retrieve the original shapes at a later time.

1 With the shapes still selected, press the Option (macOS) or Alt (Windows) key, and click the Unite button () in the Properties panel.

 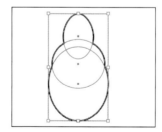

This creates a compound shape that traces the outline of what's left after the shapes are combined. You'll still be able to edit the original shapes separately.

2 Choose Select > Deselect to see the final shape.

3 With the Selection tool, double-click the black stroke of the shape to enter Isolation mode.

You double-clicked the stroke of the shape and not anywhere in the shapes because they do not have a fill.

▷ **Tip:** To edit the original shapes in a compound shape like this one, you can also select them individually with the Direct Selection tool (▷).

4 Click the edge of the ellipse at the top or drag across the path to select it.

5 Drag the selected ellipse straight down from the blue dot in the center, if you see it, or from the path stroke. As you drag, press the Shift key. When in position, release the mouse button and then the Shift key.

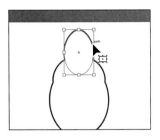 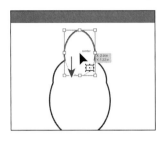 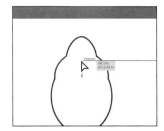

6 Press the Escape key to exit Isolation mode.

You will now expand the artwork appearance. Expanding the appearance of a compound shape maintains the shape of the compound object, but you can no longer select or edit the original objects. You will typically expand an object when you want to modify the appearance attributes and other properties of specific elements within it.

7 Click away from the shape to deselect it and then click to select it again. That way the entire object is selected, and not just the one shape.

8 Choose Object > Expand Appearance.

The Pathfinder effect is now *permanent* and the shapes are a single shape.

9 Change the Fill color in the Properties panel to an aqua.

10 Change the stroke weight to **0**.

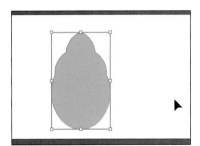

Reshaping a path

In Lesson 3 you learned about creating shapes and paths (lines). You can use the Reshape tool to stretch parts of a path without distorting its overall shape. In this section, you'll change the shape of a line, giving it a bit of curve, so you can finish the nose of one of the dinosaurs.

1 Make sure the Smart Guides are on (View > Smart Guides).

2 With the Selection tool (▶) selected, click the light green path in the middle of the artboard.

3 To make it easier to see, press Command and + (macOS) or Ctrl and + (Windows) a few times to zoom in.

4 Click Edit Toolbar (•••) at the bottom of the toolbar. Scroll in the menu that appears, and drag the Reshape tool (ψ) onto the Rotate tool (↻) in the toolbar on the left to add it to the list of tools.

● **Note:** You may want to press the Escape key to hide the extra tools menu.

5 With the Reshape tool (ψ) selected, move the pointer over the middle of the path. When the pointer changes (▷), drag to the left to add an anchor point and reshape the path.

● **Note:** You can use the Reshape tool on a closed path, like a square or circle, but if the entire path is selected, the Reshape tool will add anchor points and move the path.

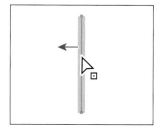
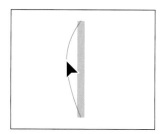
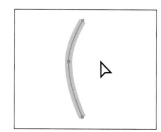

The Reshape tool can be used to drag an existing anchor point or path segment. If you drag from an existing path segment, an anchor point is created.

6 Move the pointer over the top anchor point of the path, and drag it to the left a little. Leave the path selected.

● **Note:** Only selected anchor points are adjusted when dragging with the Reshape tool.

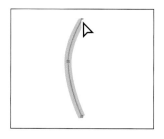
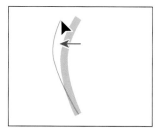
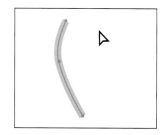

Using the Width tool

Not only can you adjust the weight of a stroke, as you did in Lesson 3, but you can alter regular stroke widths either by using the Width tool (🖉) or by applying width profiles to the stroke. This allows you to create a variable width along the stroke of a path. Next, you will use the Width tool to adjust the path you just reshaped.

Tip: You can drag one width point on top of another width point to create a discontinuous width point. If you double-click a discontinuous width point, the Width Point Edit dialog box allows you to edit both width points.

1   Select the Width tool (🖉) in the toolbar. Move the pointer over the middle of the path you just reshaped, and notice that the pointer has a plus symbol next to it (►₊) when it's positioned over the path. If you were to drag, you would edit the width of the stroke. Drag away from the line, to the right. Notice that, as you drag, you are stretching the stroke to the left and right equally. Release the mouse button when the measurement label shows Width at approximately 0.4 in.

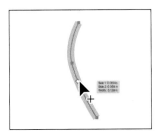
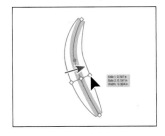
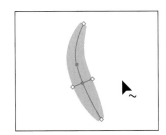

You just created a variable stroke on a path, not a shape with a fill. The new point on the original path is called the *width point*. The lines extending from the width point are the *handles*.

Tip: If you select a width point by clicking it, you can press Delete to remove it. When there is only one width point on a stroke, removing that point removes the width completely.

2   Click in an empty area of the artboard to deselect the point.

3   Move the pointer anywhere over the path, and the width point you just created will appear (an arrow is pointing to it).

4   Move the pointer over the original width point, and when you see lines extending from it and the pointer changes (►〜), drag it up and down to see the effect on the path. See the last part of the following figure for where it should approximately land.

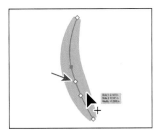

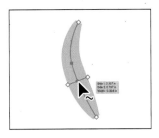
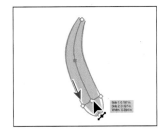

In addition to dragging to reposition a width point, you can double-click and enter values in a dialog box. That's what you'll do next.

5 Move the pointer over the top anchor point of the path, and notice that the pointer has a wavy line next to it (▶〰) and the word "anchor" appears (see the first part of the following figure). Double-click the point to create a new width point and to open the Width Point Edit dialog box.

6 In the Width Point Edit dialog box, change Total Width to **0 in**, and click OK.

▶ **Tip:** You can select a width point and Option-drag (macOS) or Alt-drag (Windows) one of the width point handles to change one side of the stroke width.

The Width Point Edit dialog box allows you to adjust the length of the width point handles, together or separately, with more precision. Also, if you select the Adjust Adjoining Width Points option, any changes you make to the selected width point affect neighboring width points as well.

7 Move the pointer over the bottom anchor point of the path, and double-click. In the Width Point Edit dialog box, change Total Width to **0 in**, and click OK.

▶ **Tip:** After defining the stroke width, you can save the variable width as a *profile* that you can reuse later from the Stroke panel or the Control panel. To learn more about variable-width profiles, search for "Apply stroke on an object" in Illustrator Help (Help > Illustrator Help).

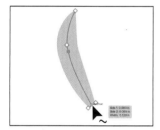 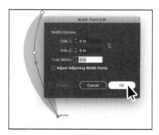 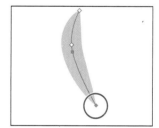

8 Move the pointer over the original width point. When the width point handles appear, drag one of them away from the center of the path to make it a little wider. Leave the path selected for the next section.

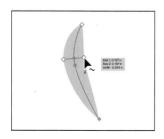 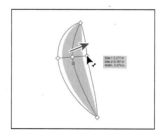 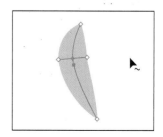

9 Change the Stroke color in the Properties panel to black.

Assemble the last dinosaur

To complete the dinosaur you see, you'll drag and position the artwork you have worked on to this point.

1 Choose View > Fit Artboard In Window.

2 With the Selection tool (▶) selected, drag the aqua dinosaur head shape and the path you reshaped onto the dinosaur to the right. Leave the black reshaped path selected.

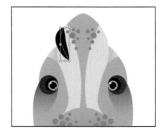

3 Choose View > Zoom In a few times to zoom in to the dinosaur.

4 Shift-drag the corner of the black path to make it smaller. Notice that the stroke weight is still the same even though the line is smaller. This happens by default.

5 Change the stroke weight in the Properties panel to **19**.

 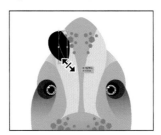 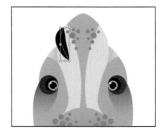

6 Drag it into the position you see in the first part of the following figure.

7 To make a copy of the reshaped path, Option-drag (macOS) or Alt-drag (Windows) it to the other side. Release the mouse button and then the key.

8 In the Properties panel, click Flip Horizontally to flip the shape.

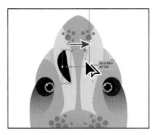 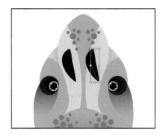 

9 Choose View > Fit All In Window.

10 Choose File > Save, and then choose File > Close.

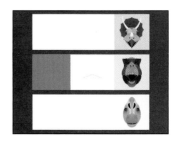

Review questions

1 Name two ways you can combine several shapes into one.

2 What is the difference between the Scissors tool (✂) and the Knife tool (✐)?

3 How can you erase with the Eraser tool (◆) in a straight line?

4 What is the main difference between shape modes and Pathfinder effects in the Properties panel or Pathfinder panel?

5 Why would you outline strokes?

Review answers

1 Using the Shape Builder tool (◉), you can visually and intuitively merge, delete, fill, and edit overlapping shapes and paths directly in the artwork. You can also use the Pathfinder effects, which can be found in the Properties panel, the Effects menu (not mentioned in this lesson), or the Pathfinder panel, to create new shapes out of overlapping objects.

2 The Scissors tool (✂) is meant to split a path, graphics frame, or empty text frame at an anchor point or along a segment. The Knife tool (✐) cuts objects along a path you draw with the tool, dividing objects. When you cut a shape with the Scissors tool, it becomes an open path. When you cut a shape with the Knife tool, the resulting shapes become closed paths.

3 To erase in a straight line with the Eraser tool (◆), press and hold the Shift key before you begin dragging with the Eraser tool.

4 In the Properties panel, when a shape mode (such as Unite) is applied, the original objects selected are permanently transformed, but you can hold down the Option (macOS) or Alt (Windows) key and the original underlying objects are preserved. When a Pathfinder effect (such as Merge) is applied, the original objects selected are permanently transformed.

5 A path, like a line, can show a stroke color but not a fill color by default. If you create a line in Illustrator and want to apply both a stroke and a fill, you can outline the stroke, which converts the line into a closed shape (or compound path).

5 TRANSFORMING ARTWORK

Lesson overview

In this lesson, you'll learn how to do the following:

- Add, edit, rename, and reorder artboards in an existing document.

- Navigate artboards.

- Work with rulers and guides.

- Position objects with precision.

- Move, scale, rotate, and shear objects using a variety of methods.

- Explore mirror repeat.

- Work with the Puppet Warp tool.

 This lesson will take about 60 minutes to complete. To get the lesson files used in this chapter, download them from the web page for this book at adobepress.com/IllustratorCIB2022. For more information, see "Accessing the lesson files and Web Edition" in the Getting Started section at the beginning of this book.

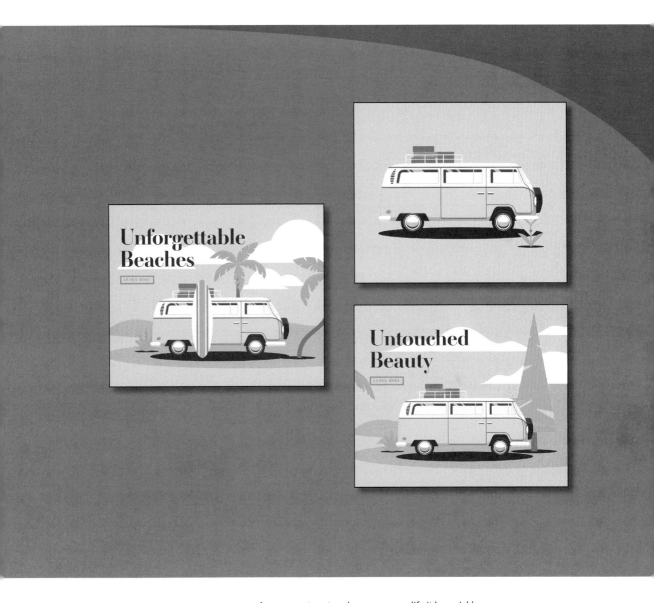

As you create artwork, you can modify it by quickly and precisely controlling objects' size, shape, and orientation. In this lesson, you'll explore creating and editing artboards, the various Transform commands, and specialized tools while creating several pieces of artwork.

Starting the lesson

In this lesson, you'll transform artwork and use it to complete an ad. Before you begin, you'll restore the default preferences for Adobe Illustrator and then open a file containing the finished artwork to see what you'll create.

Note: If you have not already downloaded the project files for this lesson to your computer from your Account page, make sure to do so now. See the "Getting Started" section at the beginning of the book.

1 To ensure that the tools function and the defaults are set exactly as described in this lesson, delete or deactivate (by renaming) the Adobe Illustrator preferences file. See "Restoring default preferences" in the "Getting Started" section at the beginning of the book.

2 Start Adobe Illustrator.

3 Choose File > Open, and open the L5_end.ai file in the Lessons > Lesson05 folder on your hard disk.

This file contains the artboards that make up a few different versions of an ad. Any data presented is purely fictitious.

Note: For more information on activating fonts, visit helpx.adobe.com/ creative-cloud/help/ add-fonts.html.

4 In the Missing Fonts dialog box, ensure that each missing font is selected, and click Activate Fonts. After some time, the font(s) should be activated, and you should see a success message in the Missing Fonts dialog box. Click Close.

5 If a dialog box appears discussing font auto-activation, you can click Skip.

6 Choose View > Fit All In Window, and leave the artwork onscreen as you work.

7 Choose File > Open. In the Open dialog box, navigate to the Lessons > Lesson05 folder, and select the L5_start.ai file on your hard disk. Click Open.

8 Choose File > Save As. If the Cloud Document dialog box opens, click Save On Your Computer.

9 In the Save As dialog box, name the file **Vacation_ads.ai**, and navigate to the Lesson05 folder. Leave Adobe Illustrator (ai) chosen from the Format menu (macOS) or Adobe Illustrator (*.AI) chosen from the Save As Type menu (Windows), and click Save.

10 In the Illustrator Options dialog box, leave the Illustrator options at their default settings, and then click OK.

Note: If you don't see Reset Essentials in the Workspace menu, choose Window > Workspace > Essentials before choosing Window > Workspace > Reset Essentials.

11 Choose Window > Workspace > Reset Essentials.

Working with artboards

Artboards represent the regions containing printable or exportable artwork, similar to pages in Adobe InDesign or artboards in Adobe Photoshop or Adobe XD. You can use artboards for creating a variety of project types, such as multipage PDF files, printed pages with different sizes or different elements, independent elements for websites or apps, or video storyboards, for instance.

Drawing a custom-sized artboard

You can add and remove artboards at any time while working on a document, and they can be different sizes, as needed. You can resize, position, reorder, and rename them in Artboard Editing mode. Next, you'll add a few artboards to your document, which has only one artboard.

1 Choose View > Fit Artboard In Window.

2 Choose Select > Deselect, if available. If any fonts were replaced in the previous section, the text objects will be selected.

3 To zoom out, press Command and – (macOS) or Ctrl and – (Windows) twice.

4 Press the spacebar to temporarily access the Hand tool (✋). Drag the artboard to the left to see the tree off the right side of the artboard.

5 Select the Selection tool (▶).

To see document options like the Edit Artboards button in the Properties panel, you cannot have content selected in your document, and the Selection tool needs to be selected.

6 Click the Edit Artboards button in the Properties panel.

Clicking the Edit Artboards button enters Artboard Editing mode and selects the Artboard tool in the toolbar. You can see a dashed line around the only artboard in the document and, if it's in view, a label "Artboard 1" in the upper-left corner of the artboard. Notice that artwork, like the palm tree, can extend beyond the edges of an artboard.

7 Move the pointer to the right of the artboard that has the "Unforgettable Beaches" text, and drag to draw an artboard around the tree. Don't worry about the size; you're going to change it soon.

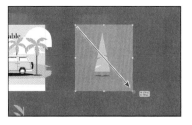

The tree is now on that new artboard.

In the Properties panel on the right, in Artboard Editing mode, you'll see lots of options for editing the selected artboard. For instance, when an artboard is selected, the Preset menu lets you change the artboard to a set size, like Letter. The sizes in the Preset menu include typical print, video, tablet, and web sizes.

8   In the Properties panel on the right, select the Width and type **336**. Select the Height value, and type **280**. Press Return or Enter to accept the height.

Notice that the unit shown is pixels.

9   Change the name to **City vacation ad** in the Artboards section of the Properties panel. Press Return or Enter to make the change.

10 Drag the artboard to the right a bit to make more room between the artboards.

By default, content on an artboard that isn't locked moves with the artboard. Looking in the Properties panel, you'll see the Move Artwork With Artboard option is selected. If you deselect that option before moving an artboard, the artwork won't move with it. In this case, the tree would not have moved.

Creating a new artboard

Next, you'll create another artboard that's the same size as the City vacation ad artboard.

1   Click the New Artboard button (▣) in the Properties panel to create a new artboard that's the same size as the City vacation ad artboard and to its right.

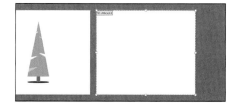

2 Change the name of the new artboard to **Mountain vacation ad** in the Properties panel. Press Return or Enter to make the change.

 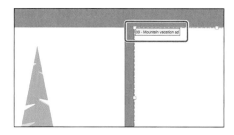

When editing artboards in Artboard Editing mode, you can see the name of each artboard in the upper-left corner of the artboard.

3 Choose View > Fit All In Window to see all of your artboards.

4 Click the Exit button at the top of the Properties panel to exit Artboard Editing mode.

▶ **Tip:** To exit Artboard Editing mode, you can also select another tool in the toolbar besides the Artboard tool (↰) or press the Escape key.

Exiting Artboard Editing mode deselects all artboards and selects the tool that was active before you entered that mode. In this case, the Selection tool is selected.

Editing artboards

After creating artboards, you can edit or delete them by using the Artboard tool (↰), menu commands, Properties panel, or Artboards panel. Next, you'll reposition and change the size of an artboard.

1 Press Command and – (macOS) or Ctrl and – (Windows) twice to zoom out.

2 Select the Artboard tool (↰) in the toolbar to enter Artboard Editing mode.

This is another way to enter Artboard Editing mode and can be useful when artwork is selected, since you can't see the Edit Artboards button in the Properties panel with artwork selected.

Tip: I'm asking you to drag the artboard a little higher so when you align the artboards later, they will move.

3 Drag the artboard named Mountain vacation ad to the left of the original artboard *and a little higher*. Don't worry about its exact position yet, but make sure it doesn't cover any artwork.

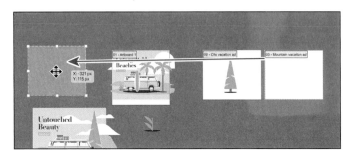

4 Click in the artboard in the center with the "Unforgettable Beaches" text to select that artboard. Choose View > Fit Artboard In Window to fit that artboard in the Document window.

Commands such as View > Fit Artboard In Window typically apply to the selected, or *active*, artboard.

5 Drag the bottom-middle point of the artboard up to resize it. When the point snaps to the bottom of the yellow-orange shape, release the mouse button.

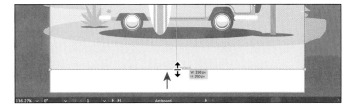

You can resize artboards to fit content or the other way around—whatever you need. Next, you'll delete the artboard named "City vacation ad" on the right since you will copy an artboard from another document to replace it.

6 Choose View > Fit All In Window to see all of your artboards.

Tip: With an artboard selected with the Artboard tool (⌐) you can also click the Delete Artboard button (▣) in the Properties panel to delete an artboard.

7 Click the City vacation ad artboard on the right and press Delete or Backspace to remove it.

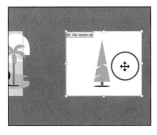
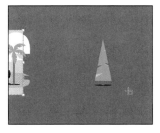

When you delete an artboard, the artwork that was on that artboard remains. In your document, you can delete all but one artboard.

8   Select the Selection tool (▶), which exits Artboard Editing mode, and drag the tree artwork below the artboard with the "Unforgettable Beaches" text on it.

Copying artboards between documents

You can copy or cut artboards from one document and paste them into another, and the artwork on those artboards comes with them. Copying artboards makes it easy to reuse content across documents. For this project, you'll copy the start of another ad design into the project you're working on to keep it all in one file.

1   Choose File > Open. Open the Bus.ai file in the Lessons > Lesson05 folder on your hard disk.

2   Choose View > Fit Artboard In Window to see the entire artboard.

Notice that the van is blue? A color swatch named "Van" is applied to it. That will be important soon.

3   Select the Artboard tool (┤┐) in the toolbar, and the only artboard in the document is selected. If it isn't, click the artboard to select it.

Be careful about clicking the artboard if it's already selected! You may make a copy on top.

● **Note:** If Move Artwork With Artboard is deselected in the Properties panel before you copy an artboard, the artwork on the artboard will not be copied with it.

4   Choose Edit > Copy to copy the artboard and the artwork on the artboard.

Artwork not on the artboard—like the palm tree off the right side of the artboard—isn't copied. Depending on how the artboard fits, you may not see it.

5   Choose File > Close to close the file without saving.

6   Back in the Vacation_ads.ai document, choose Edit > Paste to paste the artboard and the artwork.

7   In the Swatch Conflict dialog that appears, make sure that Merge Swatches is selected and select Apply To All so any other swatches do the same. Click OK.

Swatches applied to any content on the artboard that you paste are imported. If those imported swatches have the same name but different color values as swatches already in the document, a swatch conflict occurs.

In the Swatch Conflict dialog box, by selecting the "Add Swatches" option, any swatches from the Van.ai document with the same name as found in the Vacation_ads.ai file are added by appending a number to the conflicting swatch names. If you select "Merge Swatches," swatches with the same name are merged using the color values of the existing swatches. The blue van from the Bus.ai file is now green because the swatch named "Van" in the Vacation_ads.ai file is green.

Aligning and arranging artboards

To keep artboards tidy in your document, you can move and align artboards to suit your working style. One example is arranging artboards, so similar artboards are next to each other. Next, you'll select all of the artboards and align them.

▶ **Tip:** With the Artboard tool (⊹) selected, you can also press the Shift key and drag across a series of artboards to select them.

1   With the Artboard tool (⊹) still selected, Shift-click the other two artboards to select them as well.

The Shift key allows you to add artboards to the selection, rather than draw an artboard, when the Artboard tool is selected.

2   Click the Vertical Align Top button (▥) in the Properties panel on the right to align the artboards to each other.

You *might* have seen that the light orange background shape on the artboard with the "Unforgettable Beaches" text didn't move with the artboard. An arrow is pointing to it in the previous figure. That rectangle is locked, and locked objects don't move when you move an artboard.

3 Choose Edit > Undo Align to get the artboards back where they were.

4 To unlock the background object (and any other locked objects), choose Object > Unlock All.

5 Click the Vertical Align Top button (▥) in the Properties panel on the right to align the artboards to each other.

In Artboard Editing mode, you can also arrange your artboards however you like using the Rearrange All Artboards command. This option makes it possible to arrange artboards in columns and/or rows and define precise spacing between.

6 Click the Rearrange All button in the Properties panel to open the Rearrange All Artboards dialog box.

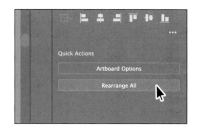

In the Rearrange All Artboards dialog box, you can arrange your artboards in columns or rows and set the spacing between each artboard to a set amount.

7 Click Arrange By Row (▦) so the three artboards can remain next to each other horizontally. Set Spacing to **40** to set an exact spacing between them. Click OK.

The artboard that was in the middle is now first in the row of artboards and the other artboards are to the right of it. That's because the Arrange By Row option ordered the artboards based on artboard number. You'll see how to change that number shortly.

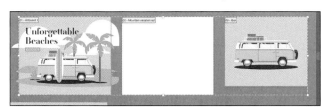

Setting options for artboards

By default, artboards are assigned a number and a name, as you've seen. When you navigate the artboards in a document, it can be helpful to name them. Next, you'll learn how to rename artboards so that the names help identify artboards more quickly, and you'll see other options you can set for each artboard.

1 While still in Artboard Editing mode, click to select the artboard named "Artboard 1." It's the artboard with the "Unforgettable Beaches" text on it.

2 Click the Artboard Options button in the Properties panel.

3 In the Artboard Options dialog box, change the name to **Beach vacation ad** and click OK.

The Artboard Options dialog box has a lot of extra options for artboards, as well as a few you've already seen, like width and height.

4 Choose File > Save.

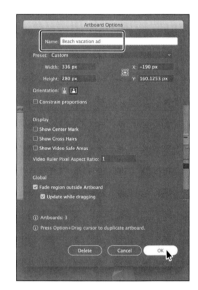

Reordering artboards

You can navigate between artboards in your document using the Next Artboard (▶) and Previous Artboard (◀) buttons in the Properties panel with the Selection tool selected, with nothing selected, and while not in Artboard Editing mode. You can do this from below the Document window. By default, artboards appear according to the order created, but you can change that order. Next, you'll reorder the artboards in the Artboards panel to navigate them in the artboard order you set.

1 Choose Window > Artboards to open the Artboards panel.

The Artboards panel allows you to see a list of all of the artboards in the document. It also allows you to reorder, rename, add, and delete artboards and choose many other artboard options without being in Artboard Editing mode.

2 With the Artboards panel open, double-click the number 3 to the left of the name "Bus" in the Artboards panel.

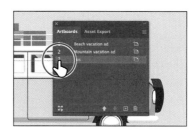

Double-clicking the number to the left of an artboard name that isn't selected in the Artboards panel makes that artboard the *active* artboard and fits it in the Document window.

3 Drag the "Bus" artboard name up until a line appears above the artboard named "Mountain vacation ad." Release the mouse button.

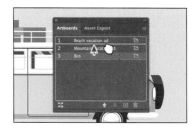

This makes the Bus artboard the second artboard in the list. When you choose artboards from the Properties panel—in this case, 1, 2, or 3—the numbering will follow what you see in the Artboards panel.

▷ **Tip:** You can also reorder the artboards by selecting an artboard in the Artboards panel and clicking the Move Up (▲) or Move Down (▼) button at the bottom of the panel.

4 Choose View > Fit All In Window.

▷ **Tip:** The Artboard Options button (▣) appears to the right of the name of each artboard in the Artboards panel. It not only allows access to the artboard options for each artboard but also indicates the orientation (vertical or horizontal) of the artboard.

Notice that the if you change the ordering of the artboards in the panel, it doesn't move the artboards around.

5 Drag the "Bus" artboard name back down below the artboard named "Mountain vacation ad." Release the mouse button.

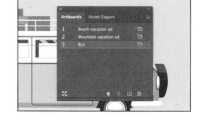

I find that keeping the artboard numbering in the order that the artboards appear in the document window is easiest when choosing artboards to show.

6 Click the Exit button at the top of the Properties panel to exit Artboard Editing mode.

7 Click the X at the top of the Artboards panel group to close it.

8 Choose View > Fit All In Window.

9 Choose File > Save.

Working with rulers and guides

Note: You could switch between the artboard and global rulers by choosing View > Rulers > and selecting Change To Global Rulers or Change To Artboard Rulers, depending on which option is currently chosen, but don't do that now.

With the artboards set up, you'll learn about aligning and measuring content using rulers and guides. Rulers help you accurately place and measure objects and distances. They appear along the top and left sides of the Document window and can be shown and hidden. There are two types of rulers in Illustrator: *artboard rulers* and *global rulers.*

The point on each ruler (horizontal and vertical) where the 0 (zero) shows is the *ruler origin.* Artboard rulers set the ruler origin to the upper-left corner of the active artboard. Global rulers set the ruler origin to the upper-left corner of the first artboard or the artboard at the top of the list in the Artboards panel, no matter which artboard is active. By default, rulers are set to artboard rulers.

Creating guides

Guides are nonprinting lines created from the rulers that help you align objects. Next, you'll create a guide so you can accurately align content to an artboard.

Tip: You can also choose View > Rulers > Show Rulers.

1 With nothing selected and the Selection tool (▶) selected, click the Show Rulers button (▦) in the Properties panel to show the rulers.

2 Click in each of the artboards, and as you do, look at the horizontal and vertical rulers (along the top and left sides of the Document window).

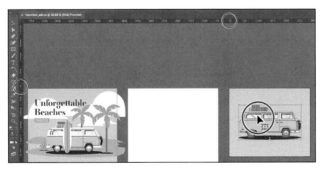

The number 0 (zero) for each ruler is in the upper-left corner of the active (selected) artboard. As you can see, the 0 point on both rulers corresponds to the edges of the active artboard.

3 With the Selection tool, click the text "Unforgettable Beaches..." in the leftmost artboard.

Notice the *very* subtle black outline around the artboard, with "1" showing in the Artboard Navigation menu (below the Document window), which indicates that the Beach vacation ad artboard is the active artboard. There can be only one active artboard at a time. Commands such as View > Fit Artboard In Window apply to the active artboard.

4 Choose View > Fit Artboard In Window.

That fits the active artboard in the window, and the ruler origin (0,0) is in the upper-left corner of that same artboard. Next you'll create a guide on the active artboard.

5 Choose Select > Deselect so you can see the document properties in the Properties panel on the right.

6 Click the Units menu in the Properties panel, and choose Inches to change the units for the entire document.

You can now see that the rulers show inches instead of pixels. For this example, you were told that text needs to be at least 0.25 inches from the edge of the ad.

7 Drag from the ruler on the left into the artboard to make a vertical guide. Continue dragging until you reach about 1/2 inch on the ruler above the document, and then release the mouse button. Don't worry about the guide being at precisely 1/2 inch.

After creating a guide, it's selected. When selected, the color of a guide matches the color of the layer it's on (blue in this case) when you move the pointer away from it.

8 With the guide still selected, change the X value in the Properties panel to **0.25** (inch), and press Return or Enter to reposition the guide.

9 Choose Select > Deselect to deselect the guide. In a few sections, you'll drag content to align it with the guide.

10 Choose File > Save.

Tip: To change the units for a document (inches, points, etc.), you can also right-click either ruler and choose the new units.

Tip: Dragging from a ruler while pressing the Shift key "snaps" a guide to the measurements on the ruler.

Tip: You can double-click the horizontal or vertical ruler to add a new guide.

Editing the ruler origin ▇◀

You can move the ruler origin to start the horizontal and vertical measurements at another location. To learn how to work with the ruler origin, check out the video *Editing the ruler origin,* which is part of the Web Edition. For more information, see the "Web Edition" section of "Getting Started" at the beginning of the book.

Transforming content

In Lesson 4, you learned how to take simple paths and shapes and create more complex artwork by editing and combining that content. That was one way to transform artwork. In this lesson, you'll learn how to scale, rotate, and transform content in other ways, using various tools and methods.

Working with the bounding box

As you've seen in this lesson and previous lessons, a bounding box appears around selected content. You can resize and rotate content using the bounding box, but you can also turn it off. Turning off the bounding box makes it so you can't resize or rotate content with the Selection tool by dragging anywhere on the bounding box.

1   With the Selection tool (▶) selected, click to select the Unforgettable Beaches text to select the text and the button that are grouped together.

2   Move the pointer over the lower-left corner of the selected group. If you were to drag right now, you would resize the content.

3   Choose View > Hide Bounding Box.

This command hides the bounding box for the group and all other artwork. Now, you can't resize the group by dragging with the Selection tool.

4   Move the pointer over the lower-left point on the LEARN MORE button, and drag the group to the left, onto the vertical guide you created. When the pointer arrow changes, the artwork is snapped to the guide, and you can release the mouse button.

If the group is not aligning to the guide, or in other words, it's not *snapping*, and the pointer isn't changing, you need to zoom in closer.

5   Choose View > Show Bounding Box to turn it back on for all artwork.

Positioning artwork using the Properties panel

At times, you may want to position objects more precisely—relative either to other objects or to the artboard. You could use the alignment options, as you saw in Lesson 2. You can also use Smart Guides (View > Smart Guides) and Transform options in the Properties panel to move objects to exact coordinates on the x and y axes and control the positioning of objects relative to the edge of the artboard. Next, you'll add content to an artboard and position it precisely.

1   Choose View > Fit All In Window to see all three artboards.

2   Click in the blank artboard in the middle to make it the active artboard.

3   Click to select the group of artwork with the Untouched Beauty text, beneath the artboards. You may need to zoom out or pan to see it.

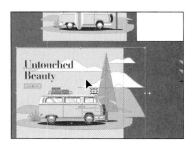

4   In the Transform section of the Properties panel, click the upper-left point of the reference point locator ( ). Change the X value to **0** and the Y value to **0**, and press Return or Enter.

> **Tip:** You could have also aligned the content to the artboard using the alignment options. You'll find there are at least a few ways to accomplish most tasks in Illustrator.

The group of content is moved into the upper-left corner of the *active* artboard. The points in the reference point locator map to the points of the bounding box for the selected content. For instance, the upper-left reference point refers to the upper-left point of the bounding box.

5   Shift-drag the lower-right corner to make the selected artwork smaller. Make sure the pink rectangle in the background just fits on the artboard. Other artwork will hang off and that's okay.

6   Choose Select > Deselect, and then choose File > Save.

Scaling objects precisely

So far in this book, you've scaled most content with the selection tools. In this part of the lesson, you'll scale artwork using the Properties panel and use an option called Scale Strokes & Effects.

1   If necessary, press Command and – (macOS) or Ctrl and – (Windows) (or choose View > Zoom Out) to see the half of a plant off the bottom edge of the artboards.

2   With the Selection tool (▶) selected, drag across the plant group to select it.

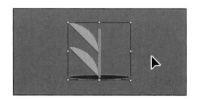

3   Press Command and + (macOS) or Ctrl and + (Windows) a few times to zoom in to it.

4   Choose View > Hide Edges so you hide the inside edges.

▷ **Tip:** When typing values to transform content, you can type different units, such as percent (%) or pixels (px), and they will be converted to the default unit, which is inches (in) in this case.

5   In the Properties panel, click the center reference point of the reference point locator (▦), if it's not selected, to resize from the center. Ensure that Maintain Width And Height Proportions is set (🔒), type **40%** in the Width (W) field, and then press Enter or Return to make it less than half the size.

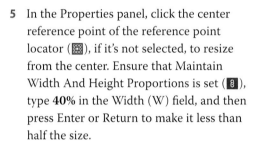

Notice that the artwork is smaller, but the stem of the plant is still the same width. That's because it is a path with a stroke applied.

By default, strokes and effects, like drop shadows, are *not* scaled along with objects. For instance, if you enlarge a circle with a 1-pt stroke, the stroke remains 1 pt. By selecting Scale Strokes & Effects before you scale—and then scaling the object—that 1-pt stroke would scale (change) relative to the amount of scaling applied to the object.

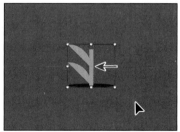

6   Choose View > Show Edges to show the inside edges again.

7   Choose Edit > Undo Scale.

8   In the Properties panel, click More Options (•••) in the Transform section. Select Scale Strokes & Effects. Type **40%** in the Width (W) field and press Enter or Return to increase the size of the artwork.

Now any strokes applied to any paths are scaled proportionally.

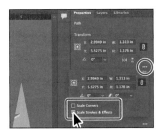 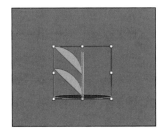

Rotating objects with the Rotate tool

There are many ways to rotate artwork, including methods that range from precise to more free-form rotation. In previous lessons, you learned that you could rotate selected content with the Selection tool. By default, objects rotate around a designated reference point in the center of content. In this part of the lesson, you'll learn about using the Rotate tool.

1 Choose View > Fit All In Window.

2 With the Selection tool (▶) selected, click to select the palm tree to the right of the van on the far left artboard.

3 Choose View > Fit Artboard In Window.

The palm tree would look better if it were rotated, giving it a more wind-blown look. You could rotate it with the Selection tool, and then drag it into place, but to save a step, you can rotate it with the Rotate tool.

4 Select the Rotate tool (↻) in the toolbar. Move the pointer over the bottom of the tree trunk—click and release to set the point that the palm tree will rotate around. It looks like an aqua crosshairs and is called the *reference point*.

5 Move the pointer anywhere around the palm tree, and drag clockwise to give the tree a bit of a lean.

▶ **Tip:** If you want to make the bottom of the palm tree look flatter, you can erase it with the Eraser tool (◆) in the toolbar.

Scale using Transform Each

Making artwork bigger or smaller is relatively straightforward. Sometimes, however, you want to make multiple objects bigger or smaller together. Using the Transform Each command, objects you scale or rotate are done in place—they don't move, and they are all transformed at once using the same settings.

Now you'll scale three clouds at one time

1   With the Selection tool (▶) selected, click to select one of the white clouds in the sky. Shift-click the other two clouds in the sky to select all three.

2   Choose Object > Transform > Transform Each.

    The Transform Each dialog box opens with multiple options like scale, moving, rotation, and more.

3   In the Transform Each dialog box, change the Horizontal Scale and Vertical Scale values to **70%**. Click OK.

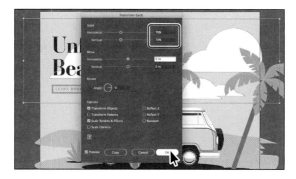

    Each of the clouds is smaller and still in the same place. In other words, each cloud scaled individually from its center.

4   Choose File > Save.

Shearing objects

Shearing an object slants, or skews, the sides of the object along the axis you specify, keeping opposite sides parallel and making the object asymmetrical. Next, you'll apply shear to a reflection in the window of the van.

1   Click to select the van and press Command and + (macOS) or Ctrl and + (Windows) a few times to zoom in.

2   Select the Rectangle tool (▭) in the toolbar. Drag to create a small rectangle in the middle of the front window of the van.

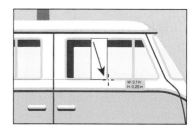

3 Change the fill color in the Properties panel to white or similar, and the Stroke Weight to **0**, if necessary.

Now you'll skew the shape to give it perspective.

4 With the shape selected, select the Shear tool (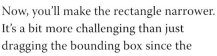), nested within the Rotate tool (⟲) in the toolbar.

5 Move the pointer above or off the right side of the shape, press the Shift key to constrain the artwork to its original height, and drag to the left. Release the mouse button and then the Shift key when you see a shear angle (S) of approximately 45.

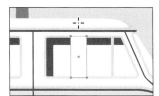 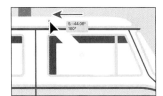

6 Change the opacity of the rectangle in the Properties panel by clicking the arrow to the right of 100% in the Opacity field and dragging the slider to change it. I changed it to 60%.

Transform using menu commands

The transform tools you find in the toolbar—rotate, move, shear, skew, reflect—are also represented as menu items when you choose Object > Transform. In a lot of cases, you can use any of those menu commands in place of a tool.

Now you'll make a copy of the window reflection using the Move command.

1 To make a copy of the rectangle, choose Object > Transform > Move.

2 In the Move dialog box, change Horizontal Position to **0.12 in** to move the rectangle that distance to the right, and make sure the Vertical Position is **0** to keep it in the same vertical position. Click Copy.

Now, you'll make the rectangle narrower. It's a bit more challenging than just dragging the bounding box since the shape is skewed. You'll drag anchor points instead to maintain the skew angle while transforming the shape.

3 Select the Selection tool (▶) and double-click the copied rectangle.

This enters Isolation mode and makes it much easier to select part of the rectangle since everything else is dimmed and can't be selected.

4 Select the Direct Selection tool (▷). Click the top-right anchor and Shift-click the bottom-right anchor to select both.

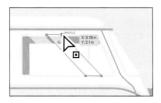 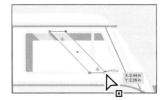

5 Press the left arrow key on your keyboard several times to move the selected anchor points to the left, making the shape narrower.

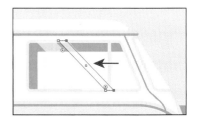

6 Press the Esc key to exit Isolation mode.

7 Choose View > Fit All In Window, and then choose File > Save.

Transforming with the Free Transform tool ▬◼

To learn how to transform artwork freely with the Free Transform tool, check out the video *Transforming with the Free Transform tool,* which is part of the Web Edition. For more information, see the "Web Edition" section of "Getting Started" at the beginning of the book.

Using repeats

You can easily repeat objects by applying one of the available repeat types: Radial, Grid, or Mirror. When you apply one of the repeats to selected artwork, Illustrator auto-generates artwork using your chosen method. If you update one of the repeat instances, all instances are modified to reflect the change.

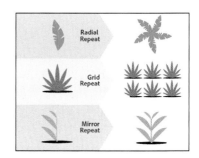

Applying a mirror repeat

To start with repeats, you'll focus on applying a mirror repeat to artwork. Mirror repeat helps create symmetrical artwork. You create half of the artwork, and Illustrator automatically makes the other half for you. In this case, you'll finish a plant that will become part of one of the ads.

1 Select the Zoom tool (🔍) and zoom into the plant below the artboards.

2 Select the Selection tool (![arrow]), and drag across the plant shapes below the artboards to select them. Make sure *not* to select the dark oval shadow.

3 Choose Object > Repeat > Mirror.

In the Repeat menu, you'll see the three options: Radial, Grid, and Mirror.

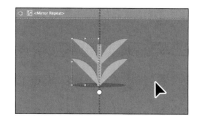

As soon as you choose Mirror, Illustrator enters an Isolation mode. The rest of the artwork is dimmed and cannot be selected, as is typical for Isolation mode. The vertical dashed line you see is called the symmetry axis. It shows the center of the symmetrical artwork, and you use it to change the distance between the halves and rotate the auto-generated half.

4 Find the circle control handle on the symmetry axis, just below the plant. Drag it left and right, to change the distance between the halves.

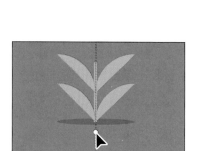

Make sure there is no gap between the plant halves.

5 Drag either circle control handle at the very top or bottom of the symmetry axis to rotate the mirrored content.

6 To reset the angle of the mirror repeat, choose 90 degrees from the Angle Of Mirror Axis in the Properties panel.

Not only can you use mirror to copy and flip artwork you've already created, but you can also add or remove artwork while editing the mirror repeat.

7 Choose Select > Deselect so no plant artwork is selected.

Note: The Shift key constrains the movement, and the Option/Alt key copies the artwork.

8   To copy one of the leaves, Shift+Option-drag (macOS) or Shift+Alt-drag (Windows) the top leaf up. Make sure to drag it to the very top of the green plant stem (the vertical green path). Release the mouse button and then the keys.

Notice that the generated artwork on the right mirrors what you are doing in real time. Any changes you make to the artwork are visible in the mirrored half.

9   Shift-drag the upper-left corner to make the leaf smaller.

10 To stop editing the mirror repeat, exit Isolation mode by pressing the Esc key. The plant should be deselected.

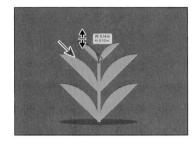

Editing a mirror repeat

When you create a mirror repeat, or any type of repeat, the artwork becomes a repeat object. In this case, the plant is now a Mirror Repeat object—sort of like a special group. Now, you'll learn how to edit the mirror repeat.

1   Click the plant to select it.

At the top of the Properties panel, you'll see "Mirror Repeat," which tells you that it's a mirror repeat object group.

2   Double-click the plant to enter Isolation mode.

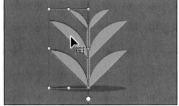

You can now see the symmetry axis and can edit the original artwork you created on the left.

3   Click away from the plant to deselect it, and then click one of the leaves and change the fill color in the Properties panel to another color. I chose a lighter green.

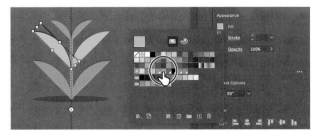

4 Press the Esc key to exit Isolation mode.

5 Choose View > Fit All In Window.

6 Drag across the plant art and oval shadow to select them. Choose Object > Group. Drag the group onto the artboard on the right with the van by itself.

If the plant is behind the artwork on the artboard, choose Bring To Front from the Arrange menu in the Properties panel.

Using grid and radial repeats ■◀

To learn how to work with the other repeat options, check out the video *Using grid and radial repeats,* which is part of the Web Edition. For more information, see the "Web Edition" section of "Getting Started" at the beginning of the book.

Adding the Puppet Warp tool to the toolbar

In Illustrator, you can easily twist and distort artwork into different positions using the Puppet Warp tool. In this section, you'll warp one of the palm trees.

1 Click the palm tree you rotated on the Beach vacation ad artboard. Zoom in by pressing Command and + (macOS) or Ctrl and + (Windows) several times.

2 Click Edit Toolbar (•••) at the bottom of the toolbar. Scroll in the menu that appears if necessary, and drag the Puppet Warp tool (✦) between two tools in the toolbar.

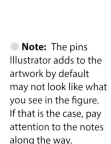

3 Press the Escape key to hide the extra tools menu.

Adding pins

With the tool now showing in the toolbar, you'll use it to warp the palm tree so it looks a little more natural and less like it's falling over.

1 Select the Puppet Warp tool (✦) in the toolbar if it isn't already selected.

By default, Illustrator identifies the best areas to transform your artwork and automatically adds pins to the artwork. The pin is circled in the figure.

Pins are used to hold part of the selected artwork to the artboard, and you can add or delete pins to transform your object. You can rotate the artwork around a pin, reposition pins to move artwork, and more.

▶ **Tip:** To edit the auto-generated half of the mirrored artwork, you need to expand the Mirror Repeat object. Choose Object > Expand. Know that if you expand a Mirror Repeat object, you cannot edit the mirror repeat using the symmetry axis, and the artwork is simply a group of individual objects.

● **Note:** The pins Illustrator adds to the artwork by default may not look like what you see in the figure. If that is the case, pay attention to the notes along the way.

2 In the Properties panel on the right, you should see Puppet Warp options. Deselect Show Mesh.

That will make it easier to see the pins and provide a clearer view of any transformations you make.

● **Note:** If your pin is in a different place, that's okay.

▶ **Tip:** You can press the Shift key and click multiple pins to select them all, or click the Select All Pins button in the Properties panel to select all of the pins.

3 Click the one pin on the tree to select it. You can tell that a pin is selected because it has a white dot in the center. Drag the selected pin to the left to see how the artwork reacts.

Notice that the whole tree moves. That's because there is only one pin. By default, pins on the artwork help to keep (pin) parts in place. Having at least three pins on your artwork usually achieves a better result.

4 Choose Edit > Undo Puppet Warp as many times as you need to return the tree to its original position.

5 Click the bottom of the brown tree trunk to add a pin. Click in the middle of the brown tree trunk to add another pin.

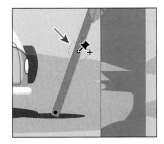

The pin at the bottom is meant to pin or hold the bottom of the tree trunk in place so that part won't move as much. The pin in the middle of the tree trunk is the one you will drag to reshape the tree.

6 Drag the pin in the middle of the trunk to reshape the tree.

You'll find that if you drag too far, odd things like path twisting may happen.

Now, you can't move pins on the artwork without moving the artwork, so if they're not in the right place for the warping you want, you need to remove pins and add them where they are needed.

7 Click the pin in the leaves to select it and press Delete or Backspace to remove it. It would better if it were in the middle of the leaves for rotation.

Notice that the leaves move once the pin is deleted.

8 Click in the middle of the leaves to add a new one.

  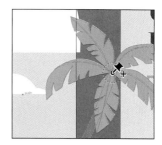

9 Drag the new pin approximately back to where the original was. Leave the pin selected.

Rotating pins

Another helpful thing you can do to pins is rotate them. In this section, you'll rotate all of the leaves and then warp one of the leaves without affecting the rest as much.

1 With the pin in the middle of the leaves still selected, you will see a dashed line around the pin. You drag that to rotate it. Move the pointer over the dashed circle, and drag to rotate the leaves around the pin until you think it looks good.

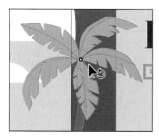 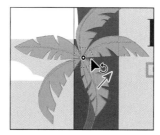

Now you'll warp a single leaf. This will require adding some more pins.

2 Click in the end of one of the leaves on the right to add a pin.

You might see the other parts of the artwork change in reaction. If that happens, select the pin in the center of the leaves again and rotate it back.

▶ **Tip:** Pressing the Option/Alt key limits the affected area directly around the pin you are dragging.

3 Drag the new pin on the end of the leaf to stretch the leaf a bit and to see how the artwork reacts.

You might see the other leaves moving as well. In this case, you want to pin the parts that are moving to keep them still.

4 Choose Edit > Undo Puppet Warp as many times as you need to return the leaf to its original position.

5 Click to set pins on the leaves around to hold them in place.

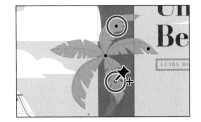

6 Drag the pin at the end of the leaf to stretch the leaf a little and see how everything reacts now.

The last thing you'll do is rotate and drag the pin at the bottom of the tree trunk.

7 Click the pin at the bottom of the tree trunk. Move it to see how the rest of the tree artwork reacts.

8 Move the pointer over the dashed circle around the pin, and drag to rotate the bottom until you think it looks good.

9 Choose Select > Deselect, and then choose View > Fit All In Window.

10 Choose File > Save, and then File > Close.

Review questions

1 Name three ways to change the size of an existing active artboard.

2 What is the *ruler origin*?

3 What is the difference between artboard rulers and global rulers?

4 Briefly describe what the Scale Strokes & Effects option in the Properties panel or Transform panel does.

5 Briefly describe what the Puppet Warp tool does.

Review answers

1 To change the size of an existing artboard, you can do any of the following:

   • Double-click the Artboard tool ( ), and edit the dimensions of the active artboard in the Artboard Options dialog box.

   • With nothing selected and the Selection tool selected, click the Edit Artboards button to enter Artboard Editing mode. With the Artboard tool selected, position the pointer over an edge or corner of the artboard, and drag to resize.

   • With the Artboard tool selected, click an artboard in the Document window, and change the dimensions in the Properties panel.

2 The ruler origin is the point where 0 (zero) appears on each ruler. By default, the ruler origin is set to be 0 (zero) in the upper-left corner of the active artboard.

3 Artboard rulers, the default rulers, set the ruler origin at the upper-left corner of the active artboard. Global rulers set the ruler origin at the upper-left corner of the first artboard, no matter which artboard is active.

4 The Scale Strokes & Effects option, which can be accessed from the Properties panel or the Transform panel, scales any strokes and effects as the object is scaled. This option can be turned on and off, as needed.

5 In Illustrator, you can use the Puppet Warp tool to easily twist and distort artwork into different positions while adding pins to hold part of it stationary.

6 USING THE BASIC DRAWING TOOLS

Lesson overview

In this lesson, you'll learn how to do the following:

- Draw curves and straight lines with the Curvature tool.

- Edit paths with the Curvature tool.

- Create dashed lines.

- Draw and edit with the Pencil tool.

- Join paths with the Join tool.

- Add arrowheads to paths.

 This lesson will take about 30 minutes to complete. To get the lesson files used in this chapter, download them from the web page for this book at adobepress.com/IllustratorCIB2022. For more information, see "Accessing the lesson files and Web Edition" in the Getting Started section at the beginning of this book.

In previous lessons you created and edited shapes. Next you'll learn how to create straight lines, curves, or more complex shapes using the Pencil and Curvature tools. You'll also explore creating dashed lines, arrowheads, and more.

Starting the lesson

In the first part of this lesson, you'll start by creating and editing free-form paths with the Curvature tool and exploring other drawing methods to create a series of logos.

Note: If you have not already downloaded the project files for this lesson to your computer from your Account page, make sure to do so now. See the "Getting Started" section at the beginning of the book.

1 To ensure that the tools function and the defaults are set exactly as described in this lesson, delete or deactivate (by renaming) the Adobe Illustrator preferences file. See "Restoring default preferences" in the "Getting Started" section at the beginning of the book.

2 Start Adobe Illustrator.

3 Choose File > Open. Locate the file named L6_end.ai, which is in the Lessons > Lesson06 folder that you copied onto your hard disk, and click Open.

This file contains the finished logos that you'll create in this lesson.

4 Choose View > Fit All In Window; leave the file open for reference, or you can close it by choosing File > Close.

5 Choose File > Open, and open the L6_start.ai file in the Lessons > Lesson06 folder on your hard disk.

6 Choose File > Save As. If the Cloud Document dialog box opens, click Save On Your Computer.

7 In the Save As dialog box, navigate to the Lesson06 folder, and open it. Rename the file to **Outdoor_logos.ai**. Choose Adobe Illustrator (ai) from the Format menu (macOS), or choose Adobe Illustrator (*.AI) from the Save As Type menu (Windows). Click Save.

8 In the Illustrator Options dialog box, leave the default settings, and then click OK.

Note: If you don't see Reset Essentials in the menu, choose Window > Workspace > Essentials before choosing Window > Workspace > Reset Essentials.

9 Choose Window > Workspace > Reset Essentials.

Creating with the Curvature tool

With the Curvature tool (✎), you can create free-form paths with straight lines and smooth, refined curves, and it is one of the easier drawing tools to master. The Curvature tool creates paths made of anchor points that are editable with any drawing or selection tools. Let's take a look.

Drawing paths with the Curvature tool

In this first part, you'll draw a curved path with the Curvature tool that will become a horizon in a logo (the red path highlighted in the figure).

1 Choose 1 Logo 1 from the Artboard Navigation menu below the Document window to fit the first artboard in the window.

2 Select the Selection tool (▶), and click the edge of the circle. To lock it, choose Object > Lock > Selection. That way, you can draw without accidentally editing the circle.

3 Select the Curvature tool (✎) in the toolbar and move the pointer into the document—an asterisk (*) next to the pointer means you will draw a new path.

4 To set the stroke and fill before you draw, make sure that the Fill is set to None (▱), that the stroke color is a dark gray swatch with the tool tip "C=0 M=0 Y=0 K=90," and that the stroke weight is 4 pt.

   The stroke and fill should be already set, since you just selected the circle and Illustrator remembers the last fill and stroke.

   With the Curvature tool, you start a path by clicking and releasing to create an anchor point. You keep creating anchor points to change the path's direction, how much it is curved, or both.

5 On the left edge of the circle, click and release to start the path that will become the horizon.

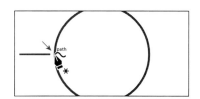

6 Move the pointer to the right, click and release to create a new point, and then move the pointer away.

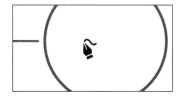
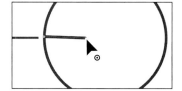

Notice the rubber band preview of the curve before and after the new point. The Curvature tool works by creating anchor points where you click. The path will "flex" around the points dynamically.

7 Move the pointer to the right. Click and release to create a point. Move the pointer around to see how the path reacts.

If you add an anchor in the wrong spot at any point, you can always move the pointer over the anchor, drag it, and then continue drawing. You'll learn all about editing paths with the Curvature tool in the next section.

8 Click and release to the right to create another anchor point.

9 Finally, to complete the horizon, move the pointer over the right edge of the circle; click and release to create the last anchor point.

10 To stop drawing and lock the path so you can't accidentally edit it in the next section, choose Object > Lock > Selection.

Drawing a river path

To continue with the Curvature tool, next you'll draw a river that begins at the horizon path you just created. You'll draw one side of the river, and then the other. The figure at the right shows an example of how the river might look. Yours may look different, and that's okay.

You may want to zoom in to the artwork for this section.

1 Move the pointer over the horizon path as you see in the figure. Click and release to start a new path.

   For the next steps, use the figures as a guide, but experiment a little!

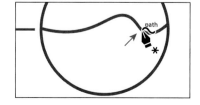

2 Move the pointer down and to the left, and click. Continue moving the pointer down, clicking and changing direction three more times to create one side of the river. Make sure the last point you create is on the circle.

 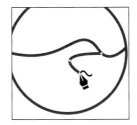  

When learning the Curvature tool, it helps to click, release, and then move the pointer around to get a feel for how it affects the path.

3 Press the Escape key to stop drawing a path.

Next you'll draw the other side of the river using a similar technique.

4 Choose Select > Deselect.

5 Move the pointer over the horizon path just to the right of the start of the path you just drew. Make sure you see the asterisk (*) next to the pointer. The asterisk means you will start a new path. Click and release to start a new path.

It's important not to click too closely to the first river path you drew because you may edit that path instead of starting a new one. If you click and begin editing the other path, press the Escape key to stop editing the first river path.

6 Move the pointer down, and click to set another point. Do this two more times to add points to create the other side of the river. Make sure the last point you create is on the edge of the circle.

7 To stop drawing the river path, press the Escape key.

Editing a path with the Curvature tool

You can also edit paths with the Curvature tool by moving or deleting anchor points or adding new ones. You can use the Curvature tool to edit a path you're drawing or any other path you've created regardless of the drawing tool used to create it. Next, you'll edit the paths you've created so far.

1 With the Curvature tool selected, click the first river path you drew on the left to select it and show the anchor points.

To edit a path with the Curvature tool, it needs to be selected.

▶ **Tip:** To close a path with the Curvature tool, hover the pointer over the first point you created in the path. When a circle appears next to the pointer (🖋₀), click to close the path.

2 Move the pointer over the anchor point circled in the first part of the following figure. When the point changes appearance (▶₀), click to select the point. Drag that point to reshape the curve a little.

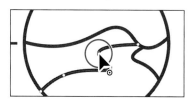 

3 Try dragging other points in the path.

You'll find that you don't need to click and release to select a path, and then drag. You can simply drag the anchor point.

Next, you'll unlock the horizon path and edit it.

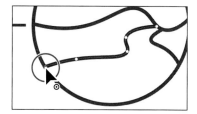

4 Choose Object > Unlock All to be able to edit the horizon path you drew.

5 With the Curvature tool selected, click the horizon path to select just that path and see the anchor points on it.

6 Move the pointer over the path just to the right of the first anchor (on the left). When a plus sign (+) appears next to the pointer (🖋₊), click to add a new point.

7 Drag the new point down a bit to reshape the path.

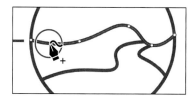 

You'll remove the point just to the right of the new point you just added so the path can have more curve.

8 Click the point to the right, and to remove it press Delete or Backspace.

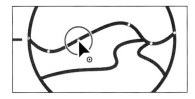 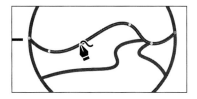

If you're wondering, instead of adding and deleting anchors, you could have just moved the anchor you deleted to reshape the path.

9 To lock the path so you don't accidentally edit it in the next section, choose Object > Lock > Selection.

Creating corners with the Curvature tool

By default, the Curvature tool creates smooth anchor points—anchor points that cause the path to curve. Paths can have two kinds of anchor points: corner points and smooth points. At a *corner point*, a path abruptly changes direction. At a *smooth point*, path segments are connected as a continuous curve. With the Curvature tool, you can also create corner points to create straight paths. Next, you'll draw a mountain for the logo using corner points.

1 With the Curvature tool (✐) selected, move the pointer over the left side of the horizon path. When the word "path" appears, telling you the point you add will start on the path, click to set the first point.

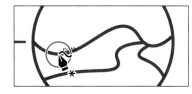

● **Note:** If the word "path" doesn't appear, make sure Smart Guides are turned on (View > Smart Guides).

2 Move the pointer up and to the right, and click to start a mountain peak.

3 Move the pointer down and to the right, and click to create a new point.

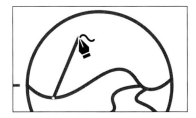 

To make the mountain peak have a point to it and not be curved, you'll convert the anchor point you just created to a corner point.

4 Move the pointer over the top anchor point on the mountain path, and when the pointer changes (▸), double-click to convert it to a corner point.

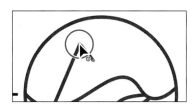

You can tell which points are smooth and which are corners by their appearance. Each point you create with the Curvature tool can have three appearances, indicating their current state: a selected point (●), a corner point that is not selected (◎), and smooth point that is not selected (○).

5   To continue drawing, move the pointer over and up, and click to create another point and start another mountain peak.

The point you just created and the point before it also need to be converted to corner points. All of the anchor points you create for the mountain path need to be corners. You'll convert the two anchor points to corner points next.

6   Double-click the last *two* anchor points you made to make them corners.

To finish the mountain path, you'll create a few more anchor points, but you will make corner points instead of smooth points by pressing a key as you create them.

7   Press Option (macOS) or Alt (Windows), and the pointer will change (🖋). Click to make a corner anchor.

8   While still pressing Option (macOS) or Alt (Windows), click a few more times to finish the mountain path. Make sure the last point you create is on the horizon path.

Feel free to adjust any anchor points. Drag a point to reshape the path, double-click a point to convert it between a corner and smooth point, or select an anchor and press Delete or Backspace to remove it from the path.

9   Press the Escape key to stop drawing.

10 Choose Select > Deselect, and then choose File > Save.

Creating dashed lines

To add some design flair to your artwork, you can add dashes to the stroke of a closed path (like a square) or an open path (like a line). You add dashes to paths in the Stroke panel, where you can specify a sequence of dash lengths and the gaps between them. Next, you'll add a dash to lines to add sun rays around the circle.

1   Select the Selection tool (▶), and click the line to the left of the circle.

2   In the Properties panel, click the word "Stroke" to show the Stroke panel. Change the following options in the Stroke panel:

▶ **Tip:** The Preserves Exact Dash And Gap Lengths button ( ) allows you to retain the appearance of the dashes without aligning to the corners or the dash ends.

*   Weight: **3 pt** (should already be set)

*   Dashed Line: Selected

*   Preserves Exact Dash and Gap Lengths ( ): Selected (The dashes won't be adjusted at all.)

*   First Dash value: **35 pt** (This creates a 35-pt dash, 35-pt gap pattern.)

*   First Gap value: **4 pt** (This creates a 35-pt dash, 4-pt gap pattern.)

*   Second Dash value: **5 pt** (This creates a 35-pt dash, 4-pt gap, 5-pt dash, 5-pt gap pattern.)

*   Second Gap value: **4 pt** (This creates a 35-pt dash, 4-pt gap, 5-pt dash, 4-pt gap pattern.) After entering the last value, press Return or Enter to accept the value and close the Stroke panel.

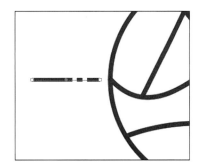

Now you'll make copies of the dashed line around the circle.

3   With the dashed line selected, select the Rotate tool ( ) in the toolbar. Move the pointer into the center of the circle, and when you see the word "center," Option-click (macOS) or Alt-click (Windows) to set the reference point (the point at which the artwork rotates around) and open the Rotate dialog box.

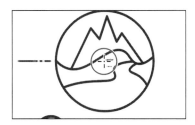

◉ **Note:** If the word "center" doesn't appear, make sure Smart Guides are turned on (View > Smart Guides).

● **Note:** To preview
the rotation, you may
need to turn off Preview
then turn it back on.

4 Select Preview to see the results of the changes you make in the dialog. Change the Angle to **−15**, and click Copy.

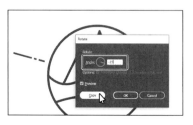

5 To copy the dashed line again using the same rotation, choose Object > Transform > Transform Again.

6 To make 10 more copies, press Command+D (macOS) or Ctrl+D (Windows) 10 times.

   That keyboard command invokes the Transform Again command you chose in the previous step.

   To finish the artwork, you'll cut off part of the circle and drag the text at the bottom of the artboard onto the logo.

7 Select the Rectangle tool (▢) in the toolbar and draw a rectangle that covers the lower part of the circle (see the following figure). Notice that the dashed stroke is applied to the rectangle.

8 Select the Selection tool (▶) and drag across the rectangle and circle (only!).

9 Select the Shape Builder tool (◉) in the toolbar. Press the Option key (macOS) or Alt key (Windows) and drag across the rectangle and bottom part of the circle to remove them. Release the mouse button and then the key. You removed the bottom part of the circle so it won't show when you drag the text into place.

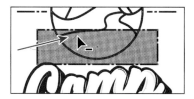

10 Select the Selection tool and drag the text at the bottom of the artboard up, onto the logo.

11 Click the Arrange button in the Properties panel and choose Bring To Front so the text is in front.

12 Choose Select > Deselect, and choose File > Save.

Creating with the Pencil tool

Another drawing tool in Illustrator is the Pencil tool. The Pencil tool (✏) lets you draw free-form open and closed paths that contain curves and straight lines and is similar to drawing on paper. As you draw with the Pencil tool, anchor points are created on the path, where necessary, according to the Pencil tool options you set. The path can easily be adjusted when the path is complete.

Drawing paths with the Pencil tool

Next you'll draw and edit a simple path to make fire for one of the logos, using the Pencil tool.

1 Choose 2 Pencil from the Artboard navigation menu in the lower-left corner of the Document window.

2 Select the Pencil tool (✏) from the Paintbrush tool (✏) group in the toolbar.

3 Double-click the Pencil tool. In the Pencil Tool Options dialog box, set the following options:

- Drag the Fidelity slider all the way to the right to Smooth. This will smooth the path and reduce the number of points on a path drawn with the Pencil tool.

- Keep Selected: Selected (the default setting)

4 Click OK.

If you move the pointer into the Document window, the asterisk (*) that appears next to the Pencil tool pointer indicates that you're about to create a new path.

5 In the Properties panel, make sure that the fill color is None (▱), the stroke color is the dark gray swatch with the tool tip "C=0 M=0 Y=0 K=90," and the stroke weight is 3 pt.

6 Starting at the red dot on the template labeled "A," drag clockwise around the dashed template path. When the pointer gets close to where you started the path (the red dot), a small circle displays next to it (✏ₒ). This means that if you release the mouse button, the path will be closed. When you see the circle, release the mouse button to close the path.

▷ **Tip:** When it comes to the Fidelity value, dragging the slider closer to Accurate usually creates more anchor points and more accurately reflects the path you've drawn. Dragging the slider toward Smooth makes fewer anchor points and a smoother, less complex path.

◉ **Note:** If the pointer looks like ✕ instead of the Pencil icon (✏), the Caps Lock key is active. Caps Lock turns the Pencil tool icon into an X for increased precision.

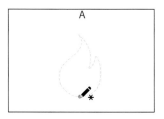
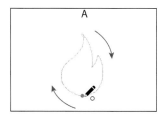
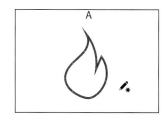

Notice that as you draw, the path may not look perfectly smooth. After releasing the mouse button, the path is smoothed based on the Fidelity value that you set in the Pencil Tool Options dialog box. Next, you'll redraw a part of the path with the Pencil tool.

7   Move the pointer on or near the path to redraw a part of it. When the asterisk next to the pointer disappears, press and drag to reshape the path, making sure the pointer begins on the original path and returns to it before releasing the mouse. If both ends of the redrawn path don't intersect with the original path, you'll end up creating a separate path alongside the original one.

8   With the fire shape selected, change the fill color to a red in the Properties panel.

Drawing straight lines with the Pencil tool

In addition to drawing free-form paths, you can create straight lines that can be constrained to 45-degree angles with the Pencil tool. Next, you'll create a log for the fire using the Pencil tool. The shape you draw could be created by drawing a rectangle and rounding the corners, but we want it to look more hand-drawn, which is why you're drawing it with the Pencil tool.

1   Move the pointer over the red dot on the left side of the path labeled "B." Press and drag up and around the top of the shape, and release the mouse button when you get to the blue dot and move the pointer away.

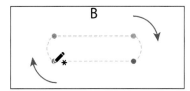 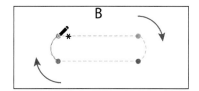

The next part of the path you draw will be straight. As you draw with the Pencil tool, you can easily continue drawing paths.

2   Move the pointer over the end of the path you just drew. When a line appears next to the Pencil tool pointer (✐), indicating that you can continue drawing the path, press Option (macOS) or Alt (Windows) and drag to the right to the orange dot. When you reach the orange dot, release the key but *not the mouse button.*

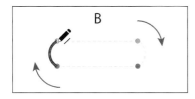 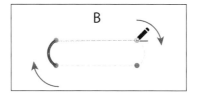

Pressing the Option (macOS) or Alt (Windows) key when you're drawing with the Pencil tool lets you create a straight path in any direction.

3 With the mouse button still held down, continue drawing around the bottom of the template path. When you reach the purple dot, keep the mouse button held down and press the Option (macOS) or Alt (Windows) key. Continue drawing to the left until you reach the start of the path at the red dot. When a small circle displays next to the Pencil tool pointer (✎), release the mouse button and then the modifier key to close the path.

▶ **Tip:** You can also press the Shift key when drawing with the Pencil tool and drag to create a straight line that is constrained to 45°.

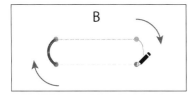 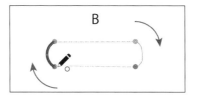

4 With the path selected, change the fill color to a brown swatch in the Properties panel.

5 Select the Selection tool (▶), and drag the fire shape down onto the log shape.

6 To bring the fire shape on top of the log shape, click the Arrange button in the Properties panel and choose Bring To Front.

7 Drag across both shapes to select them.

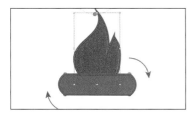 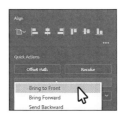 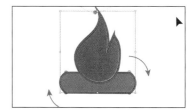

8 Copy the two shapes by choosing Edit > Copy.

9 To move to the next artboard, click the Next artboard button (▶) below the Document window in the Status bar.

10 To paste the shapes, choose Edit > Paste.

11 Drag the shapes onto the artwork as you see in the figure.

Joining with the Join tool

In earlier lessons, you used the Join command (Object > Path > Join) to join and close paths. You can also join paths using the Join tool. With the Join tool (✕✎), you can use scrubbing gestures to join paths that cross, overlap, or have open ends.

1 Select the Direct Selection tool (▷), and click the yellow circle on the artboard. The yellow circle will become the center of the flame.

2 Choose View > Zoom In a few times to zoom in.

3 Select the Scissors tool (✂), which is grouped with the Eraser tool (◆), in the toolbar.

4 Move the pointer over the top anchor point. When you see the word "anchor," click to cut the path there.

A message stating that the shape has been expanded appears at the top of the Document window. This circle, by default, was a Live Shape. After cutting the path, it's no longer a live shape.

5 Select the Direct Selection tool and drag the top anchor point up and slightly to the right.

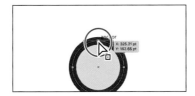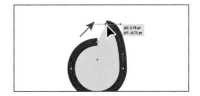

6 Drag the anchor point on the other end of the path up just to the left. A purple alignment guide will appear when the anchor point is aligned with the first anchor point.

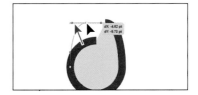

Right now the two endpoints are curved, but they need to be straight.

7 With the Direct Selection tool selected, drag across the two end points.

8 In the Properties panel on the right, click the Convert Selected Anchor Points To Corner button (▮) to straighten the ends of the path.

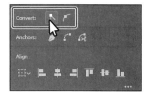

You'll learn more about converting anchor points in the next lesson.

9 Click Edit Toolbar (●●●) at the bottom of the toolbar on the left. Scroll in the menu that appears, if necessary, and drag the Join tool (➤✐) onto the Pencil tool (✐) in the toolbar to add it to the list of tools.

10 With the Join tool now selected, drag across the top two ends of the path (see the following figure).

When dragging (also called scrubbing) across paths, they will be either "extended and joined" or "trimmed and joined." In this example, the ends of the path were extended and joined. Also, the resulting joined artwork is deselected to allow you to continue working on other paths.

● **Note:** You may want to press the Escape key to hide the extra tools menu.

▶ **Tip:** Pressing the Caps Lock key will turn the Join tool pointer into a precise cursor (-¦-). This can make it easier to see where the join will happen.

● **Note:** If you were to instead join the ends of the open path by pressing Command+J (macOS) or Ctrl+J (Windows), a straight line would connect the ends.

Finishing the Camp logo

Now you'll put everything together to finish the logo.

1 Choose View > Fit Artboard In Window.

2 Select the Selection tool (▶), and select the yellow shape.

3 To bring the yellow shape on top of the other artwork, click the Arrange button in the Properties panel and choose Bring To Front.

4 Drag the yellow shape onto the fire shape, aligning it with the bottom of the shape.

5 Drag the "Camp" text at the bottom of the artboard onto the rest of the logo.

6 To bring the text on top of the other artwork, click the Arrange button in the Properties panel and choose Bring To Front.

7 Choose Select > Deselect, and choose File > Save.

Adding arrowheads to paths

You can add arrowheads to both ends of a path using the Stroke panel. There are many different arrowhead styles to choose from in Illustrator, as well as arrowhead editing options. Next, you'll apply arrowheads to a few paths to finish a logo.

1   Choose 4 Logo 3 from the Artboard Navigation menu below the Document window to switch artboards.

2   Click the curved pink path on the left to select it. Press the Shift key, and click the curved pink path to the right, to select it as well.

Note: When you draw a path, the beginning is where you start drawing, and the "end" is where you finish. If you need to swap the arrowheads, you can click the Swap Start And End Arrowheads button (⊟) in the Stroke panel.

3   With the paths selected, click the word "Stroke" in the Properties panel to open the Stroke panel. In the Stroke panel, change only the following options:

-   Stroke Weight: **3 pt**
-   Choose Arrow 5 from the Arrowheads menu on the right. This adds an arrowhead to the end of lines.
-   Scale (*directly beneath where you chose Arrow 5*): **70%**
-   Choose Arrow 17 from the Arrowheads menu on the left. This adds an arrowhead to the beginning of lines.
-   Scale (*directly beneath where you chose Arrow 17*): **70%**

Experiment with some of the arrowhead settings. Maybe try changing the Scale values or choosing different arrowheads.

4   With the paths selected, change the stroke color to white in the Properties panel.

5   Choose Select > Deselect.

6   Choose File > Save, and then choose File > Close.

Review questions

1 By default, what type of path is created by the Curvature tool, curved or straight?

2 How do you create a corner point when working with the Curvature tool?

3 How can you change the way the Pencil tool (✏) works?

4 Explain how you can redraw parts of a path with the Pencil tool.

5 How do you draw a straight path with the Pencil tool?

6 How is the Join tool different from the Join command (Object > Path > Join)?

Review answers

1 When drawing paths with the Curvature tool, curved paths are created by default.

2 When drawing with the Curvature tool, either double-click an existing point on a path to convert it to a corner or, while drawing, press Option (macOS) or Alt (Windows) and click to create a new corner point.

3 To change the way the Pencil tool (✏) works, double-click the Pencil tool in the toolbar or click the Tool Options button in the Properties panel to open the Pencil Tool Options dialog box. There you can change the fidelity and other options.

4 With a path selected, you can redraw parts of it by moving the Pencil tool pointer over the path and redrawing part of it, ending up back on the path.

5 Paths you create with the Pencil tool are free-form by default. To draw a straight path with the Pencil tool, press the Option (macOS) or Alt (Windows) key and drag to create a straight line.

6 Unlike the Join command, the Join tool can trim or extend overlapping paths or the ends of an open path as it joins, and it doesn't simply create a straight line between the anchor points you are joining. The angle created by the two paths to be joined is taken into account.

7 DRAWING WITH THE PEN TOOL

Lesson overview

In this lesson, you'll learn how to do the following:

- Draw straight and curved lines with the Pen tool.

- Edit curved and straight lines.

- Add and delete anchor points.

- Convert between smooth points and corner points.

 This lesson will take about 60 minutes to complete. To get the lesson files used in this chapter, download them from the web page for this book at adobepress.com/IllustratorCIB2022. For more information, see "Accessing the lesson files and Web Edition" in the Getting Started section at the beginning of this book.

In the previous lesson you started working with the basic drawing tools in Illustrator. In this lesson, you'll learn how to create and refine artwork using the Pen tool.

Starting the lesson

In this lesson, you'll focus on creating paths with the Pen tool. You'll start by working with a practice file to learn the fundamentals of the tool, and then you'll put the Pen tool into practice by drawing a swan.

Note: If you have not already downloaded the project files for this lesson to your computer from your Account page, make sure to do so now. See the "Getting Started" section at the beginning of the book.

1 To ensure that the tools function and the defaults are set exactly as described in this lesson, delete or deactivate (by renaming) the Adobe Illustrator preferences file. See "Restoring default preferences" in the "Getting Started" section at the beginning of the book.

2 Start Adobe Illustrator.

3 Choose File > Open, and open the L7_practice.ai file in the Lessons > Lesson07 folder on your hard disk.

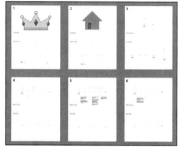

4 Choose File > Save As.

5 If the Cloud Document dialog box opens, click Save On Your Computer, otherwise continue.

6 In the Save As dialog box, navigate to the Lesson07 folder, and open it. Rename the file **Pen_practice.ai**. Choose Adobe Illustrator (ai) from the Format menu (macOS), or choose Adobe Illustrator (*.AI) from the Save As Type menu (Windows). Click Save.

7 In the Illustrator Options dialog box, leave the default settings, and then click OK.

8 Choose View > Fit All In Window.

9 Choose Window > Workspace > Reset Essentials.

Note: If you don't see Reset Essentials in the menu, choose Window > Workspace > Essentials before choosing Window > Workspace > Reset Essentials.

Why use the Pen tool?

In the previous chapter, you created curved and straight paths with the Curvature and Pencil tools. With the Pen tool (🖊) you can also create curved and straight paths, but you have even more control over the shape of the paths you draw.

The Pen tool can be used to create new vector artwork that requires more precision, as well as edit artwork you create with other drawing tools.

Since the Pen tool is in other Adobe apps, such as Photoshop and InDesign, understanding how to work with it will give you more creative freedom in Illustrator and those other apps.

Learning and mastering the Pen tool takes lots of practice.
So go through the steps in this lesson and practice, practice, practice.

What can you create with the Pen tool?

With the Pen tool, you click to create anchor points. If you create two points, you've made a straight line.

To create a curve with the Pen tool, you press and drag to create an anchor point with direction lines. Anchor point *direction lines* give you precise control over the length and slope of the path coming into and out of an anchor point.

When you create curves with the Curvature tool or Pencil tool, direction lines are created automatically, but when drawing with those tools, you don't see the direction lines, and you can't interact with them.

Curved Path

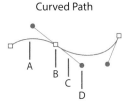

A. Path segment
B. Anchor point
C. Direction line
D. Direction point

A direction line and direction point together are called a *direction handle*.

Starting with the Pen tool

In this section, you'll set up your practice document so you can get started exploring the Pen tool.

1   Choose 1 from the Artboard Navigation menu in the lower-left corner of the Document window, if it's not already chosen. If the artboard does not fit in the document window, choose View > Fit Artboard In Window.

2   Select the Zoom tool (🔍) in the toolbar, and click once in the area on the artboard labeled "Work Area" to zoom in.

3   Choose View > Smart Guides to turn *off* Smart Guides.

    Smart Guides can be helpful when you draw, helping you align anchor points, among other things, but they make *learning* the Pen tool chaotic.

Creating straight lines to make a crown

You'll start drawing straight lines with the Pen tool to create the main path for a royal crown, like the one you see at the top of the first artboard.

1   Select the Pen tool (✒) in the toolbar.

2   In the Properties panel, click the Fill color box. In the panel that opens, make sure the Swatches option (▦) is selected, and select None (◻).

3   Click the Stroke box, and make sure that the color black is selected. Make sure the stroke weight is also **1 pt** in the Properties panel.

When you start drawing with the Pen tool, it's usually best to have no fill on the path you draw because the fill can cover parts of the path you are trying to create. You can add a fill later, if necessary.

Note: If you see ✕ instead of the Pen icon (✎ₓ), the Caps Lock key is active. Caps Lock turns the Pen tool icon into ✕ for increased precision. After you begin drawing with the Caps Lock key active, the Pen tool icon looks like this: -¦-.

4   Move the pointer into the area labeled "Work Area" on the artboard, and notice the asterisk next to the Pen icon (✎ₓ), indicating that you'll create a new path if you start drawing.

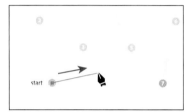

5   Move the pointer over the orange start point, "1," and click to set the first anchor point.

6   Move the pointer away from the point you just created, and you'll see a line connecting the first point and the pointer, no matter where you move the pointer.

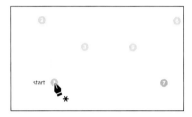 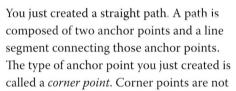

That line is called the *Pen tool preview* (or the rubber band). Later, as you create curved paths, it will make drawing them easier because it is a preview of what the path will look like. Also notice that the asterisk has disappeared from next to the pointer, indicating that you are now drawing a path.

7   Move the pointer over the gray dot labeled "2." Click and release to create an anchor point.

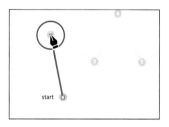

You just created a straight path. A path is composed of two anchor points and a line segment connecting those anchor points. The type of anchor point you just created is called a *corner point*. Corner points are not smooth like a curve; instead, they create an angle at the anchor point. Unlike the Curvature tool, the Pen tool creates corner points and straight lines by default.

8   Continue clicking points 3 through 7, releasing the mouse button after every click to create anchor points.

9   Select the Selection tool (▶), and leave the crown selected.

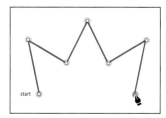

Adding some color to the crown

1   In the Properties panel, click the Fill color box. In the panel that opens, select a color fill.

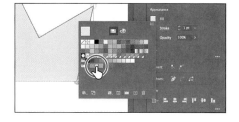

Notice that even though the crown shape is an open path (the endpoints are not connected), you can still fill it with color.

2   Choose File > Save.

Selecting and editing paths in the crown

In Lesson 2 you were introduced to selecting content with the Selection and Direct Selection tools. Next, you'll explore a few more options for selecting artwork with those same selection tools.

1   Select the Direct Selection tool (▷).

2   Move the pointer over the anchor point labeled 4; the anchor point will become a little larger than the others, and the pointer will show a small box with a dot in the center (▷) next to it, as you see in the figure. Both of these indicate that if you click, you will select the anchor point. Click to select the anchor point, and the selected anchor point is filled (appears solid), whereas the other anchor points are hollow (unselected).

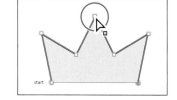

3   Drag the selected anchor point up to reposition it.

The anchor point moves, but the others remain stationary. This is one method for editing a path, as you saw in Lesson 2.

4   Click in an empty area of the artboard to deselect.

5   Move the Direct Selection pointer over the path between points 5 and 6. When the pointer changes (▷), click to select.

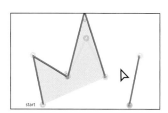

6   Choose Edit > Cut.

This removes the selected segment between anchor points 5 and 6. You can see that because the shape wasn't closed, it no longer shows the yellow fill in the whole object. Next you'll learn how to connect the paths again.

Note: If the entire path disappears, choose Edit > Undo Cut, and try selecting the line segment again.

7 Select the Pen tool (✒), and move the pointer onto the anchor point labeled 5. Notice that the Pen tool shows a forward slash (✒/), indicating that if you click, you will continue drawing from that anchor point.

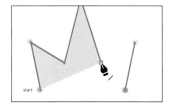

8 Click the point.

9 Move the pointer over the anchor point labeled 6. The pointer now shows a merge symbol next to it (✒₀), indicating that, if you click, you are connecting to another path. Click the point to reconnect the paths.

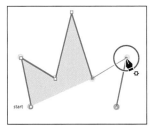 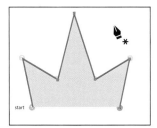

10 Choose Select > Deselect. Leave the file open for the next section.

Drawing a house with the Pen tool

In previous lessons, you learned that using the Shift key and Smart Guides in combination with shape tools constrains the shape of objects. The Shift key and Smart Guides can also constrain paths drawn with the Pen tool, allowing you to create straight paths with 45-degree angles.

Next, you'll learn how to draw straight lines *and* constrain angles as you draw with the Pen tool.

1 Choose 2 from the Artboard Navigation menu in the lower-left corner of the Document window.

2 Select the Zoom tool (🔍) in the toolbar, and click in the area labeled "Work Area" in the artboard to zoom in.

3 Click the View menu, and choose Smart Guides to turn them *on*.

4 With the Pen tool (✒) selected, in the Properties panel, make sure that the fill color is None (☐), the stroke color is Black, and the stroke weight is still 1 pt.

5 In the area labeled "Work Area," click the orange point labeled 1, where you see "start," to set the first anchor point.

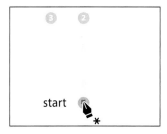

6 Move the pointer above the original anchor point to the point labeled 2. Notice the gray measurement label that appears next to the pointer. That is showing because Smart Guides are on. Click to set another anchor point.

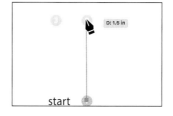

As you've learned in previous lessons, the measurement label and magenta alignment guides you might see are part of the Smart Guides. The measurement labels showing distance can be useful when you're drawing with the Pen tool.

7 Move the pointer over the anchor to the left, labeled 3. When you the pointer is aligned with the point labeled 2, it will "snap" in place. You may want to move the pointer around to feel this. Click to make the third anchor.

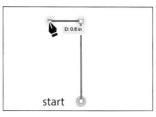

Note: You may see a vertical magenta alignment guide telling you that the point will be lined up with content like the orange house in the top half of the artboard. This is a part of the Smart Guides.

8 Click to set point 4, and then click to set point 5.

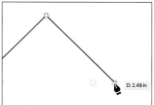

When making those points, you may have seen other magenta alignment guides telling you that the point will be lined up with other content. These guides and the snapping can sometimes make it challenging to draw freeform paths with the Pen tool.

9 Choose View > Smart Guides to turn *off* the Smart Guides.

With Smart Guides turned off, you'll need to press the Shift key to align points, which is what you'll do next. Also, with Smart Guides off, there is no measurement label, and the point is only aligning with the previous point because you are pressing the Shift key.

10 Press the Shift key, and click to set point 6 and then click to set point 7. Release the Shift key.

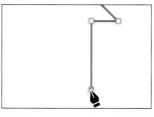

11 Move the pointer over point 1 (the first point). When the pointer shows a small circle next to it (🖋ₒ), click to close the path.

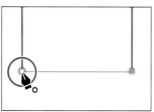

Adding some color to the house

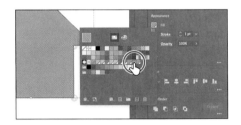

1 In the Properties panel, click the Fill color box. In the panel that opens, select a color fill.

2 Click the Stroke color box, and select None (⊠).

3 Choose Select > Deselect.

Starting with curved paths

Now that you can create corner points, you'll learn to create curves with the Pen tool. To create a curve with the Pen tool, you create anchor points and drag out direction handles to define the shape of the curve. This type of anchor point, with direction handles, is called a *smooth point*.

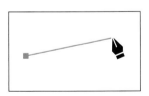

Drawing curves this way gives you some of the greatest control and flexibility in creating paths. However, mastering this technique does take some time. The goal for this exercise is not to create anything specific but to get accustomed to the feel of creating curves. First, you'll get a feel for creating a simple curved path.

1 Choose 3 from the Artboard Navigation menu in the lower-left corner of the Document window. You will draw in the area labeled "Practice."

2 Select the Zoom tool (🔍) in the toolbar, and click twice in the bottom half of the artboard to zoom in.

3 Select the Pen tool (✒) in the toolbar. In the Properties panel, make sure that the fill color is None (⊠), the stroke color is Black, and the stroke weight is still 1 pt.

4 With the Pen tool selected, click and release in an empty area of the artboard to create a starting anchor point. Move the pointer away.

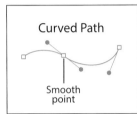

You'll see the Pen tool preview showing what the path will look like if you click and release.

5 In an empty area, press and drag to create a curved path. Release the mouse button.

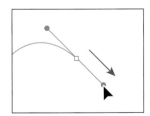

As you drag away from the point, two direction handles appear. A *Direction handle* is a direction line that has a round *direction point* at the end. The angle and length of direction handles determine the shape and size of the curve.

6. Move the pointer away from the anchor point you just created to see the path preview. Move the pointer around a bit to see how it changes.

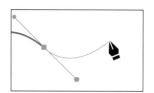

7. Continue pressing, dragging, and releasing in different areas to create a series of points.

8. Choose Select > Deselect. Leave the file open for the next section.

Drawing a curve with the Pen tool

In this part of the lesson, you'll use what you just learned about drawing curves to trace a curved shape with the Pen tool. This will require a little more precision to follow a template path.

1. Press the spacebar to temporarily select the Hand tool (✋), and drag down until you see the curve at the top of the current artboard with points labeled 1 and 2.

2. With the Pen tool (✒) selected, move the pointer over the point labeled 1. Press and drag up to the red dot, and then release the mouse button.

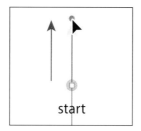

> ● **Note:** The artboard may scroll as you drag. If you lose visibility of the curve, choose View > Zoom Out until you see the curve and anchor point. Pressing the spacebar allows you to use the Hand tool to reposition the artwork.

So far you haven't drawn anything yet; you've simply created a direction line going in the same general direction that the path will go (up). Dragging out a direction line on the very first anchor point can be done to create a more curved path.

3. Press and drag from point 2 down toward the red dot. Drag the pointer around to see how the path reacts. Pulling the direction handle longer makes a steeper curve; when the direction handle is shorter, the curve is flatter. When the pointer is over the red dot, release the mouse button, and the path you are creating should follow the gray template path.

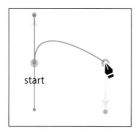
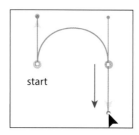

If the path you created is not aligned precisely with the template, select the Direct Selection tool (▷), and select the anchor points one at a time to show the direction handles. You can then drag the ends of the direction handles (called *direction points*) until your path better follows the template.

4   Select the Selection tool (▶), and click the artboard in an area with no objects, or choose Select > Deselect.

Deselecting the first path allows you to create a new path. If you click somewhere on the artboard with the Pen tool while the path is still selected, the new path connects to the last point you drew.

If you want to try drawing the same shape for more practice, scroll down to the Practice area in the same artboard and trace the shapes there. Make sure you deselect the previous artwork first.

Drawing a series of curves with the Pen tool

Now that you've experimented with drawing a curve, you will draw a shape that contains several continuous curves.

1   Choose 4 from the Artboard Navigation menu in the lower-left corner of the Document window. Select the Zoom tool (🔍), and click several times in the *top* half of the artboard to zoom in.

2   Select the Pen tool (🖊). In the Properties panel to the right of the document, make sure that the fill color is None (▨), the stroke color is black, and the stroke weight is still 1 pt.

3   Press and drag up from point 1, labeled "start," in the direction of the arc, stopping at the red dot. This is exactly how you started the last path.

● **Note:** Don't worry if the path you draw is not exact. You could correct the path by selecting it with the Direct Selection tool (▷) when the path is complete.

4   Move the pointer over the point labeled 2 and drag down to the red dot, adjusting the path between points 1 and 2 by dragging before you release the mouse button.

When it comes to curves, you'll find that you spend a lot of time focusing on the path segment *behind* the current anchor point you are creating. Remember, by default, there are two direction lines for an anchor point. The trailing direction line controls the shape of the segment behind the anchor point.

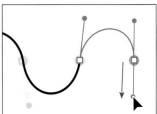

▶ **Tip:** As you are dragging out the direction handles for an anchor point, you can press and hold the spacebar to reposition the anchor point. When the anchor point is where you want it, release the spacebar and continue drawing.

5   Continue along the path, alternating between dragging up at point 3, down at point 4, and up at point 5. Put anchor points only where there are numbers, and finish with the point labeled 6.

If you make a mistake as you draw, you can undo your work by choosing Edit > Undo Pen and then draw the last point again. If your direction lines don't match the figures, that's okay.

6 When the path is complete, select the Direct Selection tool (▷), and click to select any anchor point in the path.

When an anchor point is selected, the direction handles appear, and you can readjust the curve of the path, if necessary. With a curve selected, you can also change the stroke and fill. When you do this, the next line you draw will have the same attributes. If you want to try drawing the shape again for more practice, scroll down to the bottom half of the same artboard (labeled "Practice"), and trace the shape there.

7 Choose Select > Deselect, and then choose File > Save.

Converting smooth points to corner points

When you create curves, the direction handles help to determine the shape and size of the curved segments, as you've seen. If you want to create a curved path followed by a straight line, for instance, you can remove the direction lines from an anchor point to convert a smooth point into a corner point. In this next part of the lesson, you'll practice converting between smooth points and corner points.

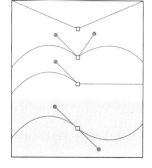

Corner point examples

Smooth point example

1 Choose 5 from the Artboard Navigation menu in the lower-left corner of the Document window.

On the top of the artboard, you can see the path that you will trace. You'll use the top artboard as a template for the exercise, creating your paths directly on top of those.

2 Select the Zoom tool (🔍), and click several times in the top part of the artboard to zoom in.

3 Select the Pen tool (✒). In the Properties panel, make sure that the fill color is None (▨), the stroke color is Black, and the stroke weight is still 1 pt.

4 Pressing the Shift key, press and drag up from point 1, labeled "start," in the direction of the arc, stopping at the red dot. Release the mouse button and then release the Shift key.

Pressing the Shift key when dragging constrains the direction handles to multiples of 45°. Next, you'll repeat the same step process for point 2.

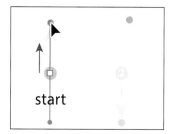

start

5 From point 2, Shift-drag down to the gold dot. When the curved path between 1 and 2 looks correct and the pointer reaches the gold dot, release the mouse button and then release the Shift key. Leave the path selected.

Now you need the path to switch directions and create another arc. You will *split* the direction lines, or move them in different directions from each other, to convert a smooth point to a corner point.

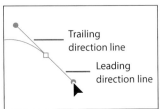

When you press and drag to create a smooth anchor point with the Pen tool, you create a leading direction line and a trailing direction line. By default, they are equal and paired together.

Note: The Option (macOS) or Alt (Windows) key essentially allows you to split the direction lines so that they are independent of each other for that anchor point.

6 Press the Option (macOS) or Alt (Windows) key, and move the pointer over the anchor point you just created (on point 2). When a convert-point icon (^) appears next to the Pen tool pointer (🖋), press and drag a new direction line up to the red dot above. Release the mouse button and then release the modifier key. If you do not see the caret (^), you might end up creating an additional loop.

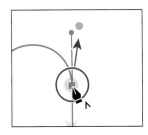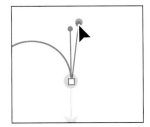

You can also Option-drag (macOS) or Alt-drag (Windows) the *end* of a direction handle (called the *direction point*). Either method "splits" the direction handles so they can go in different directions.

Tip: You can watch these steps in a video! Check out the videos that are a part of the Web Edition. For more information, see the "Web Edition" section of "Getting Started" at the beginning of the book.

7 Move the Pen tool pointer over point 3 to the right on the template path, and drag down to the gold dot. Release the mouse button when the path looks similar to the template path.

8 Press the Option (macOS) or Alt (Windows) key, and move the pointer over the last anchor point you created (at 3). When a convert-point icon (^) appears next to the Pen tool pointer (🖋), press and drag a direction line up to the red dot above. Release the mouse button, and then release the modifier key.

For the next point, you will work faster by not releasing the mouse button to split the direction handles, so pay close attention.

9 For anchor point 4, press and drag down to the gold dot until the path looks correct. This time, *do not release the mouse button*. Press the Option (macOS) or Alt (Windows) key, and drag up to the red dot for the next curve. Release the mouse button, and then release the modifier key.

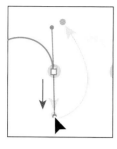
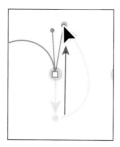

10 Continue this process using the Option (macOS) or Alt (Windows) key to create corner points. Keep doing this until the path is completed.

11 Use the Direct Selection tool to fine-tune the path, and then deselect the path.

Combining curves and straight lines

When you're drawing your own artwork with the Pen tool, you'll need to transition easily between curves and straight lines. In this next section, you'll learn how to go from curves to straight lines and from straight lines to curves.

1 Choose 6 from the Artboard Navigation menu in the lower-left corner of the Document window. Select the Zoom tool (🔍), and click several times in the top half of the artboard to zoom in.

2 Select the Pen tool (✒). Move the pointer over point 1, labeled "start," and press and drag up, stopping at the red dot. Release the mouse button.

Up to this point, you've been dragging to a gold or red dot in the templates. In the real world those obviously won't be there, so for the next point you will drag to create a point without much guidance. Don't worry, you can always choose Edit > Undo Pen and try again!

3 Press and drag down from point 2, and release the mouse button when the path between 1 and 2 roughly matches the gray template path.

This method of creating a curve should be familiar to you by now.

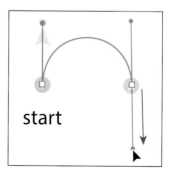

start

If you were to continue drawing by clicking point 3, even pressing the Shift key (to produce a straight line), the path would be curved (don't do either). The last point you created is a smooth anchor point and has a leading direction handle (the one you pulled

out). The previous figure shows what the path would look like if you clicked with the Pen tool on the next point. You will now continue the path as a straight line by removing the leading direction handle.

4   Move the pointer over the last point created (point 2). When the convert-point icon appears (🖋), click. This deletes the *leading* direction handle from the anchor point (not the trailing direction handle), as shown in the second part of the following figure.

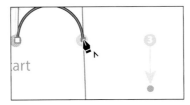   

5   Move the pointer over point 3. Pressing the Shift key, click and release to create the next point. Release the Shift key after clicking, and you've created a straight line.

6   For the next arc, move the pointer over the last point created. When the convert-point icon appears (🖋), press and drag down from that point to the red dot. This creates a new, independent direction line.

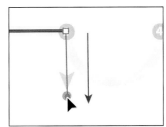

For the rest of this section, I'm going to ask you to complete the path, following the remaining part of the template. I don't include any figures, so go through the figures in the previous steps if you need guidance.

7   For the next point (point 4), press and drag up to complete the arc.

8   Click the last anchor point you just created to remove the direction line.

9   Shift-click the next point to create the second straight segment.

10 Press and drag up from the last point you created to create a direction line.

11 Press and drag down on the end point (point 6) to create the final arc.

12 Choose File > Save, and then choose File > Close.

Remember, you can always go back and work on those Pen tool templates in the L7_practice.ai file as many times as you need. Take it as slowly as you need and *practice, practice, practice.*

Creating artwork with the Pen tool

Next, you'll take what you've learned and create some artwork to be used in your project. To start you'll draw a swan, which combines curves and corners. Take your time as you practice with this shape, and use the template guides provided.

Tip: Don't forget you can always undo a point you've drawn (Edit > Undo Pen) and then try again.

1 Choose File > Open, and open the L7_end.ai file in the Lessons > Lesson07 folder to see the final artwork.

2 Choose View > Fit Artboard In Window to see the finished artwork. If you don't want to leave the artwork open, choose File > Close.

3 Choose File > Open, and open the L7_start.ai file in the Lessons > Lesson07 folder to open the file you'll be working in.

4 Choose File > Save As. If the Cloud Document dialog box opens, click Save On Your Computer, otherwise continue.

5 In the Save As dialog box, name the file **Swan.ai**, and select the Lessons > Lesson07 folder in the Save As dialog box. Leave Adobe Illustrator (ai) chosen from the Format menu (macOS) or Adobe Illustrator (*.AI) chosen from the Save As Type menu (Windows), and click Save.

6 In the Illustrator Options dialog box, leave the options set at the defaults, and then click OK.

7 Choose View > Fit Artboard In Window to ensure that you see the entire artboard.

8 Open the Layers panel (Window > Layers), and click to select the layer named "Artwork."

9 Select the Pen tool ( ) in the toolbar.

10 In the Properties panel (Window > Properties), make sure that the fill color is None ( ), the stroke color is Black, and the stroke weight is 1 pt.

Drawing the swan

Now that you have the file open and ready, you're going to put your Pen tool practice to use by drawing a beautiful swan. This next section has more than the average number of steps, so *take your time*.

● **Note:** You do not have to start at the blue square (point A) to draw this shape. You can set anchor points for a path with the Pen tool in a clockwise or counterclockwise direction.

1 With the Pen tool (✐) selected, press and drag from the blue square labeled "A" on the swan body template to the red dot. This sets the starting anchor point and direction of the first curve.

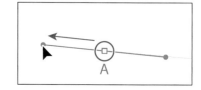

2 Move the pointer over point B. Press and drag, stopping at the gold dot. Release the mouse button.

Remember to pay attention to how the path you are creating looks as you drag the direction line. It's easier when dragging to color dots on a template, but when you're creating your own content, you'll need to focus on what the path looks like.

Next, you'll split the direction handles so the path can go in a different direction.

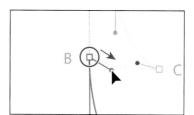

3 Move the pointer over point B again, and when the pointer changes (✐ₙ), press Option (macOS) or Alt (Windows) and drag away from the point to the red dot to create a new direction line. Release the mouse button and then the key.

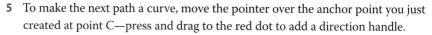

4 Move the pointer over point C. Click and release to add a point.

5 To make the next path a curve, move the pointer over the anchor point you just created at point C—press and drag to the red dot to add a direction handle.

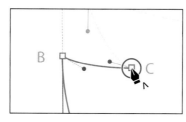
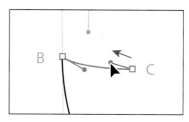

6 Move the pointer over point D. Press and drag to the red dot.

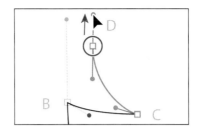

The next part of the path needs to be straight, so the direction line on point D needs to be removed.

7 Move the Pen tool pointer over point D again. When the convert-point icon (▲) appears next to the pointer, click point D to remove the leading direction handle (the handle pointing up).

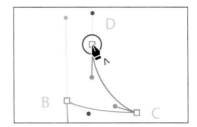

8 Click and release on point E to make a straight line.

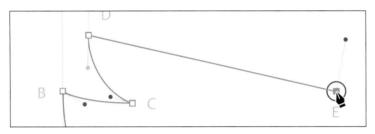

As you draw with the Pen tool, you may want to edit part of a path you previously drew. By pressing a modifier key with the Pen tool selected, you can move the pointer over a previous path segment and drag to modify it, which is what you'll do next.

9 Move the pointer over the path between points D and E. Press the Option (macOS) or Alt (Windows) key. The pointer changes appearance (▶). Drag the path up to make it curved, as you see in the figure. Release the mouse button and then the key. This adds direction handles to the anchor points at both ends of the line segment.

After releasing the mouse button, notice that as you move the pointer, you can see the Pen tool rubber banding, which means you are still drawing the path.

▶ **Tip:** You can also press Option+Shift (macOS) or Alt+Shift (Windows) to constrain the handles on each anchor point to a perpendicular direction, which ensures that the handles are the same length.

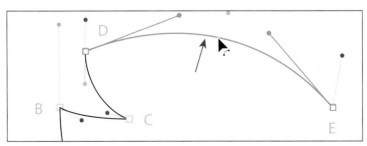

The path that continues from point E needs to be curved, so you'll need to add a leading direction handle to the point.

● **Note:** After releasing the mouse button in this step (10), if you move the pointer away and then bring it back to point E, the convert-point icon [^] will appear next to the pointer.

10 With the Pen tool pointer over point E, press and drag up to the red dot to create a new direction handle.

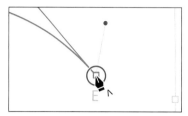 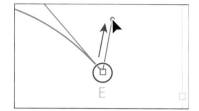

This creates a new leading direction handle and sets up the next path to be a curve.

11 Continue drawing by dragging from the anchor point at F to the red dot.

▶ **Tip:** When creating an anchor point, you can press the spacebar to move the point as you create it.

12 Drag from point G to the red dot.

The next part of the path needs to be straight, so you'll remove the leading direction handle from the point at G.

13 Move the pointer back over point G. When the convert-point icon appears (🖋̬) next to the pointer, click to remove the direction handle.

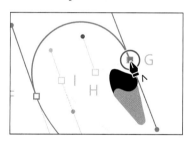 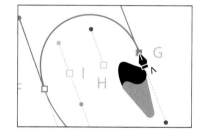

14 Click point H to create a new anchor point.

The next part of the path needs to be curved, so you will need to add a leading direction handle to point H.

15 Move the Pen tool pointer over point H again. When the convert-point icon (🖋̬) appears next to the pointer, press and drag from point H up to the red dot to add a leading direction handle.

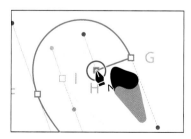 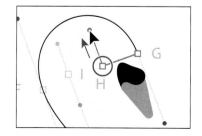

16 Continue drawing the point at I by dragging from the anchor point to the gold dot. Release the mouse button.

17 Press Option (macOS) or Alt (Windows), and when the pointer changes (↖), drag the end of the direction handle down to the red dot from the gold dot.

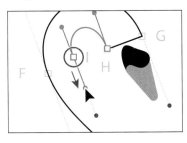 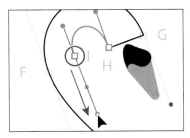

18 Drag from point J to the red dot.

Next, you'll complete the drawing of the swan by closing the path.

19 Move the Pen tool pointer over point A *without clicking*.

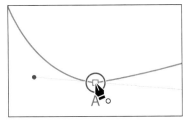

Notice that an open circle appears next to the Pen tool pointer (✎₀), indicating that the path would close if you were to click the anchor point (*don't click yet*). If you were to drag, the direction handles on either side of the point would move as a single straight line. You need to extend one of the direction handles to match the template.

20 Drag left and a little up. Notice that a direction handle shows to the right of the anchor point and is growing in the opposite direction (it's going down and to the right). Drag until the curve looks right.

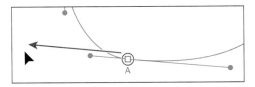

Normally, as you drag away from a point, direction lines appear before and after the point. Without the modifier key, as you drag away from a closing point, you are reshaping the path before *and* after the anchor point. Pressing the Option (macOS) or Alt (Windows) modifier key on the closing point allows you to edit the previous direction handle independently.

21 Click the Properties panel tab. Click the Fill color and select white.

22 Command-click (macOS) or Ctrl-click (Windows) away from the path to deselect it, and then choose File > Save.

Note: This is a shortcut method for deselecting a path while keeping the Pen tool selected. You could also choose Select > Deselect, among other methods.

Editing paths and points

Next you'll edit a few of the paths and points for the swan you just created.

1 Select the Direct Selection tool (⬦), and click the anchor point labeled J to select it. Drag the anchor point to the left so it roughly matches the figure.

 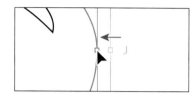

▶ **Tip:** You can drag the line segment (path) between the anchors without selecting Option/Alt as you did with the Pen tool earlier because at least one of the anchors has direction handles. Try to do this on a straight path, and it won't work.

2 Move the pointer over the part of the path between points F and G (at the top of the swan). When the pointer looks like ▸c, drag the path up and to the left a little to change the curve of the path. This is an easy way to make edits to a curved path without having to edit the direction handles for each anchor point.

Notice that the pointer changes appearance (▸c) with the pointer over the path. This indicates that you can drag the path, which will adjust the anchor points and direction handles as you drag.

3 Choose Select > Deselect, and then choose File > Save.

Deleting and adding anchor points

Most of the time, the goal of drawing paths with a tool like the Pen tool or Curvature tool is to avoid adding more anchor points than necessary. You can reduce a path's complexity or change its overall shape by deleting unnecessary points (and therefore gain more control over the shape), or you can extend a path by adding points to it. Next you'll delete anchor points from, and add anchor points to, different parts of the swan path.

1 Open the Layers panel (Window > Layers). In the Layers panel, click the eye icon (👁) for the layer named "Bird template" to hide the layer contents.

2 With the Direct Selection tool (⬦) selected, click right on the swan path to select it.

To start you'll delete a few points in the tail to simplify the swan path.

3 Select the Pen tool (✒) in the toolbar, and move the pointer over the anchor point you see in the first part of the following figure. When a minus sign (–) appears to the right of the Pen tool pointer (✒_), click to remove the anchor point.

4 Move the pointer over the anchor point in the second part of the following figure. When a minus sign (–) appears to the right of the Pen tool pointer (✒_), click to remove the anchor point.

▶ **Tip:** With an anchor point selected, you can also click Remove Selected Anchor Points (✎) in the Properties panel to delete the anchor point.

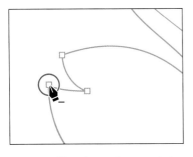
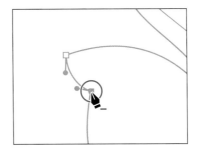

Next you'll reshape the remaining path. With the Pen tool selected, you can press Command (macOS) or Ctrl (Windows) to temporarily select the Direct Selection tool so you can edit a path and then release the key and continue drawing.

5 Press Command (macOS) or Ctrl (Windows) to temporarily select the Direct Selection tool. With the key held down, move the pointer over the anchor point shown in the figure. When the pointer shows a box next to it (▷), click to select the anchor point if it isn't already.

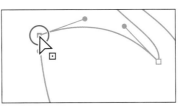

6 With the key still held down, drag the direction line pointing down from the selected anchor point to reshape the path, and release the key.

With that part of the path reshaped, now you'll add a new anchor point to the path so you can reshape it further.

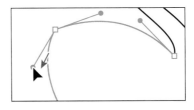

⬤ **Note:** It can be tricky to drag the end of a direction line. If you wind up missing and deselecting the path, with the modifier key still held down, click the path and then click the anchor point to see the direction handles and try again.

7 Move the pointer over the left side of the swan path, below the selected anchor point. When a plus sign (+) appears to the right of the Pen tool pointer (✒+), click to add an anchor point.

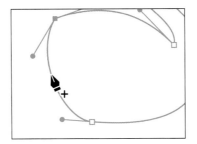

8 Press Command (macOS) or Ctrl (Windows) to temporarily select the Direct Selection tool, and drag the new anchor to the left to reshape the path. Release the key.

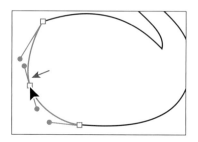

Lastly, you'll add a new anchor point to the bottom of the swan path so that in the next section you can reshape the bottom.

9 Move the pointer over the bottom part of the path. When a plus sign (+) appears to the right of the Pen tool pointer (🖋₊), click to add an anchor point.

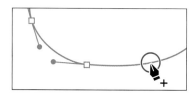

Converting between smooth points and corner points

To more precisely control the path you create, you can convert points from smooth points to corner points and from corner points to smooth points, using several methods. This will give the bird a flat bottom so it looks like it's in water.

1 Select the Direct Selection tool (▷). With the last point you added still selected, Shift-click the anchor point to the left (formerly labeled "A") to select both.

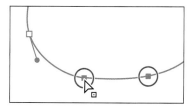

▶ **Tip:** You could also convert between corner and smooth points by double-clicking (or Option-clicking [macOS] or Alt-clicking [Windows]) an anchor point with the Curvature tool.

2 In the Properties panel, click the Convert Selected Anchor Points To Corner button (◣) to convert the anchor points to corners.

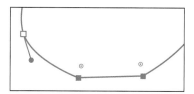

● **Note:** If the points align to the artboard after clicking the align button, try again. Make sure that Align To Key Anchor is selected in the Properties panel first.

3 Click the Vertical Align Bottom button (🇮) in the Properties panel to align the point you first selected to the second point you selected.

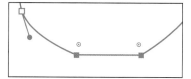

As you saw in Lesson 2, selected anchor points align to the last selected anchor point, which is known as the *key anchor*.

4 Choose Select > Deselect and then File > Save.

Converting anchors with the Anchor Point tool

The Anchor Point tool is another way to convert anchor points between smooth and corner points (⌐). With this tool, you can convert anchors as you did in the previous section, but you can adjust the paths with it simultaneously. You'll use the tool to finish the head of the swan.

1   Select the Selection tool (▶), and click the swan path to select it.

2   Press and hold on the Pen tool (✒) in the toolbar to reveal another tool. Select the Anchor Point tool (⌐).

If you click an anchor point with the Anchor point tool, the direction lines are removed and it becomes a corner point. The Anchor point tool is also used either to remove one or both of the direction handles from an anchor point, converting it to a corner point, or to drag out direction handles from an anchor point. Dragging handles out with the Anchor point tool can be a great way to restore handles that have been split.

3   Move the pointer over the point in the swan's head in the figure. When the pointer looks like ⌐, press and drag *up* from the corner point to drag the direction handles out. Drag until the neck looks similar to how it did before you started dragging.

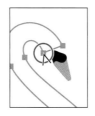 

Depending on which direction you drew the path in, dragging in one direction may reverse the direction handles.

4   Move the pointer over the anchor point to the right of the anchor point you just edited. Press and drag *down* when the pointer looks like this: ⌐. Make sure the top of the swan's head looks similar to the way it did.

 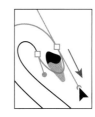

5   Select the Direct Selection tool, and drag the end of the bottom direction handle up to shorten it and make the line less curvy.

The direction handles for an anchor point are split when you create them with the Anchor Point tool, which means you can move them independently. Next you'll convert an anchor point from a smooth point (with direction handles) to a corner point.

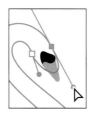 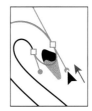

Note: Don't drag if the pointer looks like this: ▶. This means that the pointer is not over the anchor point, and if you drag, you will reshape the curve.

Tip: If you move the Anchor Point tool pointer over the end of a direction handle that is split, you can press the Option (macOS) or Alt (Windows) key and, when the pointer changes (▶), click to make the direction handles a single straight line again (not split).

Practice with the Convert Anchor point tool

Now you'll practice with the Convert Anchor point tool to finish the swan.

1   Open the Layers panel (Window > Layers). In the Layers panel, click the visibility column for the layer named "Wing" and the layer named "Background" to show the content for both.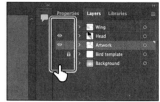

You should now see the wing of the swan on top of the swan shape you drew. It's made up of a series of simple paths that overlap each other. You need to make the right edge of the wing a corner point, not a smooth point.

2   With the Direct Selection selected, click the larger wing shape to select it and see the anchor points.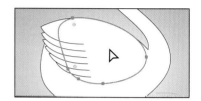

3   Select the Anchor Point tool (⊾) in the toolbar. Move the pointer over the point circled in the first part of the following figure. Click to convert the point from a curve (smooth point with direction handles) to a corner point.

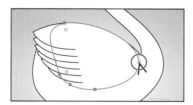 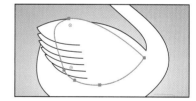

4   Select the Direct Selection tool, and drag the anchor point you converted. Snap it to the anchor point at the base of the swan's neck.

5   Move the pointer over the end of the direction handle coming from the top anchor point, and drag to change the shape of the path.

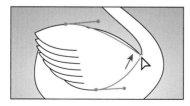 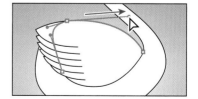

6   Choose Select > Deselect.

7   Choose View > Fit Artboard In Window.

8   Save and close the file by choosing File > Save and then File > Close.

Review questions

1 Describe how to draw straight vertical, horizontal, or diagonal lines using the Pen tool (✐).

2 How do you draw a curved line using the Pen tool?

3 What are the two types of anchor points you can create with the Pen tool?

4 Name two ways to convert a smooth point on a curve to a corner point.

5 Which tool would you use to edit a segment on a curved line?

Review answers

1 To draw a straight line, click with the Pen tool (✐) and then move the pointer and click again. The first click sets the starting anchor point, and the second click sets the ending anchor point of the line. To constrain the straight line vertically, horizontally, or along a 45° diagonal, press the Shift key as you click to create the second anchor point with the Pen tool.

2 To draw a curved line with the Pen tool, click to create the starting anchor point, drag to set the direction of the curve, and then click to end the curve.

3 With the Pen tool, you can create corner points or smooth points. Corner points allow the path to change direction and have either no direction lines or split direction lines. Smooth points have direction lines that form a straight line.

4 To convert a smooth point on a curve to a corner point, use the Direct Selection tool (▷) to select the anchor point and then use the Anchor Point tool (⌐) to drag a direction handle to change the direction. Another method is to select a point or points with the Direct Selection tool and then click the Convert Selected Anchor Points To Corner button (⌐) in the Properties panel.

5 To edit a segment on a curved line, select the Direct Selection tool and drag the segment to move it; or drag a direction handle on an anchor point to adjust the length and shape of the segment. Pressing the Option (macOS) or Alt (Windows) key and dragging a path segment with the Pen tool is another way to reshape a path.

8 USING COLOR TO ENHANCE ARTWORK

Lesson overview

In this lesson, you'll learn how to do the following:

- Understand color modes and the main color controls.
- Create, edit, and apply colors using a variety of methods.
- Name and save colors.
- Copy and paste appearance attributes from one object to another.
- Work with color groups.
- Be inspired creatively with the Color Guide panel.
- Explore the Recolor Artwork command.
- Work with Live Paint groups.

 This lesson will take about 75 minutes to complete. To get the lesson files used in this chapter, download them from the web page for this book at adobepress.com/IllustratorCIB2022. For more information, see "Accessing the lesson files and Web Edition" in the Getting Started section at the beginning of this book.

Spice up your illustrations with color by taking
advantage of color controls in Adobe Illustrator.
In this information-packed lesson, you'll discover how
to create and apply fills and strokes, use the Color
Guide panel for inspiration, work with color groups,
recolor artwork, and more.

Starting the lesson

In this lesson, you'll learn about the fundamentals of color by using the Swatches panel and more to create and edit the colors for artwork for a ski area.

● **Note:** If you have not already downloaded the project files for this lesson to your computer from your Account page, make sure to do so now. See the "Getting Started" section at the beginning of the book.

1 To ensure that the tools function and the defaults are set exactly as described in this lesson, delete or deactivate (by renaming) the Adobe Illustrator preferences file. See "Restoring default preferences" in the "Getting Started" section at the beginning of the book.

2 Start Adobe Illustrator.

3 Choose File > Open, and open the L8_end1.ai file in the Lessons > Lesson08 folder to view a final version of the artwork.

4 Choose View > Fit All In Window. You can leave the file open for reference or choose File > Close to close it.

5 Choose File > Open. In the Open dialog box, navigate to the Lessons > Lesson08 folder, and select the L8_start1.ai file on your hard disk. Click Open to open the file. This file has all the pieces already in it; they just need to be painted.

● **Note:** For more information on activating fonts, visit helpx.adobe.com/ creative-cloud/help/ add-fonts.html.

6 In the Missing Fonts dialog box, ensure that the checkboxes to the right of the names of the missing fonts are selected, and click Activate Fonts. After some time, the font(s) should be activated, and you should see a success message in the Missing Fonts dialog box. Click Close.

7 If you see a dialog box about font auto-activation, click Skip.

8 Choose View > Fit All In Window.

9 Choose File > Save As. If the Cloud Document dialog box opens, click Save On Your Computer.

10 In the Save As dialog box, navigate to the Lesson08 folder, and name the file **Snowboarder.ai**. Leave Adobe Illustrator (ai) chosen from the Format menu (macOS) or Adobe Illustrator (*.AI) chosen from the Save As Type menu (Windows), and click Save.

● **Note:** If you don't see Reset Essentials in the menu, choose Window > Workspace > Essentials before choosing Window > Workspace > Reset Essentials.

11 In the Illustrator Options dialog box, leave the options at their default settings and then click OK.

12 Choose Window > Workspace > Reset Essentials.

Exploring color modes

There are many ways to experiment with and apply color to your artwork in Adobe Illustrator. As you work with color, it's important to consider the medium in which the artwork will be published, such as print or the web. The colors you create need to be suitable for the medium. This usually requires that you use the correct color mode and color definitions for your colors.

Before starting a new document, you should decide which color mode the artwork should use, *CMYK* or *RGB*.

* **CMYK**—Cyan, magenta, yellow, and black are the colors of ink used in four-color process printing. These four colors are combined and overlapped in a pattern of dots to create a multitude of other colors.

* **RGB**—Red, green, and blue light are added together in various ways to create an array of colors. Select this mode if you are using images for onscreen presentations, the internet, or mobile apps, or maybe printing to desktop inkjet printers.

When you create a new document by choosing File > New, each new document preset, like Print or Web, has a specific color mode. For instance, the presets in the Print category use the CMYK color mode by default. You can easily change the color mode by choosing a different option from the Color Mode menu after clicking Advanced Options in the New Document dialog box.

Note: You may see a series of templates in the New Document dialog box that are different than those you see in the figure.

Once a color mode is chosen, solid colors in the document are displayed in and created from that color mode. Once a document is created, you can change the color mode of a document by choosing File > Document Color Mode and then switching to either CMYK Color or RGB Color in the menu.

Working with color

In this lesson, you'll learn about the traditional methods of coloring objects in Illustrator using a combination of panels and tools, such as the Properties panel, Swatches panel, Color Guide panel, Color Picker, and paint options in the toolbar.

● **Note:** The toolbar you see may be a double column, depending on the resolution of your screen.

In previous lessons, you learned that objects in Illustrator can have a fill, a stroke, or both. At the bottom of the toolbar, notice the Fill and Stroke boxes. The Fill box is white (in this case), and the Stroke box is black. If you click those boxes one at a time, you'll see that whichever is clicked is brought in front of the other (it's selected). When a color is chosen, it is applied to the fill or stroke, whichever is selected. As you explore more of Illustrator, you'll see these fill and stroke boxes in lots of other places, like the Properties panel, Swatches panel, and more.

As you will see in this section, Illustrator provides many ways to arrive at the color you need. You'll start by applying an existing color to a shape and then work your way through the most widely used methods for creating and applying color.

Applying an existing color

● **Note:** Throughout this lesson, you'll be working on a document with a color mode that was set to CMYK when the document was created. That means that colors you create will, by default, be composed of cyan, magenta, yellow, and black.

Every new document in Illustrator has a series of default colors available for you to use in your artwork in the form of swatches in the Swatches panel. The first color method you'll explore is applying an existing color to a shape.

1   With the Snowboarder.ai document showing, choose 1 Badge from the Artboard Navigation menu in the lower-left corner of the Document window (if it's not chosen already) and then choose View > Fit Artboard In Window.

2   With the Selection tool (▶), click the red snowboard shape to select it.

3   Click the Fill box (■) in the Properties panel on the right to reveal a panel. Click the Swatches button (▦) toward the top of the panel, if it isn't already selected, to show the default swatches (colors). Click to apply the pink swatch to change the color of the fill for the selected shape.

● **Note:** As you move the pointer over the swatches, tool tips appear revealing each swatch's name. By default, swatches are named according to their color values. If you change the name, that name will appear in the tool tip.

4   Press the Escape key to hide the panel of colors.

Creating a custom color

There are lots of ways to create your custom colors in Illustrator. Using the Color panel (Window > Color) or Color Mixer, you can apply custom colors you make to an object's fill and stroke and also edit and mix colors using different color models (CMYK, for example).

The Color panel and Color Mixer display the current fill and stroke of the selected content. You can either visually select a color from the color spectrum bar at the bottom of the panel or mix your colors in various ways. Next, you'll create a custom color using the Color Mixer.

1   With the Selection tool (▶), select the green stripe on the snowboard.

2   Click the Fill box (▦) in the Properties panel on the right to reveal the panel. Click the Color Mixer button (◉) at the top of that panel (circled in the first part of the following figure).

3   At the bottom of the panel, click in the yellow-orange part of the color spectrum to sample a yellow-orange color, and apply it to the fill (see the following figure).

▶ **Tip:** To see a larger color spectrum, you can open the Color panel (Window > Color) and drag the bottom of the panel down.

Since the spectrum bar is so small, you most likely won't achieve the same color as you see in the book. That's okay, because you'll edit it to match next.

4   In the Color Mixer panel, which should still be showing, type the following values in the CMYK fields: C=**0**, M=**20**, Y=**65**, K=**0**. Press Return or Enter after the last value entered to make a light orange color and close the panel. This ensures that we are all using the same color. Leave the shape selected.

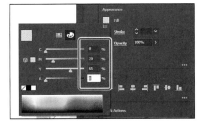 

Colors created in the Color Mixer panel are not saved anywhere except in the fill or stroke of the selected artwork. If you want to easily reuse the color you just created elsewhere in this document, you can save it as a swatch in the Swatches panel, which is what you'll do next.

Saving a color as a swatch

You can name and save different types of colors, gradients, and patterns in the document as swatches so that you can apply and edit them later. Swatches are listed in the Swatches panel in the order in which they were created, but you can reorder or organize the swatches into groups to suit your needs. All documents start with a default number of swatches, as mentioned earlier. Any colors you save or edit in the Swatches panel are available only to the current document, by default, since each document has its own defined swatches.

Next, you'll save the color you just created as a swatch so you can reuse it later.

1   With the light orange shape still selected, click the Fill box (◻) in the Properties panel to show the panel again.

2   Click the Swatches button (▦) at the top of the panel to see the swatches. Click the New Swatch button (▣) at the bottom of the panel to create a swatch from the fill color of the selected artwork.

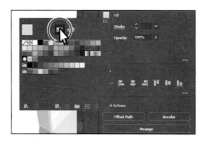 

▷ **Tip:** Naming colors can be an art form. You can name them according to their values (C=45, ...), appearance (light orange), or description (like "text header"), among other attributes.

3   In the New Swatch dialog box that appears, change the swatch name to **Light Orange**.

Notice the Global option that is selected by default? New swatches you create are global by default. A *global swatch* is a swatch that is updated everywhere it's applied anytime the color is changed, regardless of whether or not the artwork is selected. Also, the Color Mode menu lets you change the color mode of a specific color to RGB, CMYK, Grayscale, or another mode.

4   Click OK to save the swatch.

Notice that the new Light Orange swatch is highlighted in the Swatches panel (it has a white border around it). That's because it's applied to the selected shape automatically. Also, notice the little white triangle in the lower-right corner of the swatch, which indicates that it's a global swatch.

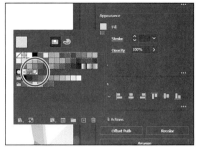

Leave the light orange shape selected and the panel showing for the next section.

Creating a copy of a swatch

One of the easiest ways to create and save a color as a swatch is to make a copy of an existing swatch and edit the color of the copy. Next, you'll create another swatch by copying and editing the swatch named "Light Orange."

1   With the shape in the snowboard still selected and the Swatches panel still showing, click the New Swatch button (⊞) at the bottom of the panel.

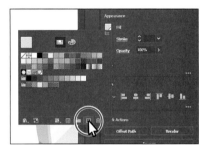

This creates a *copy* of the selected Light Orange swatch and opens the New Swatch dialog box.

▶ **Tip:** You can also choose Duplicate Swatch from the panel menu (▤) to create a copy of a selected swatch.

2   In the New Swatch dialog box, change the name to **Orange** and change the CMYK color values to C=**0**, M=**45**, Y=**90**, K=**0** to make a slightly darker orange. Click OK.

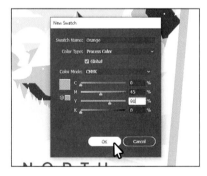

3   In the Swatches panel, click to apply the Light Orange swatch to the selected shape.

4 With the Selection tool (▶), click the word "NORTH," and then Shift-click the word "CASCADES."

5 Click the Fill box (■) in the Properties panel, and click the Orange swatch to apply it to the selected text.

6 Press the Escape key to hide the Swatches panel.

7 Choose Select > Deselect.

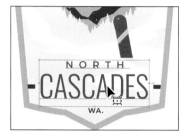 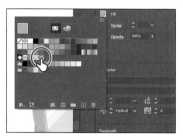 

Editing a global swatch

Next you'll edit a *global color*. When you edit a global color, all artwork with that swatch applied is updated, regardless of which artwork is and isn't selected.

1 With the Selection tool (▶), click the yellow shape in the sky, behind the clouds.

   You'll apply the Light Orange swatch to the shape and then change the color.

2 Click the Fill box (▢) in the Properties panel, and click to apply the swatch named "Light Orange." Leave the panel of swatches showing.

3 Double-click the Light Orange swatch in the panel to edit it. In the Swatch Options dialog box:

   • Select Preview to see the change.

   • Change the C (Cyan) value to **80** and click in another field in the dialog box to see the change happen.

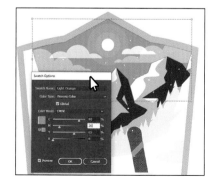

You may need to drag the dialog box by the top title bar to see the snowboard and sky shapes. All of the shapes with the global swatch applied are updated—even the shape on the snowboard that wasn't selected.

4 Change the C (Cyan) value to **3** and click OK.

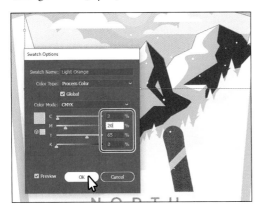

● **Note:** The cursor is in the Magenta field in the figure because I have a habit of entering a number and pressing the tab key to go to the next field, so the value is accepted.

Editing a non-global swatch

The default color swatches that come with each Illustrator document are non-global swatches by default. As a result, when you edit one of those color swatches, the artwork that uses the color will update only if that artwork is selected. Next, you'll edit the non-global pink swatch you applied to the fill of the snowboard.

1 With the Selection tool (▶) selected, click to select the pink snowboard you first changed the color for.

2 Click the Fill box (■) in the Properties panel, and you'll see that the pink swatch is applied to the fill. This was the first color you applied at the beginning of this lesson.

 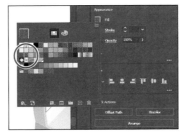

You can tell that the pink swatch you applied is *not* a global swatch because it doesn't have the small white triangle in the lower-right corner of the swatch in the Swatches panel.

3 Press the Escape key to hide the Swatches panel.

4 Click either the small blue shape on the left or to the right of the "CASCADES" text to select both since they are grouped together.

5 Click the Fill box (■) in the Properties panel, and click the same pink swatch to change the fill of both shapes.

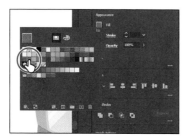

6 Choose Select > Deselect.

7 Choose Window > Swatches to open the Swatches panel as a separate panel.

8 Double-click the same pink swatch to edit it.

Most of the formatting options you find in the Properties panel can also be found in separate panels. Opening the Swatches panel, for instance, can be a useful way to work with color without having to select artwork.

● **Note:** You can change an existing swatch into a global swatch, but it requires a bit more effort. You need to either select all the shapes that swatch was applied to before you edit the swatch and make it global or edit the swatch to make it global and then reapply the swatch to your content.

9 In the Swatch Options dialog box, change the name to **Snowboard pink** and the values to C=**0**, M=**76**, Y=**49**, K=**0**, select Global to ensure that it's a global swatch, and select Preview.

Notice that the color of the snowboard or small shapes on either side of the text didn't change. That's because Global wasn't selected in the Swatch Options dialog box when the color was applied to them. After changing a non-global swatch, you need to reapply it to artwork that wasn't selected when you made the edit.

10 Click OK.

11 Click the X at the top of the Swatches panel group to close it.

12 Click to select the pink snowboard again. Shift-click one of the two shapes with the same pink applied to select them as well.

13 Click the Fill box (■) in the Properties panel, and notice that what was the pink color swatch is no longer applied.

14 Click the Snowboard pink swatch you just edited to apply it.

 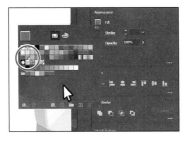 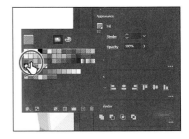

15 Choose Select > Deselect and then choose File > Save.

Using the Color Picker to create color

Another method for creating color is to use the Color Picker. The Color Picker lets you select a color in a color field or a spectrum, either by defining colors numerically or by clicking a swatch. The Color Picker is also found in Adobe applications like InDesign and Photoshop. Next, you'll create a color using the Color Picker and then save that color as a swatch in the Swatches panel.

1 Choose 2 Snowboarder from the Artboard Navigation menu in the lower-left corner of the Document window.

2 With the Selection tool (▶), click in the green jacket shape.

3 Double-click the green Fill box at the bottom of the toolbar, to the left of the document, to open the Color Picker.

● **Note:** You can't double-click the Fill box in the Properties panel to open the Color Picker.

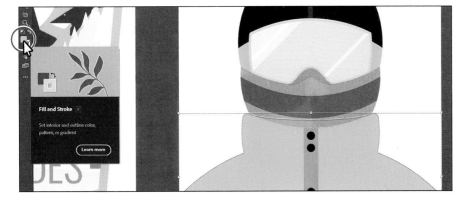

In the Color Picker dialog box, the larger color field shows saturation (horizontally) and brightness (vertically). The color spectrum bar to the right of the color field shows the hue.

4   In the Color Picker dialog box, drag up and down in the color spectrum bar to change the color range. Make sure that you wind up with the triangles in a purple color—it doesn't have to match the figure exactly.

5   Drag in the color field (where you see the circle in the following figure). As you drag right and left, you adjust the saturation, and as you drag up and down, you adjust the brightness. The color you create when you click OK (don't click yet) appears in the New Color rectangle (an arrow is pointing to it in the figure).

Don't worry about matching the color in the figure yet.

6   In the CMYK fields, change the values to C=**50**, M=**90**, Y=**5**, and K=**0**.

⬤ Note: The Color Swatches button in the Color Picker shows you the swatches in the Swatches panel and the default color books (the sets of swatches that come with Illustrator). It also lets you select a color from one. You can return to the color spectrum by clicking the Color Models button and then editing the swatch color values, if necessary.

7 Click OK, and you should see that the purple color is applied to the fill of the jacket.

8 To save the color as a swatch so you can reuse it, click the Fill box (■) in the Properties panel to show the swatches. Click the New Swatch button (▣) at the bottom of the panel, and change the following options in the New Swatch dialog box:

- Swatch Name: **Purple**
- Global: Selected (the default setting)

9 Click OK to see the color appear as a swatch in the Swatches panel.

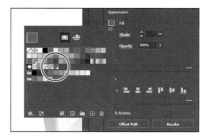

10 Choose Select > Deselect.

11 Choose File > Save.

Using Illustrator swatch libraries

Swatch libraries are collections of preset colors, such as Pantone and TOYO, and thematic libraries, such as Earthtone and Ice Cream. Illustrator has default swatch libraries that appear as separate panels and can't be edited when you open them. When you apply color from a library to artwork, the color becomes a swatch that is saved only in that document and appears in the Swatches panel. Swatch libraries are a great starting point for creating colors.

Next, you'll create a spot color using a Pantone Plus library. Those colors print using spot ink. A *spot ink* is a premixed color (not created by printing tiny dots of CMYK inks). After creating it, you'll apply it to artwork. When color is defined in Illustrator and later printed, the appearance of the color may vary, which is why most printers and designers rely on a color-matching system, like the PANTONE system, to help maintain color consistency and, in some cases, to access a wider range of colors.

● **Note:** Sometimes it's practical to use process (typically CMYK) and spot (PANTONE, for instance) inks in the same job. For example, you might use one spot ink to print the exact color of a company logo on the same pages of an annual report where photographs are reproduced using process color. You can also use a spot-color printing plate to apply a varnish over areas of a process color job. In both cases, your print job would use a total of five inks—four process inks and one spot ink or varnish.

Adding a spot color

In this section, you'll see how to open a color library, such as the PANTONE color system, and add a PANTONE Matching System (PMS) color to the Swatches panel and apply it to the snowboarder artwork.

1   Choose Window > Swatch Libraries > Color Books > PANTONE+ Solid Coated.

The Swatch Libraries option is toward the bottom of the Window menu.

2   In the PANTONE+ Solid Coated library panel, type **7562** in the Find field.

As you type, the list is filtered, showing a smaller and smaller range of swatches.

3   Click the swatch PANTONE 7562 C to add it to the Swatches panel for this document.

4   Click the X to the right of the search field to stop the filtering.

5   Close the PANTONE+ Solid Coated panel.

● **Note:** If you exit Illustrator with the PANTONE library panel still open and then relaunch Illustrator, the panel does not reopen. To automatically open the panel whenever Illustrator opens, choose Persistent from the PANTONE+ Solid Coated panel menu (▤).

6   With the Selection tool (▶), click the darker gray shape covering the mouth of the snowboarder.

7   Click the Fill box (■) in the Properties panel to show the swatches, and select the PANTONE 7562 C swatch to fill the shape.

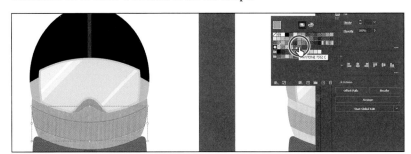

In the Swatches panel, you can identify spot-color swatches by the dot in the lower corner (▨) of the swatch, by default. Process colors do not have a spot-color icon or a dot.

8   Choose Select > Deselect and then choose File > Save.

Creating and saving a tint of a color

A *tint* is a lighter version of a color. You can create a tint from a global process color, like CMYK, or a spot color. Next, you'll create a tint of the Pantone swatch you added to the document.

1   With the Selection tool (▶), click one of the lighter gray shapes above or below the shape you applied the Pantone color to.

2   Click the Fill box in the Properties panel (▣) on the right. Select the PANTONE 7562 C swatch to fill both shapes. Leave the panel open.

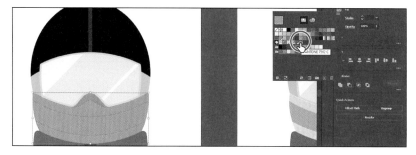

3   Click the Color Mixer button (🎨) at the top of the panel.

In the section "Creating a custom color," you created a custom color using the Color Mixer sliders. In that section, you were creating a custom color from scratch—that's why there were CMYK sliders. Now you'll see a single slider labeled "T" for tint. When using the color mixer for a global swatch, you'll create a tint instead of mixing CMYK values.

4   Drag the tint slider to the left to change the tint value to 60%.

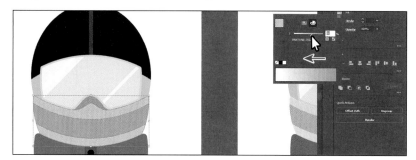

5 Click the Swatches button (▦) at the top of the panel to show the swatches. Click the New Swatch button (▣) at the bottom of the panel to save the tint.

6 Move the pointer over the swatch icon to see its name, which is PANTONE 7562 C 60%.

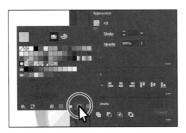 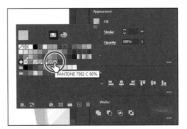

7 Choose Select > Deselect and then choose File > Save.

Converting colors

Illustrator offers commands for selected artwork that allow you to convert colors between color modes—maybe make color artwork grayscale, blend colors, invert colors, and much more. Perhaps you can no longer justify the added cost of adding a spot color. You can convert the spot color to CMYK and get something close to the original result at a lower price. Next, you'll change the snowboarder with the PANTONE 7562 C color applied to use CMYK colors instead of Pantone.

● **Note:** Currently, Convert To RGB in the Edit Color menu is dimmed (you cannot select it). That's because the document color mode is CMYK. To convert the selected content color to RGB using this method, first choose File > Document Color Mode > RGB Color.

1 Choose Select > All On Active Artboard to select all artwork on the artboard, including the shapes with the Pantone color and tint applied.

2 Choose Edit > Edit Colors > Convert To CMYK.

Any colors in the selected shapes that had Pantone applied as a spot color are now composed of CMYK. The swatches in the Swatches panel are no longer applied to the artwork.

3 Choose Select > Deselect.

Copying appearance attributes

Using the Eyedropper tool (✐), you can copy appearance attributes, such as text formatting, fill, and stroke, from one object to another. This can speed up your creative process.

1 Choose View > Fit All In Window.

▷ **Tip:** You can double-click the Eyedropper tool in the toolbar before sampling to change the attributes that the Eyedropper picks up and applies.

2 Using the Selection tool (▶), Shift-click the two light gray shapes on the snowboarder's face on the far right artboard.

3 Select the Eyedropper tool (✐) in the toolbar on the left. Click in the same shapes on the artboarder's face to the left to which you applied the tint. See the following figure.

The once gray shapes now have the attributes from the tint-filled shapes on the left artboard.

4 Select the Selection tool (▶).

5 Choose Select > Deselect and then choose File > Save.

Creating a color group

In Illustrator, you can save colors in color groups, consisting of related color swatches in the Swatches panel. Organizing colors by use, such as grouping all colors for a logo, can improve organization and efficiency, as you'll soon see. In the Swatches panel, there are a few groups by default, indicated by folders. Color groups cannot contain patterns, gradients, the None color, or the Registration color. Registration is a color that is typically composed of 100% of the four process colors: cyan (C), magenta (M), yellow (Y), and black (K), and 100% of any spot color present. Next, you'll create a color group of some of the swatches you've created to keep them organized.

1 Choose Window > Swatches to open the Swatches panel. In the Swatches panel, drag the bottom of the panel down to see more of the content.

2 Click the swatch named "Light Orange" to select it. Pressing the Shift key, click the swatch named "PANTONE 7562 60% C" to select five color swatches.

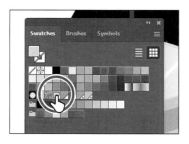

3 Click the New Color Group button (▣) at the bottom of the Swatches panel. Change Name to **Snowboarding** in the New Color Group dialog box, and click OK to save the group.

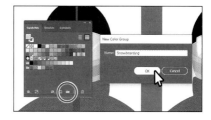

Note: If objects are selected when you click the New Color Group button, an expanded New Color Group dialog box appears. In this dialog box, you can create a color group from the colors in the artwork and convert the colors to global colors.

4 With the Selection tool (►) selected, click a blank area of the Swatches panel to deselect all in the panel.

5 Move the pointer over the folder for the new group to see the name "Snowboarding."

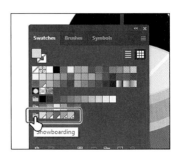

Each swatch in a color group can still be edited independently by double-clicking a swatch in the group and editing the values in the Swatch Options dialog box. You could also edit the colors in the group together by double-clicking the group folder icon.

▶ **Tip:** Aside from dragging colors in or out of a color group, you can rename a color group, reorder the colors in the group, and more.

6 Drag the tint swatch named "PANTONE 7562 C 60%" out of the color group, to the right of the last color swatch in the list. Leave the Swatches panel open.

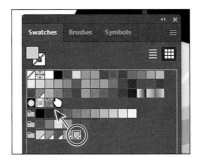 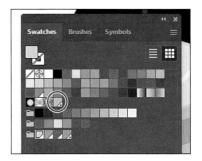

You can drag colors into or out of a color group. When dragging a color into a color group, make sure that you see a blue line appear on the right edge of a swatch within the group. Otherwise, you may drag the swatch to the wrong place. You can always choose Edit > Undo Move Swatches and try again.

Using the Color Guide panel for creative inspiration

The Color Guide panel can provide you with color inspiration as you create your artwork. You can use it to pick color tints, analogous colors, and much more, and then apply them directly to artwork, edit them using several methods, or save them as a group in the Swatches panel.

Next, you'll select a color from some artwork and then use the Color Guide panel to create new colors based on that original color.

1 Choose 3 Snowboarder Color Guide from the Artboard Navigation menu in the lower-left corner of the Document window.

2 With the Selection tool (►), click either green shape on the side of the goggles. Make sure that the Fill box is selected toward the bottom of the toolbar.

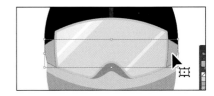

3 Choose Window > Color Guide to open the panel.

4 In the Color Guide panel, click the Set Base Color To The Current Color button (▢) (circled in the figure).

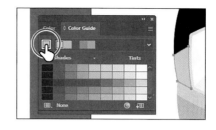

The Color Guide panel suggests colors based on the color showing in the Set Base Color To The Current Color button. The colors you see in the Color Guide panel may differ from what you see in the figure. That's okay.

Next, you'll experiment with colors using harmony rules.

5 Choose Right Complement from the Harmony Rules menu (circled in the first part of the following figure) in the Color Guide panel.

A base group of colors is created to the right of the base color (green), and a series of tints and shades of those colors appears in the body of the panel. There are lots of harmony rules to choose from, each instantly generating a color scheme based on any color you want. The base color you set (green) is the basis for generating the colors in the color scheme.

▶ **Tip:** You can also choose a different color variation (different from the default Tints/Shades), such as Show Warm/Cool or Vivid/Muted, by clicking the Color Guide panel menu icon (▤) and choosing one.

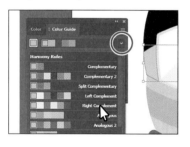
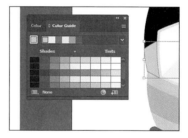

6 Click the Save Color Group To Swatch Panel button (▦) at the bottom of the Color Guide panel to save the base colors (the six colors at the top) in the Swatches panel as a group.

7 Choose Select > Deselect.

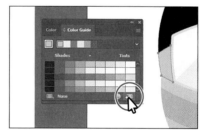

In the Swatches panel you should see the new group added. You may need to scroll down in the panel or drag the bottom of the panel down to make it taller.

8 Close the Swatches panel group.

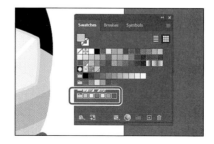

Applying colors from the Color Guide panel

After creating colors with the Color Guide panel, you can either click a color in the Color Guide panel to apply it to selected artwork or apply colors you saved in the Swatches panel as a color group. Next, you'll apply a color from the color group to the snowboarder artwork.

1 Click the purple jacket shape on the current artboard to select it.

2 Click a green color in the Color Guide panel to apply it.

3 Select the center rectangle in the jacket with the black buttons on it. Click to apply a lighter green.

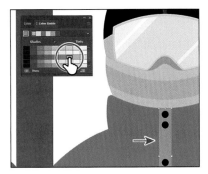

After selecting a color, it becomes the base color. If you were to click the base color (see the figure), *but don't*, then the colors in the panel would be based on that color, using the Right Complement rule you set previously.

4 Close the Color Guide panel.

5 Choose File > Save.

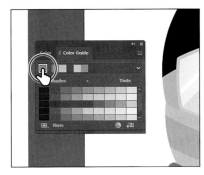

Using Recolor Artwork to edit colors in artwork

You can edit colors in selected artwork using the Recolor Artwork command. It's beneficial when global swatches weren't used in the artwork. Without using global colors in your artwork, updating a series of colors may take a lot of time. Using Recolor Artwork, you can edit colors, change sample colors from other artwork or an image, change the number of colors, map an existing color to a new color, and do much more. Next, you'll open a new document and get it ready.

1 Choose File > Open, and open the L8_start2.ai file in the Lessons > Lesson08 folder to open a new file to work with.

2 Choose File > Save As. If you see the Cloud Document dialog box, click Save On Your Computer (you most likely won't since you already chose it the last time you saved a document).

3 In the Save As dialog box, navigate to the Lesson08 folder, and name the file **Snowboards.ai**. Leave Adobe Illustrator (ai) chosen from the Format menu (macOS) or Adobe Illustrator (*.AI) chosen from the Save As Type menu (Windows), and click Save.

4 In the Illustrator Options dialog box, leave the options at their default settings and then click OK.

5 Choose 1 Snowboard Recolor from the Artboard Navigation menu in the lower-left corner of the Document window to fit the artboard in the window. You should see a brightly colored snowboard on the artboard, along with an image of some fruit and a dinosaur artwork.

Recoloring artwork

With the document open you can now recolor artwork using the Recolor Artwork dialog box.

1 Drag across the snowboard on the left to select the artwork.

2 With the snowboard artwork selected, click the Recolor button in the Properties panel to open the Recolor Artwork dialog box.

▶ **Tip:** You can also choose Edit > Edit Colors > Recolor Artwork.

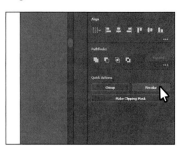

The options in the Recolor Artwork dialog box allow you to edit, sample, or reduce the colors in your *selected* artwork and to save colors you create in groups.

You'll see a big color wheel in the middle of the dialog box. The colors in the selected snowboard artwork are each represented on the color wheel as circles, called *markers*. You can edit the colors individually or together visually by dragging or precisely by double-clicking using specific color values.

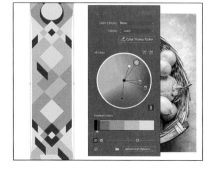

You can choose colors from a color library to change the number of colors in the selected artwork—maybe to make the artwork one single color with tints of that color applied.

3 Make sure that the Link Harmony Colors icon is disabled so you can edit colors independently. The Link Harmony Colors icon should look like this: 🔓, not like this: 🔒. It's circled in the following figure.

The lines between the color markers (circles) and the center of the color wheel are now dotted, telling you that you can edit them independently. If the Link Harmony Colors option were on and you edited one of the colors, the rest would change relative to your edited color.

4 Drag the largest orange marker (circle) into the green area to change the color.

 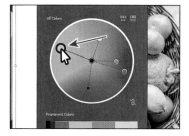

Know that if you make a mistake when editing the colors and want to start over, you can click the Reset button in the upper-right corner of the dialog box to reset the colors to their original values.

5 Double-click the now green marker (circle) to open the Color Picker. Change the color to something else, like a blue. Click OK.

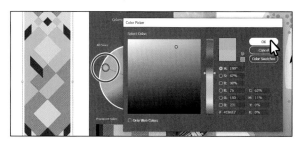

After clicking OK, notice that the marker has moved in the color wheel, and it's the only one that moved. That's because you unlinked the harmony colors before you started editing the color.

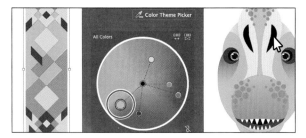

Sampling color

Next, you'll see how to sample color from an image and vector artwork to apply that color to the snowboard.

1   Click the Color Theme Picker button in the dialog box. The pointer becomes an eyedropper (🖋) that you can then click to sample color from a single raster image or vector art, for instance. You may want to drag the dialog box by the top so you can see the image of fruit and the dinosaur. Click in the image of the fruit to sample the colors from the entire image and apply them to the snowboard.

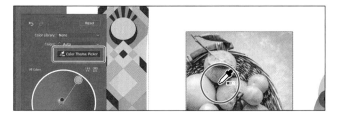

2   Click the dinosaur artwork to the right of the fruit image to sample the colors and apply it to the snowboard.

If you click a single vector object, like a shape, the color is sampled from that single object. If you click a group of objects, like the dinosaur head, the color is sampled from all of the objects within the group. With vector artwork that you sample color from, you can also select part of the artwork to sample color from. You don't need to switch tools; simply drag a selection around to sample color within the selected area.

3   Drag around a smaller area of the dinosaur artwork to sample just those colors within the selection.

Depending on what color objects were within the selection area, your dinosaur may look different, and that's okay.

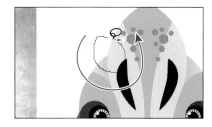

To ensure that we all see the same colors in the snowboard art going forward, next you'll click to sample the color from the dinosaur again.

4 Click the dinosaur artwork to the right of the fruit image again to sample the colors and apply it to the snowboard.

5 Click the Show Saturation And Hue On Color Wheel button toward the bottom to see brightness and hue on the color wheel (circled in the following figure).

6 Drag the slider to the right to adjust the overall saturation. When you release, the colors will change.

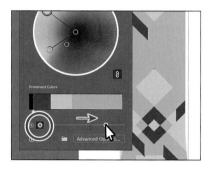

The colors in the snowboard artwork are represented on the color wheel, but they are also shown in the Prominent Colors section below the color wheel. The size of the color areas in that bar is meant to give you an idea of how much area each color occupies in the artwork. In this case, the aqua color is more prominent, so it shows as larger in the Prominent Colors section.

 **Tip:** Prominent colors are colors that are more prominent in the artwork and are categorized based on the hue and shade of the color.

7 In the Prominent Colors section of the dialog box, move the pointer between the green color and the aqua color and a slider appears between them. Drag that slider to the right to make it wider. That means more of that color will be applied to the artwork as tints and shades.

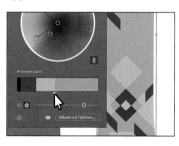

As a last step, you'll save the colors as a group in the Swatches panel.

8 Click the folder icon (📁) at the bottom of the panel and choose Save Prominent Colors to save the prominent colors as a group in the Swatches panel.

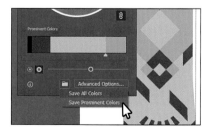

If the Swatches panel opens, you can close it.

9 Choose Select > Deselect and then choose File > Save.

Working with Live Paint

Live Paint lets you paint vector graphics intuitively by automatically detecting and correcting gaps that might otherwise affect the application of fills and strokes. Paths divide the drawing surface into areas that can be colored, whether the area is bounded by a single path or by segments of multiple paths. Painting objects with Live Paint is like coloring in a coloring book or using watercolors to paint a sketch. The underlying shapes are not edited.

Note: To learn more about Live Paint and all that it can do, search for "Live Paint groups" in Illustrator Help (Help > Illustrator Help).

Creating a Live Paint group

To start, you'll make a change to snowboard artwork, and then turn it into a Live Paint group so you can edit the colors using the Live Paint Bucket tool ( ) .

1   Choose 2 Snowboard Live Paint from the Artboard Navigation menu in the lower-left corner of the Document window.

    You'll work on the snowboard on the left—trying to match the snowboard on the right. You'll start by copying a few shapes so you can color parts of the snowboard with different colors using Live Paint.

2   With the Selection tool selected, click one of the two dark blue diamonds in the snowboard on the left. Shift-click the other dark blue diamond to select both.

3   Select the Rotate tool ( ) in the toolbar and Option-click (macOS) or Alt-click (Windows) the bottom point of the selected shapes, in the middle of the small orange triangle. The word "intersect" will most likely show. In the Rotate dialog box, change the Angle to **180** and click Copy.

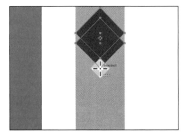 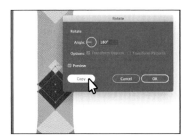 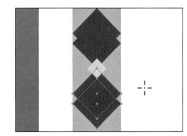

4   Select the Selection tool ( ), and drag across all of the snowboard artwork on the left to select it.

5   Choose Object > Live Paint > Make.

    The whole snowboard is now a Live Paint object. You can now see the points on the bounding box have changed ( ). One of them is circled in the figure.

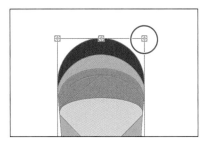

Tip: You can convert selected artwork to a Live Paint group by clicking on it with the Live Paint Bucket tool selected. You'll explore the Live Paint Bucket tool next.

Painting with the Live Paint Bucket tool

With objects converted to a Live Paint group, you can paint them with the Live Paint Bucket tool using several methods, which is what you'll do next.

● **Note:** You may want to press the Escape key to hide the extra tools menu.

1 Click Edit Toolbar ( ) at the bottom of the toolbar. Scroll in the menu that appears, and drag the Live Paint Bucket tool ( ) into the toolbar on the left to add it to the list of tools. Make sure it's selected in the toolbar.

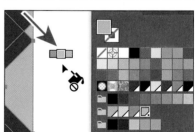

● **Note:** You may want to drag the bottom of the Swatches panel down to see more colors.

2 Open the Swatches panel by choosing Window > Swatches.

You don't have to have the Swatches panel open when working with the Live Paint Bucket tool. You can just select a color from the Fill color box in the Properties panel. It helps to have the Swatches panel open, so you can understand how color selection works with the tool.

3 Select the light green color in one of the swatch groups, as you see in the figure.

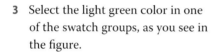

4 Move the pointer into an empty area of the artboard to see the three swatches above the pointer.

The three colors above the pointer represent the selected color (the middle, light green color), the color before it in the color group (the pink/red), and the color after it in the group (the orange).

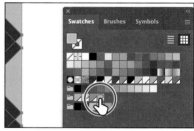

5 Click to apply the color to the area shown in the figure.

You just filled a *face*, which is an enclosed area. The color fills the area you click up to the path edges it finds.

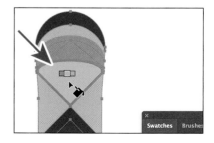

6 Click to apply the color to the area shown in the figure.

You can select another color to paint with from the Swatches panel or you can work faster and switch to another color using the arrow keys.

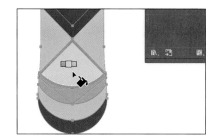

7 Press the Right Arrow key once to select the orange swatch, shown in the three swatches above the pointer.

8 Press the Right arrow key once more to select the lighter orange color in the Swatches panel group.

9 Click to apply the color to the area shown in the figure.

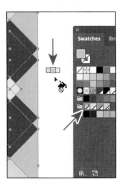
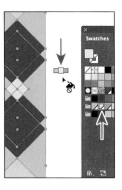

10 Click to apply the same color to the area shown in the figure.

11 Close the Swatches panel.

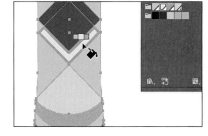

12 Choose Select > Deselect and then choose File > Save.

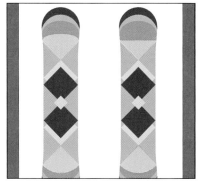

Modifying a Live Paint group

When you make a Live Paint group, each path remains editable. When you move or adjust a path, the colors that were previously applied don't just stay where they were, as they do in natural media paintings or with image-editing software. Instead, the colors are automatically reapplied to the new regions that are formed by the intersecting paths. Next you'll edit a path in the same Live Paint group.

1   Select the Selection tool (▶). Double-click the snowboard on the left to enter Isolation mode.

  A Live Paint group is similar to a regular grouped object. The individual objects in the artwork are still accessible when you double-click to enter Isolation mode. When you enter Isolation mode, you can move, transform, add, or remove shapes as well.

2   Select the Direct Selection tool (▷).

3   Move the pointer over the path between the dark pink and light green at the top of the artboard. See the first part of the following figure.

4   Click the path. When the pointer changes (▶．), drag the path down.

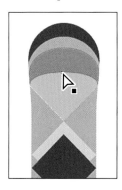  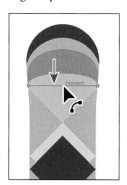

5   Press the Escape key to exit Isolation mode.

6   Choose Select > Deselect.

7   Choose View > Fit Artboard In Window.

8   Choose File > Save and then choose File > Close as many times as necessary to close all open files.

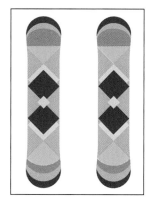

Review questions

1 Describe what a global color is.

2 How can you save a color?

3 Describe what a tint is.

4 How can you choose color harmonies for color inspiration?

5 Name two things that the Recolor Artwork dialog box allows you to do.

6 Explain what Live Paint allows you to do.

Review answers

1 A global color is a color swatch that, when you edit it, automatically updates all artwork to which it is applied. All spot colors are global; however, process colors you save as swatches are global by default, but they can be either global or non-global.

2 You can save a color for painting other objects in your artwork by adding it to the Swatches panel by doing one of the following:

- Drag the color from a Fill box, and drop it over the Swatches panel.
- Click the New Swatch button (■) at the bottom of the Swatches panel.
- Choose New Swatch from the Swatches panel menu (☰).
- Choose Create New Swatch from the Color panel menu (☰).

3 A *tint* is a lighter version of a color. You can create a tint from a global process color, like CMYK, or from a spot color.

4 You can choose color harmonies from the Color Guide panel. Color harmonies are used to generate a color scheme based on a single color.

5 You use the Recolor Artwork dialog box to change the colors used in selected artwork, create and edit color groups, or reassign or reduce the colors in your artwork, among other functions.

6 Live Paint lets you paint vector graphics intuitively by automatically detecting and correcting gaps that might otherwise affect the application of fills and strokes. Paths divide the drawing surface into areas, any of which can be colored, regardless of whether the area is bounded by a single path or by segments of multiple paths.

9 ADDING TYPE TO A PROJECT

Lesson overview

In this lesson, you'll learn how to do the following:

- Create and edit area and point type.
- Import text.
- Change text formatting.
- Fix missing fonts. ■◢
- Work with glyphs. ■◢
- Vertically align area type.
- Snap to glyphs. ■◢
- Create columns of text.
- Create and edit paragraph and character styles.
- Wrap type around an object.
- Reshape text with a warp.
- Curve text on a path.
- Create text outlines.

This lesson will take about 75 minutes to complete. To get the lesson files used in this chapter, download them from the web page for this book at adobepress.com/IllustratorCIB2022. For more information, see "Accessing the lesson files and Web Edition" in the Getting Started section at the beginning of this book.

Text is an important design element in your illustrations. Like other objects, type can be painted, scaled, rotated, and more. In this lesson, you'll create basic text and add interesting text effects.

Starting the lesson

You'll be adding type to two recipe cards during this lesson, but before you begin, you'll restore the default preferences for Adobe Illustrator. Then you'll open the finished art file for this lesson to see the illustration.

Note: If you have not already downloaded the project files for this lesson to your computer from your Account page, make sure to do so now. See the "Getting Started" section at the beginning of the book.

1   To ensure that the tools function and the defaults are set exactly as described in this lesson, delete or deactivate (by renaming) the Adobe Illustrator preferences file. See "Restoring default preferences" in the "Getting Started" section at the beginning of the book.

2   Start Adobe Illustrator.

3   Choose File > Open. Locate the file named L9_end.ai in the Lessons > Lesson09 folder. Click Open.

You will most likely see a Missing Fonts dialog box since the file is using specific Adobe fonts. Simply click Close in the Missing Fonts dialog box. You will learn all about Adobe fonts later in this lesson.

Leave the file open for reference later in the lesson, if you like. I closed it.

4   Choose File > Open. In the Open dialog box, navigate to the Lessons > Lesson09 folder, and select the L9_start.ai file on your hard disk. Click Open to open the file.

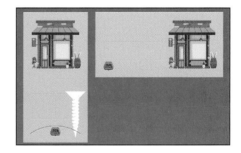

You'll add text and formatting to complete the social media ads.

5   Choose File > Save As. If the Cloud Document dialog box opens, click Save On Your Computer.

6   In the Save As dialog box, navigate to the Lesson09 folder, and name the file **HardwareStore_ads.ai**. Leave Adobe Illustrator (ai) chosen from the Format menu (macOS) or Adobe Illustrator (*.AI) chosen from the Save As Type menu (Windows), and click Save.

7   In the Illustrator Options dialog box, leave the Illustrator options at their default settings, and then click OK.

Note: If you don't see Reset Essentials in the Workspace menu, choose Window > Workspace > Essentials before choosing Window > Workspace > Reset Essentials.

8   Choose Window > Workspace > Reset Essentials.

Adding text

Type features are some of the most powerful in Illustrator. As in Adobe InDesign, you can create columns and rows of text, place text, flow text into a shape or along a path, work with letterforms as graphic objects, and more.

In Illustrator, you can create text in three main ways:

- Point type
- Area type
- Type on a path

Adding text at a point

Point type is a horizontal or vertical line of text that begins where you click and expands as you enter characters. Each line of text is independent—the line expands or shrinks as you edit it but doesn't form multiple lines unless you add a paragraph return or a soft return. Entering text this way is perfect for small amounts of text like a headline or text on a button. Next, you'll add some heading text using point type.

1 Choose 1 Vertical Ad from the Artboard Navigation menu below the document, if not selected. Then choose View > Fit Artboard In Window.

You will add some text below the building illustration, like you see in the figure.

2 Select the Type tool (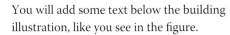) in the toolbar on the left. Click (don't drag) below the building, as you see in the previous figure. Type **RJ Hardware**.

 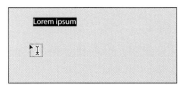 

The "Lorem ipsum" text you saw is just placeholder text that you can replace.

3 Select the Selection tool (▶), and Shift-drag the lower-right bounding point to make the text much larger.

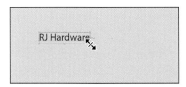 

If you scale point type without the Shift key held down, the text stretches when you drag any bounding point.

4 Practice by selecting the Type tool again and clicking to add more text. Type **Making your home beautiful**.

5 Select the Selection tool. Shift-drag a corner to make it as large as the other text you made.

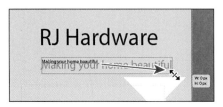

As you go through this chapter, you will refine the appearance of this text and get it into place.

Adding area type

Area type uses the edges of an object, like a rectangle, to control how text flows either horizontally or vertically. When text reaches an edge, it automatically wraps to fit inside the object. Entering text in this way is useful when you want to create one or more paragraphs, such as for a poster or a brochure.

Making your home beautiful.

Text flowing within a frame.

To create area type with the Type tool (**T**), you drag where you want the text— which creates an area type object (also called a *type object, text box, text area,* or *text object*). Next, you'll create some area type and add a heading to the ad.

1 Choose 2 Horizontal ad from the Artboard Navigation menu below the document.

2 With the Type tool (**T**) selected, move the pointer into the aqua box. Press and drag to create a small type object that is about 100 pixels in width and 100 pixels in height.

▶ **Tip:** Filling type objects with placeholder text is a preference you can change. Choose Illustrator > Preferences (macOS) or Edit > Preferences (Windows), select the Type category, and deselect Fill New Type Objects With Placeholder Text to turn the option off.

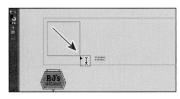 

By default, area type objects are filled with selected placeholder text that you can replace with your own.

3 Choose View > Zoom In a few times to zoom in.

4 With the placeholder text selected, type **Your local home repair specialists**. *(Without the period!)*

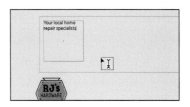

Notice how the text wraps horizontally to fit within the type object.

5 Select the Selection tool (▶), and drag the lower-right bounding point to the left and then back to the right to see how the text wraps within but doesn't resize.

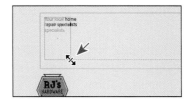

You can drag any of the eight bounding points on the type object to resize it.

6 Drag the same point to make the type object shorter so that you still see all of the text and it wraps as you see in the figure.

7 Double-click on the text to switch to the Type tool.

8 Put the cursor before the word "repair" and press Shift+Return or Shift+Enter to break the line using a soft return.

Soft returns keep the lines of text a single paragraph rather than breaking it into two. Later, when you apply paragraph formatting, this can make applying the formatting easier.

9 Select the Selection tool, and drag the text above the aqua box.

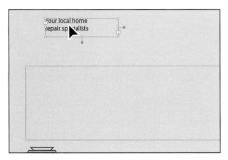

Converting between area type and point type

You can easily convert a text object from area type to point type and vice versa. This can be useful if you type a headline by clicking, which creates point type, but later want to resize and add more text without stretching the text inside.

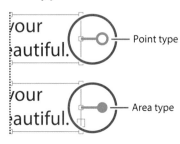
Point type

Area type

Next, you will convert a type object from point type to area type.

1 With the Type tool (**T**) selected, to the right of the RJ's Hardware logo in the lower-left of the same artboard, click to add some point type.

2 Type:
215 Grand Street · Hometown USA 555-555-5555.

> **Tip:** To add a bullet, place the cursor where you want the bullet, and then choose Type > Insert Special Character > Symbols > Bullet.

Notice that the text keeps going. We need to have the text wrap in different ways, so area type might be a better choice in this case.

3 Press the Escape key to select the Selection tool (▶).

> **Tip:** With a type object selected, you can also choose Type > Convert To Point Type or Convert To Area Type, depending on what the selected type object is.

4 Move the pointer over the annotator (—○) off the right edge of the type object. A hollow end on the annotator means it's point type. When the pointer changes (▶), double-click the annotator to convert the point type to area type.

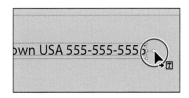
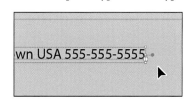

The annotator end should now be filled (—●), indicating that it is area type.

5 Drag the lower-right bounding point to wrap the text within until it looks like the figure.

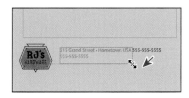

Area type auto sizing ▰◣

To learn about setting auto-resize on text objects, check out the video *Area type auto sizing*, which you'll find in the Web Edition. For more information, see the "Web Edition" section of "Getting Started" at the beginning of the book.

Importing a plain-text file

You can import text into your Illustrator document from a text file created in another application. One of the advantages of importing text from a file, rather than copying and pasting it, is that imported text retains its character and paragraph formatting (by default). For example, text from an RTF file retains its font and style specifications in Illustrator, unless you remove formatting when you import the text.

Note: To learn more about the types of text documents you can import, visit https://helpx.adobe.com/illustrator/using/importing-exporting-text.html.

In this section, you'll place text from a plain-text file into your design to get the bulk of the text for the ads in place.

1   Choose 1 Vertical Ad from the Artboard Navigation menu below the Document window to switch to the other ad.

2   Choose Select > Deselect.

3   Choose File > Place. In the Place dialog box, navigate to the Lessons > Lesson09 folder, and select the L9_text.txt file.

4   Click Place.

    In the Text Import Options dialog box that appears, you can set some options prior to importing text.

5   Leave the default settings, and click OK.

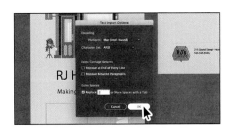

6   Move the loaded text icon into the lower-left part of the artboard, in the aqua box. Drag from the upper-left corner to make a text box. Use the figure as a guide.

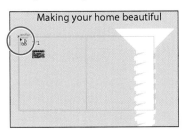
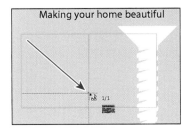
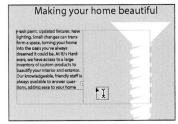

If you were to simply click with the loaded text pointer, a type object would be created that is smaller than the size of the artboard.

7   Choose File > Save.

Threading text

When working with area type, each area type object has an in port and an out port. Those ports enable you to link type objects and flow text between them.

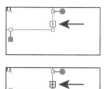

In port ── 123 Some Street / Hometown

Out port

- An empty out port indicates that all the text is visible and that the type object isn't linked.

- An arrow in a port indicates that the type object is linked to another type object.

- A red plus sign (⊞) in an out port indicates that the object contains additional text called *overflow text*. You can adjust the text, resize the type object, or thread the text to another type object to show all of the overflow text.

To *thread* or continue text from one object to the next, you have to link the objects. Linked type objects can be of any shape; however, the text must be entered in an object or along a path, not as point type (simply clicking to create text).

Next, you'll thread text between two type objects.

1   Choose View > Fit All In Window.

Note: If you double-click an out port, a new type object appears. If this happens, you can either drag the new object where you would like it to be positioned or choose Edit > Undo Link Threaded Text, and the loaded text icon will reappear.

2   With the Selection tool (▶) selected, click the out port (⊞) in the lower-right corner of the type object. Move the pointer away.

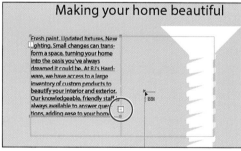

The pointer changes to a loaded text icon (⸬) when you move it away from the original type object.

3   Move the pointer to the upper-left corner of the aqua box on the horizontal ad to the right. Drag across the aqua box to make an area type object. Use the figure as a guide.

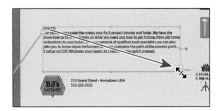

With the second type object still selected, notice the line connecting the two type objects (an arrow is pointing to it in the previous figure). This (non-printing) line is the *text thread* that tells you that the two objects are connected. If you don't see this thread (line), choose View > Show Text Threads.

The out port (▶) of the top type object on the artboard and the in port (▶) of the bottom type object on the artboard contain small arrows indicating how the text is flowing from one to the other.

▶ **Tip:** Another way to thread text between objects is to select an area type object, select the object (or objects) you want to link to, and then choose Type > Threaded Text > Create.

4   Click in the first threaded type object on the left.

5   Drag the right-middle point to the right to make it as wide as you see in the figure. Drag the bottom of that text object up until some of the text flows into the text area on the right. Leave the text selected.

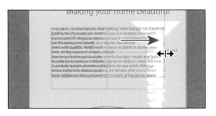
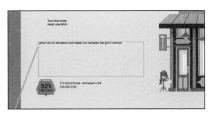

The text will flow between the type objects. If you delete the second type object, the text is pulled back into the original object as overflow text. Although not visible, the overflow text isn't deleted.

After resizing your text area, you may see more or less text in your text area on the right side artboard than you see in the second part of the previous figure, and that's okay.

Formatting type

You can format text in a lot of creative ways. You can apply formatting to one character, a range of characters, or all characters. As you'll soon see, selecting the type object, rather than selecting the text inside, lets you apply formatting options to all of the text in the object, including options from the Character and Paragraph panels, fill and stroke attributes, and transparency settings.

In this section, you'll discover how to change text attributes, such as size and font, and later learn how to save that formatting as text styles.

Changing font family and font style

In this section, you'll apply a font to text. In addition to local fonts, Creative Cloud members have access to a library of fonts for use in desktop applications such as InDesign or Microsoft Word and on websites. Trial Creative Cloud members can also access select fonts from Adobe. Fonts you choose are activated and appear alongside other locally installed fonts in the fonts list in Illustrator. By default, Adobe fonts are turned on in the Creative Cloud desktop application to activate fonts and make them available in your desktop applications.

> ● **Note:** The Creative Cloud desktop application must be installed on your computer, and you must have an Internet connection to initially activate fonts. The Creative Cloud desktop application is installed when you install your first Creative Cloud application, like Illustrator.

Activating Adobe Fonts

Next, you'll select and activate Adobe fonts so that you can use them in your project.

> ● **Note:** To learn about the Creative Cloud desktop application, visit www.adobe.com/creativecloud/desktop-app.html.

1   Ensure that the Creative Cloud desktop application has been launched and you are signed in with your Adobe ID (*this requires an internet connection*).

2   Select the Type tool (**T**), move the pointer over the text in the threaded type object on the left, and click to insert the cursor.

3   Choose Select > All or press Command+A (macOS) or Ctrl+A (Windows) to select all of the text in both threaded type objects.

4 In the Properties panel, click the arrow to the right of the Font Family menu, and notice the fonts that appear in the menu.

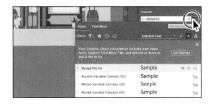

The fonts you see by default are those that are installed locally. In the font menu, an icon appears to the right of the font names in the list, indicating what type of font it is ($\bigcirc$ is an activated Adobe font, O is OpenType, $\sf{\textit{f}}$ is a variable font, $\sf{\textit{f}}$ is an SVG font, $\mathbf{T}\!\!\!T$ is TrueType, and $\boldsymbol{a}$ is Adobe Postscript).

5 Click Find More to see a list of Adobe fonts you can choose from.

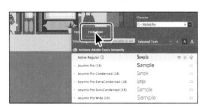

The menu content may take a few seconds to initialize. My list will look different from yours since Adobe is constantly updating the font selections.

6 Click the Filter Fonts icon ($\blacktriangledown$) to open a menu. You can filter the font list by selecting classification and property criteria. Click the Sans Serif option under Classification to filter the fonts.

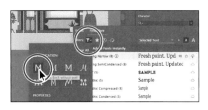

7 Scroll down in the font list to find Rajdhani. Click the arrow to the left of Rajdhani, if necessary, to see the font styles.

Tip: The fonts are activated on all computers where you've installed the Creative Cloud application and logged in. To view fonts you've activated, open the Creative Cloud desktop application and click the Fonts icon (f) in the upper right.

8 Click the Activate icon ($\bigcirc$) to the far right of the name "Rajdhani SemiBold."

If you see $\bigcirc$, or when the pointer is over the font name in the list, $\bigcirc\!\!\!x$, then the font is already activated, so you don't need to do anything.

9 Click OK in the dialog box that appears.

10 Click the Activate button ($\bigcirc$) to the far right of the name "Rajdhani Bold." Click OK in the dialog box that appears.

Once the fonts are activated (be patient; it may take some time), you may begin to use them.

11 After activating the fonts, click the words "Clear All" toward the top of the menu to remove the Sans Serif filtering and see all of the fonts again.

Applying fonts to text in Illustrator

Now that the Adobe fonts are activated, you can use them in any application. That's what you'll do next.

1 With the threaded text still selected and the Font Family menu still showing, click the Show Activated Fonts button () to filter the font list and show only activated Adobe fonts.

The list in the figure may be different than yours, and that's okay as long as you see the Rajdhani fonts.

2 Move the pointer over the fonts in the menu. You should see a preview of the font the pointer is over, which is applied to the selected text. Click the arrow to the left of Rajdhani in the menu, and choose SemiBold (or simply choose Rajdhani SemiBold).

3 With the Selection tool (▶) selected, click the "RJ Hardware..." text and Shift-click the "Making your home beautiful" and "Your local home repair specialists" text to select all three.

If you want to apply the same font to all of the text in a point type or area type object, you can simply select the object, not the text, and then apply the font.

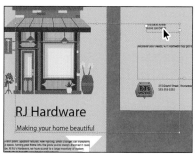

4 With the type object selected, click the font name in the Properties panel (I see Myriad Pro). Begin typing the letters **raj** (you may need to type more of the word "Rajdhani").

⯈ **Tip:** With the cursor in the Font Name field, you can also click the X on the right side of the Font Family field to clear the search field.

A menu appears beneath where you are typing. Illustrator filters through the list of fonts and displays the font names that contain "rajd," regardless of where "rajd" is in the font name and regardless of whether it's capitalized. The Show Activated Fonts () filter is still turned on from before, so you'll turn it off next.

5 Click Clear Filter (◌) in the menu that is showing to see all of the available fonts.

6 In the menu that appears beneath where you are typing, move the pointer over the fonts in the list (my list will be different from yours because of the other fonts I already had activated). Illustrator shows a live font preview of the text.

7 Click to select Rajdhani Bold to apply the font.

8 Click the 215 Grand Street • Hometown, USA... text on the horizontal ad.

9 Click the font name in the Properties panel and type the letters **raj** (for Rajdhani). Select the Rajdhani SemiBold font to apply it.

Fixing missing fonts ▰◀

To learn how to fix missing fonts, check out the video *Fixing Missing Fonts,* which is part of the Web Edition. For more information, see the "Web Edition" section of "Getting Started" at the beginning of the book.

Changing font size

By default, typeface size is measured in points (a point equals 1/72 of an inch). In this section, you will change the font size of text and also see what happens to point type that is scaled.

1 With the Selection tool, click to select the "RJ Hardware" heading on the artboard on the left.

Looking in the Character section of the Properties panel, you'll see that the font size may not be a whole number. That's because you scaled the point type earlier by dragging.

2 Choose 60 pt from the Font Size menu in the Properties panel.

3 Click the "Making your home beautiful" text to select the text object.

4 Choose 24 pt from the Font Size menu.

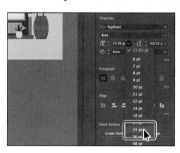

5 The font size is a little small, so click the up arrow until the text is 30 pt.

6. Click in the "Your local home repair specialists" text on the artboard on the right and practice by changing the font size to 54 pt.

   Instead of clicking the arrow next to the font size field, you can also select the value and type in **54**. Press Return or Enter to accept.

7. If the text disappears, it's too big to fit in the text box. Drag a corner until you can see the text, and then drag it above the aqua box.

Changing the color of the text

You can change the appearance of text by applying fills, strokes, and more. In this section, you'll change the fill of selected text by selecting type objects. Know that you can also select text with the Type tool to apply different color fills and strokes to text.

1. With the text "Your local home repair specialists" selected, Shift-click the "Making your home beautiful" text.

2. Click the Fill color box in the Properties panel. With the Swatches option (⊞) selected in the panel that appears, select the white swatch.

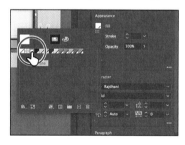

3. Click the text "RJ Hardware." Click the Fill color box in the Properties panel. Select the dark gray swatch.

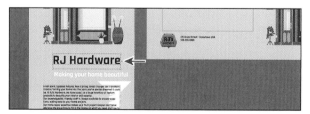

4. Choose Select > Deselect, and then choose File > Save.

Changing additional character formatting

In Illustrator, you can change a lot of text formatting besides font, font size, and color. As in InDesign, text attributes are split between character and paragraph formatting and can be found in the Properties panel, the Control panel, and two main panels: the Character panel and the Paragraph panel.

The Character panel, which you can access by clicking More Options (●●●) in the Character section of the Properties panel or by choosing Window > Type > Character, contains the formatting for selected text such as font, font size, kerning, and more. In this section, you will apply a few of the many possible attributes to experiment with the different ways you can format text.

Tip: By default, text is set to a value called Auto for leading. When looking at the Leading value in the Properties panel, you can tell it's set to Auto if the value has parentheses around it, (). To return the leading to the default auto value, choose Auto from the Leading menu.

1 With the Selection tool (▶) selected, click the "Your local home repair specialists" text.

2 In the Properties panel, change Leading (🔡) to 54 pt by selecting the value and typing **54** (or you can change to a similar value that looks good). Press Return or Enter to accept the value. Leave the text selected.

Leading is the vertical space between lines of text. Adjusting the leading can be useful for fitting text into a type object. Now, you'll make all of the headings capital letters.

3 Shift-click the "RJ Hardware" and "Making your home beautiful" text to select all.

4 With the text selected, click More Options (●●●) (circled in the following figure) in the Character section of the Properties panel to show the Character panel. Click the All Caps button (🇹🇹) to capitalize the headings.

If part of the heading "YOUR LOCAL HOME REPAIR SPECIALISTS" on the artboard on the right disappears, it's because it doesn't fit in the type area. With the Selection tool, drag a corner of the box to show all of the text.

One of the benefits of point type versus area type is that no matter what formatting you throw at point type text, the box around it will always resize to show the text.

Changing paragraph formatting

As with character formatting, you can set paragraph formatting, such as alignment or indenting, before adding new text or changing existing text appearance. Paragraph formatting applies to entire paragraphs rather than just selected content and can be found in the Properties panel, Control panel, or Paragraph panel.

You can access the Paragraph panel options by clicking More Options (••••) in the Paragraph section of the Properties panel or choosing Window > Type > Paragraph.

1   With the Type tool (**T**) selected, click in the threaded text in the artboard on the left.

2   Press Command+A (macOS) or Ctrl+A (Windows) to select all of the text between the two type objects.

3 With the text selected, click More Options (![icon]) in the Paragraph section of the Properties panel to show the Paragraph panel options.

4 Change Space After Paragraph (![icon]) to **9 pt** in the Paragraph panel.

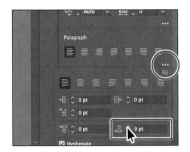 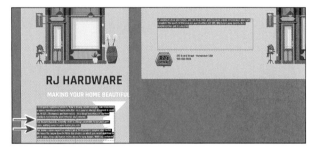

Setting a spacing value after paragraphs, rather than pressing the Enter or Return key, helps you maintain consistency and makes editing easier.

5 Select the Selection tool, and click the "Your local home repair specialists" text on the ad on the right to select it.

6 To align the text to center, click Align Center in the Paragraph section of the Properties panel.

7 Choose Select > Deselect, and then choose File > Save.

Working with glyphs ![icon]

To learn about working with the Glyphs panel, check out the video *Working with the Glyphs Panel*, which you'll find in the Web Edition. For more information, see the "Web Edition" section of "Getting Started" at the beginning of the book.

Vertically aligning area type

You can align or distribute lines of text in a frame vertically or horizontally when using vertical type. You can align text to the frame's top, center, or bottom using each paragraph's leading and paragraph spacing values. You can also justify text vertically, evenly spacing lines regardless of their leading and paragraph spacing values. Here are the different types of vertical alignment you can apply to text:

Align top   Align center   Align bottom   Vertically Justify

Next, you'll vertically align one of the headings to more easily set the spacing between it and the paragraph of text.

1   Select the Selection tool (▶) and click the heading, "YOUR LOCAL HOME REPAIR SPECIALISTS."

2   In the Area Type section of the Properties panel, click Align Bottom to align the text to the bottom of the text area.

● **Note:** You can also access the vertical text align options in the Area Type Options dialog box (Type > Area Type Options).

3   Drag the text area so it looks like the figure.

Using glyph snapping ◼️

To learn about glyph snapping, check out the video *Working with glyph snapping*, which you'll find in the Web Edition. For more information, see the "Web Edition" section of "Getting Started" at the beginning of the book.

Resizing and reshaping type objects

You can create unique type object shapes by reshaping them using a variety of methods, including adding columns to area type objects or reshaping type objects using the Direct Selection tool. To start this section, you'll place some more text on artboard 1 so you have more text to work with.

Creating columns of text

You can easily create columns and rows of text by using the Type > Area Type Options command. This can be useful for creating a single type object with multiple columns or for organizing text, such as a table or simple chart, for instance. Next, you'll add a few columns to a type object.

> Our home repair expertise makes your fix-it project simpler and faster. From old home restorations to new builds, we have the know-how to fill in the blanks on what you need and how to get it done. With our network of qualified specialists, we can also refer you to home repair technicians who can complete the parts of the process you'd rather not DIY.

Area type in columns

▶ **Tip:** You will also see the Vertical option for vertically aligning text that you explored earlier in the lesson.

1   With the Selection tool (▶) selected, click the paragraph of text in the horizontal ad (the artboard on the right).

2   Choose Type > Area Type Options. In the Area Type Options dialog box, change Number to **2** in the Columns section, and the Gutter to **14 px**. Select Preview to see the change, and then click OK.

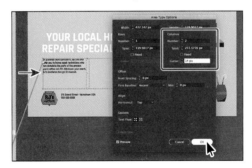

The text box is not split into two columns. There most likely isn't enough text to fill the second column. You'll fix that later.

● **Note:** You may see more or less text in your text area than in the figure, and that's okay.

3   If necessary, drag the bottom-middle bounding point down so the area type object is the size of the aqua box on the artboard.

Reshaping type objects

In this section, you'll reshape and resize a type object to better fit text.

1   With the Selection tool (▶), click the text object with the "215 Grand Street…" text.

2   Press Command and + (macOS) or Ctrl and + (Windows) several times to zoom in to the text.

3   Select the Direct Selection tool (▷). Click and release on the lower-left corner of the type object to select the anchor point.

4   Drag that point to the right to adjust the shape of the path so the text follows the contour of the RJ's Hardware logo.

5   Select the Selection tool, and drag the text closer to the logo, if necessary.

Sampling text formatting

Using the Eyedropper tool (🖊), you can quickly sample type attributes from text and apply those attributes to other text.

1   Choose 1 Vertical Ad from the Artboard Navigation menu below the Document window to switch to the other ad.

2   Select the Type tool (T) in the toolbar. At the bottom of the artboard, above the curved black line, click and type **FAMILY-OWNED SINCE 1918**.

3   Press the Escape key to select the text object and Selection tool.

Note: Your text may be a different size than the figure. That's okay because you're about to change it!

4 To sample and apply formatting from other text, select the Eyedropper tool (✐) in the toolbar, and click one of the letters in the "MAKING YOUR HOME BEAUTIFUL" text to apply the same formatting to the selected text.

5 Choose Select > Deselect and then File > Save.

Creating and applying text styles

Text styles allow you to save text formatting to apply it consistently and to be updated globally. Once a style is created, you only need to edit the saved style, and then all text formatted with that style is updated. Illustrator has two types of text styles.

- **Paragraph**—Retains character and paragraph attributes and applies them to an entire paragraph.
- **Character**—Retains character attributes and applies them to selected text.

Creating and applying a paragraph style

You'll start by creating a paragraph style for the body copy.

1 Select the Selection tool (▶). On the artboard on the left, double-click in the paragraphs of threaded text to switch to the Type tool and insert the cursor.

2 Choose Window > Type > Paragraph Styles, and click the Create New Style button (▣) at the bottom of the Paragraph Styles panel.

A new paragraph style appears in the panel and is called "Paragraph Style 1." To create a paragraph style from text, you don't have to select the text. You can insert the cursor in the text when making a paragraph style. The text formatting attributes are saved from the paragraph that the cursor is in.

3 Double-click directly on the style name "Paragraph Style 1" in the list of styles. Change the name of the style to **Body**, and press Return or Enter to confirm the name inline.

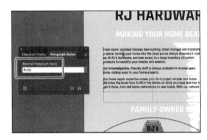

By double-clicking the style to edit the name, you apply the new style to the paragraph (where the cursor is). This means that if you edit the formatting for the Body paragraph style, only this paragraph will update.

Now you'll apply the style to all of the text in the threaded frames.

4 With the cursor in the paragraph text, choose Select > All to select it all.

5 Click the Body style in the Paragraph Styles panel to apply the formatting.

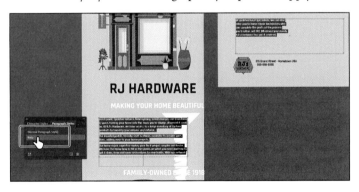

Practicing paragraph styles

With one paragraph style made, you'll practice by creating another for a few of the headlines in the document.

1 Choose Select > Deselect.

2 Select the Selection tool (▶), and click the text "215 Grand Street" in the horizontal ad on the right.

3 In the Properties panel, click the Fill color, and select the dark green swatch.

● **Note:** If you see the overset text icon (⊞) in the out port of the type object, with the Selection tool selected, drag the corner to make it larger so you can see all of the text.

4 To make a new paragraph style, click the Create New Style button (⊞) at the bottom of the Paragraph Styles panel.

5 Double-click directly on the new style name "Paragraph Style 2" (or whatever the name you see is) in the list of styles. Change the name of the style to **Blurb**, and press Return or Enter to change the name.

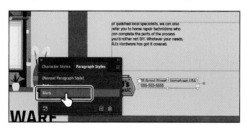

6 In the vertical ad on the left, click the text that toward the bottom of the artboard that starts with "FAMILY-OWNED..."

● **Note:** If your text is now lowercase, with the "family-owned..." text selected, choose Type > Change Case > UPPERCASE.

7 Click the Blurb style in the Paragraph Styles panel to apply the Blurb style to the text.

The Blurb formatting will suit that text better because you'll add it to the black curved path later in the lesson.

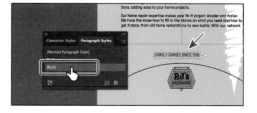

Editing a paragraph style

After creating a paragraph style, you can easily edit the style formatting. Then anywhere the style has been applied, the formatting will be updated automatically. Next, you'll edit the Body style to see firsthand why paragraph styles can save you time and maintain consistency.

1   Double-click in the paragraphs of text with the Body style applied on either artboard to insert the cursor and switch to the Type tool.

2   To edit the Body style, double-click to the *right* of the style named "Body" in the Paragraph Styles panel list.

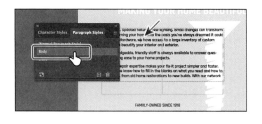

3   In the Paragraph Style Options dialog box, select the Basic Character Formats category on the left side of the dialog box.

4   Change the Font Size to **14 pt** and choose Auto from the Leading menu to ensure it's the default. The Font Size and Leading options will most likely be blank.

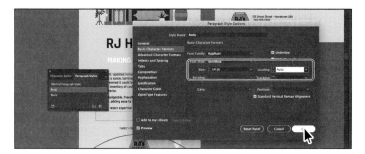

Since Preview is selected by default, you can move the dialog box out of the way to see the text change everywhere the Body style is applied.

5   Click OK. Leave the cursor in the paragraph so you can zoom into where the cursor is in the text.

Creating and applying a character style

Character styles, unlike paragraph styles, can be applied only to selected text and can contain only character formatting. Next, you will create a character style from text styling.

1   With the cursor still in the paragraph, choose View > Zoom In a few times to zoom in to the text.

▶ **Tip:** There are many more options for working with paragraph styles, most of which are found in the Paragraph Styles panel menu, including duplicating, deleting, and editing paragraph styles. To learn more about these options, search for "paragraph styles" in Illustrator Help (Help > Illustrator Help).

2   Drag across the "RJ's Hardware" text to select it.

3   In the Properties panel, click the Fill box in the Properties panel, and select the swatch named "Salmon."

4   Change the Font Style in the Properties panel to Bold.

5   In the Paragraph Styles panel group, click the Character Styles panel tab.

6   In the Character Styles panel, Option-click (macOS) or Alt-click (Windows) the Create New Style button (⊞) at the bottom of the Character Styles panel.

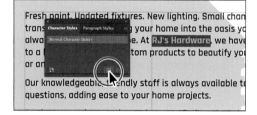

Option-clicking (macOS) or Alt-clicking (Windows) the Create New Style button in a Styles panel lets you edit the style options before the style is added to the panel.

7   In the dialog box that opens, change the following options:

- Style Name: **Biz name**
- Add To My Library: Deselected (if it appears)

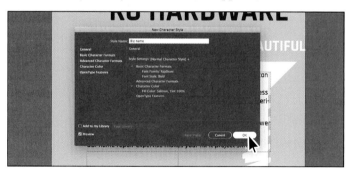

8   Click OK. The style records the attributes applied to your selected text.

9   With the text still selected, click the style named "Biz name" in the Character Styles panel to assign the style to that text, and the text will change if the style formatting changes.

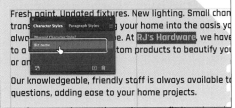

Note: If you apply the character style and a plus appears next to the style name, which indicates formatting applied to the text that is different from the style formatting, you can Option-click (macOS) or Alt-click (Windows) the style name to apply it.

10 Choose 2 Horizontal Ad from the Artboard Navigation menu in the lower-left corner of the Document window.

11 In the paragraph of text, select the "RJ's Hardware" text, and click to apply the Biz name style in the Character Styles panel.

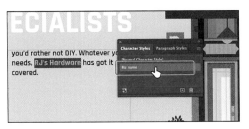

12 Choose Select > Deselect.

Editing a character style

After creating a character style, you can easily edit the style formatting, and anywhere that style is applied, the formatting is updated automatically.

1   Double-click to the right of the Biz name style name in the Character Styles panel (not the name).

2   In the Character Style Options dialog box, change the following:

- Click the Basic Character Formats category on the left side of the dialog box, and change the Font Style back to SemiBold.
- Add To My Library: Deselected (if it appears)
- Preview: Selected

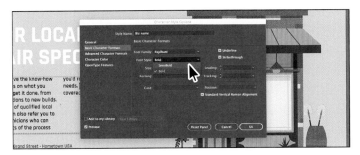

3   Click OK, and then close the Character Styles panel group.

Wrapping text

In Illustrator, you can wrap text around objects, such as imported images and vector artwork, to avoid text running over those objects or to create interesting design effects. Next, you'll wrap text around part of the artwork. In Illustrator, as in InDesign, you apply text wrap to the content that the text will wrap around.

Text wrapping around a logo

1   Choose 1 Vertical Ad from the Artboard Navigation menu below the Document window to switch to the other ad.

2   Select the Selection tool (▶), and click the white screw in the artboard on the left. See the following figure.

Text wrap needs to be applied to the object(s) that the text will wrap around.

3   Choose Object > Text Wrap > Make. Click OK if a dialog box appears.

To wrap text around an object, that object must be in the same layer as the text that will wrap around it, and the object must also be located above the text in the layer hierarchy.

4   With the artwork selected, click the Arrange button in the Properties panel, and choose Bring To Front.

The screw artwork should now be on top of the text in the stacking order, and the text should be wrapping around it.

▶ **Tip:** Try dragging the screw artwork to see how the text flows.

5   Choose Object > Text Wrap > Text Wrap Options. In the Text Wrap Options dialog box, change Offset to **15 pt**, and select Preview to see the change. Click OK.

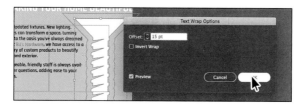

Curving text on a path

In addition to having text in point and type objects, you can have type along a path. Text can flow along the edge of an open or closed path and can lead to some uniquely creative ways to display text. In this section, you'll add some text to an open path.

Text on a path.

1   With the Selection tool (▶), select the black curved path at the bottom of the artboard on the left.

2   Press Command and + (macOS) or Ctrl and + (Windows) a few times to zoom in.

3   Select the Type tool (**T**), and move the cursor over the left end of the black path to see an insertion point with an intersecting wavy path (. ̖Į·) (see the figure). Click when this cursor appears.

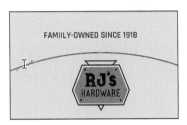
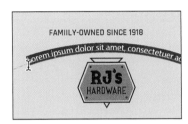

Placeholder text is added to the path, and it starts where you clicked. Your text may have different formatting than you see in the previous figure, and that's okay.

Now you'll cheat and copy the FAMILY-OWNED SINCE 1918 text onto the path.

4   Click in the "FAMILY-OWNED SINCE 1918" text and press Command+A (macOS) or Ctrl+A (Windows) to select it.

5   Choose Edit > Copy.

6   Click in the placeholder text on the path, and press Command+A (macOS) or Ctrl+A (Windows) to select it all.

7   Choose Edit > Paste to replace it.

For the next section, you may want to zoom in further!

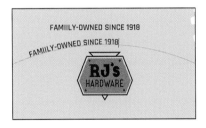

8 Select the Selection tool, and move the pointer over the line on the left edge of the text (just to the left of the "F" in "FAMILY"). When you see this cursor (⯌), press and drag to try to center the text as best you can on the path. Use the following figure as a guide.

9 Click the "FAMILY-OWNED..." text that is not on the path. Select it and delete it.

An arrow is pointing to it in the figure.

Warping text

You can create some original design effects by warping text into different shapes using envelopes (shapes). You can make an envelope out of an object on your artboard, or you can use a preset warp shape or a mesh grid as an envelope.

warped text

Reshaping text with a preset envelope warp

Illustrator comes with a series of preset warp shapes that you can warp text with. Next, you'll make a creative heading by applying a preset warp shape.

1 Choose View > Fit Artboard In Window.

2 With the Selection tool selected, click the "RJ HARDWARE" text.

3 Zoom in closely to the text by pressing Command and + (macOS) or Ctrl and + (Windows) a few times.

4 Choose Object > Envelope Distort > Make With Warp.

5 The Warp Options dialog box appears, with Preview selected. Make sure Arc Upper is chosen from the Style menu.

6 Drag the Bend, Horizontal, and Vertical Distortion sliders to see the effect on the text.

You may need to deselect and then select Preview.

Ensure the Distortion sliders are 0%, and make sure that Bend is 50%. Click OK.

Editing the envelope warp

If you want to make any changes, you can edit the text and shape that make up the envelope warp object separately. Next, you will edit the text and then the warp shape.

1 With the envelope object still selected, click the Edit Contents button () at the top of the Properties panel.

2 Select the Type tool (**T**), and move the pointer over the warped text. Notice that the unwarped text appears in blue. Change the "RJ" text to **RJ'S**.

You can also edit the preset shape, which is what you'll do next.

3 Select the Selection tool (▶), and make sure the envelope object is still selected. Click the Edit Envelope button (⊞) at the top of the Properties panel.

4 Click the Warp Options button in the Properties panel to show the same Warp Options dialog box you saw when you first applied the warp. Change the Bend to **25%**, and click OK.

> **Tip:** If you double-click with the Selection tool instead of with the Type tool, you enter Isolation mode. This is another way to edit the text within the envelope warp object. Press the Escape key to exit Isolation mode.

> **Tip:** To take the text out of the warped shape, select the text with the Selection tool and choose Object > Envelope Distort > Release. This gives you two objects: the type object and an arc lower shape.

5 With the Selection tool, drag the warped text and then the white heading that starts with "MAKING YOUR…" to center them above the paragraphs of text.

6 Choose Select > Deselect, and then choose File > Save.

Creating text outlines

Note: Bitmap fonts and outline-protected fonts cannot be converted to outlines, and outlining text that is less than 10 points in size is not recommended.

Converting text to outlines means converting text into vector shapes that you can edit and manipulate like any other vector graphic. When you create outlines from text, that text is no longer editable as text. Text outlines allow you to change the look of large display type or send a file to someone when you can't or don't want to send the font. They are rarely helpful for body text or other text formatted at small sizes. If you convert all text to outlines, the file recipient doesn't need your fonts installed to open and view the file correctly.

When type is converted to outlines, it loses its hints—instructions built into outline fonts to adjust their shape to display or print optimally at many sizes. You must also convert all text in a selection to outlines; you cannot convert a single letter within a type object. Next, you will convert the main heading to outlines.

1 Choose View > Fit All In Window.

2 With the Selection tool (▶) selected, click the "YOUR LOCAL HOME REPAIR SPECIALISTS" text, on the right artboard.

3 Choose Edit > Copy and then choose Object > Hide > Selection.

   The original text is still there; it's just hidden. This way, you can always choose Object > Show All to see the original text if you need to make changes.

4 Choose Edit > Paste In Front.

5 Choose Type > Create Outlines.

   The text is no longer linked to a particular font. Instead, it is now editable artwork.

6 For a last bit of cleanup, click the two columns of text and drag the bottom middle handle up so the text is balanced across the columns.

   Having the business name split on two lines is bothersome. To

   fix it, you could select the Type tool and insert the cursor right before "RJ's" and then add a soft return (Shift+Enter [macOS] or Shift+Return [Windows]).

7 Choose Select > Deselect.

8 Choose File > Save, and then choose File > Close.

Review questions

1 Name a few methods for creating text in Adobe Illustrator.

2 What is overflow text?

3 What is text threading?

4 What is the difference between a character style and a paragraph style?

5 What is the advantage of converting text to outlines?

Review answers

1 The following methods can be used for creating text:

- With the Type tool (**T**), click the artboard, and start typing when the cursor appears. A point type object is created to accommodate the text.

- With the Type tool, drag to create a type area object. Type when a cursor appears.

- With the Type tool, click a path or closed shape to convert it to text on a path, or click in a type object. Here's a tip: Option-clicking (macOS) or Alt-clicking (Windows) when crossing over the stroke of a *closed* path creates text around the shape.

2 Overflow text is text that does not fit within an area type object or path. A red plus sign (⊞) in an out port indicates that the object contains additional text.

3 Text threading allows you to flow text from one object to another by linking type objects. Linked type objects can be of any shape; however, the text must be entered in an area or along a path (not at a point).

4 A character style can be applied to selected text only. A paragraph style is applied to an entire paragraph. Paragraph styles are best for indents, margins, and line spacing.

5 Converting text to outlines eliminates the need to send the fonts along with the Illustrator file when sharing with others and makes it possible to add effects to type that aren't possible when the type is still editable (live).

10 ORGANIZING YOUR ARTWORK WITH LAYERS

Lesson overview

In this lesson, you'll learn how to do the following:

- Work with the Layers panel.

- Create, rearrange, and lock layers and sublayers.

- Move objects between layers.

- Merge layers into a single layer.

- Locate objects in the Layers panel.

- Copy and paste objects and their layers from one file to another.

- Apply an appearance attribute to objects and layers.

- Make a layer clipping mask.

 This lesson will take about 45 minutes to complete. To get the lesson files used in this chapter, download them from the web page for this book at adobepress.com/IllustratorCIB2022. For more information, see "Accessing the lesson files and Web Edition" in the Getting Started section at the beginning of this book.

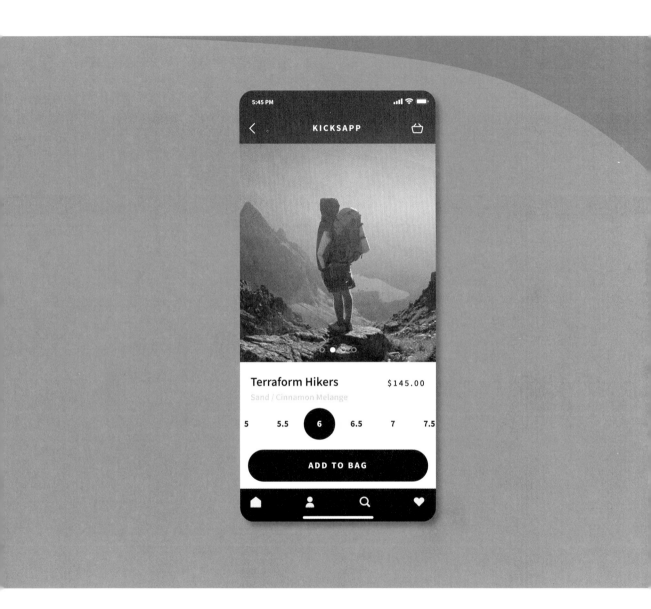

Layers let you organize your work so that it can be edited and viewed individually or together. Every Adobe Illustrator document has at least one layer. Creating multiple layers in your artwork lets you easily control how artwork is printed, displayed, selected, and edited.

Starting the lesson

In this lesson, you'll organize the artwork for an app design as you explore various ways to work with layers in the Layers panel.

Note: If you have not already downloaded the project files for this lesson to your computer from your Account page, make sure to do so now. See the "Getting Started" section at the beginning of the book.

1 To ensure that the tools function and the defaults are set exactly as described in this lesson, delete or deactivate (by renaming) the Adobe Illustrator preferences file. See "Restoring default preferences" in the "Getting Started" section at the beginning of the book.

2 Start Adobe Illustrator.

3 Choose File > Open, and open the L10_end.ai file in the Lessons > Lesson10 folder, located on your hard disk.

4 Choose View > Fit All In Window.

5 Choose Window > Workspace > Reset Essentials.

Note: If you don't see Reset Essentials in the Workspace menu, choose Window > Workspace > Essentials before choosing Window > Workspace > Reset Essentials.

6 Choose File > Open. In the Open dialog box, navigate to the Lessons > Lesson10 folder, and select the L10_start.ai file on your hard disk. Click Open.

The Missing Fonts dialog box may appear, indicating that fonts were used in the file that Illustrator can't find on your machine. The file uses Adobe fonts that you most likely don't have activated, so you will fix the missing font(s) before moving on.

Note: For more information on activating fonts, visit helpx.adobe.com/ creative-cloud/help/ add-fonts.html.

Note: For more information on resolving missing fonts, visit helpx.adobe. com/fonts/kb/resolve-missing-fonts.html.

7 In the Missing Fonts dialog box, make sure any missing fonts are selected, and click Activate Fonts. After some time, the font(s) should be activated, and you should see a success message in the Missing Fonts dialog box. Click Close.

8 If you see another dialog box asking about font auto-activation, click Skip.

9 Choose File > Save As. If the Cloud Document dialog box opens, click Save On Your Computer.

10 In the Save As dialog box, name the file **TravelApp.ai**, and select the Lesson10 folder. Leave Adobe Illustrator (ai) chosen from the Format menu (macOS) or Adobe Illustrator (*.AI) chosen from the Save As Type menu (Windows), and then click Save. In the Illustrator Options dialog box, leave the Illustrator options at their default settings, and then click OK.

11 Choose Select > Deselect (if available).

12 Choose View > Fit All In Window.

Understanding layers

Layers are like invisible folders that help you hold and manage all of the items that make up your artwork. If you shuffle those folders, you change the stacking order of your artwork. You learned about stacking order in Lesson 2.

The structure of layers in your document can be as straightforward or as complex as you want. When you create a new Illustrator document, all of the content you create is organized in a single layer. However, you can create new layers and sublayers (like subfolders) to manage your artwork, as you'll learn about in this lesson.

1 Click the L10_end.ai tab at the top of the document window to show that document.

2 Click the Layers panel tab in the upper-right corner of the workspace, or choose Window > Layers.

In addition to organizing content, the Layers panel gives you an easy way to select, hide, lock, and change your artwork's appearance attributes. In the following figure, the Layers panel shows the content for the L10_end.ai file. It may not match what you see in the file. You can refer to this figure as you progress through the lesson.

3 After reviewing the panel, choose File > Close to close the L10_end.ai file.

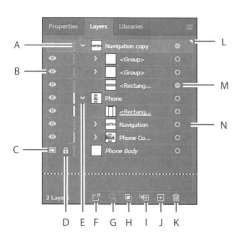

A. Layer color
B. Visibility column (eye icon)
C. Template Layer icon
D. Edit column (lock/unlock)
E. Disclosure triangle (expand/collapse)
F. Collect For Export
G. Locate Object
H. Make/Release Clipping Mask
I. Create New Sublayer
J. Create New Layer
K. Delete Selection
L. Current layer indicator (the triangle)
M. Target column (the circle)
N. Selection column (blank space to right of circle)

Note: The figure shows the top and bottom of the Layers panel. The Layers panel in the Essentials workspace is very tall, which is why the figure shows a split (dashed line) in the panel.

Creating layers and sublayers

By default, every document starts with a single layer, named "Layer 1." As you create artwork, you can rename and add layers and sublayers at any time. Placing objects on separate layers lets you more easily select and organize them because you can temporarily hide the content for a layer, lock it on a layer, and more.

For example, by placing type on a separate layer, you could lock the rest of the artwork in the document so you can focus on the type without affecting the rest of the artwork, or you could have several versions of an icon—one is showing while the rest are hidden.

Creating new layers

▶ **Tip:** Know that there is no "wrong" layer structure, but as you gain more experience with layers, you'll see what makes sense for you.

You'll start by renaming the default layer name and then create new layers using different methods. The idea for this project is to organize the artwork so you can more easily work with it later. Ideally, when you're working in Illustrator, you'll set up layers before you begin creating or editing the artwork. In this lesson, you'll organize artwork with layers *after* the artwork is created, which can be a bit more challenging. Instead of keeping all the content on a single layer, you'll create several layers and sublayers to organize the content better and make it easier to select later.

1   With the TravelApp.ai document showing, if the Layers panel isn't visible, click the Layers panel tab on the right side of the workspace, or choose Window > Layers.

    In the Layers panel, Layer 1 is highlighted, indicating that it is active. Anything you create or add to the document will go on the active layer.

2   Click the disclosure triangle (▶) to the left of the Layer 1 thumbnail to show the content on the layer.

    Each object you create is listed under that layer. By default, Illustrator shows groups as <Groups>, paths as <Paths>, images as <Images>, and so on. That makes it easier to glance at the content and see what is there.

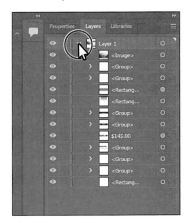

3   Click the disclosure triangle (˅) to the left of the Layer 1 thumbnail to hide the content on that layer.

4   In the Layers panel, double-click directly on the layer name "Layer 1" to edit it inline. Type **Phone Body** and then press Enter or Return.

5 Click the Create New Layer button (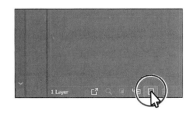) at the bottom of the Layers panel.

Layers and sublayers that aren't named are numbered in sequence. For example, the new layer is named "Layer 2." When a layer or sublayer in the Layers panel contains other items, a disclosure triangle (▶) appears to the left of the layer or sublayer name. You can click the disclosure triangle to show or hide the contents. If no triangle appears, the layer has no content on it.

6 Double-click the white layer thumbnail to the left of the layer name "Layer 2" or to the right of the name in the Layers panel to open the Layer Options dialog box. Change the name to **Navigation**, and notice all the other options available. Click OK.

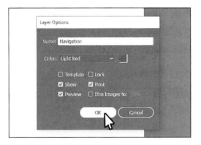

● **Note:** The Layer Options dialog box has a lot of the options you've already worked with, including naming layers, setting Preview or Outline mode, locking layers, and showing and hiding layers. You can also deselect the Print option in the Layer Options dialog box, and any content on that layer will not print.

By default, the new layer is added above the currently selected layer in the Layers panel (Phone Body, in this case) and becomes active. Notice that the new layer has a different layer color (a light red) to the left of the layer name. This will become more important later, as you select content.

Next you'll create a new layer and name it in one step, using a modifier key.

7 Option-click (macOS) or Alt-click (Windows) the Create New Layer button (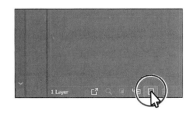) at the bottom of the Layers panel (circled in the following figure). In the Layer Options dialog box, change the name to **Phone Content** and then click OK.

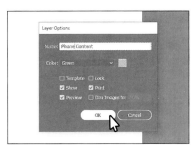

Creating a sublayer

Think of sublayers as subfolders within a layer—essentially they are a layer nested within a layer. Sublayers can be useful for organizing content within a layer without grouping or ungrouping content. Next you'll create a sublayer to put the footer content in so you can keep it together.

1   Click the layer named "Phone Content" to select it, if it isn't already, and then click the Create New Sublayer button (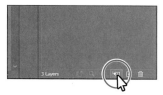) at the bottom of the Layers panel.

▷ **Tip:** To create a new sublayer and name it in one step, Option-click (macOS) or Alt-click (Windows) the Create New Sublayer button or choose New Sublayer from the Layers panel menu to open the Layer Options dialog box.

A new sublayer is created on the Phone Content layer and is selected. You can think of this new sublayer as a "child" of the "parent" layer named Phone Content.

2   Double-click the new sublayer name (Layer 4, in my case), change the name to **Footer**, and then press Enter or Return.

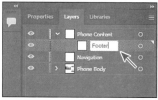

Creating a new sublayer opens the selected layer to show existing sublayers and content.

3   Click the disclosure triangle (⌄) to the left of the Phone Content layer to hide the content of the layer.

In a few sections, you'll add content to the Footer sublayer.

Editing layers and objects

By rearranging the layers in the Layers panel, you can change the stacking order of objects in your artwork. On an artboard, things higher in the list in the Layers panel are in front of objects located on layers lower in the list. Within each layer, there is also a stacking order applied to the objects on that layer. Layers are helpful for various reasons, including the ability to move objects between layers and sublayers to organize and more easily select your artwork.

Finding content in the Layers panel

When working on artwork, there may be times when you select content on the artboard and then want to locate that content in the Layers panel. This can help you determine how content is organized.

1 Drag the left edge of the Layers panel to the left to make it wider.

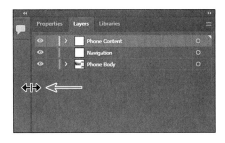

When the names of layers and objects are long enough or objects become further nested one in another, the names can become truncated—in other words, you can't see all of them.

2 With the Selection tool (▶), click the "Terraform Hikers" text on the artboard.

3 Click the Locate Object button (🔍) at the bottom of the Layers panel to reveal the selected content (a text group) within the Layers panel.

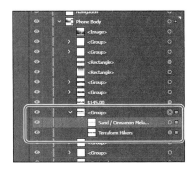

Clicking the Locate Object button will reveal the content for the layer that the selected text is on in the Layers panel. You'll see a selection indicator (▣) to the far right of the layer that the selected content is on (Phone Body), as well as a <Group> object and the individual text objects. You can see that the selected text is in a group on a layer.

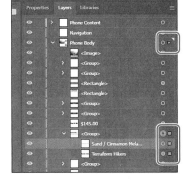

4 On the artboard, Shift-click the "$145.00" text to select it as well.

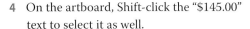
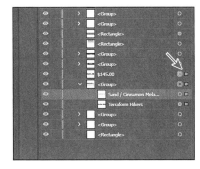

In the Layers panel, you should also see a selection indicator (■) to the far right of the $145.00 text object.

5 To group the selected text, press Command+G (macOS) or Ctrl+G (Windows).

When content is grouped, a group object (<Group>) is created that contains the grouped content.

6 Click the disclosure triangle (⌄) to the left of the selected <Group> to show the original group and the $145.00 text object that is now grouped with it.

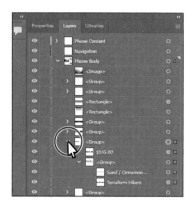

You can rename a <Group> by double-clicking the name in the Layers panel. Renaming a group doesn't ungroup it, but it can make it easier to recognize what is in the group in the Layers panel.

7 Double-click the main <Group> name and type **Description**. Press Return or Enter to accept the name.

8 To collapse the group again so you hide the content, click the disclosure triangle (⌄) to the left of Description.

9 Click the disclosure triangle (⌄) to the left of the Phone Body layer thumbnail to collapse the layer and hide the contents of the entire layer.

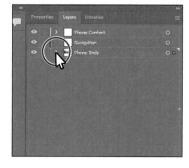

Keeping layers, sublayers, and groups collapsed is a great way to make the Layers panel less visually cluttered. The Phone Content layer and Phone Body layer are the only layers with a disclosure triangle because they're the only layers with content on them.

10 Choose Select > Deselect.

Moving content between layers

Next you'll move the artwork to the different layers to take advantage of the layers and sublayers you've created.

1 In the artwork, using the Selection tool (▶), click the text "Terraform Hikers" to select that group of content.

In the Layers panel, notice that the Phone Body layer name has the selected-art indicator (the color square); it's circled in the figure.

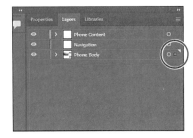

▶ **Tip:** This selection square is smaller than the selected squares you've seen up until now. A smaller selection square indicates that it's not the entire layer that's selected—just certain objects on the layer.

Also notice that the color of the bounding box, paths, and anchor points of the selected artwork matches the color of the layer (the small color strip [▮] you see to the left of the layer name in the Layers panel).

If you want to move selected artwork from one layer to another, you can drag the selected-art indicator for either a *sublayer* or *layer*. That's what you'll do next.

2 Drag the selected-art indicator (the little blue box) for the Phone Body layer straight up to the right of the target icon (◎) on the Phone Content layer.

This action moves all of the selected artwork to the Phone Content layer. The color of the bounding box, paths, and anchor points in the artwork changes to the color of the Phone Content layer, which is green (in my case).

3 Choose Select > Deselect.

4 Click the disclosure triangle (▶) for the Phone Body *and* the Phone Content layers to show the content for each layer.

▶ **Tip:** You can also press Option (macOS) or Alt (Windows) and drag the selected-art indicator to another layer to duplicate the content. Remember to release the mouse button first and then the key.

5 With the Selection tool (▶) selected, move the pointer above the ADD TO BAG button. Drag across the "ADD TO BAG" text and black rectangle at the bottom of the artboard to select a series of objects, making sure not to select the small white rectangle on the bottom edge of the artboard.

You should see the blue selection indicators to the right of that content in the Layers panel. Also, notice the icons that are selected but can't be seen on the artboard because they are behind the black rectangle at the bottom. In the next section you'll arrange those icons so they are in front. Next you'll select those objects in the Layers panel and move them to another layer.

● **Note:** You didn't need to select the artwork on the artboard to drag content from one layer to another, but it made it easier to find in the Layers panel.

6 In the Layers panel, click one of the <Group> objects that has the selection indicator to the right of the name. To select the other two groups, Command-click (macOS) or Ctrl-click (Windows) the other two <Group> objects where you see the selected indicator to the right of the name.

7 Drag any of the selected objects to the Footer sublayer in the Phone Content layer above it. When the Footer sublayer shows a highlight, release the mouse button.

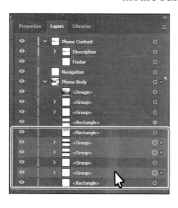 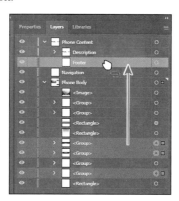 

This is another way to move artwork between layers. Any content that is dragged to another layer or sublayer is automatically at the top of the layer or sublayer ordering. The color of the bounding box, paths, and anchor points of the selected artwork now matches the color of the Footer sublayer.

8 Click the disclosure triangle (⌄) to the left of the Phone Body *and* Phone Content layers to hide the layer contents.

9 Choose Select > Deselect, and then choose File > Save.

Viewing layer content differently

In the Layers panel, you can display layers or objects individually in either Preview or Outline mode. In this section, you'll learn how to view layers in Outline mode, which can make artwork easier to select.

1   Choose View > Outline. This displays the artwork so that only its outlines (or paths) are visible.

You should be able to see the menu icons that are hidden beneath the black shape. They are circled in the figure.

Notice the eye icons () in the Layers panel now. They indicate that the content on that layer is in outline mode.

2   Choose View > Preview (or GPU Preview) to see the painted artwork.

Sometimes you may want to view part of the artwork in Outline mode while retaining the strokes and fills for the rest of the artwork. This can be useful if you need to see all artwork in a given layer, sublayer, or group.

3   In the Layers panel, click the disclosure triangle (▶) for the Phone Content layer to reveal the layer content.

4   Command-click (macOS) or Ctrl-click (Windows) the eye icon (👁) to the left of the Phone Content layer name to show the content for *only that layer* in Outline mode.

You should be able to see the icons near the bottom of the artboard again. Displaying a layer in Outline mode is also useful for selecting the anchor points or center points of objects.

5 With the Selection tool (▶) selected, click one of the mobile icons to select the group of icons.

6 Click the disclosure triangle (▶) to the left of the Footer sublayer to show the content on the sublayer.

 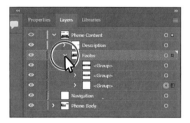

You should be able to find the group of icons in the Footer sublayer.

7 Choose Object > Arrange > Bring To Front.

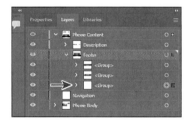 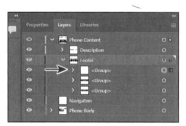

The Arrange commands move the content up or down in the layer stack on an individual layer. The Bring To Front command only brought the icons group to the top of the Footer sublayer. If you decide to create layers and organize your content and later need to move content in front of other content, it can be a bit more challenging to use the Arrange commands if that content is not on the same layer. Sometimes you wind up moving content from one layer to another or reordering layers altogether so some content can be in front of other content.

8 Click the disclosure triangle (▾) to the left of the Phone Content layer to hide the layer content.

9 Command-click (macOS) or Ctrl-click (Windows) the eye icon (👁) to the left of the Phone Content layer name to show the content for that layer in Preview mode again. You should now see the icons.

10 Choose Select > Deselect and then File > Save.

Reordering layers and content

In earlier lessons, you learned that objects have a stacking order, depending on when and how they were created. That stacking order applies to each of the layers in the Layers panel. By creating multiple layers in your artwork, you can control how overlapping objects are displayed. Next, you'll reorder content to change the stacking order.

1   With the Selection tool (▶) selected, on the artboard, drag across the content at the top of the artboard to select the header content.

After attempting to select just the header content, you'll see that the selection appears to capture other content. You can tell because the bounding box surrounding the selection covers the artboard.

2   Click the disclosure triangle (▶) to the left of the Phone Body layer name to show the content.

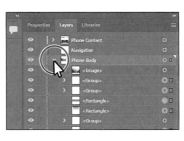

You should see the content that is selected. You need to remove a few items from the selection. There is a gradient-filled rectangle and something else.

3   To remove the rectangle with the gradient fill from the selection, Shift-click the rectangle on the artboard. See the figure.

There is still a shape that is the size of the artboard that is selected and needs to be deselected.

4   In the Layers panel, Shift-click the selection indicator to the right of the bottom <Rectangle> object to remove it from the selection.

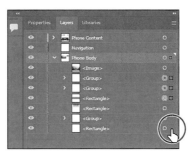

That happened to be the right thing to deselect, in this case. If it weren't, you could have Shift-clicked the selection indicator column again to reselect it and tried another object. Just as in the document, you can use the Shift key to add or remove items from a selection in the Layers panel. As I'm sure you've figured out by now, selecting the name of a layer or object in the Layers panel does not select it in the document. That's why you Shift-clicked the selection indicator and not the name of the rectangle.

5 Click the disclosure triangle () to the left of the Phone Body layer to hide the content. To move the selected content to the *Navigation* layer, where it belongs, drag the selection indicator to the right of the Phone Body layer up to the Navigation layer and release.

 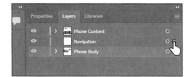

The selection indicator to the right of a layer means that there is selected content on that layer. It doesn't tell you what or how much is selected, but dragging it to another layer moves only the currently selected content.

6 With the Selection tool (▶) selected, click in a blank area, away from artwork, to deselect, if necessary. Shift-drag the image from off the left edge of the artboard into the approximate center of the artboard. Release the mouse button and then the Shift key.

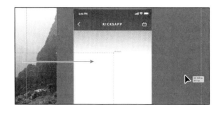

7 The image needs to be on the Phone Content layer, so with it selected, drag the selection indicator in the Layers panel up to the Phone Content layer.

Unfortunately, the image now covers the content on the Navigation layer. Next you'll reorder the layers so you can once again see the navigation content.

8 Drag the Phone Content layer down below the Navigation layer. When you see a blue line below the Navigation layer, release the mouse button to move the Phone Content layer below the Navigation layer. You should now see the navigation content since it's above the Phone Content layer content.

9 Choose Select > Deselect.

10 Choose File > Save.

Locking and hiding layers

In Lesson 2, you learned about locking and hiding content. When you lock and hide content using menu commands or keyboard shortcuts, lock, unlock, hide, and show are set in the Layers panel. The Layers panel lets you hide layers, sublayers, or individual objects from view. When a layer is hidden, the content on the layer is also locked and cannot be selected or printed. In this section, you'll lock some content and hide other content to make it easier to select things.

1 Click the image of the hiker on the artboard. Click the Locate Object button (🔍) at the bottom of the Layers panel to find it in the layers. Notice the eye icon (👁) to the far left of the <Image> name.

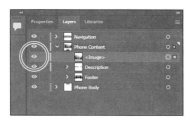

2 Choose Object > Hide > Selection.

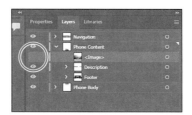

The image is hidden, and the eye for the <Image> object is gone in the Layers panel.

3 Click where the eye icon (👁) was, to the far left of the <Image> name in the Layers panel, to show the image again.

That is the same as choosing Object > Show All. But in the Layers panel, you don't have to show everything that you hide, like the command does. You can show or hide layers, sublayers, individual objects, or a combination.

4 Option-click (macOS) or Alt-click (Windows) the eye icon (👁) to the left of the Phone Body layer to hide the *other* layers.

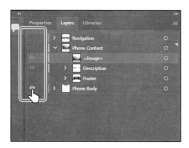

Hiding all layers except those that you want to work with can make it easier to focus on the content at hand.

5 Click the gradient-filled rectangle in the top part of the artboard. In the Layers panel, drag the selection indicator up to the Phone Content layer and release.

The rectangle will disappear since it is now on a layer that is hidden.

6 To view the artwork in Outline mode, press Command+Y (macOS) or Ctrl+Y (Windows). You should see four small circles near the center of the artboard that are meant to show navigation for an image slideshow in the app. Click to select them.

7 Drag the selection indicator in the Layers panel up to the Phone Content layer and release. The circles disappear since they are now on a layer that is hidden.

8 Press Command+Y (macOS) or Ctrl+Y (Windows) to exit Outline mode.

9 Choose Show All Layers from the Layers panel menu ( ), or Option-click (macOS) or Alt-click (Windows) the eye icon ( ) to the left of the Phone Body layer, to show all layers again.

10 Click the empty Lock column to the left of the Navigation layer to lock *all* of the content on that layer.

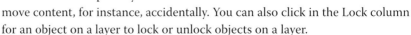

11 Try clicking the "KICKSAPP" text at the top of the artboard, and you'll wind up selecting the gradient-filled rectangle on the layer beneath.

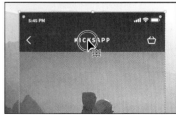

Locking a layer makes it so you can't even select the content on that layer. Locking content can be helpful if you don't want to move content, for instance, accidentally. You can also click in the Lock column for an object on a layer to lock or unlock objects on a layer.

12 Choose Select > Deselect and then choose File > Save.

Duplicating layer content

You can also use the Layers panel as another method for duplicating layers and content. Next you'll duplicate content on a layer and duplicate a layer.

1. With the Phone Content layer content showing in the Layers panel, click the name "Description" to select that group sublayer in the Layers panel. Pressing Option (macOS) or Alt (Windows), drag it down until you see a line appear just below the original. Release the mouse button and then the key to duplicate it.

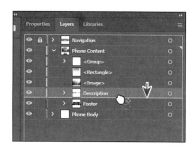

Tip: You can also Option-drag (macOS) or Alt-drag (Windows) the selected-art indicator to duplicate content. You can also select the <Description> row in the Layers panel and choose Duplicate "<Description>" from the Layers panel menu to create a copy of the same content.

Dragging with the modifier key copies the content. This is the same as selecting the content on the artboard, choosing Edit > Copy, and then choosing Edit > Paste In Place.

2. Option-click (macOS) or Alt-click (Windows) the *original* group name "Description" to select the text on the artboard.

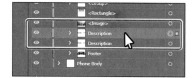

3. Drag the selected text off the artboard to the right.

Note: The original Description group was selected because if you had selected the copy and then attempted to drag it on the artboard, you would have instead dragged the original Description group that was above it in the layer stack. It really didn't matter which you dragged off the artboard, since they are the same.

You'll keep a copy of the original text in case you convert the text on the artboard to outlines. Next you'll make a copy of the Navigation layer and drag the content for the copy off the artboard. This can be a way to make a design version of the navigation off to the side.

4. Click the Navigation layer name and drag it down to the Create New Layer button (◼) at the bottom of the Layers panel.

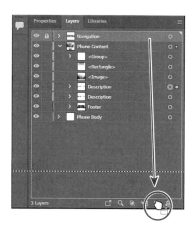

This duplicates the layer, and the content is pasted in place, on top of the original Navigation layer content. Notice that the copied layer, named "Navigation Copy" is also locked.

5 Click the lock icon (🔒) to the left of the Navigation *Copy* layer name in the panel to unlock it.

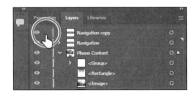

6 To select the copied content so you can move it off the artboard, click the selection indicator column to the far right of the Navigation Copy name, to select all of the layer content.

7 On the artboard, drag the selected navigation content off the artboard to the right.

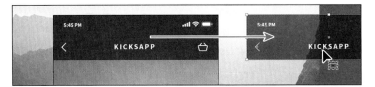

Pasting layers

To complete the app design, you'll copy and paste the remaining pieces of artwork from another file. You can paste a layered file into another file and even keep the layers intact. In this section, you'll also learn a few new things, including applying appearance attributes to layers and reordering layers.

1 Choose Window > Workspace > Reset Essentials.

2 Choose File > Open. Open the Sizes.ai file in the Lessons > Lesson10 folder on your hard disk.

3 Choose View > Fit Artboard In Window.

4 Click the Layers panel tab to show the panel and see the layer named "Sizes" that the content is on.

5 Choose Select > All and then choose Edit > Copy to select and copy the content to the clipboard.

6 Choose File > Close to close the Sizes.ai file without saving any changes. If a warning dialog box appears, click Don't Save (macOS) or No (Windows).

7 In the TravelApp.ai file, choose Paste Remembers Layers from the Layers panel menu (☰). A checkmark next to the option indicates that it's selected.

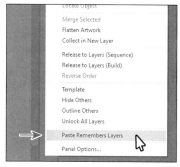

When Paste Remembers Layers is selected, artwork is pasted into the layer(s) from which it was copied, regardless of which layer is active in the Layers panel. If the option is not selected, all objects are pasted into the active layer, and the layers from the original file are not pasted in.

8   Choose Edit > Paste to paste the content into the center of the Document window.

The Paste Remembers Layers option causes the Sizes.ai layer to be pasted as a layer at the top of the Layers panel. Now you'll move the newly pasted layer into the Phone Content layer.

9   Drag the Sizes layer down on top of the Phone Content layer to move the content to the new layer. The pasted layer becomes a sublayer of the Phone Content layer.

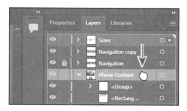

10 Drag the selected artwork on the artboard down into position.

11 Choose Select > Deselect.

Applying appearance attributes to a layer

Note: To learn more about working with appearance attributes, see Lesson 13.

Note: Clicking the target icon also selects the object(s) on the artboard. You could simply select the content on the artboard to apply an effect.

You can use the Layers panel to apply appearance attributes, such as styles, effects, and transparency to layers, groups, and objects. When an appearance attribute is applied to a layer, any object on that layer takes on that attribute. If an appearance attribute is applied only to a specific object on a layer, it affects only that object, not the entire layer. Next, you'll apply an effect to all of the artwork on one layer.

1 Click the target icon () to the right of the Navigation Copy layer in the target column.

Clicking the target icon indicates that you want to apply an effect, style, or transparency change to that layer, sublayer, group, or object. In other words, the layer, sublayer, group, or object is *targeted*. The content is also selected in the Document window. When the target button appears as a double-ring icon (either ⊚ or ⊚), the item is targeted; a single-ring icon indicates that the item is not targeted.

2 To apply an effect, choose Effect > (Illustrator Effects) Stylize > Drop Shadow.

3 In the Drop Shadow dialog box, select Preview and change the following options:

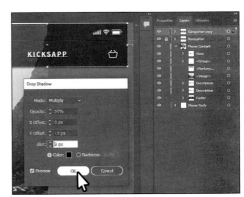

   • Mode: Multiply (default)
   • Opacity: **50%**
   • X Offset: **0 px**
   • Y Offset: **10 px**
   • Blur: **3 px**
   • Color: Selected

4 Click OK.

If you look in the Layers panel, the target icon (⊚) for the Navigation Copy layer is now shaded, indicating that the layer has at least one appearance attribute (the drop shadow added) applied to it. All content on the layer has the drop shadow applied.

5 Choose Select > Deselect.

Creating a clipping mask

The Layers panel lets you create clipping masks to control whether artwork on a layer (or in a group) is hidden or revealed. A *clipping mask* is an object or group of objects (with its shape) that masks artwork below it in the same layer or sublayer so that only artwork within the shape is visible. In Lesson 15, you'll learn about creating clipping masks that are independent of the Layers panel. Now you'll create a clipping mask from layer content.

1   Click the disclosure triangle (▶) to the left of the Phone Body layer to show its contents, and click the disclosure triangle (▼) to the left of the Phone Content layer to hide its contents.

The <Rectangle> object on the Phone Body layer will be used as the mask. In the Layers panel, a masking object must be above the objects it masks. In the case of a layer mask, the masking object must be the topmost object on a layer. You can create a clipping mask for an entire layer, a sublayer, or a group of objects. You want to mask all of the content in the Phone Content *and* Navigation layers, so the clipping object needs to be at the top of a single layer that contains the Phone Content and Navigation content.

2   Click the lock icon (🔒) to the left of the Navigation layer name in the Layers panel to unlock it.

3   Click the Phone Content layer and Shift-click the Navigation layer name in the Layers panel. See the first part of the following figure.

4   Choose Collect In New Layer from the Layers panel menu to create a new layer, and put the Phone Content and Navigation layers in it as sublayers.

You probably noticed these other options in the Layers panel menu: Merge Selected and Flatten Artwork. Merge Selected would have merged the content of the two layers into the top layer (Navigation). Flatten Artwork would have collected all of the artwork into a single layer that it chooses.

5   Double-click the new layer name directly (I see "Layer 7"), and name it **Phone**. Press Return or Enter to accept the change.

6 Drag the object named <Rectangle> from the Phone Body layer onto the new Phone layer to move it to that layer.

This path will be used as the clipping mask for all of the content on the layer.

7 Click the disclosure triangle (▶) to the left of the Phone layer to show the layer content.

Tip: To release the clipping mask, you can select the Phone layer again and click the Make/Release Clipping Mask button (▣).

8 Click the Phone layer to highlight it in the Layers panel. Click the Make/Release Clipping Mask button (▣) at the bottom of the Layers panel. The figure shows just before clicking.

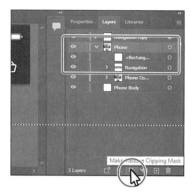

The name of the <Rectangle> content is underlined to indicate that it is the masking shape. On the artboard, the <Rectangle> content has hidden the parts of the phone content that extended outside of the shape.

Note: For a complete list of shortcuts that you can use with the Layers panel, see "Keyboard shortcuts" in Illustrator Help (Help > Illustrator Help).

Now that the artwork is complete, you may want to combine all the layers into a single layer and delete the empty layers. This is called *flattening* artwork. Delivering finished artwork in a single-layer file can prevent accidents, such as hiding layers or omitting parts of the artwork during printing. To flatten specific layers without deleting hidden layers, you can select the layers you want to flatten and choose Merge Selected from the Layers panel menu (≡). In this case, make sure to select the layer with the mask (Phone) last, so the layer mask is intact.

9 Choose File > Save and then choose File > Close.

Review questions

1 Name at least two benefits of using layers when creating artwork.

2 Describe how to reorder layers in a file.

3 What is the purpose of changing the color for a layer?

4 What happens if you paste a layered file into another file? Why is the Paste Remembers Layers option useful?

5 How do you create a layer clipping mask?

Review answers

1 The benefits of using layers when creating artwork include organizing content, selecting content more easily, protecting artwork that you don't want to change, hiding artwork that you aren't working with so that it's not distracting, controlling what prints, and applying effects to all of the content on a layer.

2 You reorder layers by selecting a layer name or its selected-art indicator in the Layers panel and dragging the layer to its new location. The order of layers in the Layers panel controls the document's layer order—topmost in the panel is frontmost in the artwork.

3 The color for a layer controls how selected anchor points and direction lines are displayed on a layer and helps you identify which layer an object resides on in your document.

4 The paste commands paste layered files or objects copied from different layers into the active layer by default. The Paste Remembers Layers option keeps the original layers intact when the objects are pasted.

5 Create a clipping mask on a layer by selecting the layer and clicking the Make/Release Clipping Mask button (▣) in the Layers panel. The topmost object in the layer becomes the clipping mask.

11 GRADIENTS, BLENDS, AND PATTERNS

Lesson overview

In this lesson, you'll learn how to do the following:

- Create and save a gradient fill.

- Apply and edit a gradient on a stroke.

- Apply and edit a radial gradient.

- Adjust the direction of a gradient.

- Adjust the opacity of color in a gradient.

- Create and edit freeform gradients.

- Blend the shapes of objects in intermediate steps.

- Create smooth color blends between objects.

- Modify a blend and its path, shape, and color.

- Create and paint with patterns.

This lesson will take about 60 minutes to complete. To get the lesson files used in this chapter, download them from the web page for this book at adobepress.com/IllustratorCIB2022. For more information, see "Accessing the lesson files and Web Edition" in the Getting Started section at the beginning of this book.

To add depth and interest to your artwork in Illustrator, you can apply gradient fills, which are graduated blends of two or more colors, patterns, or shapes. In this lesson, you'll explore how to work with each of these to complete several projects.

Starting the lesson

In this lesson, you'll explore various ways to work with gradients, blend shapes and colors, and create and apply patterns. Before you begin, you'll restore the default preferences for Adobe Illustrator. Then you'll open a finished art file for the first part of the lesson to see what you'll create.

Note: If you have not already downloaded the project files for this lesson to your computer from your Account page, make sure to do so now. See the "Getting Started" section at the beginning of the book.

Note: For more information on activating fonts, visit helpx.adobe.com/creative-cloud/help/add-fonts.html.

1 To ensure that the tools function and the defaults are set exactly as described in this lesson, delete or deactivate (by renaming) the Adobe Illustrator preferences file. See "Restoring default preferences" in the "Getting Started" section at the beginning of the book.

2 Start Adobe Illustrator.

3 Choose File > Open, and open the L11_end1.ai file in the Lessons > Lesson11 folder on your hard disk.

4 In the Missing Fonts dialog box, ensure that each font is selected (the checkbox to the right of each font name), and click Activate Fonts. After some time, the font(s) should be activated, and you should see a success message in the Missing Fonts dialog box. Click Close.

5 Choose View > Fit All In Window. If you don't want to leave the document open as you work, choose File > Close. To begin working, you'll open an art file that you need to finish.

6 Choose File > Open. In the Open dialog box, navigate to the Lessons > Lesson11 folder, and select the L11_start1.ai file on your hard disk. Click Open to open the file.

7 Choose View > Fit All In Window.

8 Choose File > Save As. If the Cloud Document dialog box opens, click Save On Your Computer.

9 In the Save As dialog box, name the file **FoodTruck.ai**, and select the Lessons > Lesson11 folder in the Save As menu. Leave Adobe Illustrator (ai) chosen from the Format menu (macOS) or Adobe Illustrator (*.AI) chosen from the Save As Type menu (Windows), and then click Save.

Note: If you don't see Reset Essentials in the workspace switcher menu, choose Window > Workspace > Essentials before choosing Window > Workspace > Reset Essentials.

10 In the Illustrator Options dialog box, leave the Illustrator options at their default settings, and then click OK.

11 Choose Reset Essentials from the workspace switcher in the Application bar.

Working with gradients

A *gradient fill* is a graduated blend of two or more colors, and it always includes a starting color and an ending color. You can create three different types of gradient fills in Illustrator. At their simplest, here they are described:

- **Linear**—One color blends into another color along a line.

- **Radial**—A beginning color radiates outward, from the center point to an ending color.

- **Freeform**—A graduated blend of color stops within a shape in an ordered or random sequence that gives the blending a smooth appearance, like natural color.

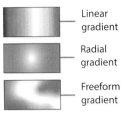

Linear gradient

Radial gradient

Freeform gradient

You can use gradients provided with Adobe Illustrator or create your gradients and save them as swatches for later use (except for freeform gradients). You can create blends between colors, add volume, or add a light and shadow effect to your artwork using gradients. As you go through this lesson, you'll see examples of each type of gradient and understand why you use each.

You can apply, create, and modify gradients with the Gradient panel (Window > Gradient) or the Gradient tool (▣) in the toolbar. In the Gradient panel, the Gradient Fill box or Stroke box displays the current gradient colors and gradient type applied to the fill or stroke of an object.

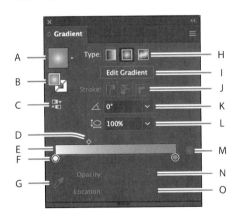

- **A.** Gradient
- **B.** Fill box/ Stroke box
- **C.** Reverse gradient
- **D.** Gradient midpoint
- **E.** Gradient slider (the color bar)
- **F.** Color stop (the circle)
- **G.** Color Picker
- **H.** Gradient type
- **I.** Edit Gradient
- **J.** Stroke gradient type
- **K.** Angle
- **L.** Aspect ratio
- **M.** Delete stop
- **N.** Opacity
- **O.** Location

Note: If you opened the Gradient panel, what you see won't match the figure, and that's okay.

In the Gradient panel under the gradient slider (labeled "E" in the previous figure), the leftmost gradient stop (labeled "F") is called a *color stop*. This marks the starting color; the right gradient stop (the orange circle to the far right) marks the ending color. A color stop is the point at which a gradient completely changes from one color to the next. Between the color stops, the color is blending or transitioning from one color to another. You can add more color stops by clicking below the gradient slider. Double-clicking a color stop opens a panel where you can choose a color from swatches or color sliders.

Applying a linear gradient to a fill

A starting color blends into an ending color along a straight line with the simplest two-color linear gradient. To begin the lesson, you'll apply a gradient fill that comes with Illustrator to the brown background shape to give the idea of a sunset.

1   With the Selection tool (▶) selected, click the brown rectangle in the background, behind the food truck.

2   Click the Fill box (▦) in the Properties panel, click the Swatches button (▦), and select the gradient swatch named "White, Black." Leave the swatches showing. The figure shows right before clicking.

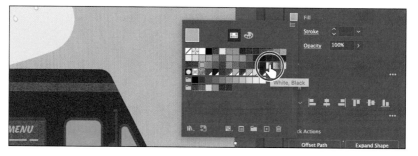

The default black-and-white gradient is applied to the fill of the selected shape.

Editing a gradient

Next, you'll edit the colors in the default black-and-white gradient you applied.

1   With the swatches panel still showing (click Fill color if it's not still showing), click the Gradient Options button at the bottom of the panel to open the Gradient panel (Window > Gradient), and perform the following in the Gradient panel:

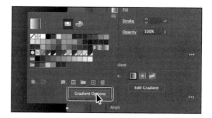

- Make sure that the Fill box is still selected (circled in the following figure) so that you edit the fill color and not the stroke color.

- Double-click the black color stop on the right side of the gradient slider (an arrow is pointing to it in the figure) to edit the color in the Gradient panel. In the panel that appears, click the Color button (▦) to open a color panel.

- Click the menu icon (▤), and choose CMYK from the menu, if CMYK values aren't showing.

- Change the CMYK values to C=**0**, M=**49**, Y=**100**, and K=**0** to make an orange. Press Return or Enter after entering the last value.

▶ **Tip:** To move between text fields, press the Tab key. Press Enter or Return to apply the last value typed.

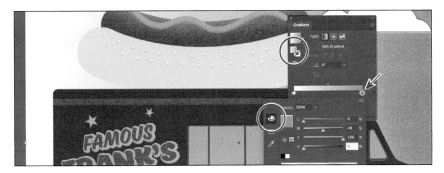

2 Double-click the white, leftmost white gradient stop to select the starting color of the gradient (an arrow is pointing to it in the following figure).

- Click the Swatches button (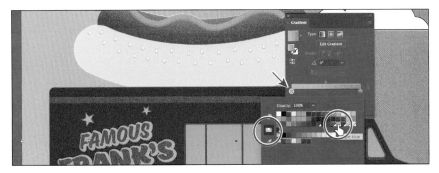) in the panel that appears.
- Click to select the blue swatch named "Light blue."

Saving a gradient as a swatch

Next, you'll save the gradient as a swatch in the Swatches panel. Saving a gradient is a great way to be able to apply it to other artwork easily and maintain consistency in the gradient appearance across artwork.

1 In the Gradient panel, click the Gradient menu arrow (▾) to the left of the word "Type," and click the Add To Swatches button at the bottom of the panel that appears.

The Gradient menu you saw lists all the default and saved gradients that you can apply.

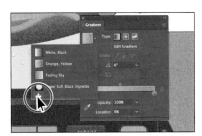

2 Click the X at the top of the Gradient panel to close it.

> **Tip:** You can also save a gradient by selecting an object with a gradient fill or stroke, clicking the Fill box or Stroke box in the Swatches panel (whichever the gradient is applied to), and then clicking the New Swatch button (▣) at the bottom of the Swatches panel.

3 With the background rectangle still selected, click the Fill box in the Properties panel. With the Swatches option (![]) selected, double-click the "New Gradient Swatch 1" thumbnail to open the Swatch Options dialog box.

4 In the Swatch Options dialog box, type **Background** in the Swatch Name field, and then click OK.

5 Click the Show Swatch Kinds Menu button (![]) at the bottom of the Swatches panel, and choose Show Gradient Swatches from the menu to display only gradient swatches in the Swatches panel.

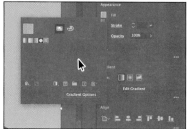

The Swatches panel lets you sort colors based on type, like gradient swatches.

6 With the shape still selected on the artboard, apply some of the different gradients to the shape fill by selecting them in the Swatches panel.

7 Click the gradient named "Background" (the one you just saved) in the Swatches panel to make sure it's applied.

8 Click the Show Swatch Kinds Menu button (![]) at the bottom of the Swatches panel, and choose Show All Swatches from the menu.

9 Save the file by choosing File > Save, and leave the shape selected.

Adjusting a linear gradient fill

Once you have applied a gradient to the fill of artwork, you can adjust the gradient's direction, origin, and beginning and endpoints using the Gradient tool. Now you'll adjust the gradient fill in the selected shape so the colors follow the sunset.

1 With the Selection tool (![]) selected, double-click the rectangle to isolate it.

This is a great way to enter Isolation mode for a single shape so you can focus on it without the other content (in this case) on top of it.

2 Click the Edit Gradient button in the Properties panel.

Clicking the Edit Gradient button selects the Gradient tool (■) in the toolbar and enters gradient editing mode. With the Gradient tool, you can apply a gradient to an object's fill or edit an existing gradient fill.

Notice the horizontal gradient slider in the middle of the artwork, like the one found in the Gradient panel. The slider is called the *gradient annotator*. The gradient annotator is a slider that indicates the direction and length of the gradient. You can use the gradient annotator on the art to edit the gradient without opening the Gradient panel. The two-color circles on either end represent the color stops. The tiny circle on the left shows the starting point of the gradient, and the tiny square on the right is the ending point. The diamond you see in the middle of the annotator is the midpoint of the gradient.

3   With the Gradient tool selected, drag from the top of the shape down to the bottom of the shape to change the position and direction of the starting and ending colors of the gradient.

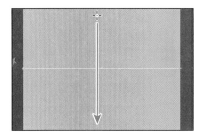
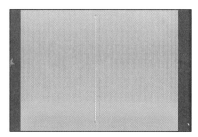

Where you begin dragging is where the first color starts, and where you end is where the last color stops. As you drag, you see a live preview of the gradient as it's adjusted in the object.

4   With the Gradient tool, move the pointer just off the bottom of the small black square at the *bottom* of the gradient annotator. A rotation icon (⟳) appears. Drag to the right to rotate the gradient in the rectangle, and then release the mouse button.

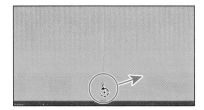

5 Double-click the Gradient tool in the toolbar to open the Gradient panel (if it isn't already open).

6 Make sure that the Fill box is selected in the panel (circled in the figure) so you can edit the gradient applied to the fill, and then change the Angle value to **−90** by typing in the value. Press Return or Enter.

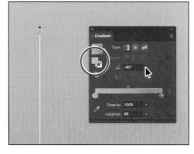

Make sure the gradient shows blue on top and orange at the bottom.

7 Choose Object > Lock > Selection to lock the shape (so you don't accidentally move it later) and to make selecting other artwork easier.

8 Select the Selection tool, and press the Escape key to exit Isolation mode.

You should be able to select other artwork again.

Applying a linear gradient to a stroke

You can also apply a gradient blend to the stroke of an object. Unlike with a gradient applied to the fill of an object, you cannot use the Gradient tool to edit a gradient on the stroke of an object. However, a gradient on a stroke has more options available in the Gradient panel than does a gradient fill. Next, you'll add colors to a stroke to give a hot dog bun a three-dimensional appearance.

1 With the Selection tool (▶) selected, click in the center of the yellow path sitting on top of the truck to select that path.

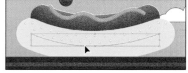

The yellow object looks like a shape, but it's actually a path with a large stroke. That's why you need to select it from the center of the path and not just anywhere in the yellow fill.

● **Note:** After clicking the Stroke box in the toolbar, the Color panel group may open. If it does, you can close it.

2 Click the Stroke box at the bottom of the toolbar on the left, and click the Gradient box below the Stroke box in the toolbar to apply the last used gradient for the current session.

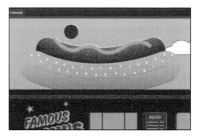

Editing a gradient on a stroke

For a gradient applied to a stroke, you can choose different alignments on the stroke: within, along, or across. In this section, you'll explore how to align a gradient to the stroke and edit the gradient's colors.

1   In the Gradient panel (Window > Gradient), make sure the Stroke box is selected (an arrow is pointing to it in the figure) so you can edit the gradient applied to the stroke. Leave Type as Linear Gradient (circled in the figure), and click the Apply Gradient Across Stroke button (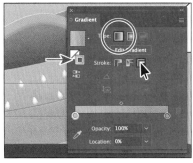) to change the gradient type.

Note: You can apply a gradient to a stroke in three ways: within a stroke (default) (▣), along a stroke (▣), and across a stroke (▣).

With this type of path, aligning the gradient across the stroke can give the path a three-dimensional appearance.

2   Double-click the blue color stop, and with the Swatches option selected, select the swatch named Peach to apply it.

3   Double-click the orange color stop on the right, and with the Swatches option selected, select the swatch named "Red" to apply it.

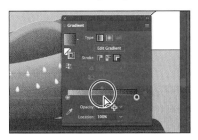
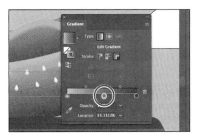

4   Move the pointer below the gradient slider, between the two color stops, in the Gradient panel. When the pointer with a plus sign (▷₊) appears, click to add another color stop, as you see in the first part of the following figure.

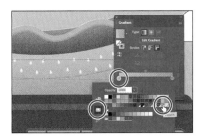
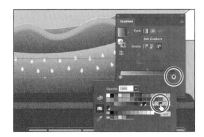

5 Double-click that new color stop and, with the swatches selected ( ), click the swatch named "Orange red."

6 Press the Escape key to hide the swatches and return to the Gradient panel.

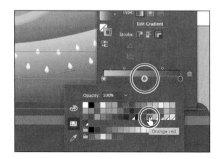

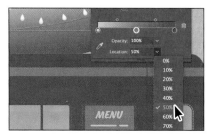

7 With the color stop still selected (you can tell it's selected because it has a highlight around it), choose 50% from the Location menu.

The color is now exactly halfway between the other colors in the gradient. You could have also dragged the color stop along the gradient slider to change the Location value.

Next you'll add a new color to the gradient by dragging to create a copy of a color stop in the Gradient panel.

▶ **Tip:** When copying a color stop by pressing Option or Alt, if you release the mouse button on top of another color stop, you'll swap the two color stops instead of creating a duplicate.

8 Pressing the Option (macOS) or Alt (Windows) key, drag the peach color stop on the far left end to the right; release the mouse button when you see *roughly* 70% in the Location value, and then release the modifier key.

Looking at the hot dog, the color you just added isn't necessary, so you'll remove it.

9 Drag the new color stop at 70% down, away from the gradient slider. When you see that it's gone from the slider, release the mouse button to remove it.

10 Click the X at the top of the Gradient panel to close it.

Applying a radial gradient to artwork

With a radial gradient, the starting color (leftmost color stop) defines the center point of the fill, which radiates outward to the ending color (rightmost color stop). Radial gradients help give elliptical shapes a circular type of gradient. Next, you'll create and apply a radial gradient fill to the pink circle above the hot dog to make ketchup.

1   With the Selection tool (▶) selected, click the pink circle above the hot dog.

2   Click the Fill box in the Properties panel, and change the fill color to the White, Black gradient.

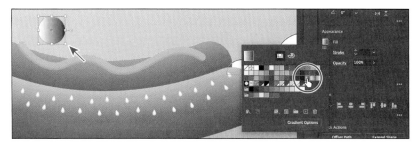

3   Click the Gradient Options button at the bottom of the Swatches panel to open the Gradient panel.

4   Click the Fill box in the Gradient panel to edit the fill and not the stroke. See the first part of the following figure.

5   Click the Radial Gradient button to convert the linear gradient to a radial gradient.

 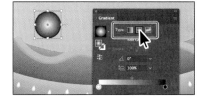

6   Choose File > Save.

Editing the colors in the radial gradient

Previously in this lesson, you edited gradient colors in the Gradient panel. You can also edit the colors directly on artwork with the Gradient tool, which you'll do next.

1 Select the Gradient tool (▨) in the toolbar.

2 In the Gradient panel, with the circle still selected, click the Reverse Gradient button (▦) to swap the white and black colors in the gradient.

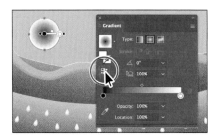

3 To zoom in to the circle, press Command and + (macOS) or Ctrl and + (Windows) a few times.

Notice that the gradient annotator starts from the center of the shape and points to the right on the circle. If you move the pointer over the gradient slider, a dashed circle around the gradient annotator indicates that it's a radial gradient. You can set additional options for radial gradients, as you'll soon see.

4 Move the pointer over the gradient annotator in the ellipse, and double-click the black color stop in the center of the ellipse to edit the color (it's circled in the following figure). In the panel that appears, click the Swatches button (▦), if it's not already selected. Select the swatch named "Orange red."

5 Press Escape to hide the Swatches panel.

6 Double-click the white color stop on the circle. In the panel that appears, make sure that the Swatches option is selected, and select the swatch named "Red."

7 Press the Escape key to hide the panel.

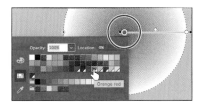 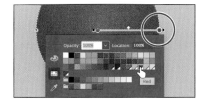

8 Choose File > Save.

Adjusting the radial gradient

Next, you'll move the gradient within the circle and adjust the size to make the circle look more three-dimensional by changing the aspect ratio, radius, and origin of the radial gradient.

1 With the Gradient tool (▨) selected in the toolbar and the circle still selected, move the pointer in the upper-right part of the circle (see the first part of the following figure). Drag toward the center of the circle to change the gradient in the circle.

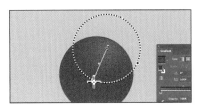

2   Move the pointer over the gradient annotator on the artwork so you can see the dashed ring around the gradient.

You can rotate this ring to change the angle of the radial gradient. The black point on the ring ( ) is for changing the shape of the ring (called the *aspect ratio*), and the double-circle point ( ) is for changing the size of the gradient (called the *spread*).

3   Move the pointer over the double-circle on the dashed circle ( ) (see the first part of the following figure). When the pointer changes ( ), drag toward the center of the circle a little. Release the mouse button to make the gradient smaller.

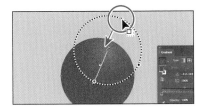

4   Move the pointer over the black circle ( ) on the dashed ring. When the pointer changes ( ), drag to make the gradient wider. Leave the Gradient panel open.

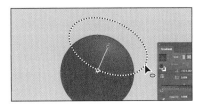

In the Gradient panel, you just changed the aspect ratio ( ) by dragging the black circle. The aspect ratio changes a radial gradient into an elliptical gradient and makes the gradient better match the shape of the artwork.

Note: As the aspect ratio gets smaller, the ellipse flattens and widens.

5   Select the Selection tool ( ), and Shift-drag the corner of the circle to make it about half its size. Drag it onto the top of the hot dog.

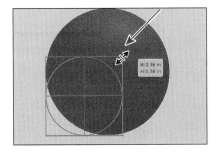

6 Make copies by Option-dragging (macOS) or Alt-dragging (Windows) the circle as many times as you want to make the ketchup on the hot dog. You may need to zoom out and pan.

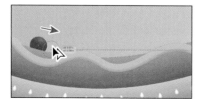 

7 Choose Select > Deselect, and then choose File > Save.

Applying gradients to multiple objects

You can apply a gradient to multiple objects by selecting all the objects, applying a gradient color, and then dragging across the objects with the Gradient tool.

Now you'll apply a linear gradient fill to the windows of the food truck.

1 Choose View > Fit Artboard In Window.

2 With the Selection tool (▶) selected, click one of the blue windows on the truck. Shift-click the other two to select all three windows.

3 Click the Fill box in the Properties panel. In the panel that appears, make sure the Swatches button (▦) is selected, and select the Background gradient swatch.

4 Select the Gradient tool (▦) in the toolbar.

You can see that every object now has the gradient fill applied separately. With the Gradient tool selected, you can see that each object has its own annotator bar.

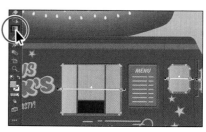

5 Looking at the following figure for guidance, start from a point above the windows, and drag across the middle of the area they occupy.

Dragging across multiple shapes with the Gradient tool allows you to apply a gradient across those shapes.

Adding transparency to gradients

By specifying varying opacity values for the different color stops in your gradient, you can create gradients that fade in or out and that show or hide underlying artwork. Next, you'll apply a gradient that fades to transparent in a cloud shape.

1   Select the Selection tool (▶), and click to select the white cloud in the design.

2   In the Gradient panel, ensure that the white Fill box is selected so you are editing the fill and not the stroke.

3   Click the Gradient menu arrow (▼), and then select White, Black to apply the generic gradient to the fill (you might need to scroll up in the menu to see it).

4   Select the Gradient tool (▨) in the toolbar, and drag from just above the cloud down to the bottom edge at a slight angle.

5   With the pointer over the shape, double-click the black color stop at the bottom. Make sure the Swatches button (▦) is selected, and then select the light sage color named "Cloud" from the swatches. Choose 0% from the Opacity menu. Press Return or Enter to hide the swatches.

   The color is completely transparent at the end of the gradient, but you'll see the Cloud color in the gradient through the cloud.

6 Drag the bottom color stop up to shorten the gradient a little.

7 Select the Selection tool (▶), and set the stroke weight in the Properties panel to **0** to remove it.

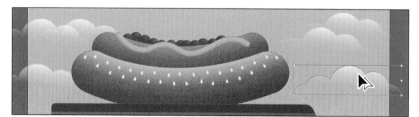

8 Make a series of cloud copies by Option-dragging (macOS) or Alt-dragging (Windows) the cloud a few times, and drag them around the sky.

9 Choose File > Save.

Applying a freeform gradient

Aside from creating linear and radial gradients, you can also create freeform gradients. Freeform gradients are made of a series of color stops that you can place anywhere within a shape randomly or as a path. The colors blend between the color stops to create a freeform gradient. Freeform gradients help add color blends that follow the contour of a shape, adding more realistic shading and more to artwork. Next, you'll apply a freeform gradient to the truck.

1 Select the Selection tool (▶), and click to select the purple/blue truck shape.

2 Select the Gradient tool (▦) in the toolbar.

3 Click the Freeform Gradient option (▦) in the Properties panel on the right.

4 Ensure that the Points option is selected in the Gradient section of the Properties panel (an arrow is pointing to it in the figure).

● **Note:** By default, Illustrator chooses color from surrounding artwork. This is because the preference Illustrator > Preferences > General > Enable Content Aware Defaults (macOS) or Edit > Preferences > General > Enable Content Aware Defaults (Windows) is on by default. You can deselect this option to create your own color stops.

By default, a freeform gradient is applied in Points mode. Illustrator automatically adds individual solid color stops to the object with colors that blend into each other. The number of color stops Illustrator automatically adds depends on the shape and surrounding artwork. *The color for each stop and the number of stops you see may not be the same as what is shown in the figures, and that's okay.*

Editing a freeform gradient in Points mode

You can add, move, edit, or delete the color stops independently to change the overall gradient with Points mode selected. In this section, you'll edit the default individual color stops in the freeform gradient.

1 Double-click the color stop you see in the figure to show the color options. With the swatches showing, select the Freeform-Red swatch to apply it.

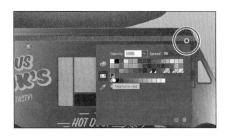

With each color stop, you can drag it, double-click to edit its color, and more.

2 Drag the Freeform-Red color stop to the spot you see in the figure. You can see that the gradient blending changes as you drag it.

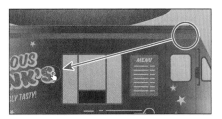

Next you'll remove a few color stops, as well as edit and move color stops.

3 Click the color stop near the upper-left corner. Mine is light blue, but yours may be a different color. Press Delete or Backspace to remove it. If you see a color stop near the lower-left corner of the truck shape, select it and delete it as well. Notice how the gradient changes.

4 Double-click the color stop at the front of the truck (mine is white), and change the color to the Freeform-Red swatch.

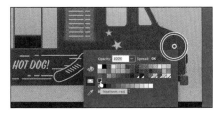

Note: If you don't see a color stop where you see one in the figure, you can click in that area to add one.

5   Double-click the color stop near the bottom middle of the truck and change the color to the swatch named, "Orange red." Press the Escape key to hide the swatches.

The orange red color of the color stop you just edited needs to be more spread out. To do that, you can adjust the spread of the color.

6   Move the pointer over the orange red color stop you just changed the color for. When you see the dotted circle appear, drag the widget at the bottom of the circle away from the color stop.

The color from that stop will "spread" farther away from the color stop.

Applying color stops in Lines mode

You can also add multiple solid colors that blend along a line in Lines mode. In this section, you'll add more color to the truck using Lines mode.

1   Click near the top middle part of the truck to add a new color stop.

2   Double-click the new color, and change the color to an orange swatch.

Note: The first part of the following figure shows a white color stop added. Yours may be a different color, and that's okay.

3   In the Gradient panel or Properties panel, select Lines to be able to draw a gradient along a path.

Note: The first part of the following figure shows the gradient before clicking to add the next color stop.

4   Click the orange color stop you just added. Move the pointer to the right, and you'll see the path preview. Click to create a new color stop. You should see that it's the same orange color.

5   Click to make a final color stop down and to the right. The color stop should also be orange.

The color stops are part of a curved path.

6   Drag the middle color stop down to reshape the path that the color gradient follows.

7   Close the Gradient panel.

8   Choose Select > Deselect, and then choose File > Save.

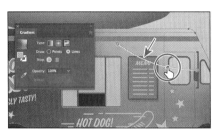

Working with blended objects

You can blend two distinct objects to create and distribute shapes evenly between two objects. The two shapes you blend can be the same or different. You can also blend between two open paths to create a smooth transition of color between objects, or you can combine blends of colors and objects to create color transitions in the shape of a particular object.

The following are examples of different types of blended objects you can create:

Blend between two of the same shape.

Blend between two of the same shapes, each with a different color fill.

Blend between two different shapes with different fill colors.

Blend between two of the same shape along a path.

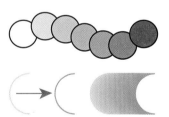

Smooth color blend between two stroked lines (original lines on left, blend on right).

When you create a blend, the blended objects are treated as one object, called a *blend object*. If you move one of the original objects or edit the anchor points of the original object, the blend changes accordingly. You can also expand the blend to divide it into distinct objects.

Creating a blend with specified steps

Next you'll use the Blend tool (⬚) to blend two shapes to create a shooting star for the side of the truck.

1 Choose View > Fit Artboard In Window. Choose View > Zoom Out a few times until you see the artwork off the upper-right corner of the artboard.

2 Zoom in to the stars.

Tip: You can add more than two objects to a blend.

3 Select the Blend tool (⬚) in the toolbar. Move the pointer around the shape; you'll see the little box in the center changing from black to white. Black means you will click an anchor; white means the fill. Click when it's white (⬚*).

Note: If you wanted to end the current path and blend other objects, you would first click the Blend tool in the toolbar and then click the other objects, one at a time, to blend them.

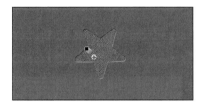 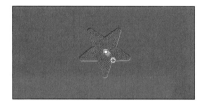

By clicking, you are telling Illustrator that this will be the starting point of the blend. Nothing will appear to happen.

4 Move the pointer over the center of the large yellow star to the right. When the pointer looks like ⬚+, click to create a blend between these two objects.

Tip: To edit the blend options for an object, you can also select the blend object and then double-click the Blend tool. You can also double-click the Blend tool (⬚) in the toolbar to set tool options *before* you create the blend object.

5 With the blended object still selected, choose Object > Blend > Blend Options. In the Blend Options dialog box, choose Specified Steps from the Spacing menu. Change Specified Steps to **10** to see what it looks like—there are 10 copies between the two stars. You may need to deselect and select Preview to see the change. Click OK.

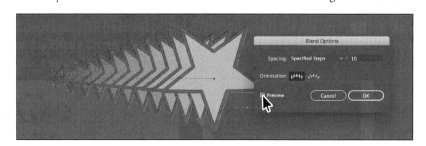

Modifying a blend

Now you'll edit one of the shapes in the blend as well as the spine of the blend you just created so the shapes blend along a curve.

1   Select the Selection tool (▶) in the toolbar, and double-click anywhere on the blend object to enter Isolation mode.

This temporarily ungroups the blended objects and lets you edit each original shape, as well as the spine. The *spine* is a path along which the steps in a blended object are aligned. By default, the spine is a straight line.

2   Choose View > Outline.

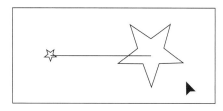

In Outline mode, you can see the outlines of the two original shapes and a straight path (spine) between them. These three objects are what a blend object is composed of, by default. It can be easier to edit the path between the original objects in Outline mode.

3   Click the edge of the larger star to select it. Move the pointer off a corner, and when the rotate arrows (↱) appear, drag to rotate it a little.

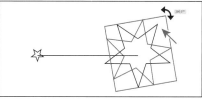

4   Choose Select > Deselect, and remain in Isolation mode.

Next, you'll curve the spine (path) that the blend follows.

5   Select the Pen tool (✒) in the toolbar. Press the Option key (macOS) or Alt key (Windows), and move the pointer over the path between the shapes. When the pointer changes (▶.), drag the path up and to the left a little, as in the figure.

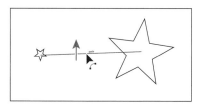
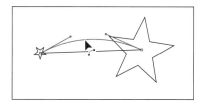

6   Choose View > Preview (or GPU Preview).

7   Press the Escape key to exit Isolation mode.

8   Choose Select > Deselect.

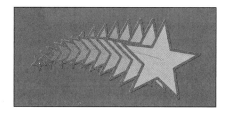

Creating and editing a smooth color blend

You can choose several options for blending the shapes and colors of objects to create a new object. When you choose the Smooth Color blend option in the Blend Options dialog box, Illustrator combines the shapes and colors of the objects into many intermediate steps, creating a smooth, graduated blend between the original objects, as you see in the figure above.

If objects are filled or stroked with different colors, the steps are calculated to provide the optimal number for a smooth color transition. If the objects contain identical colors, gradients, or patterns, the number of steps is based on the longest distance between the bounding box edges of the two objects. Now you'll combine two shapes to see how the sesame seeds on the hot dog were made.

1 Zoom out or pan in the window with the Hand tool to see two tear-drop shapes below the stars that you just blended.

You'll blend these two shapes together to give them a more three-dimensional appearance.

2 Select the Selection tool (▶), and click the smaller shape on the left. Shift-click the larger shape on the right to select both.

▶ **Tip:** You can also click the Blend Options button in the Properties panel to edit the options for a selected blend object.

● **Note:** Creating smooth color blends between paths can be difficult in certain situations. For instance, if the lines intersect or the lines are too curved, unexpected results may occur.

3 Choose Object > Blend > Make.

This is another way to create a blend and can be useful if creating a blend using the Blend tool proves challenging.

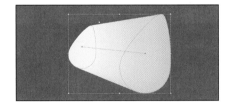

4 With the blend object still selected, double-click the Blend tool (⬚) in the toolbar. In the Blend Options dialog box, make sure that Smooth Color is chosen from the Spacing menu. Click OK.

5 Choose Select > Deselect.

Next, you'll edit the paths that make up the blend.

6 Select the Selection tool (▶), and double-click within the color blend to enter Isolation mode. Click the smaller path on the left to select it. Drag it to the right until it looks like the figure. Notice that the colors are now blended.

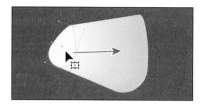 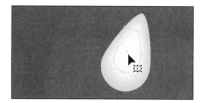

7 Press the Escape key to exit Isolation mode.

8 Choose Select > Deselect.

9 To see the artboard again, choose View > Fit Artboard In Window. To zoom out so you can see the artwork you blended off the right edge of the artboard, press Command and – (macOS) or Ctrl and – (Windows) a few times.

10 Drag the star onto the truck as in the figure. If the star artwork is behind the other artwork, choose Object > Arrange > Bring To Front.

11 Make a copy by Option-dragging (macOS) or Alt-dragging (Windows), releasing the mouse button and then the key.

12 To flip the artwork, click the Flip Horizontally button (◀▷) in the Properties panel.

13 Rotate the stars by moving the pointer off a corner, and when you see rotate arrows (↰), drag to rotate it a little.

14 Drag the stars into place.

If you want to drag the sesame seed off the right edge of the artboard onto the hot dog bun, do that now.

15 Choose File > Save, and then choose File > Close.

Creating patterns

In addition to process colors, spot colors, and gradients, the Swatches panel can also contain pattern swatches. A *pattern* is artwork saved in the Swatches panel that can be applied to the stroke or fill of an object. Illustrator provides sample swatches of each type in the default Swatches panel as separate libraries and lets you create your own patterns as well. In this section, you will focus on creating, applying, and editing patterns.

Applying an existing pattern

You can design patterns from scratch and customize existing patterns with any of the Illustrator tools. Patterns can start with artwork (a tile) that is repeated (tiled) within a fill or stroke, starting at the ruler origin and continuing to the right. Next, you'll apply a pattern that comes with Illustrator to the road.

1   Choose File > Open. In the Open dialog box, navigate to the Lessons > Lesson11 folder, and select the L11_start2.ai file on your hard disk. Click Open to open the file.

2   Choose File > Save As. If the Cloud Document dialog opens, click Save On Your Computer.

3   In the Save As menu dialog box, name the file **FoodTruck_pattern.ai**, and select the Lessons > Lesson11 folder. Leave Adobe Illustrator (ai) chosen from the Format menu (macOS) or Adobe Illustrator (*.AI) chosen from the Save As Type menu (Windows) and then click Save. In the Illustrator Options dialog box, leave the Illustrator options at their default settings, and then click OK.

4   Choose View > Fit All In Window.

5   With the Selection tool (▶) selected, click to select the dark gray road (rectangle).

● **Note:** You'll learn all about the Appearance panel in Lesson 13.

▶ **Tip:** To explore other pattern swatches in Illustrator, choose Window > Swatch Libraries > Patterns, and then select a pattern library.

6   Click More Options (⬤⬤⬤) in the Appearance section of the Properties panel to open the Appearance panel (or choose Window > Appearance).

7   Click the Add New Fill button at the bottom of the Appearance panel.

This adds a copy of the existing fill to the shape. The new fill is layered on top of the existing stroke and fill.

8   Click the new fill box to the right of the word "Fill" to show a panel of swatches. An arrow is pointing to it in the second part of the following figure. Select the Mezzotint Dot swatch.

The pattern swatch fills the shape as a second fill on top of the first. The swatch named "Mezzotint Dot" is found in a default pattern library.

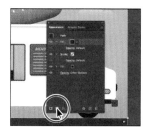
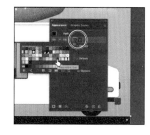
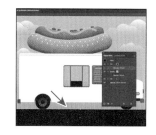

9   In the Appearance panel, just below the *top* word "Fill," click the word "Opacity" to open the transparency panel (or choose Window > Transparency). Change the Opacity value to **90**. Press the Escape key to hide the panel.

Note: If you don't see the word "Opacity" below the top Fill row, click the disclosure triangle (▶) to the left of the top word "Fill" to show it.

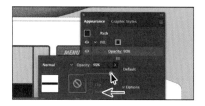

10 Choose Select > Deselect, and then close the Appearance panel.

Creating your own pattern

In this section, you'll create your own custom pattern. Each pattern you create is saved as a swatch in the Swatches panel for the document you're working in.

1   Choose View > Fit Artboard In Window. Choose View > Zoom Out a few times until you see the artwork off the left side of the artboard.

2   With the Selection tool (▶) selected, click the FRANK'S text off the left edge of the artboard to select a group of objects.

    You'll create a pattern from this group of objects.

Note: You don't need to have anything selected when you create a pattern. You can add content to a pattern when you edit it in Pattern Editing mode, as you'll see.

3   Choose Object > Pattern > Make.

4   Click OK in the dialog box that appears.

    When you create a pattern, Illustrator enters Pattern Editing mode, which is similar to the Isolation mode you've worked with. Pattern Editing mode allows you to create and edit patterns interactively, while previewing the changes to the pattern on the artboard.

Note: A pattern can be composed of shapes, symbols, or embedded raster images, among other objects that you can add in Pattern Editing mode. For instance, to create a flannel pattern for a shirt, you can create three overlapping rectangles or lines, each with varying appearance options.

All other artwork is not visible and cannot be edited while in this mode. The Pattern Options panel (Window > Pattern Options) also opens, giving you all the necessary options to create and edit your pattern.

5 Choose Select > All On Active Artboard to select the artwork.

6 Press Command and + (macOS) or Ctrl and + (Windows) to zoom in.

The series of lighter-colored copies around the artwork in the center are repetitions of the pattern. They are there for a preview and are a little dimmed so you can focus on the original. The blue box around the original group of objects is the *pattern tile* (the area that repeats).

▶ **Tip:** We use the word "vinyl" here because this pattern could be used to print a large vinyl graphic or decal that is then applied over the original paint of the food truck.

7 In the Pattern Options panel, change Name to **Truck vinyl**.

8 Try choosing different options from the Tile Type menu to see the effect on the pattern. Before continuing, make sure Hex By Column is selected.

The name in the Pattern Options panel becomes the name of the swatch saved in the Swatches panel and can be useful to distinguish multiple versions of a pattern swatch, for instance. Tile Type determines how the pattern is tiled. You have three main Tile Type choices: the default grid pattern, a brick-style pattern, and the hex pattern.

9 Choose 1 x 1 from the Copies menu at the bottom of the Pattern Options panel. This will remove the repeat and let you temporarily focus on the main pattern artwork.

10 Choose Select > Deselect.

11 Click to select the single star below "FAMOUSLY TASTY" and delete it.

12 Drag the shooting star to the right a *little*. See the second part of the figure.

You can add, delete, and transform artwork at this point to make up the repeating content for your pattern.

13 In the Pattern Options panel, choose 5 x 5 from the Copies menu to see the repeat again.

14 Select the Size Tile To Art option in the Pattern Options panel.

The Size Tile To Art selection fits the tile area (the blue hexagon) to the bounds of the artwork, changing the spacing between the repeated objects. With Size Tile To Art deselected, you could manually change the width and the height of the pattern definition area in the Width and Height fields to include more content or edit the spacing between. You can also edit the tile area manually with the Pattern Tile Tool button (🔡) in the upper-left corner of the Pattern Options panel.

If you set the spacing values (H Spacing or V Spacing) to negative values, the artwork in the pattern tile will overlap. By default, when objects overlap horizontally, the left object is on top; when objects overlap vertically, the top object is on top. You can set the overlap values to Left In Front, Right In Front to change overlap horizontally, or to Top In Front, Bottom In Front to change the overlap vertically (they are the small buttons in the Overlap section of the panel).

Tip: The H Spacing and V Spacing values can be either positive or negative, and they move the tiles apart or bring them closer together either horizontally (H) or vertically (V).

15 Click Done in the bar along the top of the Document window. If a dialog box appears, click OK.

16 Choose File > Save.

Tip: If you want to create pattern variations, you can click Save A Copy in the bar along the top of the Document window when in Pattern Editing mode. This saves the current pattern in the Swatches panel as a copy and allows you to continue creating.

Applying your pattern

You can assign a pattern using a number of different methods. In this section, you'll use the Fill color box in the Properties panel to apply your pattern.

1 Choose View > Fit Artboard In Window.

2 With the Selection tool (▶), click the white truck shape.

3 Click the Fill color in the Properties panel and select the yellow/orange color with the tool tip that shows as "C=0 M=33 Y=100 K=0."

4 Click More Options (⚬⚬⚬) in the Appearance section of the Properties panel to open the Appearance panel (or choose Window > Appearance).

5 Click the Add New Fill button (▣) at the bottom of the Appearance panel to add a copy of the existing fill to the shape.

6 In the top "Fill" row, click the fill box to show a panel of swatches (see the following figure). Select the Truck Vinyl pattern swatch.

7 Close the Appearance panel.

Editing your pattern

Next, you'll edit the Truck Vinyl pattern swatch in Pattern Editing mode.

1 With the truck shape still selected, click the Fill box in the Properties panel. Double-click the Truck Vinyl pattern swatch to edit it in Pattern Editing mode.

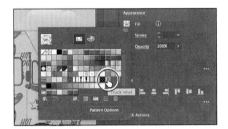

2 Press Command and + (macOS) or Ctrl and + (Windows) to zoom in.

3 In Pattern Editing mode, with the Selection tool (▶) selected, click the "FAMOUS FRANK'S" text.

4 In the Properties panel, change the stroke color to a dark red swatch.

5 Click Done in the gray bar along the top of the Document window to exit Pattern Editing mode.

6 Choose View > Fit Artboard In Window.

7 Choose Select > Deselect, and then choose File > Save.

8 Choose File > Close.

Review questions

1 What is a *gradient*?

2 How do you adjust the blend between colors in a linear or radial gradient?

3 Name two ways you can add colors to a linear or radial gradient.

4 How can you adjust the direction of a linear or radial gradient?

5 What is the difference between a gradient and a blend?

6 When you save a pattern in Illustrator, where is it saved?

Review answers

1 A gradient is a graduated blend of two or more colors or tints of the same color. Gradients can be applied to the stroke or fill of an object.

2 To adjust the blend between colors in a linear or radial gradient, with the Gradient tool (▇) selected and with the pointer over the gradient annotator or in the Gradient panel, drag the diamond icons or the color stops of the gradient slider.

3 To add colors to a linear or radial gradient, in the Gradient panel, click beneath the gradient slider to add a gradient stop to the gradient. Then double-click the color stop to edit the color, using the panel that appears, to mix a new color or to apply an existing color swatch. You can select the Gradient tool in the toolbar, move the pointer over the gradient-filled object, and then click beneath the gradient annotator that appears in the artwork to add or edit a color stop.

4 Drag across artwork with the Gradient tool to adjust the direction of a linear or radial gradient. You can also rotate the gradient using the Gradient tool and change the radius, aspect ratio, starting point, and more.

5 The difference between a gradient and a blend is the way that colors combine—colors blend together within a gradient and between objects in a blend.

6 When you save a pattern in Illustrator, it is saved as a swatch in the Swatches panel. By default, swatches are saved with the currently active document.

12 USING BRUSHES TO CREATE AN AD

Lesson overview

In this lesson, you'll learn how to do the following:

- Use four brush types: Calligraphic, Art, Bristle, and Pattern.

- Apply brushes to paths.

- Paint and edit paths with the Paintbrush tool.

- Change brush color and adjust brush settings.

- Create new brushes from Adobe Illustrator artwork.

- Work with the Blob Brush tool and the Eraser tool.

This lesson will take about 60 minutes to complete. To get the lesson files used in this chapter, download them from the web page for this book at adobepress.com/IllustratorCIB2022. For more information, see "Accessing the lesson files and Web Edition" in the Getting Started section at the beginning of this book.

The variety of brush types in Adobe Illustrator
lets you create a myriad of effects by painting with the
Paintbrush tool or drawing with the drawing tools. You
can work with the Blob Brush tool; choose from the
Art, Calligraphic, Pattern, Bristle, and Scatter brushes;
and create new brushes based on your artwork.

Starting the lesson

In this lesson, you will learn how to work with the different brush types in the Brushes panel, change brush options, and create your own brushes. Before you begin, you'll restore the default preferences for Adobe Illustrator. Then you'll open the finished art file for the lesson to see the finished artwork.

● **Note:** If you have not already downloaded the project files for this lesson to your computer from your Account page, make sure to do so now. See the "Getting Started" section at the beginning of the book.

1 To ensure that the tools function and the defaults are set exactly as described in this lesson, delete or deactivate (by renaming) the Adobe Illustrator preferences file. See "Restoring default preferences" in the "Getting Started" section at the beginning of the book.

2 Start Adobe Illustrator.

3 Choose File > Open. In the Open dialog box, navigate to the Lessons > Lesson12 folder, and select the L12_end.ai file on your hard disk. Click Open to open the file.

4 If you want, choose View > Zoom Out to make the finished artwork smaller, and then adjust the window size and leave the artwork on your screen as you work. (Use the Hand tool [✋] to move the artwork to where you want it in the Document window.) If you don't want to leave the artwork open, choose File > Close.

To begin working, you'll open an existing art file.

5 Choose File > Open. In the Open dialog box, navigate to the Lessons > Lesson12 folder, and select the L12_start.ai file on your hard disk. Click Open to open the file.

6 Choose View > Fit All In Window.

7 Choose File > Save As. If the Cloud Document dialog box opens, click Save On Your Computer to save it locally.

8 In the Save As dialog box, name the file **UpLiftAd.ai**, and select the Lesson12 folder. Leave Adobe Illustrator (ai) chosen from the Format menu (macOS) or Adobe Illustrator (*.AI) chosen from the Save As Type menu (Windows) and then click Save.

9 In the Illustrator Options dialog box, leave the Illustrator options at their default settings, and then click OK.

● **Note:** If you don't see Reset Essentials in the workspace switcher menu, choose Window > Workspace > Essentials before choosing Window > Workspace > Reset Essentials.

10 Choose Reset Essentials from the workspace switcher in the Application bar to reset the workspace.

Working with brushes

You can decorate paths with patterns, figures, brush strokes, textures, or angled strokes using brushes. You can also modify the brushes provided with Illustrator and create brushes.

You can apply brush strokes to existing paths or use the Paintbrush tool to draw a path and apply a brush stroke simultaneously. You can change the color, size, and other brush features, and you can edit paths after brushes are applied (including adding a fill).

Types of brushes

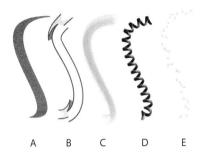

A   B   C   D   E

A. Calligraphic brush

B. Art brush

C. Bristle brush

D. Pattern brush

E. Scatter brush

There are five types of brushes that appear in the Brushes panel (Window > Brushes): Calligraphic, Art, Bristle, Pattern, and Scatter.

In this lesson, you will discover how to work with all except the Scatter brush.

▶ **Tip:** To learn more about Scatter brushes, search for "Scatter brushes" in Illustrator Help (Help > Illustrator Help).

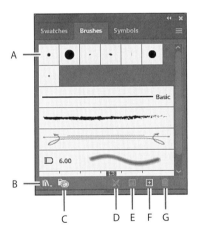

A. Brushes

B. Brush Libraries Menu

C. Libraries panel

D. Remove Brush Stroke

E. Options of selected object

F. New Brush

G. Delete Brush

Using Calligraphic brushes

The first type of brush you'll learn about is the Calligraphic brush. Calligraphic brushes resemble strokes drawn with the angled point of a calligraphic pen. Calligraphic brushes are defined by an elliptical shape whose center follows the path, and you can use these brushes to create the appearance of hand-drawn strokes made with a flat, angled pen tip.

Calligraphic brush examples.

Applying a Calligraphic brush to artwork

To get started, you'll filter the types of brushes shown in the Brushes panel so that it shows only Calligraphic brushes.

1   Choose Window > Brushes to open the Brushes panel. Click the Brushes panel menu icon (☰), and choose List View.

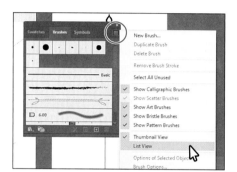

2   Click the Brushes panel menu icon (☰) again, and deselect the following, but leave the Calligraphic brushes visible:

  •   Show Art Brushes
  •   Show Bristle Brushes
  •   Show Pattern Brushes

A checkmark next to the brush type in the Brushes panel menu indicates that the brush type is visible in the panel. You can't deselect them all at once, so you'll have to keep clicking the menu icon (☰) to access the menu.

Your panel will wind up looking like the figure.

3   Select the Selection tool (▶) in the toolbar, and click pink text object at the top of the artboard to select it. The text has been converted to paths because it was edited to create the appearance you see.

4   To zoom in, press Command and + (macOS) or Ctrl and + (Windows) a few times.

5   Select the 5 pt. Flat brush in the Brushes panel to apply it to the pink text shapes.

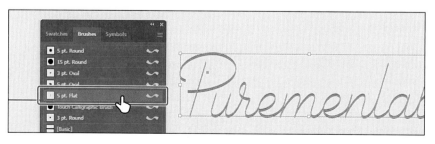

6   Change the Stroke weight to **5 pt** in the Properties panel to see the effect of the brush, and then change it to **1 pt**.

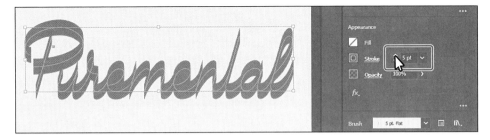

Similarly to drawing with an actual calligraphic pen, when you apply a Calligraphic brush, such as the 5 pt. Flat brush, the more vertically you draw a path, the thinner the path's stroke appears.

7   Click the Stroke color in the Properties panel, make sure the Swatches option (![icon]) is selected, and select Black. Press the Escape key to hide the Swatches panel, if necessary.

8   Choose Select > Deselect and then choose File > Save.

Editing a brush

To change the options for a brush, you can double-click the brush in the Brushes panel. When you edit a brush, you can also choose whether to change artwork that the brush has been applied to. Next you'll change the appearance of the 5 pt. Flat brush you've been painting with.

1   In the Brushes panel, double-click the brush thumbnail to the left of the text "5 pt. Flat," or to the right of the name in the Brushes panel, to open the Calligraphic Brush Options dialog box.

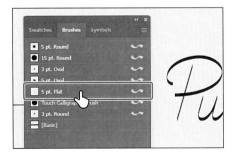

●   **Note:** The edits you make will change the brush for this document only.

▶ **Tip:** The Preview window in the dialog box (below the Name field) shows the changes that you make to the brush.

2 In the dialog box make the following changes:

- Name: **8 pt. Angled**
- Angle: **35°**
- Choose Fixed from the menu to the right of Angle. (When Random is chosen, a random variation of brush angles is created every time you draw.)
- Roundness: **15%** (This setting makes the brush stroke more or less round.)
- Size: **8 pt**

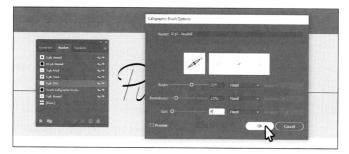

3 Click OK.

4 In the dialog box that appears, click Apply To Strokes so the brush changes will affect the text shapes that have the brush applied.

5 Choose Select > Deselect, if necessary, and then save the file by choosing File > Save.

Drawing with the Paintbrush tool

The Paintbrush tool allows you to apply a brush as you paint. Painting with the Paintbrush tool creates vector paths that you can edit with the Paintbrush tool or other drawing tools. Next you'll use the Paintbrush tool to paint part of the "t" in the text with a Calligraphic brush from a brush library.

1 Select the Paintbrush tool ( ) in the toolbar.

2 Click the Brush Libraries Menu button ( ) at the bottom of the Brushes panel, and choose Artistic > Artistic_Calligraphic.

A brush library panel with various brushes appears.

Illustrator comes with a host of brush libraries that you can use in your artwork. Each brush type, including those discussed previously, has a series of libraries to choose from.

3 Click the Artistic_Calligraphic panel menu icon (), and choose List View. Click the brush named "15 pt. Flat" to add it to the Brushes panel.

4 Close the Artistic_Calligraphic brush library panel.

Selecting a brush from a brush library, such as the Artistic_Calligraphic library, adds that brush to the Brushes panel for the active document only.

5 Make sure the fill color is None (◻), the stroke color is Black, and the stroke weight is **1 pt** in the Properties panel.

With the pointer in the Document window, notice that the Paintbrush pointer has an asterisk next to it (🖌︎*), indicating that you are about to paint a new path.

6 Move the pointer to the left of the "t" in Puremental (see the first part of the following figure). Paint a curving path from left to right.

● **Note:** This Calligraphic brush creates random angles on the paths, so yours may not look like what you see in the figures, and that's okay.

7 Select the Selection tool, and click to select the new path you drew. Change the stroke weight to 0.5 pt in the Properties panel on the right.

8 Choose Select > Deselect (if necessary), and then choose File > Save.

Editing paths with the Paintbrush tool

Now you'll use the Paintbrush tool to edit paths.

1   With the Selection tool (▶) selected, click to select the Puremental text shapes.

2   Select the Paintbrush tool (✏) in the toolbar. Move the pointer over the capital "P"; see the figure for where. An asterisk will not appear next to the pointer when it's positioned anywhere over a selected path. Drag to redraw the path. The selected path is edited from the point at which you began drawing.

Notice that the letter shapes are no longer selected after you finish drawing with the Paintbrush tool. By default, paths are deselected.

3   Press and hold the Command (macOS) or Ctrl (Windows) key to toggle to the Selection tool, and click to select the curved path you drew on the letter "t." After clicking, release the key to return to the Paintbrush tool.

4   With the Paintbrush tool, move the pointer over some part of the selected path. When the asterisk disappears next to the pointer, drag to the right to redraw the path.

Next you'll edit the options of the Paintbrush tool to change how it paints.

5 Double-click the Paintbrush tool (✏) in the toolbar to display the Paintbrush Tool Options dialog box, and make the following changes:

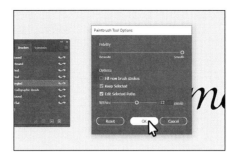

- Fidelity: Drag the slider all the way to Smooth (to the right).

- Keep Selected: Selected.

6 Click OK.

The Paintbrush Tool Options dialog box changes the way the Paintbrush tool functions. For the Fidelity option, the closer to Smooth you drag the slider, the smoother the path will be, and the fewer points it will have. Also, because you selected Keep Selected, the paths remain selected after you finish drawing them.

7 With the Paintbrush tool selected, once again press and hold the Command (macOS) or Ctrl (Windows) key to toggle to the Selection tool, and click to select the curved path you drew on the letter "t." Release the key. Try repainting the path once more.

Notice that now, after painting, the path is still selected, so you could edit it further if you needed to. Know that if you want to draw a series of overlapping paths with the Paintbrush tool, setting the tool option to *not* remain selected after you finish drawing paths is best. That way, you can draw overlapping paths without altering previously drawn paths.

8 Choose Select > Deselect, if necessary, and then choose File > Save.

Removing a brush stroke

You can easily remove a brush stroke applied to artwork where you don't want it. Now you'll remove the brush stroke from the stroke of a path.

1   Choose View > Fit Artboard In Window to see everything.

2   Select the Selection tool (▶), and click the black path with what looks like a chalk scribble down its length (see the following figure).

When creating the artwork, I was trying out different brushes on the artwork. The brush applied to the stroke of the selected path needs to be removed.

▶ **Tip:** You can also select the [Basic] brush in the Brushes panel to remove a brush applied to a path.

3   In the Brushes panel, click the Remove Brush Stroke button (✖) at the bottom to remove it.

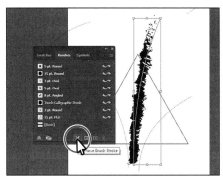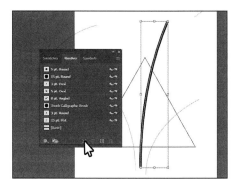

Removing a brush stroke doesn't remove the stroke color and weight; it just removes the brush applied.

4   Change the stroke weight to **1 pt** in the Properties panel.

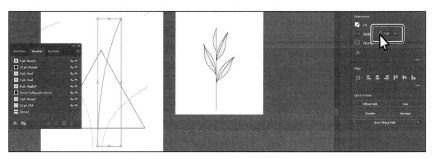

5   Choose Select > Deselect, and then choose File > Save.

Using Art brushes

Art brushes stretch artwork or an embedded raster image evenly along the length of a path. As with other brushes, you can edit the brush options to affect how the brush looks and is applied to paths.

Applying an existing Art brush

Next you'll apply an existing Art brush to the lines on either side of the text you edited at the top of the ad.

Art brush examples.

1   In the Brushes panel, click the Brushes panel menu icon (☰), and deselect Show Calligraphic Brushes. Then choose Show Art Brushes from the same panel menu to make the Art brushes visible in the Brushes panel.

2   Click the Brush Libraries Menu button (📚) at the bottom of the Brushes panel, and choose Decorative > Elegant Curl & Floral Brush Set.

3   Click the Elegant Curl & Floral Brush Set panel menu icon (☰), and choose List View. Click the brush named "Floral Stem 3" in the list to add the brush to the Brushes panel for this document.

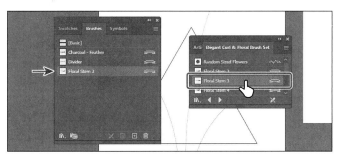

4   Close the Elegant Curl & Floral Brush Set panel group.

5   With the Selection tool selected, click the path to the left of the text up top.

6   To zoom in, press Command and + (macOS) or Ctrl and + (Windows) a few times.

7   Shift-click the path to the right of the text to select it as well.

8   Click the Floral Stem 3 brush in the Brushes panel.

9   Click the Group button in the Properties panel to keep them together.

10 Choose Select > Deselect, and then choose File > Save.

Creating an Art brush

In this section, you'll create a new Art brush from existing artwork. You can make Art brushes from embedded raster images or from vector artwork, but that artwork must not contain gradients, blends, other brush strokes, mesh objects, graphs, linked files, masks, or text that has not been converted to outlines.

1   Choose 2 from the Artboard menu in the Properties panel to navigate to the second artboard with the tea leaves artwork on it.

2   With the Selection tool (▶) selected, click the leaves artwork to select it (see the following figure).

3   In the Brushes panel, with the artwork still selected, click the New Brush button (■) at the bottom of the Brushes panel.

    This begins the process of creating a new brush from the selected artwork.

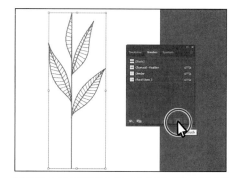

▶ **Tip:** You can also create an Art brush by dragging artwork into the Brushes panel and choosing Art Brush in the New Brush dialog box that appears.

4   In the New Brush dialog box, select Art Brush, and then click OK.

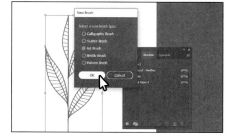

5 In the Art Brush Options dialog box that appears, change the name to **Tea Leaves**. Click OK.

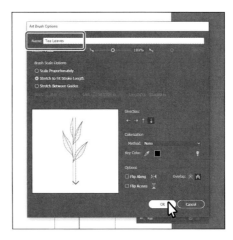

6 Choose Select > Deselect.

7 Choose 1 from the Active Artboard menu in the Properties panel to navigate back to the first artboard.

8 With the Selection tool selected, Shift-click to select the vertical curved lines over the triangle in the center of the artboard.

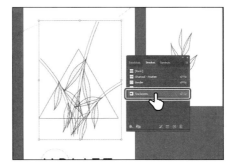

9 Click the brush named "Tea Leaves" in the Brushes panel to apply it.

Notice that the original tea leaf artwork is stretched along each path. This is the default behavior of an Art brush. Unfortunately, it's upside-down from how it should be. You'll fix that next.

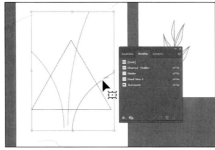

Editing an Art brush

Next you'll edit the Tea Leaves brush you applied to the path and update the appearance of the paths on the artboard.

1 With the paths still selected on the artboard, in the Brushes panel, double-click the brush thumbnail to the left of the text "Tea Leaves" (or to the right of the name in the Brushes panel) to open the Art Brush Options dialog box.

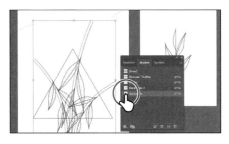

2 In the Art Brush Options dialog box, select Preview to see the changes as you make them, and move the dialog box so you can see the line with the brush applied. Make the following changes:

- Stretch Between Guides: Selected. These guides are not physical guides on the artboard. They are used to indicate the portion of the art that stretches or contracts to make the Art brush fit the path length. Any part of the art that is not within the guides will be able to stretch or contract. The Start and End settings are how you indicate where the guides are positioned on the original art.

- Start: **7.375 in**

- End: **10.8588 in** (default setting)

- Flip Along: **Selected**

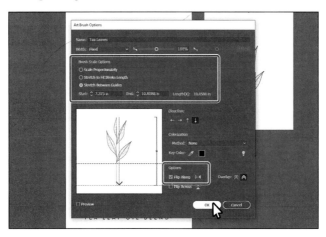

3 Click OK.

4 In the dialog box that appears, click Apply To Strokes to apply the change to the paths that have the Tea Leaves brush applied.

Now you'll make a copy of the brush and make it so the artwork on the center path stretches along the path like it does without the guides set in the options.

5 Choose Select > Deselect and then click the larger, center path with the Tea Leaves brush applied (see the following figure).

6 In the Brushes panel, drag the Tea Leaves brush to the New Brush button at the bottom to make a copy.

7 Double-click the Tea Leaves brush *copy* thumbnail in the Brushes panel to edit it.

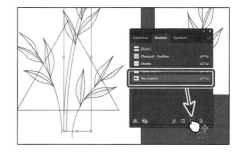

8 In the Art Brush Options dialog box, select Scale Proportionately from the Brush Scale Options section so artwork is scaled proportionally along the path. Click OK.

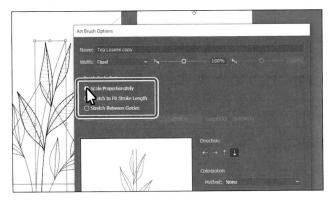

9 In the dialog box that appears, click Apply To Strokes to apply the change to the one path that has the Tea Leaves Copy brush applied.

10 Deselect the path.

11 Shift-click the remaining paths around the artboard and apply either the Tea Leaves or Tea Leaves Copy brush. Arrows are pointing to the paths in the figure.

12 Choose Select > Deselect.

Using Pattern brushes

Pattern brushes paint a pattern made up of separate sections or tiles. When you apply a Pattern brush to artwork, different tiles of the pattern are applied to different path sections, depending on where the section falls on the path—the end, middle, or corner. There are hundreds of interesting Pattern brushes that you can choose from when creating your projects, from grass to cityscapes. Next, you'll apply an existing Pattern brush to a triangle in the middle of the ad.

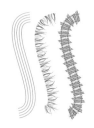

Pattern brush examples.

1   Choose View > Fit Artboard In Window.

2   In the Brushes panel, click the panel menu icon (▤), choose Show Pattern Brushes, and then deselect Show Art Brushes.

3   With the Selection tool (▶) selected, click the triangle in the middle of the ad.

4   Click the Brush Libraries Menu button (▥.) at the bottom of the Brushes panel, and choose Borders > Borders_Geometric.

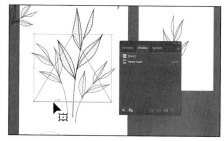

5   Click the brush named "Geometric 17" to apply it to the paths and add the brush to the Brushes panel for this document. Close the Borders_Geometric panel group.

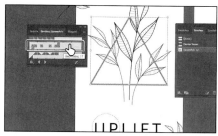

6   Change the stroke weight in the Properties panel to **2 pt**.

> **Tip:** You'll also see the Options Of Selected Object button (▤) at the bottom of the Brushes panel or in the Properties panel.

7   Click the Options Of Selected Object button (▤) in the Properties panel to edit the brush options for only the selected path on the artboard.

8   Select Preview in the Stroke Options (Pattern Brush) dialog box. Change the Scale to **120%** either by dragging the Scale slider or by typing in the value. Click OK.

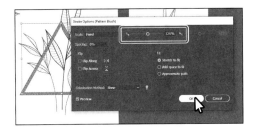

When you edit the brush options of the selected object, you see only some of the brush options. The Stroke Options (Pattern Brush) dialog box is used to edit the properties of the path with the brush applied without updating the corresponding brush.

9 Choose Select > Deselect, and then choose File > Save.

Creating a Pattern brush

You can create a Pattern brush in several ways. For a simple pattern applied to a straight line, for instance, you can select the content that you're using for the pattern and click the New Brush button ( ) at the bottom of the Brushes panel.

The pattern you
will create.

To create a more complex pattern to apply to objects with curves and corners, you can select artwork in the Document window to be used in a pattern brush, create swatches in the Swatches panel from the artwork that you are using in the Pattern brush, and even have Illustrator autogenerate the Pattern brush corners.

In Illustrator, only a side tile needs to be defined. Illustrator automatically generates four different types of corners based on the art used for the side tile. These four autogenerated options fit the corners perfectly. Next, you'll create a Pattern brush for decoration around the UPLIFT text.

1 With nothing selected, choose 2 from the Artboard menu in the Properties panel to navigate to the second artboard.

2 With the Selection tool ( ) selected, click to select the artwork at the top of the artboard.

3 To zoom in, press Command and + (macOS) or Ctrl and + (Windows) a few times.

4 Click the panel menu icon (▤) in the Brushes panel, and choose Thumbnail View.

Notice that Pattern brushes in the Brushes panel are segmented in Thumbnail view. Each segment corresponds to a pattern tile.

5 In the Brushes panel, click the New Brush button (▣) to create a pattern out of the artwork.

6 In the New Brush dialog box, select Pattern Brush. Click OK.

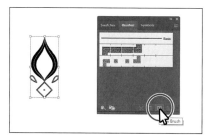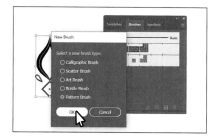

A new Pattern brush can be made regardless of whether artwork is selected. If you create a Pattern brush without artwork selected, it is assumed that you will add artwork by dragging it into the Brushes panel later or by selecting the artwork from a pattern swatch you create as you edit the brush. You will see the latter method later in this section.

7 In the Pattern Brush Options dialog box, name the brush **Decoration**.

Pattern brushes can have up to five tiles—the side, start, and end tiles, plus an outer-corner tile and an inner-corner tile to paint sharp corners on a path.

You can see all five tiles as buttons below the Spacing option in the dialog box. The tile buttons let you apply different artwork to different parts of the path. You can click a tile button for the tile you want to define, and then you select an autogenerated selection (if available) or a pattern swatch from the menu that appears.

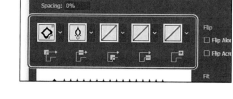

▶ **Tip:** Move the pointer over the tile squares in the Pattern Brush Options dialog box to see a tool tip indicating which tile it is.

▶ **Tip:** Selected artwork becomes the side tile, by default, when creating a Pattern brush.

8 Under the Spacing option, click the Side Tile box (the second tile from the left). The decorative artwork that was originally selected is in the menu that appears, along with None and any pattern swatches found in the Swatches panel.

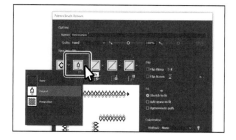

9 Click the Outer Corner Tile box to reveal the menu. You may need to click twice, once to close the previous menu and another click to open this new one.

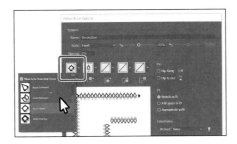

The outer-corner tile has been generated automatically by Illustrator, based on the original decorative artwork. In the menu, you can choose from four types of corners that are autogenerated:

- **Auto-Centered:** The side tile is stretched around the corner and centered on it.

- **Auto-Between:** Copies of the side tile extend all the way into the corner, with one copy on each side. They are then stretched into shape.

- **Auto-Sliced:** The side tile is sliced diagonally, and the pieces come together, similar to the miter joint at each corner of a wooden picture frame.

- **Auto-Overlap:** Copies of the tiles overlap at the corner.

10 Choose Auto-Between from the Outer Corner Tile box menu. This generates the outer corner of any path that the Pattern brush will be applied to from the selected decorative artwork.

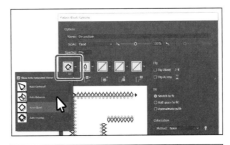

11 Click OK. The Decoration brush appears in the Brushes panel.

12 Choose Select > Deselect.

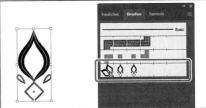

Applying a Pattern brush

In this section, you'll apply the Decoration Pattern brush to a circle around the text in the center of the first artboard. As you've seen, when you use drawing tools to apply brushes to artwork, you first draw the path with the drawing tool and then select the brush in the Brushes panel to apply the brush to the path.

1 Choose 1 from the Active Artboard menu in the Properties panel to navigate to the first artboard with the ad artwork on it.

2 With the Selection tool (▶) selected, click the circle around the "UP" in "UPLIFT."

3 Choose View > Zoom In a few times to zoom in.

4 With the path selected, click the Decoration brush in the Brushes panel to apply it.

5 Choose Select > Deselect.

The path is painted with the Decoration brush. Because the path does not include sharp corners, outer-corner and inner-corner tiles are not applied to the path.

Editing the Pattern brush

Tip: For more information on creating pattern swatches, see "About patterns" in Illustrator Help.

Now you'll edit the Decoration Pattern brush using a pattern swatch that you create.

1 Choose 2 from the Active Artboard menu in the Properties panel to navigate to the second artboard.

2 With the Selection tool (▶), click the same decoration artwork at the top of the artboard. Change the stroke color to a light green color, as in the figure. Press the Escape key to hide the panel.

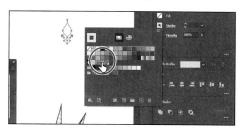

3 Click the Swatches panel tab in the Brushes panel group to show the Swatches panel.

4 Drag the decoration artwork into the Swatches panel.

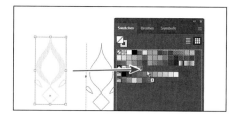 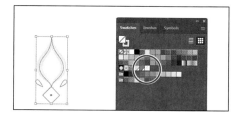

The artwork is saved as a new pattern swatch in the Swatches panel. After you create a Pattern brush, you can delete the pattern swatches from the Swatches panel, if you don't plan to use them for additional artwork.

5 Choose Select > Deselect.

6 Choose 1 from the Active Artboard menu in the Properties panel to navigate to the first artboard with the main scene artwork on it.

7 Click the Brushes panel tab to show the panel, and double-click the Decoration Pattern brush to open the Pattern Brush Options dialog box.

8 Click the Side Tile box, and choose the pattern swatch named New Pattern Swatch 1, which you just created, from the menu that appears.

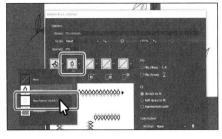

Tip: You can also change the pattern tiles in a Pattern brush by pressing the Option (macOS) or Alt (Windows) key and dragging artwork from the artboard onto the tile of the Pattern brush you want to change in the Brushes panel.

9 Change Scale to **50%**. Click OK.

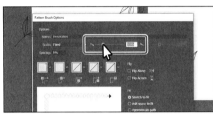

10 In the dialog box that appears, click Apply To Strokes to update the Decoration brush and the brush applied to the circle.

11 With the Selection tool selected, click to select the triangle with the Geometric 17 brush applied. You may want to zoom in.

12 Click the Decoration brush in the Brushes panel to apply it.

Notice that the corners appear (an arrow is pointing to one in the figure). The path is painted with the side tile from the Decoration brush and the outer-corner tile.

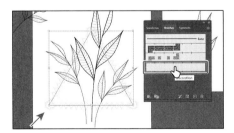

13 Click to apply the Geometric 17 brush again.

14 Choose Select > Deselect, and then choose File > Save.

Using Bristle brushes

Bristle brushes allow you to create strokes with the appearance of a natural brush with bristles. Painting with a Bristle brush using the Paintbrush tool creates vector paths with the Bristle brush applied.

In this section, you'll start by adjusting options for a brush to change how it appears in the artwork and then paint with the Paintbrush tool and a Bristle brush.

Bristle brush examples.

Changing Bristle brush options

As you've seen, you can change the appearance of a brush by adjusting its settings in the Brush Options dialog box, either before or after brushes have been applied to artwork. In the case of Bristle brushes, it's usually best to adjust the brush settings before painting since it can take some time to update the brush strokes.

1   In the Brushes panel, click the panel menu icon (▤), choose Show Bristle Brushes, deselect Show Pattern Brushes, and choose List View.

Tip: Illustrator comes with a series of default Bristle brushes. Click the Brush Libraries Menu button (▥) at the bottom of the Brushes panel, and choose Bristle Brush > Bristle Brush Library.

2   Double-click the thumbnail for the default Mop brush, or double-click directly to the right of the brush name in the Brushes panel, to change the options for that brush. In the Bristle Brush Options dialog box, make the following changes:

- Shape: **Round Fan**

- Size: **10 mm** (The brush size is the diameter of the brush.)

- Bristle Length: **150%** (This is the default setting. The bristle length starts from the point where the bristles meet the handle of the bristle tip.)

- Bristle Density: **33%** (This is the default setting. The bristle density is the number of bristles in a specified area of the brush neck.)

- Bristle Thickness: **70%** (The bristle thickness can vary from fine to coarse [from 1% to 100%].)

- Paint Opacity: **75%** (This is the default setting. This option lets you set the opacity of the paint being used.)

- Stiffness: **50%** (This is the default setting. Stiffness refers to the rigidness of the bristles.)

3   Click OK.

Painting with a Bristle brush

Now you'll use the Mop brush to draw some strokes behind the artwork to add some texture to the background of the ad. Painting with a Bristle brush can create an organic, fluid path.

1 Choose View > Fit Artboard In Window.

2 With the Selection tool (▶) selected, click to select the "UPLIFT" text.

   This selects the layer that the text shapes are on so that any artwork you paint will be on the same layer. The "UPLIFT" text shapes are on a layer that is beneath most of the other artwork on the artboard.

3 Choose Select > Deselect.

4 Select the Paintbrush tool (✐) in the toolbar. Choose the Mop brush from the Brush menu in the Properties panel or the Brushes panel, if it's not already chosen.

Tip: You can also select the brush in the Brushes panel, if it's open.

5 Make sure that the fill color is None (▱) and the stroke color is the same light green from the Decoration brush, in the Properties panel. Press the Escape key to hide the Swatches panel.

6 Change the stroke weight to **5 pt** in the Properties panel.

7 Move the pointer to the right of the triangle in the middle of the page (see the figure). Drag slightly down and to the left, across the artboard, and then back again to the right to make a sideways V shape. Release the mouse button when you reach the end of the path you want to draw.

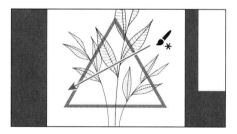
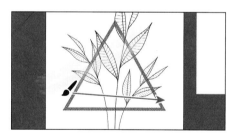

8 With the Paintbrush tool, use the Mop brush to paint more paths around the artboard. These paths are meant to add texture to the ad.

   I added pink paths to the figure to show you where we added two more paths to the ad.

Grouping Bristle brush paths

Next you'll group the paths you drew with the Mop brush to make it easier to select them later.

1   Choose View > Outline to see all of the paths you just created.

Next you'll select all of the Bristle brush paths you painted and group them together.

2   Choose Select > Object > Bristle Brush Strokes to select all of the paths created with the Paintbrush tool using the Mop brush. In the figure, I added pink paths to show you where my paths were.

3   Click the Group button in the Properties panel to group them together.

4   Choose View > Preview (or GPU Preview).

5   Choose Select > Deselect, and then choose File > Save.

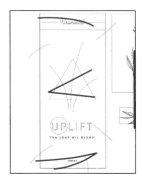

Working with the Blob Brush tool

You can use the Blob Brush tool () to paint filled shapes that intersect and merge with other shapes of the same color. With the Blob Brush tool, you can draw with Paintbrush tool artistry. Unlike the Paintbrush tool, which lets you create open paths, the Blob Brush tool lets you create a closed shape with only a fill (no stroke) that you can then easily edit with the Eraser or Blob Brush tool. Shapes that have a stroke cannot be edited with the Blob Brush tool.

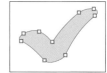

Path created with the Paintbrush tool.

Shape created with the Blob Brush tool.

Drawing with the Blob Brush tool

Next you'll use the Blob Brush tool to add color to one of the leaf shapes.

1   With the Selection tool selected (▶), click the largest bunch of leaves in the center of the artboard (over the triangle).

2   Press Command and + (macOS) or Ctrl and + (Windows) a few times.

3   Deselect the leaves by clicking in an empty area of the artboard.

4   Press and hold down on the Paintbrush tool (✐) in the toolbar, and select the Blob Brush tool ().

5 Click the Swatches panel tab in the Brushes panel group to show the Swatches panel. Select the Fill box to edit the fill color, and then select the same light green swatch you've been using up to this point. Select the Stroke color box, and select None (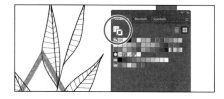) to remove the stroke.

When drawing with the Blob Brush tool, if a fill and stroke are set before drawing, the stroke color becomes the fill color of the shape made by the Blob Brush tool. If only a fill is set before drawing, it ultimately becomes the fill of the shape created.

6 Move the pointer near the largest bunch of leaves in the center. To change the Blob Brush size, press the right bracket key ( ]) several times to increase the size of the brush.

Notice that the Blob Brush pointer has a circle around it. That circle indicates the size of the brush. Pressing the left bracket key ([ ) will make the brush size smaller.

7 Drag around the outside of the leaf shape to loosely draw another leaf shape.

When you draw with the Blob Brush tool, you create filled, closed shapes. Those shapes can contain several types of fill, including gradients, solid colors, patterns, and more.

8 Select the Selection tool and click the artwork you just made. Notice that it's a filled shape, not a path with a stroke.

9 Click in an empty area of the artboard to deselect, and select the Blob Brush tool in the toolbar again.

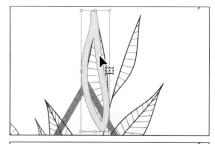

10 Drag to fill in the shape and maybe add a bit more to it.

As long as the new artwork is overlapping the existing artwork and it has the same stroke and fill, it will merge into one shape.

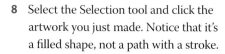

▷ **Tip:** If you want, try adding more shapes to the other leaves following the same steps.

Editing with the Eraser tool

Tip: As you draw with the Blob Brush and Eraser tools, it is recommended that you use shorter strokes and release the mouse button often. You can undo the edits that you make, but if you draw in one long stroke without releasing the mouse button, undoing removes the entire stroke.

As you draw and merge shapes with the Blob Brush tool, you may draw too much and want to edit what you've done. You can use the Eraser tool (◆) in combination with the Blob Brush tool to mold the shape and to correct any changes you don't like.

1 With the Selection tool (▶), click to select the green shape you just made.

2 Click the Arrange button in the Properties panel, and choose Send To Back to put it behind the path with the Tea Leaves Copy brush applied.

Selecting the shape(s) before erasing also limits the Eraser tool to erasing only the selected shape(s). As with the Paintbrush or Blob Brush tools, you can also double-click to set options for the Eraser tool. In this case, you'll use it as is and simply adjust the brush size.

3 Select the Eraser tool (◆) in the toolbar. Move the pointer near the green shape you made. To change the eraser size, press the right bracket key ( ]) several times to increase the size of the brush.

The Blob Brush and Eraser tools both have pointers that include a circle that indicates the diameter of the brush.

4 Move the pointer just off the upper-left of the green shape and, with the Eraser tool selected, press and drag along the edge to remove some of it. Try switching between the Blob Brush tool and the Eraser tool to edit the shape.

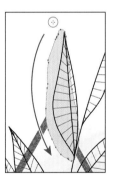 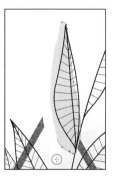 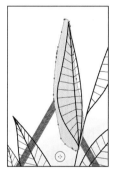

5 Choose Select > Deselect and then choose View > Fit Artboard In Window.

In the figure, you can see that I added more green shapes I created with the Blob Brush and Eraser tools for some practice.

6 Choose File > Save, and close all open files.

Review questions

1   What is the difference between applying a brush to artwork using the Paintbrush tool (✎) and applying a brush to artwork using one of the drawing tools?

2   Describe how artwork in an Art brush is applied to content.

3   Describe how to edit paths with the Paintbrush tool as you draw. How does the Keep Selected option affect the Paintbrush tool?

4   For which brush types must you have artwork selected on the artboard before you can create a brush?

5   What does the Blob Brush tool (✎) allow you to create?

6   How do you ensure that only certain artwork is erased when using the Eraser tool?

Review answers

1   When painting with the Paintbrush tool (✎), if a brush is chosen in the Brushes panel and you draw on the artboard, the brush is applied directly to the paths as you draw. To apply brushes using a drawing tool, you select the tool and draw in the artwork. Then you select the path in the artwork and choose a brush in the Brushes panel. The brush is applied to the selected path.

2   An Art brush is made from artwork (vector or embedded raster). When you apply an Art brush to the stroke of an object, the artwork in the Art brush, by default, is stretched along the selected object stroke.

3   To edit a path with the Paintbrush tool, drag over a selected path to redraw it. The Keep Selected option keeps the last path selected as you draw with the Paintbrush tool. Leave the Keep Selected option selected when you want to easily edit the previous path as you draw. Deselect the Keep Selected option when you want to draw layered paths with the paintbrush without altering previous paths. When Keep Selected is deselected, you can use the Selection tool (▶) to select a path and then edit it.

4   For Art (and Scatter) brushes, you need to have artwork selected in order to create a brush using the New Brush button (▣) in the Brushes panel.

5   Use the Blob Brush tool (✎) to create and edit filled shapes that you can intersect and merge with other shapes of the same color or to create artwork from scratch.

6   To ensure that only certain artwork is erased, select the artwork.

13 EXPLORING CREATIVE USES OF EFFECTS AND GRAPHIC STYLES

Lesson overview

In this lesson, you'll learn how to do the following:

- Work with the Appearance panel.

- Edit and apply appearance attributes.

- Duplicate, enable, disable, and remove appearance attributes.

- Reorder appearance attributes.

- Apply and edit a variety of effects.

- Save and apply an appearance as a graphic style.

- Apply a graphic style to a layer.

- Scale strokes and effects.

This lesson will take about 60 minutes to complete. To get the lesson files used in this chapter, download them from the web page for this book at adobepress.com/IllustratorCIB2022. For more information, see "Accessing the lesson files and Web Edition" in the Getting Started section at the beginning of this book.

You can change the look of an object without changing its structure simply by applying attributes, such as fills, strokes, and effects, from the Appearance panel. Since the effects are live, they can be modified or removed at any time. This allows you to save the appearance attributes as graphic styles and apply them to another object.

Starting the lesson

In this lesson, you'll change the appearance of artwork for a birthday invite using the Appearance panel, various effects, and graphic styles. Before you begin, you'll need to restore the default preferences for Adobe Illustrator. Then you'll open a file containing the final artwork to see what you'll create.

Note: If you have not already downloaded the project files for this lesson to your computer from your Account page, make sure to do so now. See the "Getting Started" section at the beginning of the book.

1 To ensure that the tools function and the defaults are set exactly as described in this lesson, delete or deactivate (by renaming) the Adobe Illustrator preferences file. See "Restoring default preferences" in the "Getting Started" section at the beginning of the book.

2 Start Adobe Illustrator.

3 Choose File > Open, and open the L13_end.ai file in the Lessons > Lesson13 folder on your hard disk.

   This file displays a completed illustration for a birthday card.

Note: You will need an internet connection to activate fonts.

4 In the Missing Fonts dialog box that most likely will appear, click Activate Fonts to activate all of the missing fonts. After they are activated and you see the message stating that there are no more missing fonts, click Close.

   If you can't get the fonts to activate, go to the Creative Cloud desktop application and click the Fonts icon (*f*) in the upper right to see what the issue may be (refer to the section "Changing font family and font style" in Lesson 9 for more information on how to resolve it).

   You can also just click Close in the Missing Fonts dialog box and ignore the missing fonts as you proceed. A third method is to click the Find Fonts button in the Missing Fonts dialog box and replace the fonts with a local font on your machine. You can also go to Help (Help > Illustrator Help) and search for "Find missing fonts."

5 If a dialog box appears referring to font auto-activation, then click Skip.

6 Choose View > Fit Artboard In Window. Leave the file open as a reference or choose File > Close to close it.

To begin working, you'll open an existing art file.

7 Choose File > Open. In the Open dialog box, navigate to the Lessons > Lesson13 folder, and select the L13_start.ai file on your hard disk. Click Open to open the file.

The L13_start.ai file uses the same fonts as the L13_end.ai file. If you've activated the fonts already, you don't need to do it again. If you didn't open the L13_end.ai file, then the Missing Fonts dialog box will most likely appear for this step. Click Activate Fonts to activate all of the missing fonts. After they are activated and you see the message stating that there are no more missing fonts, click Close.

8 Choose File > Save As. If the Cloud Document dialog box opens, click Save On Your Computer, otherwise continue.

9 In the Save As dialog box, name the file **BirthdayInvite.ai**, and select the Lesson13 folder. Leave Adobe Illustrator (ai) chosen from the Format menu (macOS) or Adobe Illustrator (*.AI) chosen from the Save As Type menu (Windows), and then click Save.

10 In the Illustrator Options dialog box, leave the Illustrator options at their default settings, and then click OK.

11 Choose Reset Essentials from the workspace switcher in the Application bar to reset the workspace.

⬤ **Note:** If you don't see Reset Essentials in the workspace switcher menu, choose Window > Workspace > Essentials before choosing Window > Workspace > Reset Essentials.

12 Choose View > Fit Artboard In Window.

Using the Appearance panel

An *appearance attribute* is an aesthetic property—like a fill, stroke, transparency, or effect—that affects the look of an object but usually does not affect its basic structure. Up to this point, you've been changing appearance attributes in the Properties panel, Swatches panel, and more. Appearance attributes like these can also be found in the Appearance panel for selected artwork. In this lesson, you'll focus on using the Appearance panel to apply and edit appearance attributes.

To begin exploring appearance options, you'll see how to edit the color fill of the cake stand and then add another fill on top to give it more dimension.

1 Select the Selection tool (▶), and click to select the black base of the cake stand.

▷ **Tip:** You can also choose Window > Appearance to open the Appearance panel.

2 Click More Options (•••) in the Appearance section of the Properties panel on the right (an arrow is pointing to it in the following figure) to open the Appearance panel.

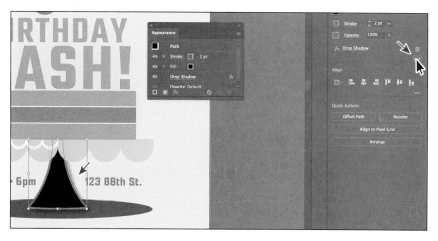

▷ **Tip:** You may want to drag the bottom of the Appearance panel down to make it taller, as you see in the figure.

The Appearance panel (Window > Appearance) shows what the selected content is (a path, in this case) and the appearance attributes applied to it (stroke, fill, etc.). The different options available in the Appearance panel are shown here:

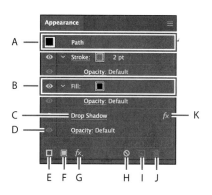

A. Selected artwork and thumbnail

B. Attribute row

C. Link to edit an effect

D. Visibility column

E. Add New Stroke

F. Add New Fill

G. Add New Effect

H. Clear Appearance

I. Duplicate Selected Item

J. Delete Selected Item

K. Indicates that an effect is applied

You can view and adjust the appearance attributes for a selected object, group, or layer in the Appearance panel. Fills and strokes are listed in stacking order; top to bottom in the panel correlates to the front to back in the artwork. Effects applied to artwork are listed from top to bottom in the order they are applied to the artwork. An advantage of using appearance attributes is that they can be changed or removed without affecting the underlying artwork or any other attributes applied to the object in the Appearance panel.

Editing appearance attributes

You'll start by changing the appearance of artwork using the Appearance panel.

1   With the cake stand selected, in the Appearance panel, click the black Fill box in the fill attribute row as many times as needed until the Swatches panel appears. Select the swatch named "Aqua" to apply it to the fill.

Note: You may need to click the Fill box more than once to open the Swatches panel. The first click of the Fill box selects the Fill row in the panel, and the next click shows the Swatches panel.

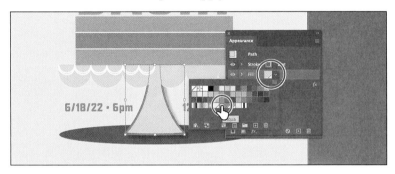

2   Press the Escape key to hide the Swatches panel.

3   Click the words "2 pt" in the pink Stroke row to show the Stroke Weight option. Change the stroke weight to **0** to remove it (the Stroke Weight field will be blank).

So far, everything you've changed could have been done in the Properties panel. Now you'll explore something unique to the Appearance panel—hiding an effect (not deleting it).

Tip: In the Appearance panel, you can drag an attribute row, such as Drop Shadow, to the Delete Selected Item button (🗑) to delete it, or you can select the attribute row and click the Delete Selected Item button.

Tip: You can view all hidden attributes (attributes you have turned off) by choosing Show All Hidden Attributes from the Appearance panel menu (☰).

4 Click the visibility column (👁) to the left of the Drop Shadow attribute name in the Appearance panel. I dragged the bottom of the Appearance panel down to make it taller in the figures.

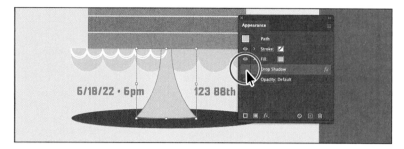

Appearance attributes can be temporarily hidden or deleted so that they are no longer applied to the selected artwork.

5 With the Drop Shadow row selected (click to the right of the link "Drop Shadow" if it isn't selected), click the Delete Selected Item button (🗑) at the bottom of the panel to completely remove the shadow, rather than just turning off the visibility. Leave the shape selected.

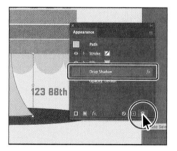
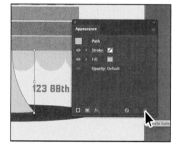

Adding another fill to content

Artwork and text in Illustrator can have more than one stroke and fill applied. This can be a great way to add interest to design elements like shapes and paths, and adding multiple strokes and fills to text can be a great way to make your text pop.

Next you'll add another fill to the cake stand to add texture over the color fill.

1 With the cake stand shape still selected, in the Appearance panel, click the Add New Fill button (🔲) at the bottom of the Appearance panel.

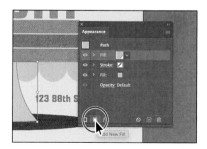

A second Fill row is added to the Appearance panel. By default, new fill or stroke attribute rows are added directly above a selected attribute row or, if no attribute rows are selected, at the top of the Appearance panel list.

2 Click the *bottom* (original) aqua Fill box in the fill attribute row a few times until the Swatches panel appears. Click the pattern swatch named "6 lpi 10%" to change the fill.

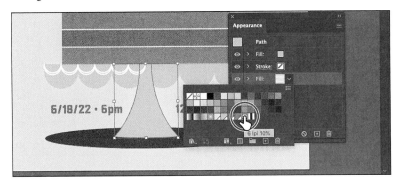

3 Press the Escape key to hide the Swatches panel.

The pattern doesn't show in the selected artwork because the second fill you added in the first step is covering the "6 lpi 10%" fill. The two fills are stacked on top of each other.

4 Click the eye icon (👁) to the left of the top aqua fill row to hide it.

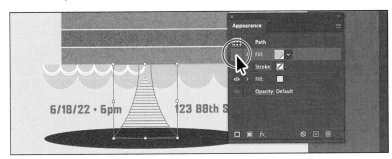

You should now see the pattern fill in the shape. In the next section, you'll reorder the attribute rows in the Appearance panel so the pattern is on top of the color fill.

5 Click where the eye icon was to the left of the top fill attribute row to make it visible again.

6 Choose Select > Deselect, and then choose File > Save.

Adding multiple strokes and fills to text

Aside from adding multiple strokes and fills to artwork, you can also do the same for text. The text remains editable, and you can use a number of effects to achieve the look that you want. Now you'll take the "BIRTHDAY BASH!" text and make it pop with a few strokes and fills.

1 Select the Type tool (T), and select the text "BIRTHDAY BASH!"

Notice that "Type: No Appearance" appears at the top of the Appearance panel. This is referring to the type object, not the text within. You will also see the word "Characters." Formatting for the text (not the type object) is listed below the word "Characters." You should see the stroke (none) and the fill (pink).

Also notice that you cannot add another stroke or fill to the text since the Add New Stroke and Add New Fill buttons are dimmed at the bottom of the panel. To add new strokes or fills to text, you need to select the type *object*, not the text within.

▶ **Tip:** You could also click Type: No Appearance at the top of the Appearance panel to select the type object (not the text within).

2 Select the Selection tool (▶). The type object will now be selected (not the text).

3 Click the Add New Fill button (▣) at the bottom of the Appearance panel to add a fill and a stroke above the word "Characters."

The new black fill is covering the original pink fill of the text. If you were to double-click the word "Characters" in the Appearance panel, you would select the text and see the formatting options for it (fill, stroke, etc.).

4 Click the fill attribute row to select it, if it's not already selected. Click the black Fill box, and select the pattern swatch named 0 to 50% Dot Gradation.

Note: Why would I name a swatch 0 to 50% Dot Gradation? Actually, I didn't. That pattern swatch can be found in Illustrator by default (Window > Swatch Libraries > Patterns > Basic Graphics > Basic Graphics_Dots).

5 Press the Escape key to hide the swatches.

At this point, I am going to stop instructing you to close panels, hoping that this is becoming habit.

When you apply a fill to a text object, an extra stroke with no color is also applied. You don't have to use it.

6 If necessary, click the disclosure triangle (▶) to the left of the fill row to show other properties, like Opacity. Click the word "Opacity," which is indented below the fill row, to show the Transparency panel, and change Opacity to **40%**.

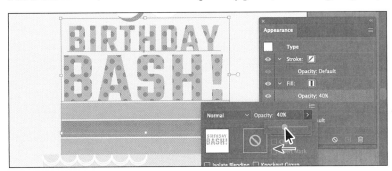

Each appearance row (stroke, fill) has its own opacity that you can adjust. The bottom Opacity appearance row in the panel affects the transparency for the entire selected object. Next you'll add two strokes to the text using the Appearance panel. This is another great way to achieve unique design effects with a single object.

7 Click the Stroke box () a few times in the Appearance panel to show the swatches. Select the white swatch.

8 Ensure that the Stroke Weight is **1 pt**.

9 Click the Add New Stroke button (■) at the bottom of the Appearance panel.

A second stroke, which is a copy of the original, is now added to the text. This is a great way to add interest to your designs without having to make copies of shapes and put them on top of each other to add multiple strokes and fills.

10 With the new (top) stroke attribute row selected, select the swatch named Orange to apply it.

11 Ensure that the Stroke Weight is **1 pt**.

12 Click the word "Stroke" in the same attribute row to open the Stroke panel. Click the Round Join option (⬛) in the Corner section of the panel to *slightly* round the corners of the stroke. Press Return or Enter to accept the value and hide the Stroke panel. Leave the type object selected.

Clicking underlined words in the Appearance panel, as in the Properties panel, shows more formatting options—usually a panel such as the Swatches or Stroke panel. Appearance attributes, such as Fill or Stroke, can have other options, such as Opacity or an effect applied to only that attribute. These additional options are listed as a subset under the attribute row and can be shown or hidden by clicking the disclosure triangle () on the left end of the attribute row.

Reordering appearance attributes

The ordering of the appearance attribute rows can greatly change how your artwork looks. In the Appearance panel, fills and strokes are listed in stacking order—top to bottom in the panel correlates to front to back in the artwork. You can reorder attribute rows in a way similar to dragging layers in the Layers panel to rearrange the stacking order. Next you'll change the appearance of artwork by reordering attributes in the Appearance panel.

1 With the text still selected, press Command and + (macOS) or Ctrl and + (Windows) to zoom in.

2 In the Appearance panel, click the eye icon to the left of the white Stroke row to hide it temporarily. You can also click the arrows to the left of all Stroke and Fill rows to hide the Opacity for each.

3 Drag the orange stroke row in the Appearance panel down below the word "Characters." When a line appears below the word "Characters," release the mouse button to see the result.

Note: You can drag the bottom of the Appearance panel to make it taller.

 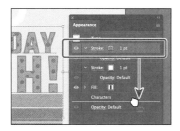 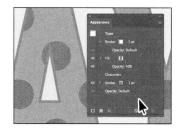

The orange stroke is now behind all fills and the white stroke. The word "Characters" represents where the stroke and fill (the pink color) of the text (not the text object) sits in the stacking order.

4 Click where the eye icon (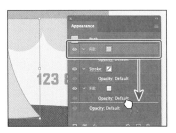) was for the white stroke row to show it again.

5 Select the Selection tool (▶), and click to select the cake stand you edited earlier.

6 In the Appearance panel, drag the aqua Fill row down below the pattern Fill row, and release.

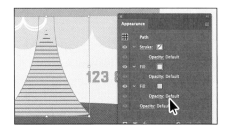

Moving the aqua fill attribute below the pattern fill attribute changes the look of the artwork. The pattern fill is now on top of the solid color fill.

7 Choose Select > Deselect, and then choose File > Save.

Using live effects

In most instances effects alter the appearance of an object without changing the underlying artwork. They're added to the object's appearance attribute, which you can edit, move, hide, delete, or duplicate, at any time, in the Appearance panel.

There are two types of effects in Illustrator: *vector effects* and *raster effects*. In Illustrator, click the Effect menu to see the different types of effects available.

Artwork with a drop shadow effect applied.

- **Illustrator effects (vector):** The top half of the Effect menu contains vector effects. You can apply most of these effects only to vector objects or to the fill or stroke of a vector object in the Appearance panel. The following vector effects can be applied to both vector and bitmap objects: 3D effects, SVG filters, Warp effects, Transform effects, Drop Shadow, Feather, Inner Glow, and Outer Glow.

- **Photoshop effects (raster):** The bottom half of the Effect menu contains raster effects. You can apply them to either vector or bitmap objects.

In this section, you will first explore how to apply and edit effects. You will then explore a few of the more widely used effects in Illustrator to get an idea of the range of effects available.

Note: When you apply a raster effect, the original vector data is rasterized using the document's raster effects settings, which determine the resolution of the resulting image. To learn about document raster effects settings, search for "Document raster effects settings" in Illustrator Help.

Applying an effect

Effects are applied using the Properties panel, the Effect menu, and the Appearance panel, and they can be applied to objects, groups, or layers. In this section, you'll apply a drop shadow to the brush handles and make it more transparent.

1 Choose View > Fit Artboard In Window.

2 With the Selection tool (▶) selected, click the green scalloped shape above the cake stand. Shift-click the cake stand to select it as well.

3 Click the Group button in the Properties panel to group them.

4 Click the Add New Effect button (𝘧𝘹.) at the bottom of the Appearance panel, or click the Choose An Effect button (𝘧𝘹.) in the Appearance section of the Properties panel. Choose Stylize > Drop Shadow from the Illustrator Effects section of the menu that appears.

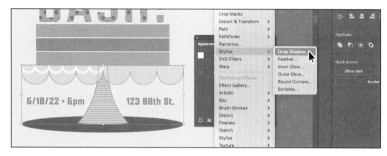

5 In the Drop Shadow dialog box that opens, select Preview and change the following options:

- Mode: Multiply (the default setting)
- Opacity: **20%**
- X Offset: **0 in**
- Y Offset: **0.03 in** (you'll need to type this value in)
- Blur: **0.03 in** (you'll need to type this value in)
- Color: Selected

6 Click OK.

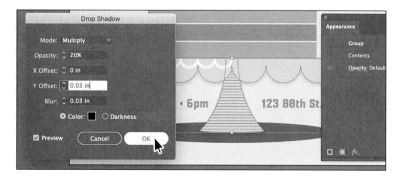

Since the drop shadow is applied to the group, it appears around the perimeter of the group, not on each object independently. If you look in the Appearance panel right now, you'll see the word "Group" at the top and the Drop Shadow effect applied. The word "Contents" refers to the content within the group. Each object in a group can have its own appearance properties.

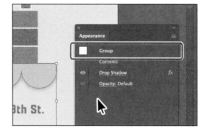

7 Choose File > Save.

Editing an effect

● **Note:** If you attempt to apply an effect to artwork that already has the same effect applied, Illustrator will warn you that the same effect is already applied.

Effects are live and can be edited after being applied to an object. You can edit the effect in the Properties panel or Appearance panel by selecting the object with the effect applied and then clicking the effect's name, or in the Appearance panel, double-clicking the attribute row. This displays the dialog box for that effect. Changes you make to the effect update in the artwork. In this section, you will apply a shadow to the "BIRTHDAY BASH!" text, but with a twist. You'll apply it to one of the strokes, not the whole object.

1 Click the "BIRTHDAY BASH!" text.

▷ **Tip:** If you were to choose Effect > Drop Shadow, the Drop Shadow dialog box would appear, allowing you to make changes before applying the effect.

2 In the Appearance panel, select the white Stroke row so the effect you apply is only applied to that appearance.

3 Choose Effect > Apply Drop Shadow. If you need, click the arrow to the left of word Stroke in the white stroke row to see the Drop Shadow.

The Apply Drop Shadow menu item applies the last used effect with the same options set.

4 In the Appearance panel, click the text "Drop Shadow" beneath the white Stroke row to edit the effect options.

5 In the Drop Shadow dialog box, select Preview to see the changes. Change the Opacity to **40%**, the X Offset and Y Offset to **0.01**, and the Blur to **0.02 in**. Click OK. Leave the text object selected.

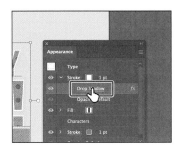

Styling text with a Warp effect

Text can have all sorts of effects applied, including warp, as you saw in Lesson 9. The difference between the warp you applied in Lesson 9 and the Warp effect you are about to apply, is that this one is an effect and can be turned on and off, edited, or removed easily. Next you will use the Warp effect to warp the "BIRTHDAY BASH!" text.

1   In the Appearance panel, click the word "Type" at the top of the panel. It's highlighted in the following figure.

Clicking "Type" targets the text, not just the stroke. The more you apply effects, the more you realize how much flexibility you have when applying them.

▶ **Tip:** You can also click the Choose An Effect button (![fx]) at the bottom of the Appearance panel.

2   With the text still selected, click the Choose An Effect button (![fx]) in the Appearance section of the Properties panel. Choose Warp > Rise from the menu.

This is another way to apply an effect to content and will be handy if you have the Appearance panel open.

3   In the Warp Options dialog box, select Preview to see the changes. Try choosing styles from the Style menu and then choose Arc Upper. Set Bend to **15%**.

4   Try adjusting the Horizontal and Vertical Distortion sliders to see the effect. Make sure that the Distortion values are returned to **0** and then click OK. Leave the text selected.

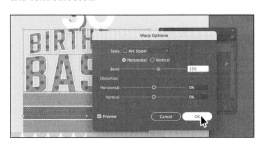

Temporarily disabling effects to make edits

You can edit text with a Warp effect applied, but sometimes it's easier to turn off the effect, make the change to the text, and then turn the effect back on.

1 With the text selected, click the visibility icon (👁) to the left of the "Warp: Arc Upper" row in the Appearance panel to temporarily turn off the effect.

Notice that the text is no longer warped on the artboard.

▶ **Tip:** If your text is too wide, you can select it and change the font size, making it a bit smaller.

2 Select the Type tool (T) in the toolbar, and change the text to **BIRTHDAY PARTY**.

3 Select the Selection tool (▶) in the toolbar. This selects the type object, not the text.

4 Click the visibility column to the left of the Warp: Arc Upper row in the Appearance panel to turn on visibility for the effect.

The text is once again warped, but since the text changed, the amount of warp may need to be different due to the overall size of the text.

5 In the Appearance panel, click the underlined Warp: Arc Upper text to edit the effect. In the Warp Options dialog box, change Bend to **30%**. Click OK.

You may need to drag the text down onto the cake.

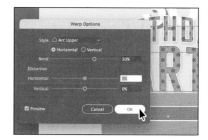

6 Choose Select > Deselect, and then choose File > Save.

Applying other effects

Next, you'll apply a few other effects to finish parts of the artwork. Know that you can apply multiple effects to the same objects to get the appearance you are after.

Now you'll add a creative stroke to the candle at the top of the cake and give the orange stroke on the "BIRTHDAY PARTY" text some depth and perspective.

1 With the Selection tool (▶) selected, drag across the two birthday candles (30) to select the candle flames and numbers. Drag them up so they are sitting on top of the text.

2 Choose Select > Deselect.

3 Click the birthday candle (3) at the top of the cake.

4 Change the yellow stroke in the Appearance panel to pink so it's easier to see.

5 With the stroke attribute row selected, in the Appearance panel, click the Add New Effect button (*fx.*) at the bottom of the panel, and choose Path > Offset Path to apply it to the pink stroke only.

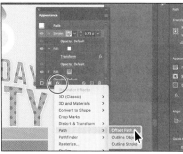

6 In the Offset Path dialog box, change Offset to **-0.03** in, select Preview, and then click OK.

7 Change the pink stroke in the Appearance panel back to yellow.

Now you'll add depth to the "BIRTHDAY PARTY" text.

8 With the Selection tool selected, click the "BIRTHDAY PARTY" text.

9 In the Appearance panel, click the orange stroke row to select it.

The effect you apply will now affect only the selected stroke. I dragged the bottom of the Appearance panel down to see more.

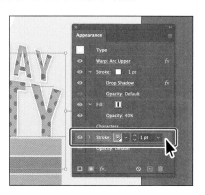

10 In the Appearance panel, click the Add New Effect button (*fx.*) at the bottom of the panel, and choose Distort & Transform > Transform.

11 In the Transform Effect dialog box, select Preview and change the following:

- Horizontal Move: **0.01 in**
- Vertical Move: **0.01 in**
- Copies: **5**

12 Click OK.

The Transform effect, in this case, will copy the stroke 5 times and move those copies to the right and down.

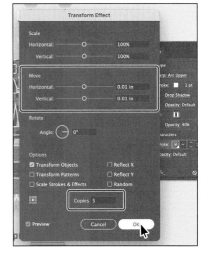

13 In the Appearance panel, click the disclosure triangle (▸) to the left of the word "Stroke" for the orange stroke to toggle it open (if it's not already open).

Notice that the Transform effect is a subset of Stroke. This indicates that the Transform effect is applied to only that stroke.

14 Choose Select > Deselect, and then choose File > Save.

Applying a Photoshop effect

As described earlier in the lesson, raster effects generate pixels rather than vector data. Raster effects include SVG filters, all of the effects in the bottom portion of the Effect menu, and the Drop Shadow, Inner Glow, Outer Glow, and Feather commands in the Effect > Stylize submenu. You can apply them to either vector or bitmap objects. Next, you'll apply a Photoshop effect (raster) to the candle flames on top of the cake.

1 Click the flame above the 3 candle and Shift-click the other flame above the 0 (zero) candle to select both.

2 Choose Effect > Texture > Grain.

When you choose a raster (Photoshop) effect, the Filter Gallery dialog box opens for most, but not all, effects. Similarly to working with filters in Adobe Photoshop, where you can also access a Filter Gallery, in the Illustrator Filter Gallery you can try different raster effects to see how they affect your artwork.

3 With the Filter Gallery dialog box open, you can see the type of filter (Grain) displayed at the top. In the lower-left corner of the dialog box, click the plus (+) to zoom in to the art. I had to click it a bunch of times.

The Filter Gallery dialog box, which is resizable, contains a preview area (labeled A), effect thumbnails that you can click to apply (labeled B), settings for the currently selected effect (labeled C), and the list of effects applied (labeled D). If you want to apply a different effect, expand a category in the middle panel of the dialog box (labeled B), and click an effect thumbnail.

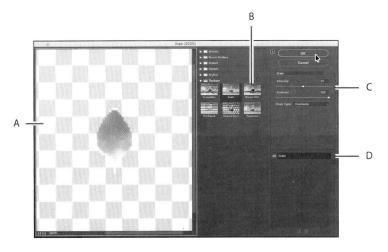

Note: The Photoshop effect will essentially rasterize your beautiful vector flame when you print or output the file. In a tip on the next page, I discuss setting it to display, print, and output at a higher resolution.

4 Change the Grain settings in the upper-right corner of the dialog box as follows (if necessary):

- Intensity: **51**
- Contrast: **100**
- Grain Type: **Contrasty**

5 Click OK to apply the raster effect to the flames.

6 Choose Select > Deselect, and then choose File > Save.

▶ **Tip:** Does the flame art look pixelated after applying the effect? Choose Effect > Document Raster Effects Settings. In the dialog box that opens, choose High (300 ppi) from the Resolution menu, and click OK. Better? The resolution of all raster effects when you output (and preview) is controlled by the settings in that dialog box. While you're working, make sure to change the Resolution setting back to Screen (72 ppi) if Illustrator becomes slower and less responsive.

Working with 3D and Materials ▬◼

To learn about other working with 3D and Materials, check out the video *Working with 3D Effects,* which is part of the Web Edition. For more information, see the "Web Edition" section of "Getting Started" at the beginning of the book.

Using graphic styles

A *graphic style* is a saved set of appearance attributes that you can reuse. By applying graphic styles, you can quickly change the appearance of objects and text globally.

The Graphic Styles panel (Window > Graphic Styles) lets you create, name, save, apply, and remove effects and attributes for objects, layers, and groups. You can also break the link between an object and an applied graphic style to edit that object's attributes without affecting other objects that use the same graphic style.

For example, if you have a map that uses a shape to represent a city, you can create a graphic style that paints the shape green and adds a drop shadow. You can then use that graphic style to paint all the city shapes on the map. If you decide to use a different color, you can change the fill color of the graphic style to blue. All the objects that use that graphic style are then updated to blue.

Applying an existing graphic style

You can apply graphic styles to your artwork from graphic style libraries that come with Illustrator. Next, you'll explore a built-in graphic style and apply it to the purple shadow shape below the cake stand.

1   Choose Window > Graphic Styles. Click the Graphic Styles Libraries Menu button (![icon]) at the bottom of the panel, and choose 3D Effects.

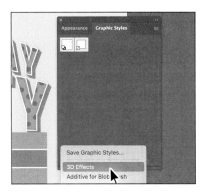

2   With the Selection tool (▶), click to select the purple "shadow" ellipse below the cake stand (see the following figure).

3   Click the 3D Effect 4 thumbnail and then click the 3D Effect 11 thumbnail in the 3D Effects panel.

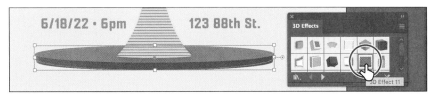

You should now see the two additional graphic styles, 3D Effect 4 and 3D Effect 11, shown in the Graphic Styles panel. Both graphic styles are added to the Graphic Styles panel for the active document only.

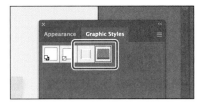

4   Close the 3D Effects panel.

When you clicked the first style (3D Effect 4), appearance attributes from that style were applied to the selected artwork. Clicking the second style (3D Effect 11) replaced the appearance attributes of the first style with the new attributes.

5   With the artwork still selected, click the Appearance panel tab to see the appearance of the selected artwork.

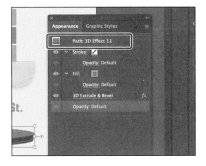

You may need to scroll in the panel, but notice Path: 3D Effect 11 at the top of the panel list. This indicates that the graphic style named "3D Effect 11" is applied.

6   Click the Graphic Styles panel tab to show the panel again.

> **Tip:** You can right-click a graphic style thumbnail in the Graphic Styles panel to show a preview of the graphic style on the selected artwork. Previewing a graphic style is a great way to see how it will affect the selected object, without actually applying it.

Creating and applying a graphic style

Now you'll create a new graphic style from the number 3 candle and apply that graphic style to the number 0 candle.

1   With the Selection tool (▶) selected, click the number 3 candle on top of the cake.

▶ **Tip:** When you make a graphic style by selecting an object, you can then either drag the object directly into the Graphic Styles panel or, in the Appearance panel, drag the appearance thumbnail at the top of the listing into the Graphic Styles panel.

2   Click the New Graphic Style button (▣) at the bottom of the Graphic Styles panel.

The appearance attributes from the selected candle are saved as a graphic style.

3   In the Graphic Styles panel, double-click the new graphic style thumbnail. In the Graphic Style Options dialog box, name the new style **Candle**. Click OK.

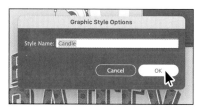

4   Click the Appearance panel tab, and at the top of the Appearance panel you'll see "Path: Candle."

This indicates that a graphic style named "Candle" is applied to the selected artwork.

● **Note:** You could also have grouped the candles together and applied the graphic style to the group. If you ever were to ungroup the candles, the graphic style would be removed because it was applied to the group.

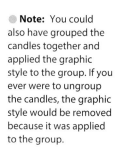

5   With the Selection tool, click the number 0 candle. In the Graphic Styles panel, click the graphic style named "Candle" to apply the styling.

Leave the candle selected.

Applying a graphic style to text

When you apply a graphic style to a type area, the fill color of the graphic style overrides the fill color of the text by default. If you deselect Override Character Color from the Graphic Styles panel menu (▤), the fill color in the text (if there is one) will be preserved.

You can right-click and hold down the mouse button on a graphic style to preview the graphic style on the text. If you choose Use Text For Preview from the Graphic Styles panel menu (▤), you can view the style on the letter "T" in the panel.

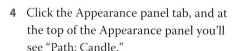

Updating a graphic style

You can also update a graphic style, and all artwork with that style applied will update as well. If you edit the appearance of artwork that a graphic style is applied to, the graphic style is overridden, and the artwork will not update when the graphic style is updated.

1 With the candle still selected, look in the Graphic Styles panel; you will see that the Candle graphic style thumbnail is highlighted (it has a border around it), indicating that it's applied.

2 Click the Appearance panel tab.

3 With the candle selected, in the orange Fill row in the Appearance panel, click the Fill color box a few times to open the Swatches panel. Select the swatch named "Aqua." Press the Escape key to hide the swatches.

Notice that the "Path: Candle" text at the top of the Appearance panel is now just "Compound Path," telling you that the graphic style is no longer applied to the selected artwork.

4 Click the Graphic Styles panel tab to see that the Candle graphic style no longer has a highlight (border) around it, which means that the graphic style is no longer applied.

5 Press the Option (macOS) or Alt (Windows) key, and drag the selected shape on top of the Candle graphic style thumbnail in the Graphic Styles panel. Release the mouse button, and then release the modifier key when the thumbnail is highlighted.

> **Tip:** You can also update a graphic style by selecting the graphic style you want to replace. Then you select artwork (or target an item in the Layers panel) that has the attributes you want to use, and choose Redefine Graphic Style "Style name" from the Appearance panel menu.

Both candles now look the same since the Candle graphic style was applied to both objects.

6 Choose Select > Deselect and then choose File > Save.

7 Click the Appearance panel tab. You should see "No Selection: Candle" at the top of the panel (you may need to scroll up).

Applying a graphic style to a layer

When a graphic style is applied to a layer, everything on that layer has that same style applied. Now you'll apply a drop shadow graphic style to the layer named Cake, which will apply the style to every object currently on that layer and anything you add later. Instead of applying the graphic style to each part of the cake, you are applying a graphic style this way to save time and effort.

1 Click the Layers panel tab on the right to show the Layers panel. Click the target icon (⊙) for the Cake layer.

This selects the layer content (three rectangles that are the cake layers) and targets the layer for any appearance attributes.

2 Click the Graphic Styles panel tab, and then click the graphic style named Drop Shadow to apply the style to the layer and all its contents.

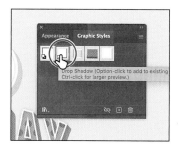

The target icon in the Layers panel for the Cake layer (⊙) is now shaded. Also, in the Graphic Styles panel, graphic style thumbnails that show a small box with a red slash (☒) indicate that the graphic style does not contain a stroke or fill. It may just be a drop shadow or outer glow, for instance.

3 Click the Appearance panel tab, and you should see, with all of the artwork on the Cake layer still selected, the words "Layer: Drop Shadow." You can close the Appearance panel group.

This is telling you that the layer target icon is selected in the Layers panel and that the Drop Shadow graphic style is applied to that layer.

Applying multiple graphic styles

You can apply a graphic style to an object that already has a graphic style applied. This can be useful if you want to add properties to an object from another graphic style. After you apply a graphic style to selected artwork, you can then Option-click (macOS) or Alt-click (Windows) another graphic style thumbnail to add the graphic style formatting to the existing formatting, rather than replacing it.

Scaling strokes and effects

In Illustrator, by default, when scaling (resizing) content, any strokes and effects that are applied do not change. For instance, suppose you scale a circle with a 2-pt stroke from small to the size of the artboard. The shape may change size, but the stroke will remain 2 points by default. That can change the appearance of scaled artwork in a way that you didn't intend, so you'll need to watch out for that when transforming artwork. Next you'll make white path on the cake larger.

1 Choose Select > Deselect, if necessary.

2 Choose View > Fit Artboard In Window, if necessary.

3 Click the white curvy lines on the aqua cake base (the scalloped shape).

4 In the Properties panel (Window > Properties), notice the stroke weight of 1 pt.

5   Click More Options () in the
    Transform section of the Properties
    panel, and select Scale Strokes &
    Effects at the bottom of the panel that
    appears. Press the Escape key to hide
    the options.

    Without this option selected, scaling
    the artwork will not affect the stroke
    weights or effects when it is scaled. You
    are selecting this option, so the artwork
    will scale larger and not remain the
    same stroke weight.

6   Pressing the Shift key, drag the lower-
    right corner of the path to make it larger. Drag until it's the width of the green
    scalloped shape it's on. Release the mouse button and then the key.

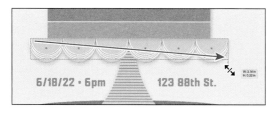

    After scaling the artwork, if you look in
    the Properties panel, see that the stroke
    weight has gotten bigger.

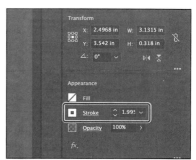

7   Choose Select > Deselect.

8   Choose File > Save, and then choose
    File > Close.

Review questions

1 How do you add a second fill or stroke to artwork?

2 Name two ways to apply an effect to an object.

3 When you apply a Photoshop (raster) effect to vector artwork, what happens to the artwork?

4 Where can you access the options for effects applied to an object?

5 What's the difference between applying a graphic style to a *layer* versus applying it to *selected artwork*?

Review answers

1 To add a second fill or stroke to artwork, click the Add New Stroke button (■) or Add New Fill button (▢) at the bottom of the Appearance panel. We didn't cover this in the lesson, but you can also choose Add New Stroke/Add New Fill from the Appearance panel menu. A stroke is added to the top of the appearance list. It has the same color and stroke weight as the original.

2 You can apply an effect to an object by selecting the object and then choosing the effect from the Effect menu. You can also apply an effect by selecting the object, clicking the Choose An Effect button (fx.) in the Properties panel or the Add New Effect button (fx.) at the bottom of the Appearance panel, and then choosing the effect from the menu that appears.

3 Applying a Photoshop effect to artwork generates pixels rather than vector data. Photoshop effects include all of the effects in the bottom portion of the Effect menu and the Drop Shadow, Inner Glow, Outer Glow, and Feather commands in the Effect > Stylize submenu. You can apply them to either vector or bitmap objects.

4 You can edit effects applied to selected artwork by clicking the effect link in the Properties panel or Appearance panel to access the effect options.

5 When a graphic style is applied to a single object, other objects on that layer are not affected. For example, if a triangle object has a Roughen effect applied to its path and you move it to another layer, it retains the Roughen effect.

After a graphic style is applied to a layer, everything you add to the layer has that style applied to it. For example, if you create a circle on Layer 1 and then move that circle to Layer 2, which has a Drop Shadow effect applied, the circle adopts that effect.

14 CREATING ARTWORK FOR A T-SHIRT

Lesson overview

In this lesson, you'll learn how to do the following:

- Work with existing symbols.

- Create, modify, and redefine a symbol.

- Store and retrieve artwork in the Symbols panel.

- Understand Creative Cloud libraries.

- Work with Creative Cloud libraries.

- Work with global editing.

 This lesson will take about 45 minutes to complete. To get the lesson files used in this chapter, download them from the web page for this book at adobepress.com/IllustratorCIB2022. For more information, see "Accessing the lesson files and Web Edition" in the Getting Started section at the beginning of this book.

In this lesson, you'll explore a variety of useful concepts for working smarter and faster in Illustrator: using symbols, working with Creative Cloud libraries to make your design assets available anywhere, and editing content using global editing.

Starting the lesson

In this lesson, you'll explore concepts such as symbols and the Libraries panel to create artwork for a T-shirt. Before you begin, you'll restore the default preferences for Adobe Illustrator. Then, you'll open the finished art file for this lesson to see what you'll create.

Note: If you have not already downloaded the project files for this lesson to your computer from your Account page, make sure to do so now. See the "Getting Started" section at the beginning of the book.

1 To ensure that the tools function and the defaults are set exactly as described in this lesson, delete or deactivate (by renaming) the Adobe Illustrator preferences file. See "Restoring default preferences" in the "Getting Started" section at the beginning of the book.

2 Start Adobe Illustrator.

3 Choose File > Open, and open the L14_end1.ai file in the Lessons > Lesson14 folder on your hard disk.

You're going to create artwork for a T-shirt design.

4 Choose View > Fit All In Window and leave the file open for reference, or choose File > Close.

5 Choose File > Open. In the Open dialog box, navigate to the Lessons > Lesson14 folder, and select the L14_start1.ai file on your hard disk. Click Open to open the file.

6 Choose View > Fit All In Window.

7 Choose File > Save As. If the Cloud Document dialog box opens, click Save On Your Computer.

8 In the Save As dialog box, navigate to the Lesson14 folder, and name the file **TShirt.ai**. Leave Adobe Illustrator (ai) chosen from the Format menu (macOS) or Adobe Illustrator (*.AI) chosen from the Save As Type menu (Windows), and click Save.

9 In the Illustrator Options dialog box, leave the Illustrator options at their default settings, and then click OK.

10 Choose Reset Essentials from the workspace switcher in the Application bar.

Working with symbols

A *symbol* is a reusable art object that is stored in the Symbols panel (Window > Symbols). For example, if you create a symbol from a flower you drew, you can then quickly add multiple *instances* of that flower symbol to your artwork, which saves you from having to draw each flower. All instances in the document are linked to the original symbol in the Symbols panel. When you edit the original symbol, all instances of that symbol (a flower, in this example) that are linked to the original are updated. You can turn all those flowers from white to red instantly! Not only do symbols save time, but they also greatly reduce file size.

● **Note:** Illustrator comes with a series of symbol libraries, which range from tiki icons to hair to web icons. You can access those symbol libraries in the Symbols panel or by choosing Window > Symbol Libraries and easily incorporate them into your own artwork.

- Choose Window > Symbols to open the Symbols panel. The symbols you see in the Symbols panel are the symbols you can use with this document. Each document has its own set of saved symbols. The features of the Symbols panel are shown here:

A. Symbol thumbnail
B. Symbol Libraries Menu
C. Place Symbol Instance
D. Break Link To Symbol
E. Symbol Options
F. New Symbol
G. Delete Symbol

Using default Illustrator symbol libraries

You'll start by adding to your project a symbol from one of the many symbol libraries that come with Illustrator.

1 Select the Selection tool (▶) in the toolbar and click in the larger artboard to make it the active artboard.

2 Choose View > Fit Artboard In Window to fit the active artboard in the Document window.

3 Click the Hide Smart Guides button in the Properties panel to turn the Smart Guides off temporarily.

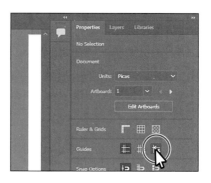

▶ **Tip:** You can also choose View > Smart Guides to turn them off.

4 Open the Symbols panel (Window > Symbols) if it isn't already.

5 Click the Symbol Libraries Menu button (![icon]) at the bottom of the panel, and choose Tiki from the menu.

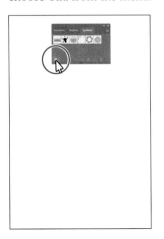 

The Tiki library opens as a free-floating panel. The symbols in this library that comes with Illustrator are not part of the file that you are working on, but you can import any of the symbols into the document and use them in the artwork.

Tip: If you want to see the symbol names along with the symbol pictures, click the Symbols panel menu (![icon]) and then choose Small List View or Large List View.

6 Move the pointer over the symbols in the Tiki panel to see their names as tool tips. Click the symbol named "Fish" to add it to the Symbols panel.

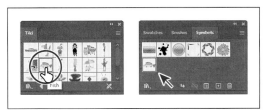

When you add symbols to the Symbols panel, they are saved with the active document only.

Tip: You can also copy a symbol instance on the artboard and paste as many as you need. This is the same as dragging a symbol instance out of the Symbols panel onto the artboard.

7 Close the Tiki panel.

8 With the Selection tool (![icon]) selected, drag the Fish symbol from the Symbols panel onto the artboard into the approximate center of the artboard. Do this a total of *two times* to create two instances of the fish next to each other.

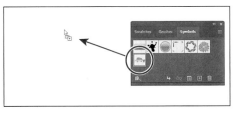 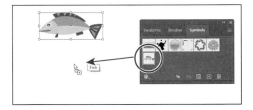

Each time you drag a symbol like the fish onto the artboard, an instance of the original symbol is created. Next you'll resize one of the symbol instances.

9   With one of the Fish symbol instances selected, Shift-drag the upper-right bounding point toward the center to make it a little smaller while also constraining its proportions. Release the mouse button and then the key.

Note: Although you can transform symbol instances in many ways, specific properties of instances from static symbols like the fish cannot be edited. For example, the fill color is locked because it is controlled by the original symbol in the Symbols panel.

A symbol instance is treated like a group of objects and can have only certain transformation and appearance properties changed (scale, rotate, move, transparency, and more). You cannot edit the individual artwork that makes up an instance without breaking the link to the original symbol. With the symbol instance still selected on the artboard, notice that, in the Properties panel, you see "Symbol (Static)" and symbol-related options.

10 With the same fish instance still selected, make a copy of it by pressing Option (macOS) or Alt (Windows) and dragging a copy. Release the mouse button and then the key.

Creating a copy of an instance is the same thing as dragging an instance of a symbol from the Symbols panel.

11 To resize the new fish instance, Shift-drag a corner to make it smaller. Release the mouse button and then the key.

You may want to zoom in to the fish to make it easier to scale and position them.

12 Drag all three fish instances into position, as in the following figure.

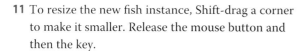

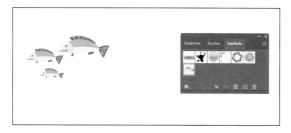

13 Choose Select > Deselect, and then choose File > Save.

Editing a symbol

In this next section, you'll edit the original Fish symbol, and all instances in the document will be updated. There are several ways to edit a symbol, and in this section you will focus on one method.

1 With the Selection tool (▶) selected, double-click any of the Fish symbol instances on the artboard. A warning dialog box appears, stating that you are about to edit the original symbol and that all instances will update. Click OK.

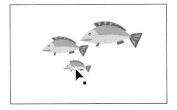  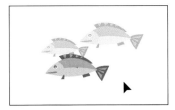

Tip: There are a lot of ways to edit a symbol. You can select the symbol instance on the artboard and then click the Edit Symbol button in the Properties panel, or double-click a symbol thumbnail in the Symbols panel.

This takes you into symbol editing mode, so you can't edit any other objects on the page. The Fish symbol instance you double-clicked will show as the size of the original symbol artwork. That's because in symbol editing mode, you are looking at the *original* symbol artwork rather than the transformed instance (if you double-clicked one that was resized). You can now edit the artwork that makes up the symbol.

2 Select the Zoom tool (🔍), and drag across the fish to zoom in closely.

3 Select the Direct Selection tool (▷), and click to select the light green head of the fish. See the first part of the following figure.

4 Click the Fill color box in the Swatches panel, and select the Color Mixer (🎨). Press the Shift key and drag the Cyan (C) slider to the right a little to change all of the CMYK colors proportionally.

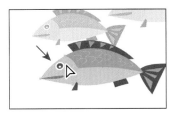 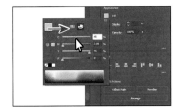

5 Double-click away from the symbol content, or click the Exit Symbol Editing Mode button (◀) in the upper-left corner of the Document window, until you exit symbol editing mode so that you can edit the rest of the content.

Notice that all of the Fish symbol instances on the artboard have been changed.

Working with dynamic symbols

As you just saw, editing a symbol updates all of the instances in your document. Symbols can also be *dynamic*, which means you can change specific appearance properties of individual instances using the Direct Selection tool (▷) without editing the original symbol. In this section, you'll make the Fish symbol dynamic, and then you'll edit each instance separately.

1   In the Symbols panel, select the Fish symbol thumbnail, if it's not already selected. Click the Symbol Options button (▣) at the bottom of the Symbols panel.

2   In the Symbol Options dialog box, select Dynamic Symbol, and click OK. The symbol and its instances are now dynamic.

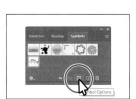

You can tell if a symbol is dynamic by looking at the thumbnail in the Symbols panel. If there is a small plus sign (+) in the lower-right corner of the thumbnail, it is a dynamic symbol.

3   With the Direct Selection tool (▷) selected, click within the fish head of the smallest fish instance. See the following figure.

    With part of the symbol instance selected, notice the words "Symbol (Dynamic)" at the top of the Properties panel, telling you it's a dynamic symbol.

4   Click the Fill box in the Properties panel. With the Swatches option (▦) selected, change the fill color to another color in the Swatches panel.

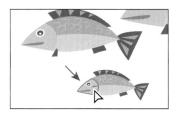
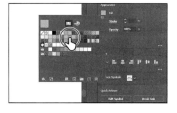

One fish now looks a little different from the others. Know that if you were to edit the original symbol, like you did previously, all symbol instances would still update, but that blue-green part of the smallest fish instance would remain different.

Creating a symbol

Illustrator also lets you create and save symbols. You can make symbols from objects, including paths, compound paths, text, embedded (not linked) raster images, mesh objects, and groups of objects. Symbols can even include active objects, such as brush strokes, blends, effects, or other symbol instances. Next, you'll create a symbol from existing artwork.

1 Choose 2 Symbol Artwork from the Artboard Navigation menu in the Status bar below the Document window.

2 With the Selection tool (▶) selected, click the flower on the artboard to select it.

3 Click the New Symbol button (▣) at the bottom of the Symbols panel to make a symbol from the selected artwork.

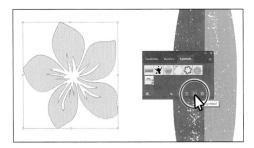

4 In the Symbol Options dialog box that opens, change the name to **Flower**. Ensure that Dynamic Symbol is selected, just in case you want to edit the appearance of one of the instances later. Click OK to create the symbol.

▶ **Tip:** You can drag the symbol thumbnails in the Symbols panel to change their ordering. Reordering symbols in the Symbols panel has no effect on the artwork. It is simply a way to organize your symbols.

In the Symbol Options dialog box, you'll see a note explaining no difference between a movie clip and a graphic type in Illustrator. If you don't plan on exporting this content to Adobe Animate, you don't need to worry about choosing an export type. After creating the symbol, the flower artwork on the artboard becomes an instance of the Flower symbol, and the symbol appears in the Symbols panel.

Now you'll create another symbol by dragging artwork into the Symbols panel.

5 Drag the surfboard artwork into a blank area of the Symbols panel. In the Symbol Options dialog box, change the name to **Surfboard** and click OK.

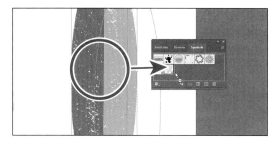

6 Choose 1 T-Shirt from the Artboard menu in the Status bar below the Document window.

7 Drag the Flower symbol from the Symbols panel onto the artboard four times, and position the instances around the fish, as you see in the following figure.

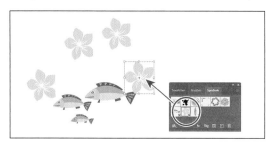

8 Resize and rotate each of the flower instances on the artboard using the Selection tool, making them different sizes. Make sure to press the Shift key to constrain the proportions as you scale.

9 Choose Select > Deselect and then choose File > Save.

Breaking a link to a symbol

At times you will need to edit a specific instance on the artboard in ways that require you to break the link between the original symbol artwork and an instance. As you've learned, you can make specific changes, such as scaling, opacity, and flipping, to a symbol instance, and saving the symbol as dynamic only lets you edit certain appearance attributes using the Direct Selection tool. When you break the link between a symbol and an instance, that instance will no longer update if the symbol is edited.

Next, you'll see how to break the link to a symbol instance so you can make a change to just that one.

Tip: You can also break the link to a symbol instance by selecting the symbol instance on the artboard and then clicking the Break Link To Symbol button (🔗) at the bottom of the Symbols panel.

1   Turn on the Smart Guides by choosing View > Smart Guides.

2   With the Selection tool (▶) selected, drag *three* copies of the Surfboard symbol on top of the other artwork already on the artboard. Arrange them as you see in the following figure.

3   Select each symbol instance and resize it, making the center artboard taller than the other two. I wound up making all three larger. Don't forget to Shift-drag a corner in order to resize proportionally.

4   Select the center surfboard, and in the Properties panel, click the Break Link button.

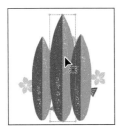

This surfboard is now a group of paths, and you'll see "Group" at the top of the Properties panel. You should be able to edit the artwork directly now. This content will no longer update if the Surfboard symbol is edited.

5   Select the Zoom tool (🔍), and drag across the top of the selected surfboard artwork on the artboard to zoom in.

6   Choose Select > Deselect.

7   Select the Direct Selection tool, and drag across the top of the middle surfboard. Move the pointer over the anchor points at the top of the surfboard and when you see the word "anchor," drag one of them down a little to reshape the top.

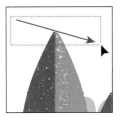
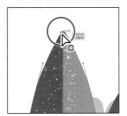

8   Choose Select > Deselect.

Now you'll arrange the surfboards behind the flowers and fish.

9   Select the Selection tool (▶) and Shift-click all three of the surfboards to select them all. Choose Object > Arrange > Send To Back.

10 Click the Group button in the Properties panel to group them together.

The symbolism tools

The Symbol Sprayer tool (⊞) allows you to spray symbols on the artboard, creating symbol sets. The symbolism tools are not in the default toolbar. To access them, click Edit Toolbar (•••) at the bottom of the toolbar, and drag any of the symbolism tools into the toolbar.

A *symbol set* is a group of symbol instances that you create with the Symbol Sprayer tool. This can be really useful if, for instance, you were to create grass from individual blades of grass. Spraying the blades of grass speeds up this process greatly and makes it much easier to edit individual instances of grass or the sprayed grass as a group. You can create mixed sets of symbol instances by using the Symbol Sprayer tool with one symbol and then using it again with another symbol.

You use the symbolism tools to modify multiple symbol instances in a set. For example, you can disperse instances over a larger area using the Symbol Scruncher tool or gradually tint the color of instances to make them look more realistic.

—From Illustrator Help

Replacing symbols

You can easily replace a symbol instance in the document with another symbol. You can also replace a symbol like a fish if you made changes to the dynamic symbol instance. That way, the symbol instance matches the original symbol artwork again. Next you'll replace one of the Fish symbol instances.

1   With the Selection tool (▶), select the smallest Fish symbol instance, the one whose head you recolored. You might need to zoom out or pan to see it.

    When you select a symbol instance, you can tell which symbol it came from because the symbol for the selected instance is highlighted in the Symbols panel.

2   In the Properties panel, click the arrow to the right of the Replace Symbol field to open a panel showing the symbols in the Symbols panel. Click the Flower symbol in the panel.

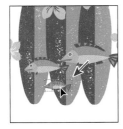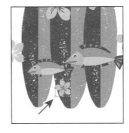

If the original symbol instance you are replacing had a transformation applied, such as a rotation, the symbol instance replacing it would have the same transformations applied.

Note: After making edits to a dynamic symbol instance with the Direct Selection tool, you can reselect the entire instance with the Selection tool and click the Reset button in the Properties panel to reset the appearance to the same as the original symbol.

3   With the Flower symbol instance still selected on the artboard, in the Properties panel click the arrow to the right of the Replace Symbol field and click the Fish symbol in the panel.

The change you made to the Fish symbol instance earlier (changing the color of the head) is gone, and the original Fish symbol artwork replaces the flower.

4   Choose Select > Same > Symbol Instance.

This is a great way to select all instances of a symbol in the document.

5   Click the Group button in the Properties panel to keep them together as a group.

6   Choose Select > Deselect, and close the Symbols panel group.

7   Choose File > Save.

Symbol layers

When you edit a symbol using any of the methods described, open the Layers panel, and you will see that the symbol has its own layering.

Similar to working with groups in Isolation mode, you see the layers associated with that symbol only, not the document's layers. In the Layers panel, you can rename, add, delete, show/hide, and reorder content for a symbol.

Working with Creative Cloud libraries

Creative Cloud libraries are an easy way to gather project elements that you can use—such as images, colors, text styles, Adobe Stock assets, and more—between applications like Adobe Photoshop, Illustrator, InDesign, and Adobe mobile apps.

Creative Cloud libraries connect to your creative profile, putting the creative assets you have saved at your fingertips. When you create content in Illustrator and save it to a Creative Cloud library, that asset is available to use in all of your Illustrator files. Those assets are automatically synced, and you can share them with anyone with a Creative Cloud account. As your creative team works across Adobe desktop and mobile apps, your shared library assets are always up to date and ready to use anywhere. In this section, you'll explore libraries and use assets you save there in your project.

Note: To use Creative Cloud libraries, you will need to be signed in with your Adobe ID and have an internet connection.

Adding assets to a Creative Cloud library

The first thing you'll learn about is how to work with the Libraries panel (Window > Libraries) in Illustrator and add assets to a Creative Cloud library. You'll open an existing document in Illustrator and capture assets from it.

1   Choose File > Open. In the Open dialog box, navigate to the Lessons > Lesson14 folder, and select the Sample.ai file on your hard disk. Click Open.

Note: The Missing Fonts dialog box may appear. You need an internet connection to activate the fonts. The activation process may take a few minutes. Click Activate Fonts to activate all the missing fonts. After they are activated and you see the message stating that there are no more missing fonts, click Close. If a dialog box referring to auto-activation appears, click Skip. If you have an issue with activation, you can go to Help (Help > Illustrator Help) and search for "Find missing fonts."

2   Choose View > Fit Artboard In Window.

Using this document, you will capture artwork, text, and colors to be used in the TShirt.ai document.

3   Choose Window > Libraries, or click the Libraries panel tab to open the Libraries panel.

4   In the Libraries panel, click Your Library (or My Library if you see it) to open the default library, if it isn't already open.

To start you have one library to work with, called "Your Library." You can add your design assets to this default library and you can create more libraries—maybe to save assets for specific clients or projects.

Note: In earlier versions of Illustrator, the default library was named "My Library." If you don't see a library named "Your Library," feel free to use another library or create a new library by clicking + Create New Library and naming it.

5   Choose Select > Deselect, if anything is selected.

6 Select the Selection tool (▶), and click the text object that contains the text "PLAY ZONE." Drag the text into the Libraries panel. When a plus sign (+) appears in the panel, release to save the text object in the default library. If you see a missing profile warning dialog box, click OK.

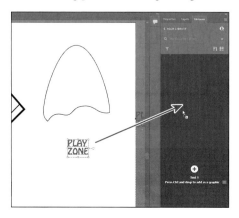

The text object is now saved in the currently selected library and is still editable as text—retaining the text formatting as well. As you save assets and formatting in the Libraries panel, the content is organized by asset type.

● **Note:** Your library content may be organized in groups, like you see in the figures, or not.

7 To change the name of the saved text object, double-click the name "Text 1" in the Libraries panel and change it to **SURF ZONE**. Press Enter or Return to accept the name change. That name will make more sense when you update the text to "SURF ZONE" later in the lesson.

You can change the names of other assets like graphics, colors, character styles, and paragraph styles saved in the Libraries panel as well. In the case of character and paragraph styles you save, you can also move the pointer over the asset and see a tool tip that shows the saved formatting.

8 With the PLAY ZONE text still selected on the artboard, click the plus sign (+) at the bottom of the Libraries panel, and choose Text Fill Color from the menu to save the blue color.

9   Click the T-shirt artwork to select it. Drag the selected artwork into the Libraries panel. When a plus sign (+) and a name (such as "Artwork 1") appear, release the mouse button to add the artwork as a graphic.

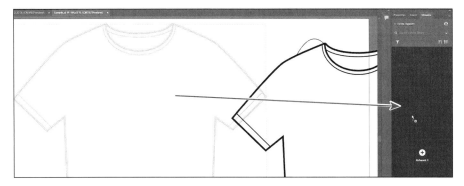

The assets you store as graphics in a Creative Cloud library remain editable vectors wherever you use the graphic.

10 Click the shape on the artboard above the PLAY ZONE text. You'll simply copy this artwork since you will use it to mask or hide parts of the surfboards. Choose Edit > Copy.

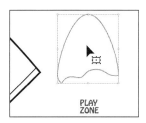

11 Choose File > Close to close the Sample.ai file and return to the TShirt.ai file. Don't save the file if asked.

Notice that even with a different document open, the Libraries panel still shows those assets in the library. The libraries and their assets are available no matter which document is open in Illustrator.

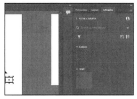

12 Choose Edit > Paste to paste the shape. Drag it to the right of the surfboards.

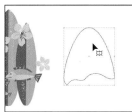

Using library assets

Now that you have some assets in the Libraries panel, once those assets are synced with your Creative Cloud account, they will be available to other applications and apps that support libraries, as long as you are signed in with the same Creative Cloud account. Next you'll use some of those assets in the TShirt.ai file.

1 While still on the 1 T-Shirt artboard, choose View > Fit Artboard In Window.

2 Drag the SURF ZONE asset from the Libraries panel onto the artboard.

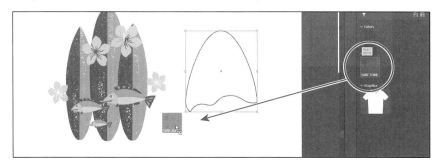

Tip: To apply a color or style saved in the Libraries panel, select artwork or text and click the library item to apply it. When it comes to text styles in the Libraries panel, if you apply them to text in a document, a style of the same name and formatting will appear in the Paragraph Styles panel or Character Styles panel (depending on which you selected in the Libraries panel).

Tip: Text saved in a Creative Cloud library can be dragged onto existing text and the text from the library will be added to the text object.

Tip: If you right-click text saved in a library, you can choose to place the text with formatting (styles) or without.

3 Click to place the text.

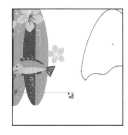 

4 With the Type tool selected, click in the "PLAY ZONE" text, select the word "PLAY," and type **SURF**.

5 Select the Selection tool (▶), and drag the T-shirt graphic asset from the Libraries panel onto the artboard. You will need to click the artboard after dragging to place it. Don't worry about position for now.

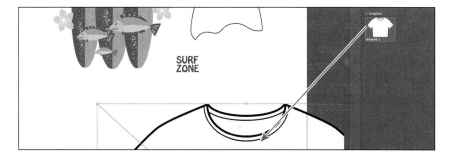

6 Choose Select > Deselect.

Updating a library asset

When you drag a graphic from your Creative Cloud library to an Illustrator project, it is automatically placed as a linked asset. You can tell that an asset you dragged from a library is linked by the X that appears on the object bounding box when it's selected in the document. If you make a change to a library asset, the linked instances will update in your projects. Next you'll see how to update the asset.

1   In the Libraries panel, double-click the T-shirt asset thumbnail. The artwork will appear in a new, temporary document.

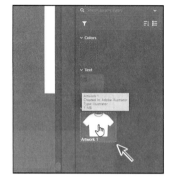

▶ **Tip:** You can also edit a linked library asset like the T-shirt by clicking Edit Original (▨) at the bottom of the Links panel.

2   With the Selection tool (▶) selected, click to select the T-shirt shape. In the Properties panel, change the stroke color to a lighter gray with the tool tip "C=0 M=0 Y=0 K=40."

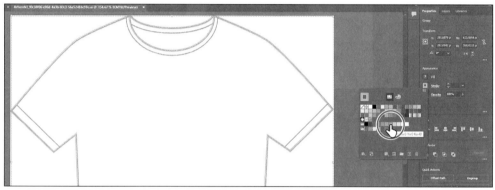

3   Choose File > Save, and then choose File > Close.

In the Libraries panel, the graphic thumbnail should update to reflect the appearance change you made. Back in the TShirt.ai document, the T-shirt graphic on the artboard should have updated. If it hasn't, with the T-shirt artwork still selected on the artboard, click the text "Linked File" at the top of the Properties panel. In the Links panel that shows, with the T-shirt asset row selected, click the Update Link button (🔁) at the bottom of the panel.

4   Click the T-shirt artwork. To embed the graphic, click the Properties panel tab to see the panel again. Click the Embed button in the Quick Actions section of the panel.

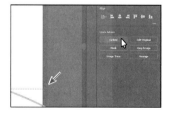

The asset is no longer linked to the library item and will not update if the library item is updated.

That also means the artwork is now editable in the TShirt.ai document. Libraries panel artwork that is embedded after it has been placed will typically have a clipping mask applied. Next you'll move and scale the artwork.

5   With the Selection tool (▶) selected and the T-shirt artwork still selected, click the Arrange button in the Properties panel and choose Send To Back. The artwork is now behind all other content. Drag it into the approximate center of the artboard.

6   To lock the T-shirt artwork, press Command+2 (macOS) or Ctrl+2 (Windows).

7   Click the shape you pasted into the document and drag it on top of the surfboards. Shift-drag a corner to make it bigger; then release the mouse button and key when finished. See the figure for approximate position and size.

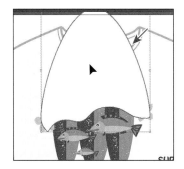

The shape will be used as a mask to hide parts of the surfboards. You'll learn more about creating and editing masks in Lesson 15.

8   With the shape selected, Shift-click the artwork in the surfboard group.

9   Choose Object > Clipping Mask > Make.

The surfboard artwork that's outside of the shape is now hidden.

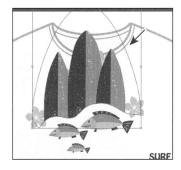

10 To arrange the surfboard group behind the fish and flowers, click the Arrange button in the Properties panel and choose Send To Back. This will put the artwork behind the T-shirt. Then click the Arrange button and choose Bring Forward so it's on top of the T-shirt.

11 Drag across the flowers, fish, and surfboards to select it all. You might need to arrange them like you see in the following figure. Click the Group button in the Properties panel to group it.

▷ **Tip:** You may also want to adjust text formatting like leading, font size, and more in the Properties panel.

12 Drag that new group into position, along with the text. You may want to enlarge the text in the Properties panel. If you do make it larger, you will need to resize the text area so all of the text shows.

13 Choose Select > Deselect.

14 Choose File > Save, and then choose File > Close.

Working with global editing

There will be times where you create multiple copies of artwork and use it across multiple artboards within a single document. If you need to make changes to an object everywhere it's used, you can use global editing to edit all similar objects. In this section, you'll open a new file with icons and make a global edit to its content.

1 Choose File > Open, and open the L14_start2.ai file in the Lessons > Lesson14 folder on your hard disk.

2 Choose File > Save As. If the Cloud document dialog box opens, click Save On Your Computer. In the Save As dialog box, navigate to the Lesson14 folder, and name the file **Icons.ai**. Leave Adobe Illustrator (ai) chosen from the Format menu (macOS) or Adobe Illustrator (*.AI) chosen from the Save As Type menu (Windows), and click Save.

3 In the Illustrator Options dialog box, leave the Illustrator options at their default settings, and then click OK.

4 Choose View > Fit All In Window.

5 With the Selection tool selected, click the black circle behind the larger microphone icon.

Suppose you need to edit all of the circles behind each of the icons. In that case, you can select them using several methods, including the Select > Similar commands, assuming they all share similar appearance attributes. You can also use global editing, which selects objects that share attributes, such as stroke, fill, or size, on the same artboard or all artboards.

▶ **Tip:** You can also start global editing by choosing Select > Start Global Edit.

6 Click Start Global Edit in the Quick Actions section of the Properties panel.

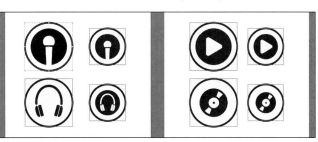

All circles (in this case) are now selected, and you can edit them. The object you originally selected has a red highlight, and the similar objects have a blue highlight. You can also use the Global Edit options to further narrow down the objects that will be selected, which is what you'll do next.

Note: The Appearance option is enabled by default when the selection includes plug-in art or mesh art.

7 Click the arrow to the right of the Stop Global Edit button to open a menu. Select Match > Appearance to select all of the circles with the same appearance attributes as the selected circle. Leave the menu showing.

 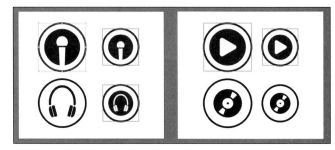

8 Select Match > Size from the Global Edit menu to further refine the search to include objects that have the same shape, appearance properties, and size. There should now be only two circles selected.

 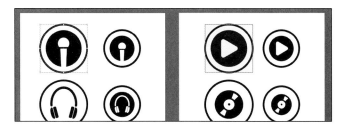

You can further refine your selection by choosing to search for similar objects on certain artboards.

9 Click the Stroke color in the Properties panel, make sure the Swatches option is selected, and apply a color to the stroke. If you see a warning dialog box, click OK.

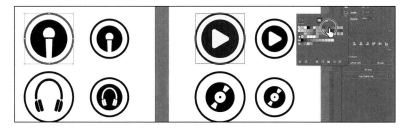

10 Click away from the panel to hide it, and both of the selected objects should change appearance.

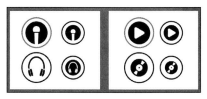

11 Choose Select > Deselect, and then choose File > Save.

12 Choose File > Close.

Review questions

1 What are three benefits of using symbols?

2 How do you edit an existing symbol?

3 What is a dynamic symbol?

4 In Illustrator, what type of content can you save in a library?

5 Explain how to embed a linked library graphic asset.

Review answers

1 Three benefits of using symbols are as follows:

   • You can edit one symbol, and all instances are updated.

   • You can map artwork to 3D objects (not discussed in the lesson).

   • Using symbols reduces file size.

2 To update an existing symbol, double-click the symbol icon in the Symbols panel, double-click an instance of the symbol on the artboard, or select the instance on the artboard, and then click the Edit Symbol button in the Properties panel. Then you can make edits in Isolation mode.

3 When a symbol is saved as dynamic, you can change certain appearance properties of instances using the Direct Selection tool (▷) without editing the original symbol.

4 In Illustrator, currently you can save colors (fill and stroke), type objects, graphic assets, and type formatting.

5 By default, when a graphic asset is dragged from the Libraries panel into a document, a link is created to the original library asset. To embed a graphic asset, select the asset in the document and click Embed in the Properties panel. Once embedded, the graphic will no longer update if the original library asset is edited.

15 PLACING AND WORKING WITH IMAGES

Lesson overview

In this lesson, you'll learn how to do the following:

- Place linked and embedded graphics in an Illustrator file.

- Transform and crop images.

- Create and edit clipping masks.

- Use text to mask an image.

- Make and edit an opacity mask.

- Work with the Links panel.

- Embed and unembed images.

 This lesson will take about 60 minutes to complete. To get the lesson files used in this chapter, download them from the web page for this book at adobepress.com/IllustratorCIB2022. For more information, see "Accessing the lesson files and Web Edition" in the Getting Started section at the beginning of this book.

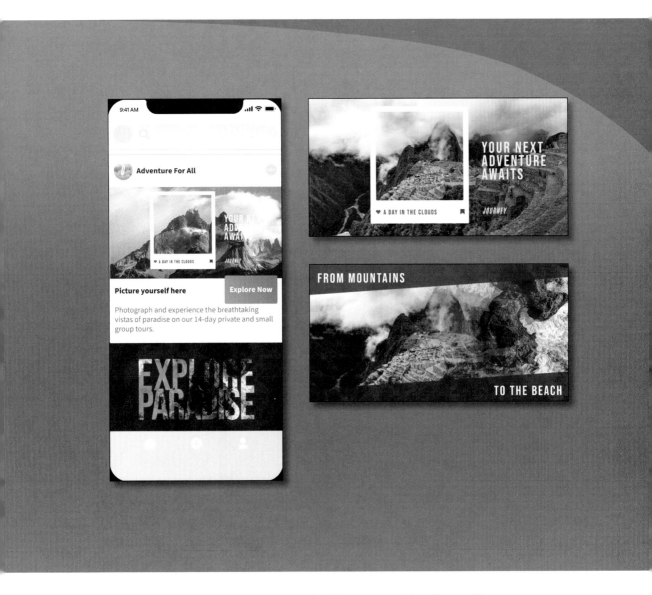

You can easily add images to an Adobe Illustrator file. This is a great way to incorporate raster images into your vector artwork to combine the two.

Starting the lesson

Before you begin, you'll need to restore the default preferences for Adobe Illustrator. Then you'll open the finished art file for this lesson to see what you'll create.

Note: If you have not already downloaded the project files for this lesson to your computer from your Account page, make sure to do so now. See the "Getting Started" section at the beginning of the book.

1 To ensure that the tools function and the defaults are set exactly as described in this lesson, delete or deactivate (by renaming) the Adobe Illustrator preferences file. See "Restoring default preferences" in the "Getting Started" section at the beginning of the book.

2 Start Adobe Illustrator.

3 Choose File > Open, and open the L15_end.ai file in the Lessons > Lesson15 folder that you copied onto your hard disk.

This file contains a few social images and an app design for a travel company. The fonts in the L15_end.ai file have been converted to outlines (Type > Create Outlines) to avoid having missing fonts, and the images are embedded.

4 Choose View > Fit All In Window and leave it open for reference, or choose File > Close.

5 Choose File > Open. In the Open dialog box, navigate to the Lessons > Lesson15 folder, and select the L15_start.ai file on your hard disk. Click Open to open the file.

This is an unfinished version of the social content for a travel company. You will add graphics to it and edit them in this lesson.

Note: You need an internet connection to activate fonts. The process may take a few minutes.

6 The Missing Fonts dialog box will most likely appear. Click Activate Fonts to activate all the missing fonts. After they are activated and you see the message stating that there are no more missing fonts, click Close.

If you see another dialog box asking about font auto-activation, click Skip.

If you can't get the fonts to activate, you can go to the Creative Cloud desktop application and click the Fonts icon (*f*) in the upper right to see what the issue may be (refer to the section "Changing font family and font style" in Lesson 9 for more information on how to resolve it).

You can also just click Close in the Missing Fonts dialog box and ignore the missing fonts as you proceed. A third method is to click the Find Fonts button in the Missing Fonts dialog box and replace the fonts with a local font on your machine.

● **Note:** You can also go to Help (Help > Illustrator Help) and search for "Find missing fonts."

7   Choose File > Save As. If the Cloud Document dialog box opens, click Save On Your Computer.

8   In the Save As dialog box, navigate to the Lesson15 folder, and open it. Name the file **SocialTravel.ai**. Leave Adobe Illustrator (ai) chosen from the Format menu (macOS) or Adobe Illustrator (*.AI) chosen from the Save As Type menu (Windows), and then click Save.

9   In the Illustrator Options dialog box, leave the Illustrator options at their default settings. Click OK.

10 Choose Window > Workspace > Reset Essentials to reset the Essentials workspace.

11 Choose View > Fit All In Window.

Combining artwork

You can combine Illustrator artwork with images from other graphics applications in a variety of ways for a wide range of creative results. Sharing artwork among applications lets you combine continuous-tone paintings and photographs with vector art. Illustrator lets you create certain types of raster images, and Adobe Photoshop excels at many additional image-editing tasks. The images edited or created in Photoshop can then be inserted into Illustrator.

This lesson steps you through the process of creating a composite image, including combining bitmap images with vector art and working between applications. You will add photographic images created in Photoshop to social content created in Illustrator. Then you'll mask an image and replace a placed image.

Placing image files

You can bring raster artwork from Photoshop or other applications into Illustrator using the Open command, the Place command, the Paste command, drag-and-drop operations, and the Libraries panel. Illustrator supports most Adobe Photoshop data, including layer comps, layers, editable text, and paths. This means that you can transfer files between Photoshop and Illustrator and still be able to edit the artwork.

When placing a file using the File > Place command, no matter what type of image file it is (JPEG, GIF, HEIC, PSD, AI, etc.), it can be either embedded or linked. *Embedding* files stores a copy of the image in the Illustrator file, which often increases the Illustrator file size to reflect the addition of the placed file. *Linking* files creates a link to external files, and that link is placed in the Illustrator file. A linked file does not significantly add to the size of the Illustrator file. Linking to files can be a great way to ensure that image updates are reflected in the Illustrator file. The linked file must always accompany the Illustrator file, or the link will break, and the placed file will not appear in the Illustrator artwork.

Placing an image

First, you'll place a JPEG (.jpg) image in your document.

1 Choose File > Place.

● **Note:** On macOS, you may need to click the Options button in the Place dialog box to reveal the Link option.

2 Navigate to the Lessons > Lesson15 > images folder, and select the Mountains2.jpg file. Make sure that Link is selected in the Place dialog box.

3 Click Place.

The pointer should now show the loaded graphics cursor. You can see "1/1" next to the pointer, indicating how many images are being placed (1 of 1), and a thumbnail so you can see what image you are placing.

4 Move the loaded graphics cursor off the left side of the mobile design on the artboard on the left (see the figure), and click to place the image. Leave the image selected.

The image appears on the artboard at 100% of its original size, with the upper-left corner of the image placed where you clicked. You could also have dragged with the loaded graphics cursor to size the image as you placed it. The "X" on a selected image indicates that the image is linked (with edges showing, View > Show Edges).

Notice in the Properties panel (Window > Properties) that, with the image selected, you see the words "Linked File" at the top, indicating that the image is linked to its source file. By default, a placed image is linked to the source file, so if the source file is edited (outside of Illustrator), the placed image in Illustrator is also updated. Deselecting the Link option while placing embeds the image file in the Illustrator file.

Transforming a placed image

You can duplicate and transform placed raster images just as you do other objects in an Illustrator file. Unlike with vector artwork, with raster images you need to consider the image resolution, since raster images with lower resolution may look pixelated when printed. Working in Illustrator, if you make an image smaller, the resolution of the image increases. If you make an image larger, the resolution decreases. Transformations performed on a linked image in Illustrator, and any resulting resolution changes, do not change the original image. The changes affect only how the image is rendered in Illustrator. Next you'll transform the Mountains2.jpg image.

1   With the Selection tool (▶) selected, press and hold the Shift key and drag the lower-right bounding point toward the center of the image until it is just wider than the artboard. Release the mouse button and then release the key.

▶ **Tip:** Much as with other artwork, you can also Option+Shift-drag (macOS) or Alt+Shift-drag (Windows) the image's bounding box to resize from the center while maintaining the image proportions.

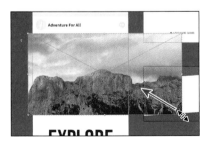

2   In the Properties panel, click the text "Linked File" at the top of the Properties panel to see the Links panel. With the Mountains2.jpg file selected in the Links panel, click the Show Link Info arrow in the lower-left corner of the panel to see information about the image.

You can see the scale percentage as well as rotation information, size, and much more. Specifically, notice that the PPI (pixels per inch) value is approximately 100. PPI refers to the current resolution of the image. If you scale a placed raster image like you just did, the image resolution in Illustrator will change (the original placed image isn't affected). Generally, if you scale the image to be larger, the resolution becomes lower. Conversely, if you scale an image to be smaller, the resolution becomes higher. Other transformations, like rotation, can also be applied to images using the various methods you learned in Lesson 5.

3   Press the Escape key to hide the panel.

4   Click the Flip Horizontally button (⬚) in the Properties panel to flip the image horizontally, across the center.

5   Leave the image selected, and choose File > Save.

Cropping an image

▶ **Tip:** You can turn off the Content Aware feature by choosing Illustrator > Preferences > General (macOS) or Edit > Preferences > General (Windows) and deselecting Enable Content Aware Defaults.

In Illustrator, you can mask or hide part of an image, as you'll learn about in this lesson, but you can also crop images to *permanently* remove part of an image. While cropping an image, you can define the resolution, which can be a useful way to reduce file size and improve performance. When cropping an image, on Windows 64-bit and macOS, Illustrator uses the power of Adobe Sensei to automatically identify the visually significant portions of the selected image, called Content-Aware cropping. Next you'll crop part of the image of the mountains.

1 With the image still selected, click the Crop Image button in the Properties panel. Click OK in the warning dialog box that appears.

Tip: To crop a selected image, you can also choose Object > Crop Image or right-click the image and choose Crop Image from the context menu.

A linked image, like the mountain image, becomes embedded after you crop it. Illustrator automatically identifies the visually significant portions of the selected image, and a default cropping box is displayed on the image. You can adjust the dimensions of this cropping box, if needed. The rest of the artwork is dimmed, and you cannot select it until you are finished cropping.

2 Drag the crop handles so the bottom and top of the image are cut off and the image stops at the edge of the artboard on the right and left. The crop you see initially may be different from the figure, and that's okay. Use the second part of the following figure as a guide for the final crop.

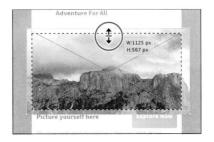

You can drag the handles that appear around the image to crop different parts of the image. You can also define a size in the Properties panel (width and height) to crop to.

3 Click the PPI (resolution) menu in the Properties panel.

The PPI is the resolution of the image. Any options in the PPI menu that are higher than the original resolution of the image are disabled. The maximum value that you can enter equals the resolution of the original image, or 300 PPI for linked artwork.

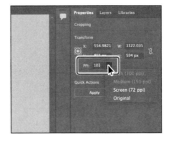

Note: Depending on the size of your image, the "Medium (150 ppi)" option may not be dimmed, and that's okay.

Choosing a lower resolution than the original can be useful if you want to save file size, but may result in an image that is not suitable for printing.

Note: If you cannot drag up or down, try dragging right or left.

4 Move the pointer over the center of the image, and drag the crop area up a little to include more of the top of the image in the final crop.

Tip: You can press Return or Enter to apply the cropping or press the Escape key to cancel the cropping process.

5 Click Apply in the Properties panel to *permanently* crop the image.

Since the image is embedded when cropping, the crop does not affect the original image file you placed.

6 If you need to, drag the image into place, as in the following figure.

7 To send the image behind the other content on the artboard, click the Arrange button in the Properties panel and choose Send Backward. Do this a few times so the image is behind the artwork *and* text, as you see in the figure.

8 Choose Select > Deselect, and then choose File > Save.

Placing a Photoshop document

When you place a Photoshop file as either a local document (.PSD) or cloud document (.PSDC) with multiple layers in Illustrator, you can change image options when the file is imported. For instance, if you place a Photoshop file, you can choose to flatten the image or even to preserve the original Photoshop layers in the file. Next you'll place a Photoshop file, set import options, and embed it in the Illustrator file.

1 Choose File > Place.

2 In the Place dialog box, navigate to the Lessons > Lesson15 > images folder, and select the PhotoFrame.psd file. In the Place dialog box, set the following options (on macOS, if you don't see the options, click the Options button):

- Link: **Deselected** (Deselecting the Link option embeds an image file in the Illustrator file. Embedding the Photoshop file allows for more options when it is placed, as you'll see.)

- Show Import Options: **Selected** (Selecting this option will open an Import Options dialog box where you can set import options before placing.)

3 Click Place.

The Photoshop Import Options dialog box appears because you selected Show Import Options in the Place dialog box and because the file has multiple layers.

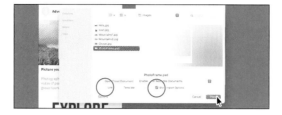

Note: The Import Options dialog box will not appear if the image only contains a locked Background layer, even though you select Show Import Options in the Place dialog box.

4 In the Photoshop Import Options dialog box, set the following options:

- Layer Comp: Beach (A layer comp is a snapshot of a state of the Layers panel that you create in Photoshop. In Photoshop, you can create, manage, and view multiple versions of a layout in a single Photoshop file. Any comments associated with the layer comp in Photoshop will appear in the Comments area.)

- Show Preview: **Selected** (Preview displays a preview of the selected layer comp.)

- Convert Layers To Objects: **Selected** (This option and the next one are available only because you deselected the Link option and chose to embed the Photoshop image.)

- Import Hidden Layers: **Selected** (to import layers hidden in Photoshop)

Note: You may not see a preview in the dialog box, and that's okay.

5 Click OK. If you see an error when placing, simply try again.

6 Move the loaded graphics cursor into the upper-left corner of the top artboard on the right. Drag from the upper-left corner of the artboard to the lower-right corner of the artboard to place and size the image. Make sure it covers the artboard.

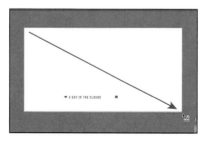

Rather than flatten the file, you have converted the PhotoFrame.psd Photoshop layers to layers that you can show and hide in Illustrator. When placing a Photoshop file in particular, if you had left the Link option selected (to link to the original PSD file), the only option in the Options section of the Photoshop Import Options dialog box would have been to flatten the content. Notice that, with the image still selected on the page, the Properties panel shows the word "Group" at the top. The Photoshop layers are grouped together when preserved and placed.

7   To send the image behind the content on the artboard, choose Object > Arrange > Send To Back.

8   Click the Layers panel tab in the upper right of the application window to open the Layers panel. Drag the left edge of the Layers panel to the left to make it wider so you can read the names.

● **Note:** If the PhotoFrame.psd file is not the last (bottom) object in the Layers panel, drag it down to match what you see in the figure.

9   To reveal the image content in the Layers panel, click the Locate Object button (🔍) at the bottom of the panel.

Notice the sublayers of PhotoFrame.psd. These sublayers were layers in Photoshop and appear in the Layers panel in Illustrator because you chose not to flatten the image when you placed it.

When you place a Photoshop file with layers and you choose to convert the layers to objects in the Photoshop Import Options dialog box, Illustrator treats the layers as separate sublayers in a group. The Photoshop image has a white picture frame in it, but there was already one on the artboard, so next you'll hide the white frame that came with the Photoshop file along with one of the images.

10 In the Layers panel, click the eye icon (👁) to the left of the Pic Frame sublayer and the Beach image to hide them both. Click the visibility column for the mountains image layer (my mountain layer is named "<Background> 0") to show the image.

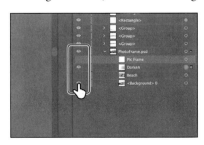

Placing multiple images

In Illustrator you can also place multiple image files in a single action. Next you'll place several images at once and position them.

1   Choose File > Place.

2   In the Place dialog box, in the Lessons > Lesson15 > images folder, select the Hills.jpg file. Command-click (macOS) or Ctrl-click (Windows) the image named Icon.jpg to select both image files. On macOS, click the Options button, if necessary, to reveal other options. Deselect Show Import Options, and make sure that the Link option is *not* selected to embed the images.

Note: The Place dialog box you see in Illustrator may show the images in a different view, like List view, and that's okay.

3   Click Place.

4   Move the loaded graphics cursor onto the left side of the artboard with the "Adventure For All" text. Press the Right or Left Arrow key (or Up and Down Arrow keys) a few times to see that you can cycle between the image thumbnails. Make sure that you see the Icon image thumbnail, and then drag to place the image at a small size, as you see in the following figure.

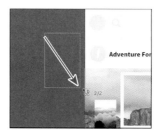

You can either click to place an image at 100% or drag to place an image and size it as you place it in the Document window. By dragging when you place an image, you are resizing the image. Resizing an image in Illustrator will most likely result in a different resolution than the original. Also, whichever thumbnail is showing in the loaded graphics cursor when you click or drag in the Document window is the image that is placed. To discard an asset that is loaded and ready to be placed, use the arrow keys to navigate to the asset and then press the Escape key.

5 Move the loaded graphics cursor into the bottom-right artboard. Move it over the upper-left corner of the artboard, and drag past the lower-right corner of the artboard to place and scale the image. Leave the image selected.

 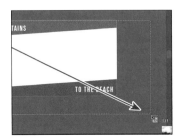 

6 Click the Properties panel tab to show the panel. To arrange the image behind the other content on the artboard, click the Arrange button in the Properties panel, and choose Send To Back.

7 Leave the image selected, and choose File > Save.

Placing cloud documents

In Illustrator, you can place Adobe Photoshop cloud documents. Here's how:

- Choose File > Place.
- In the native OS Place dialog box, click Open Cloud Document to open the asset picker for cloud documents.

  After selecting a file, like a Photoshop cloud document (.PSDC) in the asset picker, you can select Linked or not to link to the cloud asset and click Place.

Masking images

To achieve certain design effects, you can apply a clipping mask (clipping path) to content. A *clipping mask* is an object whose shape masks other artwork so that only areas that lie within the shape are visible. In the first part of the figure to the right is an image with a white circle on top. In the second part of the figure, the white circle was used to mask or hide part of the image.

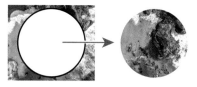

Image with a
white circle on top.

The image, with part of it now masked (hidden) by the circle.

Only vector objects can be clipping paths; however, any artwork can be masked. You can also import masks created in Photoshop files. The clipping path and the masked object are referred to as the *clipping set*.

● **Note:** You will hear people use the phrases "clipping mask," "clipping path," and "mask." Usually they mean the same thing.

Applying a simple mask to an image

In this section, you'll see how to let Illustrator create a simple mask for you on the Hills.jpg image so that you can hide parts of the image.

1   With the Hills.jpg image still selected, in the Properties panel, click the Mask button in the Quick Actions section.

▶ **Tip:** You can also apply a clipping mask by choosing Object > Clipping Mask > Make.

Clicking the Mask button applies a clipping mask to the image in the shape and size of the image. In this case, the image doesn't look any different.

2   Click the Layers panel tab to show it again. Click the Locate Object button (🔍) at the bottom of the panel.

Notice the <Clipping Path> and <Image> sublayers that are contained within the <Clip Group> sublayer. The <Clipping Path> object is the clipping path (mask) that was created, and the <Clip Group> layer is a set that contains the mask and the object that is masked (the embedded image).

Editing a clipping path (mask)

To edit a clipping path, you need to be able to select it. Illustrator offers several ways to do this. Next you'll edit the mask you just created.

Tip: You can also double-click a clip group (object masked with a clipping path) to enter Isolation mode. You can then either click the masked object (the image in this case) to select it or click the edge of the clipping path to select the clipping path. After you are finished editing, you can then exit Isolation mode using a variety of methods, discussed in previous lessons (like pressing the Escape key).

1   Click the Properties panel tab to show the panel. With the Hills.jpg image still selected on the artboard, click the Edit Contents button (▣) at the top of the Properties panel.

2   Click the Layers panel tab, and notice that the <Image> sublayer (in the <Clip Group> layer) is showing the selected-art indicator (small color box) to the far right of the sublayer name. That means it's selected on the artboard.

 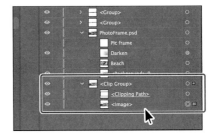

3   Click the Properties panel tab, and in the Properties panel, click the Edit Clipping Path button (▣) at the top of the Properties panel. Back in the Layers panel, the <Clipping Path> will now be selected.

 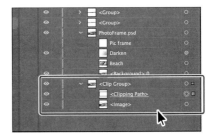

When an object is masked, you can edit the mask, the object that is masked, or both. Use these two buttons to select which to edit. When you first click to select an object that is masked, you will edit both the mask and the masked object.

Tip: You can also edit a clipping path with transformation options, like Rotate, Skew, and so on, or by using the Direct Selection tool (▷).

4   With the Selection tool (▶) selected, drag the lower-right bounding point of the selected mask so it fits the artboard.

5   With the Properties panel showing, click the Edit Contents button (▣) at the top of the Properties panel to edit the image, *not* the mask.

6 With the Selection tool (▶), be careful to drag from within the bounds of the mask to reposition the image more in the center of the mask, and release the mouse button. Notice that you are moving the image and not the mask.

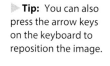 **Tip:** You can also press the arrow keys on the keyboard to reposition the image.

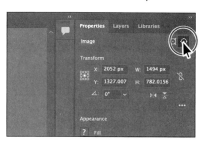 

With the Edit Contents button (⊙) selected, you can apply many transformations to the image, including scaling, moving, rotating, and more.

7 Choose View > Fit All In Window.

8 Choose Select > Deselect, and then choose File > Save.

Masking with a shape

You can also mask content with a shape that you create. In this section, you'll take a circle and mask an image to make a small image icon.

1 Select the gray circle to the left of the "Adventure For All" text and drag it on top of the Icon.jpg image.

The circle will be behind the image.

2 To zoom in to the circle, press Command and + (macOS) or Ctrl and + (Windows) four or so times.

3 To arrange the circle on top of the image, click the Arrange button in the Properties panel, and choose Bring To Front.

4 Shift-click the image to select the circle and the image. To mask the image with the circle, click the Make Clipping Mask button in the Quick Actions section of the Properties panel.

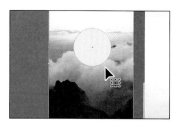  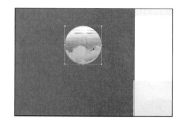

Parts of the image that are outside the bounds of the circle are now hidden.

5   To resize and reposition the image, double-click in the circle to enter
    Isolation mode. In Isolation mode, you can edit the image and the mask (the
    circle) separately. Move the pointer over the image and click to select it (be
    careful not to click the edge of the circle).

6   Shift-drag a corner of the image to make it smaller. Release the mouse button
    and then the key.

7   Move the pointer over the image, and when the pointer looks like ⬚, drag the
    image to reposition it.

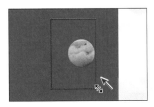 

8   Press the Escape key to exit Isolation mode.

9   Click away from the masked image to deselect it, and then drag the circle onto
    the artboard, to the left of the "Adventure For All" text.

10 Choose Object > Arrange > Send
    Backward a bunch of times so it's
    behind the white icon.

11 Choose Select > Deselect, and then
    choose View > Fit All In Window to
    see everything again.

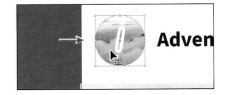

Masking an object with text

In this section, you'll use text as a mask for an image you placed. In this example,
the text will remain editable rather than converting to outlines. Also, you'll use one
of the images you previously placed as part of the Photoshop file.

1   With the Selection tool (▶) selected, click the PSD file on the top-right artboard
    that you placed earlier.

2   In the Layers panel, click the Locate Object button (🔍) to highlight the image
    content in the Layers panel.

3   Click the visibility column to the left of the Beach image to show it.

4   Click the Selected Art column in the Layers panel to select only that image.

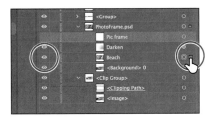

5 Choose Edit > Copy, and then choose Edit > Paste.

6 To paste another copy, choose Edit > Paste, and drag it to an empty area.

There are now three copies of the image showing.

7 In the Layers panel, click the eye icon (👁) to the left of the Beach image in the PhotoFrame.psd group to hide it again.

8 Drag a copy of the image on top of the large "EXPLORE PARADISE" text. Don't worry about exact positioning.

9 Click the Properties panel tab to show the panel. Click the Arrange button in the Properties panel and choose Send To Back. You may need to reposition the image to look like the figure.

You should see the "EXPLORE PARADISE" text now. To create a mask from text, the text needs to be on top of the image.

10 To duplicate the image, choose Edit > Copy, and then choose Edit > Paste In Front.

11 Hide the copy by choosing Object > Hide > Selection.

12 Click the image under the text and Shift-click the "EXPLORE PARADISE" text to select them both.

13 In the Properties panel, click the Make Clipping Mask button. The image should now be masked by the text.

Finishing the masked text

Lastly, you'll add a dark rectangle beneath the text to visually separate it from the image beneath.

1 In the Layers panel, click the visibility column for the hidden Beach image at the bottom of the Layers panel to show it.

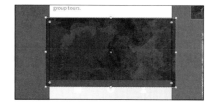

2 Select the Rectangle tool (▢) in the toolbar and draw a rectangle that is the size of the selected image and that covers it (see the following figure).

3 Click the Fill box in the Properties panel, and select a dark gray swatch.

4 Change the Opacity to **80%** in the Properties panel.

5 To send the rectangle behind the masked image, click the Arrange button, and choose Send To Back.

6 To bring it in front of the image that is not masked, click the Arrange button, and choose Bring Forward.

7 Choose Select > Deselect.

Creating an opacity mask

An *opacity mask* is different from a clipping mask because it allows you to mask an object and also alter the transparency of artwork. You can make and edit an opacity mask using the Transparency panel. In this section, you'll create an opacity mask for the copied beach image so that it fades into another image.

1 With the Selection tool (▶) selected, select the final copied beach image, and drag it into the position you see in the figure.

2 Select the Rectangle tool (▢) in the toolbar, and drag to create a rectangle that covers most of the beach image. See the following figure. This will become the mask.

3   Press the D key to set the default stroke (black, 1 pt) and fill (white) for the new rectangle to more easily select and move it.

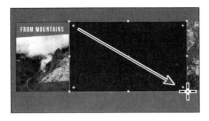 

4   Select the Selection tool (▶) and, while pressing the Shift key, click the beach image to select it as well.

5   Click the Properties panel tab to see the Properties panel again. Click the word "Opacity" to open the Transparency panel. Click the Make Mask button, and leave the artwork selected and the panel showing.

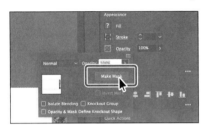 

● **Note:** If you had wanted to create a mask with the same dimensions as the image, instead of drawing a shape, you could have simply clicked the Make Mask button in the Transparency panel.

After clicking the Make Mask button, the button now shows as "Release." If you were to click the button again, the image would no longer be masked.

Editing an opacity mask

Next you'll adjust the opacity mask that you just created.

1   Choose Window > Transparency to open the Transparency panel.

You'll see the same panel you did when you clicked Opacity in the Properties panel. When you click Opacity to reveal the Transparency panel, you will need to hide the panel for the changes you make in this section to take place. In the free-floating Transparency panel, changes will happen automatically.

2   In the Transparency panel, Shift-click the mask thumbnail (as indicated by the white rectangle on the black background) to disable the mask.

Notice that a red X appears on the mask in the Transparency panel and that the entire beach image reappears in the Document window. Hiding the mask can be useful to see all of the masked object again if you need to do anything with it.

▶ **Tip:** To disable and enable an opacity mask, you can also choose Disable Opacity Mask or Enable Opacity Mask from the Transparency panel menu.

3 In the Transparency panel, Shift-click the mask thumbnail to enable the mask again.

Tip: To show the mask by itself (in grayscale if the original mask had color in it) on the artboard, you can also Option-click (macOS) or Alt-click (Windows) the mask thumbnail in the Transparency panel.

4 Click to select the mask thumbnail on the right side of the Transparency panel. If the mask isn't selected on the artboard, click to select it with the Selection tool (▶).

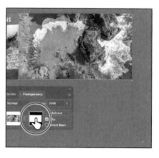

Clicking the opacity mask in the Transparency panel selects the mask (the rectangle) on the artboard. With the mask selected, you can't edit other artwork on the artboard. Also, notice that the document tab shows (<Opacity Mask>/Opacity Mask), indicating that you are now editing the mask.

5 Click the Layers panel tab to show the Layers panel, and click the disclosure triangle (▶) for the <Opacity Mask> layer to reveal the contents, if necessary.

6 With the mask selected in the Transparency panel and on the artboard, use the Properties panel to change the fill color to a white-to-black linear gradient called White, Black.

You'll now see that where there is white in the mask, the beach image is showing, and where there is black, it is hidden. The gradient mask gradually reveals the image.

7 Make sure that the Fill box toward the bottom of the toolbar is selected.

8 Select the Gradient tool (▮) in the toolbar. Move the pointer to the right side of the beach image. Starting where you see the red X in the figure, drag to the left so that more of the image shows on the right edge of the artboard.

Notice that the mask thumbnail in the Transparency panel now shows the gradient. Next you'll move the image but not the opacity mask. With the image thumbnail selected in the Transparency panel, the image and the mask are linked by default, so if you move the image, the mask moves as well.

9 In the Transparency panel, click the image thumbnail so you are no longer editing the mask (an arrow is pointing to it in the figure). Click the link icon (⬚) between the image thumbnail and the mask thumbnail.

   This allows you to move just the image or the mask, but not both.

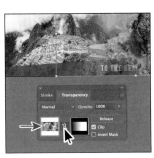

Note: You have access to the link icon only when the image thumbnail, not the mask thumbnail, is selected in the Transparency panel.

10 With the Selection tool, drag the beach image to the left. As you drag, you can still see the image, so you can position it where you want.

Note: The position of the beach image does not have to match the figure exactly.

11 In the Transparency panel, click the broken link icon (⬚) between the image thumbnail and the mask thumbnail to link the two together again.

12 Drag the beach image to the left to cover more of the mountains image.

13 Shift-click the mountains image to select it as well, and to send both behind the text on the artboard, choose Object > Arrange > Send To Back.

14 Choose Select > Deselect, and then choose File > Save.

Working with image links

Note: Learn about working with links and Creative Cloud library items in Lesson 14.

When you place images in Illustrator and either link to them or embed them, you can see a listing of these images in the Links panel. You use the Links panel to see and manage all linked or embedded artwork. The Links panel displays a small thumbnail of the artwork and uses icons to indicate the artwork's status. From the Links panel, you can view the images that have been linked to and embedded, replace a placed image, update a linked image that has been edited outside of Illustrator, or edit a linked image in the original application, such as Photoshop.

Finding link information

When you place an image, it can be helpful to see where the original image is located, what transformations have been applied to the image (such as rotation and scale), and more. Next you'll explore the Links panel to discover image information.

1   Choose Window > Workspace > Reset Essentials.

2   Choose Window > Links to open the Links panel.

Tip: You can also double-click the image in the Links panel list to see the image information.

3   Select the Icon.jpg image in the Links panel. Click the Show Link Info arrow in the lower-left corner of the Links panel to reveal the link information at the bottom of the panel.

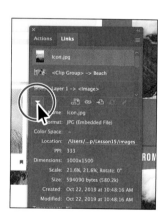

Note: The link information you see may be different than what you see in the figure, and that's okay.

Looking in the Links panel, you'll see a listing of all the images you've placed. You'll see information about the image, such as the fact that it's embedded (Embedded File), the resolution, transformation information, and more. If you see a cloud icon (☁) in the Links panel, that means a graphic was placed from a Creative Cloud library or Cloud document and is linked to that asset.

4   Click the Go To Link button (▣) below the list of images.

The Icon.jpg image will be selected and centered in the Document window.

5   Choose Select > Deselect, and then choose File > Save.

Embedding and unembedding images

When placing an image, if you deselect the Link option, the image is embedded in the Illustrator file. That means that the image data is stored within the Illustrator document. You can choose to embed an image later, after placing and linking to it. Also, you might want to use embedded images outside of Illustrator or to edit them in an image-editing application like Photoshop. Illustrator allows you to unembed images, which saves the embedded artwork to your file system as a PSD or TIFF file (you can choose) and automatically links it to the Illustrator file. Next you will unembed an image in the document.

1 Choose View > Fit All In Window.

2 Click to select the Hills.jpg image (the mountains) on the lower-right artboard.

The Hills.jpg image was embedded when you originally placed it. If you move the cursor over the image name in the Links panel, you will see a tool tip that shows as "Embedded Link."

With an embedded image, you may need to make an edit to that image in a program like Adobe Photoshop. You will need to unembed that image to make edits to it, which is what you'll do next to the image.

3 Click the Unembed button in the Properties panel.

4 In the dialog box that appears, navigate to the Lessons > Lesson15 > images folder (if you are not already there). Make sure Photoshop (*.PSD) is chosen from the File Format menu (macOS) or the Save As Type (Windows) menu, and click Save.

▶ **Tip:** You can also choose Unembed from the Links panel menu (☰).

See the "X" that shows on the image now, when it's selected? That means the image is linked and not embedded. If you were to edit the Hills.psd file in Photoshop, for instance, the image would be updated in Illustrator since it is linked.

5 Choose Select > Deselect.

Replacing an image

You can easily replace a linked or embedded image with another image to update the artwork. The replacement image is positioned exactly where the original image was, so no adjustment should be necessary if the new image has the same dimensions. If you scaled the image that you are replacing, you may need to resize the replacement image to match the original. Next you'll replace an image.

1   Click the Mountains2.jpg image on the artboard on the left. It was the first image you placed.

In the Links panel, what is now highlighted might be named something like "Layer 1 -> <Image>."

2   In the Links panel, click the Relink button (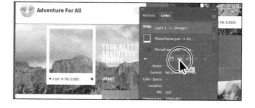) below the list of images.

3   In the dialog box that opens, navigate to the Lessons > Lesson15 > images folder, and select the Mountains1.jpg image. Make sure that the Link option is selected. Click Place to replace the image.

To the right of the Mountains1.jpg name in the Links panel, you should now see a link icon (🔗) telling you that image is linked.

4   Choose Select > Deselect, and then choose File > Save.

5   Choose File > Close as many times as necessary to close all open files.

Review questions

1 Describe the difference between linking and embedding in Illustrator.

2 How do you show options when importing images?

3 What kinds of objects can be used as masks?

4 How do you create an opacity mask for a placed image?

5 Describe how to replace a placed image with another image in a document.

Review answers

1 A *linked file* is a separate, external file connected to the Illustrator file by a link. A linked file does not add significantly to the size of the Illustrator file. The linked file must accompany the Illustrator file to preserve the link and to ensure that the placed file appears when you open the Illustrator file. An *embedded file* becomes part of the Illustrator file. The increased Illustrator file size reflects the addition of the embedded file. Because the embedded file is part of the Illustrator file, no link can be broken. You can update linked and embedded files using the Relink button ( ) in the Links panel.

2 When placing an image using the File > Place command, in the Place dialog box, select the Show Import Options option. Selecting this will open the Import Options dialog box, where you can set options before placing. In macOS, if you don't see the options in the Import Options dialog box, click the Options button.

3 A mask can be a simple or compound path, and masks (such as an opacity mask) may be imported with placed Photoshop files. You can also create layer clipping masks with any shape that is the topmost object of a group or layer.

4 You create an opacity mask by placing the object to be used as a mask on top of the object to be masked. Then you select the mask and the object(s) to be masked, and either click the Make Mask button in the Transparency panel or choose Make Opacity Mask from the Transparency panel menu.

5 To replace a placed image with a different image, select the image in the Links panel. Then click the Relink button ( ) (or Relink From CC Libraries button [ ]), and locate and select the replacement image. Click Place or Relink (if you clicked Relink From CC Libraries button).

16 SHARING PROJECTS

Lesson overview

In this lesson, you'll learn how to do the following:

- Package a file.
- Create a PDF.
- Create pixel-perfect drawings.
- Use the Export For Screens command.
- Work with the Asset Export panel.

 This lesson will take about 30 minutes to complete. To get the lesson files used in this chapter, download them from the web page for this book at adobepress.com/IllustratorCIB2022. For more information, see "Accessing the lesson files and Web Edition" in the Getting Started section at the beginning of this book.

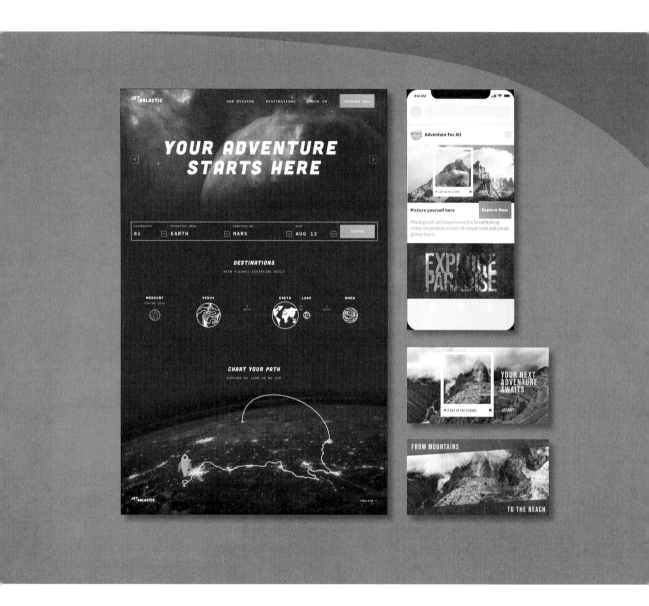

You can use various methods to share and export your projects as PDFs or to optimize your Illustrator content for use on the web, in apps, and in onscreen presentations.

Starting the lesson

Before you begin this lesson, you'll restore the default preferences for Adobe Illustrator and open the first lesson file.

Note: If you have not already downloaded the project files for this lesson to your computer from your Account page, make sure to do so now. See the "Getting Started" section at the beginning of the book.

Note: The projects for this lesson were designed by Meng He (mynameismeng.com).

1 To ensure that the tools function and the defaults are set exactly as described in this lesson, delete or deactivate (by renaming) the Adobe Illustrator preferences file. See "Restoring default preferences" in the "Getting Started" section at the beginning of the book.

2 Start Adobe Illustrator.

3 Choose File > Open. In the Open dialog box, navigate to the Lessons > Lesson16 folder. Select the L16_start1.ai file, and click Open.

4 In the warning dialog that appears, select Apply To All, and then click Ignore.

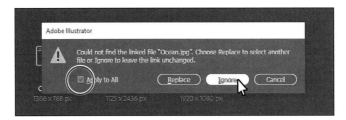

There is at least one image, Ocean.jpg, linked to the Illustrator document that Illustrator can't find on your system. Instead of replacing the missing image(s) from this dialog box, later in the lesson, you will open the Links panel so you can see which are missing and replace them there.

5 *If you skipped Lesson 15,* the Missing Fonts dialog box will most likely appear. Click Activate Fonts to activate all missing fonts (your list may not match the figure). After they are activated and you see the message stating that there are no more missing fonts, click Close.

6 If a dialog box appears referring to font auto-activation, then click Skip.

Note: If you don't see Reset Essentials in the Workspace menu, choose Window > Workspace > Essentials before choosing Window > Workspace > Reset Essentials.

7 Choose Window > Workspace > Reset Essentials to ensure that the workspace is set to the default settings.

8 Choose View > Fit All In Window.

9 Choose Select > Deselect, if available.

Fixing the missing image link

After the document is open, since you ignored the missing link dialog box when it opened, you should fix the missing images if you hope to print or export this document. If you create a PDF or print this document without fixing the missing link(s), Illustrator uses a low-resolution version of each missing image.

1   To open the Links panel, choose Window > Links.

2   In the Links panel, select the first Ocean.jpg image; it has an icon (⊗) to the right of its name telling you the image is missing. At the bottom of the panel, click the Go To Link button (⊡) to show which image is missing.

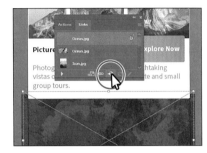

To fix the missing link, you will relink the missing image to the original image.

3   At the bottom of the panel, click the Relink button (🔗) to link the missing image to the original.

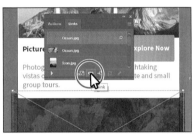

4   In the dialog box that opens, navigate to the Lessons > Lesson16 > images folder, select the Ocean image, and ensure that Link is selected. Click Place.

The Ocean.jpg image you just relinked will now show a link icon (⊘) telling you it's linked to that image.

5   Choose Select > Deselect, and then choose File > Save.

6   Close the Links panel group.

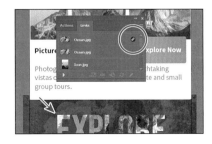

Packaging a file

When you *package* a file, you create a folder that contains a copy of the Illustrator document, any necessary fonts, copies of the linked graphics, and a report that contains information about the packaged files. This is an easy way to hand off all necessary files for an Illustrator project. Next you'll package the open file.

Note: If the file needs to be saved, a dialog box will appear to notify you.

1 Choose File > Package. If you are asked to save the file, save it. In the Package dialog box, set the following options:

   - Click the folder icon (🗀), and navigate to the Lesson16 folder, if you are not already there. Click Choose (macOS) or Select Folder (Windows) to return to the Package dialog box.
   - Folder name: **Social**
   - Options: Leave at default settings.

Note: The Create Report option, when selected, will create a package report (summary) as a .txt (text) file, which is placed in the package folder by default.

The Copy Links option *duplicates* all of the linked files to the new folder it creates. The Collect Links In Separate Folder option creates a folder called Links and copies the links into it. The Relink Linked Files To Document option updates the links within the Illustrator document to link to the new copies.

2 Click Package.

3 In the next dialog box, which discusses font licensing restrictions, click OK.

   Clicking Back would allow you to deselect Copy Fonts (Except Adobe Fonts And Non-Adobe CJK Fonts).

4 In the final dialog box to appear, click Show Package to see the package folder.

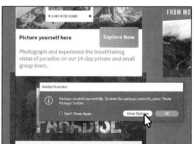

In the package folder there should be a copy of the Illustrator document and a folder named Links that contains any linked images. The L16_start1 Report text file contains information about the document contents.

5 Return to Illustrator.

Creating a PDF

Portable Document Format (PDF) is a universal file format that preserves the fonts, images, and layout of source documents created on a wide range of applications and platforms. Adobe PDF is the standard for the secure, reliable distribution and exchange of electronic documents and forms worldwide. Adobe PDF files are compact and complete and can be shared, viewed, and printed by anyone with the free Adobe Acrobat Reader or other PDF-compatible software.

You can create different types of PDF files from within Illustrator. You can create multipage PDFs, layered PDFs, and PDF/X-compliant files. Layered PDFs allow you to save one PDF with layers that can be used in different contexts. PDF/X-compliant files ease the burden of color, font, and trapping issues in printing. Next, you'll save this project as a PDF so you can send it to someone else to view.

1   Choose File > Save As. If you see the Cloud Document dialog box, click Save On Your Computer to save the file locally.

2   In the Save As dialog box, choose Adobe PDF (pdf) from the Format menu (macOS) or Adobe PDF (*.PDF) from the Save As Type menu (Windows).

Note: When creating a PDF, to save all of the artboards to one PDF, select All, or to save a subset of the artboards to one PDF, select Range and type the range of artboards. For example, in a document with three artboards, a range can be "1-3" to save all three artboards or "1,3" to save the first and third artboards.

3   Navigate to the Lessons > Lesson16 folder, if necessary. At the bottom of the dialog box, you can choose to save all of the artboards in the PDF or a range of artboards. Select All; then click Save.

4   In the Save Adobe PDF dialog box, click the Adobe PDF Preset menu to see all of the different PDF presets available. Ensure that [Illustrator Default] is chosen, and click Save PDF.

Note: If you want to learn about the options and other presets in the Save Adobe PDF dialog box, choose Help > Illustrator Help and search for "Creating Adobe PDF files."

There are many ways to customize the creation of a PDF. Creating a PDF using the [Illustrator Default] preset creates a PDF in which all Illustrator data is preserved. PDFs created with this preset can be reopened in Illustrator without any loss of data. If you are planning on saving a PDF for a particular purpose, such as viewing on the web or printing, you may want to choose another preset or adjust the options.

5   Choose File > Close to close the PDF without saving.

Creating pixel-perfect drawings

When creating content for use on the web, in mobile apps, in onscreen presentations, and more, images saved from vector art must look sharp. To enable designers to create pixel-accurate designs, you can align artwork to the pixel grid using the Snap To Pixel option. The *pixel grid* is a grid of 72 squares per inch, vertically and horizontally, viewable when you zoom to 600% or higher with Pixel Preview mode enabled (View > Pixel Preview).

Pixel-aligned is an object-level property that enables an object to align its vertical and horizontal paths to the pixel grid. This property remains with the object when the object is modified. When this property is selected, any vertical or horizontal path in the object is aligned to the pixel grid.

Previewing artwork in Pixel Preview

When you export assets in a format such as GIF, JPEG, or PNG, any vector artwork is rasterized in the resulting file. Turning on Pixel Preview is a great way to see what the artwork will look like when rasterized. First, you'll turn on Pixel Preview and view the artwork.

1 Choose File > Open. In the Open dialog box, navigate to the Lessons > Lesson16 folder. Select the L16_start2.ai file, and click Open.

2 Choose File > Document Color Mode, and you will see that RGB Color is chosen.

When designing for onscreen viewing (web, apps, etc.), RGB (Red, Green, Blue) is the preferred color mode for documents in Illustrator. When creating a new document (File > New), you can choose which color mode to use with the Color Mode option. In the New Document dialog box, choosing any document profile *except* Print sets Color Mode to RGB by default.

3 Select the Selection tool ( ), and click to select the Earth icon in the middle of the page. Press Command and + (macOS) or Ctrl and + (Windows) several times to zoom in closely to the selected artwork.

4 Choose View > Pixel Preview to preview a rasterized version of the entire design.

> **Tip:** After you create a document, you can change the document color mode using File > Document Color Mode. This sets the default color mode for all new colors you create and the existing swatches. RGB is the correct color mode to use when creating content for the web, for apps, or for onscreen presentations.

Preview mode.

Pixel Preview mode.

Aligning new artwork to the pixel grid

With Pixel Preview on, you'll see the pixel grid if you zoom in far enough. When Snap To Pixel (View > Snap To Pixel) is enabled, shapes drawn, modified, or transformed snap to the pixel grid and appear crisp. Most artwork, including most Live Shapes, align to the pixel grid automatically. In this section, you'll view the pixel grid and learn how to align new content to it.

1   Choose View > Fit Artboard In Window.

2   With the Selection tool (▶) selected, click to select the blue button shape with the text "SEARCH" on it.

3   Press Command and + (macOS) or Ctrl and + (Windows) several times until you see 600% in the View menu in the lower-left corner of the Document window (in the Status bar).

Tip: You can turn off the pixel grid by choosing Illustrator > Preferences > Guides & Grid (macOS) or Edit > Preferences > Guides & Grid (Windows) and deselecting Show Pixel Grid (Above 600% Zoom).

By zooming in to at least 600% and with Pixel Preview turned on, you can see a pixel grid appear. The pixel grid divides the artboard into 1-pt (1/72-inch) increments. For the next steps, you need to see the pixel grid (zoom level of 600% or greater).

4   Press Delete or Backspace to remove the rectangle.

5   Select the Rectangle tool (▭) in the toolbar. Draw a rectangle roughly the size of the one you just deleted.

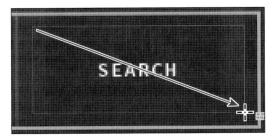
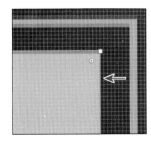

Note: As of this writing, the creation tools affected by Snap To Pixel are the Pen tool; the Curvature tool; shape tools, like the Ellipse tool and the Rectangle tool; the Line Segment tool; the Arc tool; the grid tools; and the Artboard tool.

You might notice that the edges of the rectangle look a little fuzzy. That's because Snap To Pixel was turned off in this document when shapes like this one were created, so the straight edges of the rectangle aren't snapping (aligning) to the pixel grid by default.

6   Press Delete or Backspace to remove the rectangle.

7   Choose View > Snap To Pixel to turn on Snap To Pixel.

Now, any shapes that are drawn, modified, or transformed will snap to the pixel grid, if possible. By default, Snap To Pixel is turned on when you create a new document that uses the Web or Mobile document profile.

Tip: You can also click the Snap To Pixel option in the Properties panel with nothing selected and the Selection tool selected, or you can select the Snap To Pixel option (▣) on the right end of the Control panel (Window > Control).

8 With the Rectangle tool selected, draw a simple rectangle to make the button, and notice that the edges appear cleaner.

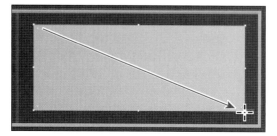

The vertical and horizontal segments of the drawn artwork snap to the pixel grid. In the next section, you'll see that you can snap existing artwork to the pixel grid. In this case, I had you redraw the shape just to see the difference.

9 Click the Arrange button in the Properties panel, and choose Send To Back to arrange it behind the "SEARCH" text.

Tip: You can press the arrow keys to move the selected artwork. The artwork will snap to the pixel grid.

10 Select the Selection tool, and drag the rectangle into position as you see in the figure.

As you drag, you may notice that the artwork is snapping to the pixel grid.

Aligning existing artwork to the pixel grid

You can also align existing artwork to the pixel grid in several ways, which is what you will do in this section.

1 Press Command and – (macOS) or Ctrl and – (Windows) once to zoom out. The grid should disappear because the zoom level is less than 600%.

2 Select the Selection tool (▶), and click to select the blue stroked rectangle surrounding the rectangle you drew.

Note: In this instance, the Align To Pixel Grid button in the Properties panel and the Object > Make Pixel Perfect command will do the same thing.

3 Click the Align To Pixel Grid button in the Properties panel to the right (or choose Object > Make Pixel Perfect).

The rectangle was created when View > Snap To Pixel wasn't selected. After you aligned the rectangle to the pixel grid, the horizontal and vertical straight edges were snapped to the closest pixel grid lines. Live Shapes and Live Corners are preserved when this is done.

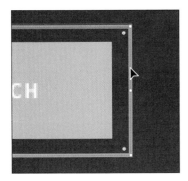

Objects that you pixel-align that have no straight vertical or horizontal segments are not modified to align to the pixel grid. For example, because a rotated rectangle does not have straight vertical or horizontal segments, it is not moved to produce crisp paths when the pixel-aligned property is set for it.

4   Click to select the blue "V" to the left of the button. You may need to scroll to the left. Choose Object > Make Pixel Perfect.

You will see a message in the Document window: "Selection Contains Art That Cannot Be Made Pixel Perfect." In this case, this means there are no vertical or horizontal straight edges to align.

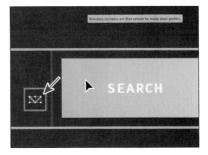

Note: The Align To Pixel Grid button does not appear in the Properties panel when an open path is selected.

5   Click the blue square surrounding the "V" (see the figure). Press Command and + (macOS) or Ctrl and + (Windows) several times to zoom in closely to the selected artwork.

6   Drag the top bounding point up to make the square a bit larger.

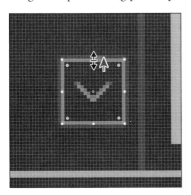
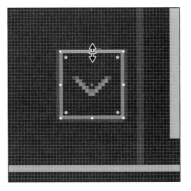

After dragging, notice that resizing the shape using the corner or side handles only fixes the *corresponding* edges (snaps them to the pixel grid).

Note: Moving artwork is constrained to whole pixels when transforming via the Selection tool, Direct Selection tool, Live Shape center widget, arrow keys, and Artboard tool. The Direct Selection tool snaps anchor points and handles to pixel or subpixel locations depending on the stroke settings of the path. This snap is similar to how the Pen tool snaps when you're creating artwork with it.

7 Choose Edit > Undo Scale so it remains square.

8 Click the Align To Pixel Grid button in the Properties panel to ensure that all of the vertical or horizontal straight edges are aligned to the pixel grid.

Unfortunately, when aligning something that small, it may move. In this case, it is no longer aligned with the center of the "V." You will need to align the "V" with the square.

9 Press the Shift key, and click the "V" to select it as well. Release the Shift key, and click the edge of the square to make it the key object.

10 Click the Horizontal Align Center button (⬛) and the Vertical Align Center button (⬛) to align the "V" to the square.

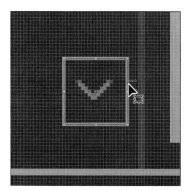  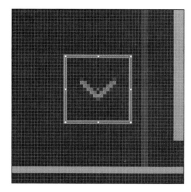

11 Choose Select > Deselect (if available), and then choose File > Save.

Exporting artboards and assets

▶ **Tip:** To learn more about working with web graphics, search for "File formats for exporting artwork" in Illustrator Help (Help > Illustrator Help).

In Illustrator, using the File > Export > Export For Screens command and the Asset Export panel, you can export entire artboards, perhaps to show a design in progress or just selected assets. You can export in several file formats: JPEG, SVG, PDF, PNG, or OBJ. These formats are optimized for use on the web, on devices, and onscreen presentations and are compatible with most browsers, yet each has different capabilities. Once selected, the artwork is automatically isolated from the rest of the design and saved as an individual file.

Exporting artboards

In this section, you'll see how to export artboards in your document, which can be helpful when you want to show someone a design you are working on or capturing a design for use in a presentation, website, or app.

1 Choose View > Pixel Preview to turn it off.

2 Choose View > Fit Artboard In Window.

3 Choose File > Export > Export For Screens.

In the Export For Screens dialog box that appears, you can choose between exporting artboards and exporting assets. Once you decide what to export, you can set the export settings on the right side of the dialog box.

4 With the Artboards tab selected, on the right side of the dialog box, ensure that All is selected.

You can choose to export all or a specific range of artboards. This document has only one artboard, so selecting All is the same as selecting a range of 1. Selecting Full Document will export all artwork in a single file.

5 Click the folder icon (📁) to the right of the Export To field. Navigate to the Lessons > Lesson16 folder, and click Choose (macOS) or Select Folder (Windows). Click the Format menu, and choose JPG 80.

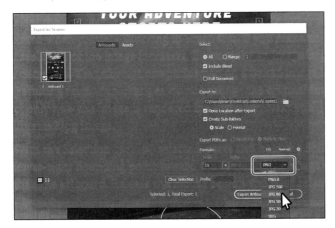

In the Formats section of the Export For Screens dialog box, you can set a Scale factor for the exported asset, create (or in this case edit) a suffix for the filename, and change the format. You can also export multiple versions with different scale factors and formats by clicking the + Add Scale button. You might need to scroll in the Formats area to see it.

6 Click Export Artboard.

The Lesson16 folder should open, and you should see a folder named "1x" and, in that folder, the JPEG image.

7 Close the folder, and return to Illustrator.

▶ **Tip:** To avoid creating subfolders, like the folder "1x," you can deselect Create Sub-folders in the Export For Screens dialog box when exporting.

Exporting assets

Using the Asset Export panel, you can quickly and easily export individual assets in file formats such as JPEG, PNG, PDF, and SVG. The Asset Export panel lets you collect assets that you might export frequently and can be an excellent tool for web and mobile workflows because it allows for the export of multiple assets with a single click. In this section, you'll open the Asset Export panel and see how to collect the artwork in the panel and then export it.

1 With the Selection tool (▶) selected, click to select the artwork labeled "VENUS" toward the middle of the artboard.

2 Press Command and + (macOS) or Ctrl and + (Windows) several times to zoom in to the artwork.

3 Press the Shift key, and click to select the artwork labeled "EARTH" to the right of the selected artwork.

4 With the artwork selected, choose Window > Asset Export to open the Asset Export panel.

The Asset Export panel is where you can save content for export now or later. It can work in conjunction with the Export For Screens dialog box to set export options for the selected assets, as you'll see.

5 Drag the selected artwork into the top part of the Asset Export panel. When you see a plus sign (+) appear, release the mouse button to add the artwork to the Asset Export panel. Each group or individual object is a different asset.

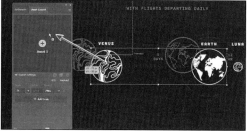

The assets are tied to the original artwork in the document. In other words, if you update the artwork in the document, the corresponding asset is updated in the Asset Export panel. Every asset you add to the Asset Export panel is saved with the panel and will stay there until you delete it from either the document or the Asset panel.

6 Click the name of the item in the Asset Export panel corresponding to the VENUS graphic and rename it **Venus**. Click the name of the item in the Asset Export panel corresponding to the EARTH graphic and rename it **Earth**. Press Return or Enter to accept the last name.

Tip: If you Option-drag (macOS) or Alt-drag (Windows) multiple objects into the Asset Export panel, the selected content will become a single asset in the Asset Export panel.

The asset name that appears is based on what the artwork is named in the Layers panel if you drag the asset into the panel. Also, how you name assets in the Asset Export panel is up to you. I name them so I can more easily keep track of what each asset is used for.

7 Click the Venus asset thumbnail to select it in the Asset Export panel.

As you add assets to the panel using various methods, you will need to first select the assets you'd like to export.

8 In the Export Settings area of the Asset Export panel, choose SVG from the Format menu, if necessary.

SVG is perfect for a website, but sometimes a co-worker may ask for a PNG version or other format of the same logo as well.

Note: If you are creating assets for use on iOS or Android, you could click iOS or Android to display a list of scaled export presets appropriate to each platform.

9 Click the + Add Scale button to export the artwork in another format (in this case). Adding a scale makes the Scale value of the additional format something other than 1x, by default.

10 Choose 1x from the Scale menu so the second asset is exported at 100% of the size of the artwork on the artboard, and ensure that Format is set to PNG.

In this case, an SVG file *and* a PNG file will be created for every selected asset in the Asset Export panel. You can also set a scale (1x, 2x, etc.) if you need multiple scaled versions of the selected assets—perhaps for Retina and non-Retina displays for raster formats like JPEG or PNG. You can also add a suffix to the exported filename. A suffix could be something like "@1x" to indicate the 100% scaled version of an exported asset.

Tip: You can also click the Launch The Export For Screens Dialog button (▣) at the bottom of the Asset Export panel. This will open the Export For Screens dialog box, where you can adjust all the same settings, including a few more.

11 With the Venus thumbnail selected at the top of the Asset Export panel, click the Export button at the bottom of the Asset Export panel to export the selected asset. In the dialog box that appears, navigate to the Lessons > Lesson16 > Asset_Export folder, and click Choose (macOS) or Select Folder (Windows) to export the assets.

Both the SVG file (Venus.svg) and the PNG file (Venus.png) will be exported to the Asset_Export folder in separate folders.

12 Choose File > Close as many times as necessary to close all open files.

Review questions

1 Describe what packaging an Illustrator document does.

2 Why do you align content to the pixel grid?

3 Describe how you export an artboard.

4 Name image file types that can be chosen in the Export For Screens dialog box and Asset Export panel.

5 Describe the generic process for exporting assets with the Asset Export panel.

Review answers

1 *Packaging* is used to gather all of the necessary pieces of an Illustrator document. Packaging creates a copy of the Illustrator file, the linked images, and the necessary fonts (if desired), and gathers those copies into a folder.

2 Aligning content to the pixel grid creates a crisp appearance at the edges of artwork. When Snap To Pixel is enabled for supported artwork, all the horizontal and vertical segments in the object are aligned to the pixel grid.

3 To export an artboard, choose File > Export > Export As (not covered in the lesson) or File > Export > Export For Screens. In the Export For Screens dialog box that appears, you can choose between exporting artboards and exporting assets. You can choose to export all or a specific range of artboards.

4 The image file types that can be chosen in the Export For Screens dialog box and the Asset Export panel are PNG, JPEG, SVG, PDF, and OBJ.

5 To export assets using the Asset Export panel, the artwork to be exported needs to be collected in the Asset Export panel. Once it's in the panel, you can select the asset(s) to be exported, set the export settings, and then export.

INDEX

brushes *(continued)*
    Paintbrush tool, 331, 334–337
    Pattern, 344–349
    previewing changes to, 334
    removing strokes made by, 338
    size setting for, 350, 353
    types of, 331
Brushes panel, 331, 333, 338
bullet character, 246

C

Calligraphic brushes, 331–338
    applying to artwork, 332–333
    editing options for, 333–334
    Paintbrush tool and, 334–337
    removing strokes made by, 338
canvas, rotating, 54
Caps Lock key
    Join tool and, 181
    Knife tool and, 119, 121
    Pen tool and, 188
    Pencil tool and, 177
cascading documents, 55
center point widget, 87
Character panel, 256
character styles, 262, 273
    creating and applying, 265–267
    editing, 267
Character Styles panel, 266–267
characters
    formatting applied to, 256–257
    styles applied to, 262, 265–267
circles, creating/editing, 13, 94–96
Classroom in a Book training series, 1
Clear Filter button, 253
clip groups, 108, 420
clipping masks
    applying to images, 419
    creating, 295–296, 297
    editing, 420–421
    explained, 295, 419
    releasing, 296
    See also masks
clipping paths, 108, 419, 420–421

clipping set, 419
closed paths, 87
Cloud Document dialog box, 11, 32, 437
cloud documents, 7, 32, 418
cloud icon, 428
CMYK color mode, 213, 214, 226
Collect in New Layer option, 295
color groups, 227–228
Color Guide panel, 228–230
    applying colors from, 230
    using for inspiration, 228–229
color harmonies, 229, 232, 239
color markers, 232–233
Color Mixer panel, 215
color modes, 213, 438
Color panel, 215
Color Picker, 221–223
color stops, 301
    freeform gradient, 314–315
    Lines mode for applying, 316–317
    radial gradient, 310
    stroke gradient, 307–308
color swatches, 216–221
    applying colors with, 15–16
    creating copies of, 217–218
    editing, 16, 218–221
    global, 216, 218–219, 220, 239
    libraries of, 223, 224
    non-global, 219–221
    saving colors as, 216–217, 223, 239
    spot-color, 224
Color Theme Picker, 233
colors, 214–234
    applying, 15–16, 214, 230
    blending, 320–321
    Color Picker for, 221–223
    converting between modes, 226
    copying with Eyedropper, 226–227
    creating custom, 215
    editing, 16, 18–19, 231–233
    gradient, 307–308, 310
    grouping, 227–228

Isolation mode, 77–78, 81, 108, 271, 420, 422

J

Join command, 117, 180

Join tool, 117, 180–181, 183

joining paths, 117–118, 180–181

K

key anchor points, 73, 206

key objects, 71

keyboard shortcuts
    displayed in tool tips, 34
    Fit Artboard in Window, 47
    Hand tool, 50
    Layers panel, 296
    modifying on macOS, 49
    resizing brushes, 353
    zooming in/out, 46

Knife tool, 118–121, 137

L

layer comps, 415

Layer Options dialog box, 279

layers, 274–297
    appearance attributes applied to, 294
    arranging content on, 286
    clipping masks for, 295–296, 297
    colors for, 279, 297
    creating new, 278–279
    duplicating content of, 291–292
    effects applied to, 294
    explanation of, 277
    finding content on, 280–282
    flattening, 296
    graphic styles applied to, 380–381, 383
    hiding, 289–290
    locking, 290
    moving content between, 283–284
    naming/renaming, 278, 279
    pasting, 292–293, 297
    Photoshop files with, 416
    reordering, 287–288, 297
    sublayers and, 280
    symbol, 396

viewing, 285–286

Layers panel
    eye icon, 204, 285, 290, 423
    features overview, 277
    finding content in, 280–282
    keyboard shortcuts, 296
    opening, 278
    target icon, 294, 380

leading, text, 256

lesson files, 2, 3

libraries
    brush, 334–335, 344, 350
    graphic style, 377
    swatch, 223, 224
    symbol, 387, 388
    See also Creative Cloud Libraries

Libraries panel, 397–399, 400, 401

Library folder (macOS), 4

Line Segment tool, 102

linear gradients, 301
    adjusting, 304–306
    applying to fills, 302
    applying to strokes, 306

lines
    creating/editing, 102–103
    drawing dashed, 175–176
    Pen tool for drawing, 187–188
    Pencil tool for drawing, 178–179
    rotating, 102, 175–176
    See also straight lines

Lines mode, 316–317

Link Harmony Colors icon, 232

link icon, 19, 427, 435

linked images, 410, 428–430
    embedded images vs., 410, 429, 431
    finding information about, 428
    fixing missing, 435
    replacing, 430, 431

links
    image, 410, 428–430, 435
    Library asset, 401
    opacity mask, 427
    symbol, 387, 393–394
    text, 248

Links panel, 401, 412, 428, 429, 430, 435

Live Corners widget, 90, 91–92, 99

Live Paint Bucket tool, 235, 236–237

Live Paint groups, 235–238, 239
    creating, 235
    modifying, 238
    painting objects in, 236–237

Live Shapes, 13, 88, 111

Locate Object button, 281, 416, 419, 422

locking
    layers, 290
    objects, 66

M

macOS commands, 2

magenta alignment guides, 12, 63, 98, 191

magnification level, 46

Make Mask button, 425

Make Pixel Perfect option, 441

marquee selections, 65

Mask button, 419

masks, 419–427, 431
    applying to images, 419
    editing clipping, 420–421
    opacity, 424–427
    shape, 421–422
    text, 422–424
    See also clipping masks

measurement label, 87, 98

measurement units, 151, 154

merging
    layer content, 295
    shapes, 14–15
    swatches, 146

mirror repeats, 158–161
    applying, 158–160
    editing, 160–161

Missing Fonts dialog box, 140, 212, 276, 300, 358, 397

Mop brush, 350, 351, 352

Move dialog box, 157

N

naming/renaming
    artboards, 148
    colors, 216
    groups, 282
    layers, 278, 279

native format, 85

Navigator panel, 50

nested groups, 78–79

New Artboard button, 142

New Brush dialog box, 340, 346

New Document dialog box, 10, 84–85

New Swatch dialog box, 216, 217, 223

Next artboard button, 70, 148

non-global swatches, 219–221

O

objects
    aligning, 70–75
    arranging, 79–80
    blended, 317–321
    coloring, 214
    distributing, 72
    gradients applied to, 312–313
    grouping, 17, 75–79, 282
    hiding, 66–67, 81
    key, 71
    locating, 281
    locking, 66
    painting, 235, 236–237
    repeat, 158–161
    rotating, 155
    scaling, 154–155
    selecting, 61–70
    shearing, 156–157
    similar, 68–69
    stacking order of, 79, 280, 287
    text or type, 244, 246
    unlocking, 67–68, 147
    See also artwork

Offset Path effect, 373

online content, 2–3

opacity
    appearance attribute, 365

Pearson's Commitment to Diversity, Equity, and Inclusion

Pearson is dedicated to creating bias-free content that reflects the diversity of all learners. We embrace the many dimensions of diversity, including but not limited to race, ethnicity, gender, socioeconomic status, ability, age, sexual orientation, and religious or political beliefs.

Education is a powerful force for equity and change in our world. It has the potential to deliver opportunities that improve lives and enable economic mobility. As we work with authors to create content for every product and service, we acknowledge our responsibility to demonstrate inclusivity and incorporate diverse scholarship so that everyone can achieve their potential through learning. As the world's leading learning company, we have a duty to help drive change and live up to our purpose to help more people create a better life for themselves and to create a better world.

Our ambition is to purposefully contribute to a world where:

- Everyone has an equitable and lifelong opportunity to succeed through learning.

- Our educational products and services are inclusive and represent the rich diversity of learners.

- Our educational content accurately reflects the histories and experiences of the learners we serve.

- Our educational content prompts deeper discussions with learners and motivates them to expand their own learning (and worldview).

While we work hard to present unbiased content, we want to hear from you about any concerns or needs with this Pearson product so that we can investigate and address them.

- Please contact us with concerns about any potential bias at https://www.pearson.com/report-bias.html.

Contributors

Brian Wood is a content developer and the author of more than twenty training books (Adobe Illustrator, Adobe InDesign, Adobe Muse, Adobe XD, and more), as well as training videos on Adobe Dreamweaver & CSS, InDesign, Illustrator, XD, Adobe Acrobat, Muse and others. In addition to training many clients large and small, Brian speaks regularly at national conferences, such as Adobe MAX, as well as events hosted by AIGA and other industry organizations. To learn more, check out www.youtube.com/askbrianwood or visit www.brianwoodtraining.com.

Production Notes

The *Adobe Illustrator Classroom in a Book (2022 release)* was created electronically using Adobe InDesign 2021. Art was produced using Adobe InDesign, Adobe Illustrator, and Adobe Photoshop.

References to company names, websites, or addresses in the lessons are for demonstration purposes only and are not intended to refer to any actual organization or person.

Images

Photographic images and illustrations are intended for use with the tutorials.

Typefaces used

Adobe Myriad Pro and Adobe Warnock Pro are used throughout this book. For more information about OpenType and Adobe fonts, visit www.adobe.com/type/opentype/.

Team credits

The following individuals contributed to the development of this edition of the *Adobe Illustrator Classroom in a Book (2022 release)*:

Writer: Brian Wood
Adobe Press Executive Editor: Laura Norman
Adobe Press Senior Production Editor: Tracey Croom
Keystroke Editors: Jean-Claude Tremblay
Technical Editor: Victor Gavenda
Project Design: Danielle Fritz, Matthew Fleming, Meng He, Trey Shively, and Brian Wood
Compositor: Brian Wood
Proofreader: Kim Wimpsett
Indexer: James Minkin
Interior Design: Mimi Heft

Lesson project credits

The following individuals contributed artwork for the lesson files for this edition of the *Adobe Illustrator Classroom in a Book (2022 release)*:

Danielle Fritz (www.behance.net/danielle_fritz): Lessons: 00, 1–5, 8, 9, 12, and 13.

Matthew Fleming (matthew@matthewjayfleming.com): Lesson 11.

Meng He (www.mynameismeng.com): Lessons 10, 15, and 16.

Trey Shively (@tshiv): Lesson 14.

Image credits

In Chapter 1, a photo of flowers by **Markus Winkler** on Unsplash.com was used: unsplash.com/photos/34Dl4UKIItU/

In Chapter 3, a photo of a lemon by **Lauren Mancke** on Unsplash.com was used: unsplash.com/photos/sil2Hx4iupI

In Chapter 8, a photo of a basket with fruit by **Monika Grabkowska** on Unsplash.com was used: unsplash.com/photos/VSYjkfzj3nw

Throughout Chapter 10, the following is used:

Photo by **Danka & Peter** on Unsplash.com: unsplash.com/photos/tvicgTdh7Fg

Throughout Chapter 15 and 16, the following images are used:

Photo by **David Marcu** on Unsplash.com: unsplash.com/photos/f2SeKHyjqk4

Photo by **Andreas Kind** on Unsplash.com: unsplash.com/photos/pGdKXbqTOQ4

Photo by **Mason Panos** on Unsplash.com: unsplash.com/photos/8Lv4uJEoHmo

Photo by **Jeremiah Berman** on Unsplash.com: unsplash.com/photos/9dmycbFE7mQ

Photo by **Rodrigo Flores** on Unsplash.com: unsplash.com/photos/nk_JKocDkDo

Throughout Chapter 16, two photos by **NASA** (@nasa) on Unsplash.com are used:

unsplash.com/photos/rTZW4f02zY8
unsplash.com/photos/Q1p7bh3SHj8

The fastest, easiest, most comprehensive way to learn
Adobe Creative Cloud

Classroom in a Book®, the best-selling series of hands-on software training books, helps you learn the features of Adobe software quickly and easily.

The **Classroom in a Book** series offers what no other book or training program does—an official training series from Adobe Systems, developed with the support of Adobe product experts.

To see a complete list of our Classroom in a Book titles covering the 2022 release of Adobe Creative Cloud go to:
adobepress.com/CC2022

Adobe Photoshop Classroom in a Book (2022 release)
ISBN: 9780137621101

Adobe Illustrator Classroom in a Book (2022 release)
ISBN: 9780137622153

Adobe InDesign Classroom in a Book (2022 release)
ISBN: 9780137622962

Adobe Dreamweaver Classroom in a Book (2022 release)
ISBN: 9780137623303

Adobe Premiere Pro Classroom in a Book (2022 release)
ISBN: 9780137625123

Adobe After Effects Classroom in a Book (2022 release)
ISBN: 9780137623921

Adobe Animate Classroom in a Book (2022 release)
ISBN: 9780137623587

Adobe Photoshop Lightroom Classic Classroom in a Book (2022 release)
ISBN: 9780137625154

 **Adobe Press**